THE CHINESE CONUNDRUM

Engagement or Conflict

New, updated and expanded edition

Vince Cable

ALMA BOOKS

ALMA BOOKS LTD
Thornton House
Thornton Road
Wimbledon Village
London SW19 4NG
United Kingdom
www.almabooks.com

The Chinese Conundrum: Engagement or Conflict first published by
Alma Books Limited in 2021

This new, updated and expanded edition, first published in 2023

Printed and bound by CPI Group (UK) Ltd, Croydon, CR0 4YY

MIX
Paper | Supporting
responsible forestry
FSC® C171272

ISBN: 978-1-84688-470-2

CONTENTS

The Chinese Conundrum

Engagement or Conflict

Foreword

There is a vast outpouring of books and papers on China. Why would I want to add to it? I am not a China scholar, do not speak or read the Chinese language and have never lived in China. My direct experience is confined to business visits over a thirty-year period.

What motivated me to write this book – and an earlier, shorter pamphlet (*China: Engage! Avoid the New Cold War*) – was the rapid deterioration in the political climate around China's relations with Britain and most of the Western world. I was closely involved, in a ministerial capacity, during the early part of the last decade, in what was called the "Golden Era" of cordial relationships between China and the UK and positive perceptions built around commercial diplomacy.

There is now a much more negative perception of China, reflecting more authoritarian and ideological politics within China and assertiveness externally under President Xi; a more confrontational consensus in the USA over technology, trade, human rights and security and military threats; and, to a degree, home-grown doubts. Particularly within the Conservative Party, but not exclusively, China is viewed with hostility and as a "threat". Engagement through trade and foreign investment, overseas students, joint research, cultural events and social media (such as TikTok), which until very recently was seen as beneficial or innocuous, is now viewed with suspicion.

Recent events, such as the declaration of "no-limits friendship" with Russia and refusal to condemn the invasion of Ukraine, have reinforced the negativity. That negative narrative is, at best, one-sided and a questionable guide to the future. I felt that I should assemble and analyse the evidence we have, from commentators and analysts coming from different perspectives.

3

Getting the balance right is important, since China is already, arguably, an economic superpower alongside the USA, and is likely – though not certain – to grow in relative economic and political importance. Since Britain, outside the European Union, is now trying to define itself as "Global Britain" and even as an Asia-Pacific power, it matters that we get the relationship with China right. In addition to trade relationships, Britain is also being drawn into military commitments in the Asia-Pacific, prompted mainly by fears of China in the region and pressure to support allies, notably the USA and Australia. Such military involvement may prove to be momentous if pessimists are correct that attempted containment of China will lead to conflict.[1]

My own involvement with China goes back to my membership of Shell's scenario-planning team and being invited to carry out scenarios specific to China as part of the challenge process before the company made an irrevocable commitment to large investments in China, especially the Nanhai petrochemicals joint venture in Guangdong province.

This exercise opened my eyes to the extraordinary pace and achievements of Chinese development, but also to its less attractive features (my Shell China counterpart, a young woman with children, was unjustly imprisoned at the behest of an aggrieved commercial party). The project went ahead, is deemed to be a considerable success and has been expanded since. I was left with a great admiration for the Shell scenario process and make use of it in Chapter 7. The scenario approach is ideally suited to an environment of extreme uncertainty, such as we have now, when there is the possibility of China emerging to a dominant position in an integrated world economy; or what has been called a "great split" into a confrontation between rival power blocks; or possibly a China which fails to deal with its economic and political challenges and turns inward. I deal with these different possibilities.

When I spent some time, in the 1990s, at Chatham House, I embarked upon and published a comparative study of development in China and India, with which I had had more acquaintance.² It seemed then, and more so now, that the trajectories of these two populous and remarkable countries – in terms of economic, politics and environmental stewardship particularly – will shape the planet's future later this century. I believed then that India's more gradual and democratic approach must win out. Now I am not so sure.

It was my role in the Coalition government, as President of the Board of Trade as well as Secretary of State for BIS, that led me into close involvement with Chinese decision-makers, British firms, universities and others who were trying to do business in China and with Chinese firms investing in the UK. It was one of the top priorities of that government to boost commercial and wider relationships with the big emerging economies such as China, India, Brazil, Indonesia, Russia, the Gulf states and Turkey among others, while continuing to operate from a home base within the EU and its common standards and values. Several of these countries had unattractive governments with poor human-rights records, but reality required us to engage with them for commercial and security reasons.

The UK was, hitherto, seriously underperforming commercially in comparison to other European countries, especially Germany, and we needed to make a major effort to catch up. In practical terms that meant a great deal of travelling to those countries – especially China – for promotion and negotiation, as well as welcoming their representatives and investors here. On most metrics, the efforts were productive in realizing trade and investment opportunities beneficial to the UK as well as China. That was the "Golden Era" – a phrase which now invites derision.

Short ministerial visits, hobnobbing with the rich and powerful and communicating with officials through translators do not provide the best vantage point for deepening knowledge of a country. The national and provincial officials with whom I had to deal were clever, polished and open to debate and ideas (at least in private) but represented only the governing elite. I was also fortunate to be able to meet, thanks to the British embassy and consulates, some of the brave people speaking up for labour, women and LGBT rights, or victims of environmental and health scandals, who were under surveillance.

I also had to deal with, and encourage, Chinese companies who were interested in the UK. Among them was Huawei, which was to become a serious source of friction later. Since Huawei was engaged in sensitive communications work, I insisted on comprehensive and honest briefings on the security implications. I was categorically assured by people who ought to know that Huawei presented no security risk to the UK that was not being adequately managed. I was – and am – puzzled by claims made subsequently that the company was, all along, a security risk. The concept of "security risks" has now expanded to include the Chinese-owned TikTok – whose short videos provide entertainment to millions of teenagers worldwide – and the Chinese software helping cities to monitor traffic and population movements. Those of us who are sceptical of unevidenced claims that Chinese "threats" lurk round every corner are becoming used to being regarded as "naive". It is surely no coincidence that the idea of China as a "threat" is growing strongly in the USA as Congressmen and state governments seek to outbid each other in anti-Chinese rhetoric and security warnings.

It was clear all along that there was a politically unattractive side to the China economic "miracle". My Lib Dem colleagues were exercised about human rights, as in Tibet, and the issue featured in our dialogue with the Chinese. It was also clear that the Chinese had their own definition of human rights, centring on basic economic and social needs and security, and that Western insistence that China follow western ideas of universal standards was often counterproductive (though China's breaches of human rights, as in Xinjiang, have also led to censure within the United Nations system). Getting the right balance of engagement, competition, independence, criticism and confrontation was and is crucial in dealings with China, as with Britain's other major commercial and political partners whose alleged misdeeds are serious, such as Saudi Arabia and the Gulf states or Turkey.

In assembling material for the book, I made use as much as possible of the large and growing volume of published material which is, of necessity, from Western (mainly US) sources. I also sought the views of as many UK-based Chinese and China-based expatriates as I was able to contact. Most of my writing took place during the Covid pandemic – a time of minimum face-to-face contact and a growing sense of isolation by and from China with a hardening of attitudes on both sides. The extreme lockdown measures in Shanghai and other cities also did serious damage to the Chinese economy and to its interconnectedness with the rest of the world, with potentially severe long-term consequences. Lack of meaningful contact contributed to the fact that there are wildly different interpretations of events.

Much of the analysis, even in scholarly sources, is steeped in strong biases, which could be characterized as "pro-" or "anti-" China. The anti-China literature can be summarized as follows: China is an aggressive, expansionist power which bullies its neighbours and critics and is trying to dominate the world; the size and performance of the Chinese economy and technology is a good deal less impressive than it is cracked up to be (or so impressive that they will overwhelm us); the politics is even nastier than we thought it was and deteriorating; human-rights abuse is on an industrial scale, with totalitarian systems of surveillance and control and suppression of minorities amounting to "genocide"; the country's values and interests are totally incompatible with ours – and it must be confronted politically and perhaps militarily.

The "pro-China" material, by contrast, will stress the scale and success of China's economic renaissance and its role in improving economic and social welfare; the economic benefits of trade and investment links with China; the need to accommodate a new economic superpower within a rules-based system; the scope for common action on shared problems, like climate change; the importance of constructive engagement and dialogue. I have tried to be balanced but have been accused of the latter heresy based on my more prescriptive booklet.[3]

7

The debate has often degenerated into partisan invective on both sides. When Australia caused offence by calling for an inquiry into the origins of the pandemic, a Chinese state media boss described Australia as "gum stuck to the bottom of China's shoe – sometimes you have to find a rock and scrape it off". At the same time, anyone in the West seen as "pro-Chinese" can also expect a volley of abuse. Martin Jacques's provocatively titled *When China Rules the World* earned him the following attack from a fellow political scientist: "Embarrassingly starry-eyed, servile and naïve"[4] (though he is one of the few Western authors of serious books on China to have confronted the sensitive issue of Chinese racism).

My fundamental objective however is not to be "pro-" or "anti-" China, or to act as an apologist for or denouncer of China, but to try to ensure that the debate on our relations with China, especially in the UK, reflect different standpoints and narratives and is open to critical questioning. Western critics of China will often say that they have nothing against the Chinese people, only the government. But I often meet Chinese visitors, students and expatriates who dislike the current regime in Beijing but are strongly patriotic, proud of China's rise and its many achievements and resentful or hurt by Western criticism of China and "preaching".

In order to avoid the extremes and excessive reliance on anecdotage, visitors' tales and impressionistic reporting, I try where possible to use recognized, reputable, official international economic sources (the IMF and World Bank), public-opinion analysis from the likes of the Pew Centre and Edelman and measures of political freedom or corruption from respected NGOs such as Freedom House and Transparency International – although all of these could be accused of "Western bias".

I am very indebted to Andrew Cainey of RUSI and to Zhenbo Hou of RBC Global Asset Management for detailed comments on an early draft of this book. The Dean of the School of Public Policy at the LSE, Professor Andrés Velasco, hosted an online seminar on the book. Since the publication of the hardback edition, the book has been extensively discussed in public debates, interviews, academic events and private conversations. I am grateful for the constructive criticism, updates and corrections which I have been given and I have tried to reflect them in this edition. I also wish to thank Alessandro Gallenzi and Elisabetta Minervini of Alma Books, who encouraged and promoted this project and have been immensely supportive. The book would never have been written without the unfailing help and support of my wife Rachel, who indulges my determination to write. Any errors and biases are mine alone.

Chapter 1

Changing Perceptions

Within a very short period, relations between China and the rest of the world, and especially the United States and its Western allies, have deteriorated badly. What was characterized in the UK as a "Golden Era" is now discussed in the language of a new Cold War. Surveys of public attitudes mirror the rhetoric of politicians and chart a sharp decline from "favourable" to "unfavourable" perceptions of China, at least in richer countries.[1] The fact that China was the source of the global pandemic has played a major part in that decline, but it is not the only factor.

Such changes in perception have been sudden but are not new. Over the two centuries or so in which there has been close interaction between China and Western powers, the West could be broadly described as following a succession of different approaches: curiosity, condescension, plunder, conversion, withdrawal, re-engagement, partnership, competition and now, disillusion, apprehension and perhaps fear. The Chinese, for their part, have passed from disdain and disinterest to defeatism, deference and humiliation; to revolution and upheaval; to modernization, integration and development; and now to assertiveness and perhaps ascendancy. On both sides there has also been a consistent sense of cultural – and perhaps racial – superiority, which has been the source of much misunderstanding and offence.

These sweeping generalizations do not take account of nuance and particular events and individuals: the emergence of President Xi, who has led China in a more authoritarian manner, and more forceful abroad; the Trump administration, which may or may not prove to have been an aberration; the more nuanced approach of the Biden administration, with its attempts to create coalitions of democratic countries to confront China; the re-emergence of Taiwan as a flashpoint; the influence of Japan, aligned with the West but not belonging to it; and the complex and ambiguous relationships with China's other neighbours and the Chinese diaspora. But beneath the shifting sands of changing attitudes and alignments, there is the solid reality of differential growth and economic development. We have witnessed the realization of the oft-quoted prediction attributed to Napoleon: "Let China sleep: when she awakes, she will shake the world." Napoleon himself probably never said anything of the kind, but whoever said it was right.[2]

The predicted awakening has led to specific points of dispute and conflict, as well as opportunities, but also what looks like an existential crisis in the Western world. That sense of crisis reflects two underlying trends: one is a shift in the economic centre of gravity of the world economy towards Asia in general and China in particular.[3] The other is political: the drift away from the values of "liberal democracy" to different and more authoritarian models of government of which China's is pre-eminent and seemingly successful – at least, so far.[4] The seeming inevitability of the West's relative decline is captured in the title of Martin Jacques's influential book – *When China Rules the World*[5] – in Kishore Mahbubani's *Has China Won?*[6] or Arvind Subramanian's *Eclipse: Living in the Shadow of China's Economic Dominance*.[7] We do not need to buy fully into the melodramatic message behind the titles – and the Chinese regime's use of it – to recognize a fundamental shift in economic strength, with its inevitable political consequences.

There is also a more specific debate about the competition for hegemonic power between the USA and China. This in part about economic leadership, as in Bergsten's *The United States v China*.[8] But it can also be seen as a long-term geopolitical struggle for dominance.[9] There is also a counter-narrative from those who see China's growing power as overstated and who argue that the United States – and, even more, the West as a whole – has such overwhelming underlying economic strengths, military capacity and cultural and political appeal that there is little threat to its hegemonic status.[10] Perhaps the argument is about time horizons which is why it is useful to start at the beginning.

The beginnings

Most accounts of China's interactions with the West written from the perspective of the Anglosphere tend to start with the visit of Lord Macartney in 1793, at the behest of George III, to initiate a formal trading relationship with Britain. From a Chinese point of view, this represented one recent episode in a long history of engagement with the global economy and disengagement from it.

Romans were familiar with Chinese products, notably silk, but not their provenance: they arrived in their provinces via a complex sea journey involving Indian and Arab trading networks.[11] In so far as it is possible to tell – and Angus Maddison's epic compilation work of long-term economic statistics adds numbers to anecdote[12] – China was the world's pre-eminent economy and trading nation over the following centuries, with India the only serious rival. The port of Canton (now Guangzhou) became a major trading city, home to a large, cosmopolitan merchant community. As in later centuries, Chinese engagement with the outside world rested on stable, confident government at home. When there was a period of domestic upheaval, trade and traders were often the casualties. In the ninth century, for example, there was a crisis in the Tang dynasty which led to a scapegoating of foreigners: in 878, a rebel army sacked Canton and massacred tens of thousands of Muslims, Jews and Christians. The practical effect was to displace China's entrepôt centres further north. But trade continued.

Western understanding of China percolated through by means of travellers' tales. The likes of Marco Polo, journeying to China on the land route (the "Belt" in the new version of the Silk Road, the "Belt and Road"), brought back stories of the magnificence of the imperial court and cities in the late thirteenth century, as well as the extent of China's trading operations from Canton.[13] Exploration by way of the sea routes (the "Road") was reported at second hand by Arab traders, and entered Western consciousness via fantastical stories, such as those of Sinbad the Sailor.

Europe appears to have had little awareness of the three centuries of Chinese naval might (from 1132 to 1433), between the establishment of a permanent navy with sophisticated marine engineering, huge vessels and advanced (imported) navigation systems and the last of Admiral Zheng He's "treasure fleet" voyages of exploration to Africa. There followed a period of deliberate introversion. The benefits and costs of early globalization were nonetheless experienced through the spread of high-value goods on the one hand and, on the other, plague carried by fleas along the arms of both the Belt and the Road.

Knowledge of China was built up through early trading encounters following Portuguese maritime penetration of Asia. Jesuit missionaries fed back an essentially positive view of Chinese values, aesthetics and institutions, eulogized by Voltaire among others.[14] Others were less flattering, but there was a fascination with China in the mid-eighteenth century.[15] Well-informed and thoughtful analysts like the economist Adam Smith were able to dissect the strengths and weaknesses of the Chinese economy. In *The Wealth of Nations*, published in 1776, Smith observed that its impressive development had reached a limit: "Long one of the richest, that is most fertile, best cultivated, most industrious, and most populous countries in the world", China had "acquired that full complement of riches which the nature of its laws and institutions permits it to acquire".[16]

Lack of further economic growth combined with a rising population had led him to see what would later be seen as a "Malthusian trap" characterized by hunger: "The poverty of the lower ranks of people in China far surpasses the most beggarly nations in Europe." He noted the widespread occurrence of infanticide: "Marriage is encouraged in China, not by the profitableness of its children, but by the liberty of destroying them." He saw a solution in trade: "A country which neglects or despises foreign commerce [...] cannot transact the same quantity of business which it might do with different laws and institutions."[17] Smith was to provide a theoretical framework, which was then used by less scrupulous British trade practitioners to force open the Chinese economy in ways that poisoned future relationships.

There was already a somewhat hostile narrative about China, centring on the frustrations of British traders. In 1741 a representative of the East India Company (EIC), George Anson, found obstructive, bureaucratic and dishonest Chinese officials in Canton sufficiently exasperating to write a widely read pamphlet "helping to build a ground-swell of anti-Chinese feeling in Britain and elsewhere in the West".[18]

Underlying the complaints about what would now be called non-tariff barriers to trade was a serious imbalance in payments, in ways that are recognizable in disputes today, as between the USA and China. Then, there was a rapidly growing demand in the UK and the USA for tea. Together with exports of silk and porcelain, tea exports led to large Chinese trade surpluses, since China had little interest in imports. The same contemptuous attitude to foreigners and their products that led to the retreat from trade in the Ming dynasty was repeated in the Qing era: foreigners were "culturally inferior and geographically marginal".[19] As a result, Chinese exports were paid for not in goods, but in silver bullion – which covered around 90% of British imports from China in the eighteenth century.[20] Bullion formed the basis of Chinese money supply, and so boosted the economy (and inflation), with the opposite effect in the West.

The century of humiliation

The British response to this imbalance in trade was to send Lord Macartney in 1793 with a large trade mission to open the Chinese market for imports, of which he carried a sample. The exotic and technologically sophisticated gizmos which he took attracted no interest, and Emperor Qianlong (Ch'ienlung) sent a polite letter to King George declining the offer to trade in them and declining the proposal to station an envoy in Beijing. Macartney rationalized his failure with a prescient metaphor: "The Empire is an old, crazy, first-rate man-of-war which has [...] contrived to stay afloat for these hundred and fifty years past and to overawe its neighbours merely by her bulk and appearance [...] until (with lesser men at the helm will drift) [...] dashed to pieces on the shore."[21]

As it happens, there was a boom in demand in China for Indian cotton, which helped to ease the EIC's payments problems. But it was short-lived and, at any rate, inadequate. An alternative gradually emerged in the form of opium shipped from India. Even before Lord Macartney's visit, the trade had already built up to around 600,000 lbs per year. But it subsequently grew sixfold in the next forty years, despite strong Chinese opposition to drug-dealing. Personal fortunes were built in the opium trade by enterprising pioneers like William Jardine and James Matheson.

Although opium looms large in the present-day litany of Western crimes in China, some historians have cast doubt on the scale, or even the nature, of the problem. Opium had long been consumed in China, as in the West, without much opprobrium. Although it became widely used as a social drug, recreational use was hampered by the price, usually prohibitively high except for the elite. One historian has suggested that later in the nineteenth century, when use was more widespread, "only about one Chinese person in a hundred inhaled enough opium to be even at risk of addiction".[22] One per cent was, however, still a lot of people.

Those who minimize the social consequences of the opium trade suggest that the righteous indignation expressed by the Chinese court was fuelled by considerations of economic policy. With rising opium imports, the trade surplus disappeared, and silver flowed out in growing volumes, depressing the Chinese economy (the crossover point was 1806). There was an argument between legalizers and prohibitionists in the Chinese court about narcotics, much as today in the West. The legalizers argued that a regulated but legal trade could better control the amount of opium coming in and silver flowing out, reduce corruption and raise tax revenue. But the prohibitionists won the argument. Attempts, after 1838, to suppress the trade and destroy opium seizures with renewed vigour led to growing conflict with merchants and British traders.[23]

That conflict in turn led to the first of the (hopelessly one-sided) Opium Wars. Chinese defeat led, under the subsequent Treaty of Nanking (1842), to the cession of Hong Kong Island to the British, opening up a new set of ports for trade, together with reparations for damage and the granting to British nationals of "extraterritorial" exemption from Chinese law. There followed a long period of humiliating concessions to Western powers (and later Japan) through what became known as the "Unequal Treaties", of which there were thirteen until the end of the century (followed by further concessions after the Boxer Uprising, before the Qing dynasty finally collapsed in 1912).

Martin Jacques described China in the late nineteenth century as a "semi-colony with troops free to roam its territory, the treaty ports resembling mini-colonies, missionaries enjoying licence to proselytize Western values wherever they went and foreign companies able to establish subsidiaries with barely any taxation or duties. China was humiliated and impoverished".[24] That is indeed the Chinese view of their history, reinforced in schools and by official propaganda, and it colours their present perception of the West. There is however a counterview: "A disproportionate role in China's troubles would subsequently be attributed to this intervention. Post-imperial guilt exaggerates the responsibility of foreigners for China's woes."[25] Such amnesia or self-justification is not merely the preserve of historians, but influences perceptions today: "To this day, the Treaty of Nanking burns in Chinese national consciousness. That not one American in a hundred has heard of it does not augur well for Sino-American relations in the twenty-first century".[26]

More was involved, however, than retrospective guilt or value judgements refined in a different century. There were mainstream politicians in Britain at the time who were appalled by what was happening in China. William Ewart Gladstone, a future Liberal Prime Minister, campaigned as a young backbencher for the prohibition of the opium trade. Robert Peel, the Tory Prime Minister, whose legislation abolishing the Corn Laws established the principle of "free trade" as central to British economic and foreign policy, led the condemnation – when he was leader of the opposition – of the 1840 attacks on China in the First Opium War.

But it was a Whig (Liberal) Prime Minister, Melbourne, who had dispatched the Fleet in defence of the traders, and another Liberal, Palmerston, who, as Foreign Secretary, condemned the violence and insults directed at British residents and then criticized the seizure of Hong Kong as a woefully inadequate response to Chinese provocation.[27] Victorian liberalism had different facets, the dominant one being of the muscular variety, which argued that there were universal values and standards of political and commercial behaviour – which happened to be British – that should be enforced. Such attitudes persist in Western liberal democracies today and lie behind some of the continued friction over "human rights".

The Western powers were geographically peripheral in their coastal enclaves. They were, nonetheless, important catalysts in the slow, painful disintegration of the imperial regime. In the mid-nineteenth century, China experienced one of the most extreme paroxysms of violence in history in the form of the Taiping Rebellion.[28] The uprising lasted thirteen years, cost perhaps twenty million lives and included such episodes as the "symbolic" beheading of 100,000 people in Canton to re-establish the authority of a regional governor.[29] Inevitably, the conflict spilt over into the coastal concessions, and the Western powers used the conflict to extend their grip over China's trade.

An army that included Western troops sacked Beijing, and participants such as Charles Gordon (later of Khartoum) reported back home the sense of Chinese wretchedness: the rabble of disorganized troops, the brutalized population and contemptuous Western soldiers destroying fine historic buildings like the Old Summer Palace.[30] One commentator was Karl Marx, who saw the mid-century upheaval as a symptom of the decay of the old order and an omen of future collapse leading to republican revolution: "Dissolution must surely follow as that of any mummy carefully preserved in a hermetically sealed coffin whenever it is brought into contact with the open air."[31]

After the rebellion was defeated, there was a period of relative political stability overseen by the court of the Dowager Empress Cixi. There was an attempt by some of her ministers to modernize, making use of Western technology: the period of "self-strengthening". This opening provided opportunities for Western – mainly British – exporters and investors and for financiers to lubricate the business opportunities. The possibility that China might follow in the footsteps of the progressive Emperor Meiji in Japan proved illusory, however. Indeed, when Chinese and Japanese forces clashed in Korea in a short but brutal war in 1894, the supposedly modernized Chinese armies were humiliated. Attempts to graft Western technology onto a decaying structure were doomed to fail. After yet another demonstration of Chinese weakness, the Western powers, threatening more military intervention, pressed for more concessions – a process called "splitting the melon".

The racial divide

It had been the habit of the Chinese court, and many Chinese, to dismiss foreigners as of inferior races, and this attitude explained their complacency and the disastrous underestimation of the threat posed by the Western (and Japanese) arrivals. The prejudice was also reciprocated. Perceptions of the Chinese as inferior were reinforced by the endless defeats of Chinese armies in their encounters with foreign forces on land and at sea and the subservient role they were then required to observe.

But another powerful factor came into play from the middle of the nineteenth century: Chinese emigration, especially to the United States. The first big influx came in the wake of the "gold rush" in California in 1848–49, but the migrants spread across America working as shopkeepers and laundrymen, building railways, working in manufacturing, labouring on plantations in the deep South and becoming successful merchants. The Chinese community, almost all of them men, amounted to around 100,000 by 1880, out of a total population of 50 million – a minuscule fraction, but a very conspicuous one, marked out by a distinctive language, diet and appearance that set it apart.

Racial prejudice against the Chinese, by working-class white men who saw them as competition in the workplace (and for women), was rampant and led to widespread acts of violence, such as the Los Angeles riots of 1871, when twenty Chinese men were lynched by a white mob. At least five American presidents were preoccupied with the political problem of how to manage Chinese immigration, and the result was a Chinese Exclusion Act, justified by the Republican president William Henry Harrison as a "duty to defend our civilization by excluding alien races whose ultimate assimilation with our people is neither possible nor desirable".[32]

Along with migration, events in China cemented what was becoming a widespread view of the Chinese in the Western world – that they were an inferior race, threatening but also deserving of contempt. Popular literature and political discourse perpetuated the idea of the "Yellow Peril".[33] These negative stereotypes were reinforced by the Boxer Uprising of 1898–1901, in which strong anti-Western feeling, fuelled by what were seen as pressures and outrages perpetrated by Western powers, was channelled into attacks on missionaries and their Chinese converts. The Boxer Rebellion was only the latest of several violent spasms which racked the failing Qing dynasty in the latter part of the nineteenth century – but, unlike the others, it was not directed at the imperial throne, but specifically at foreigners. What had caused indignation in China were the missionaries, around whom swirled many rumours of depraved behaviour, and who often took no account of Chinese sensibilities.[34]

Because the Boxer rebellion was an attack on Westerners and their values, it mobilized public sentiment back home: people were outraged by the murder of Western civilians (around two hundred, including some women and children) and aroused by the relief of the beleaguered legations under siege in Peking. A multinational expeditionary force of 54,000 (of which 21,000 were Japanese) suppressed the uprising with some brutality, on what were facetiously called "punitive picnics".[35] The military campaign was followed up by penal reparations imposed on the Chinese government, which had given tacit support to the uprising. The reparations amounted to double the annual budget income of the Chinese administration, plus interest charges, and would be paid over half a century. The so-called Boxer Protocol of 1901, incorporating these and other concessions, added to the sense of humiliation and shame, which in turn fuelled Chinese nationalism: "Faced with such a coalition – Britain, France, Russia, Germany, Austria, Italy and Japan – the Chinese could only feel that the whole world was against them."[36] Such resentments boosted the various political forces which would destroy the dynasty in the 1911 revolution.[37]

The nuances of Chinese politics and the upheavals which followed were mostly lost on Western public opinion, which often managed to conflate, in an unflattering portrait of "Asiatics", a condescending depiction of the Chinese with alarm about "threats" from the Mongol hordes and the newly assertive Japanese military and industrial machine (which resoundingly defeated Tsarist Russia in a war in 1905). Negative stereotypes of the Chinese, particularly, as undesirable and inferior, were reinforced by racial theorists – not just in Germany, following the scientific fad of eugenics, but by literary figures such as Jack London and by popular stories, films and comics like those depicting the villain Fu Manchu. Popular prejudice and racial stereotyping in turn gave legitimacy to overtly racist policy measures in the USA, South Africa and Australia, whose objectives were widely shared in Europe.

It would be good, but perhaps naive, to think that such racial attitudes have totally vanished over a century later and no longer tinge Western perceptions. It is more realistic to face the fact that such prejudice lingers. And, moreover, it is reciprocated. Martin Jacques is one of the few authors to probe the politically sensitive and awkward subject of Chinese racism, which almost certainly did not disappear with the imperial court, but continues in a clear sense of hierarchy with Han Chinese at the top, followed by white people (albeit with periods of deference in the past) and others, including non-Han Chinese, seen as inferior: "The fact that the Chinese sense of superiority survived more than a century of being hugely outperformed by the West is testament to its deeply ingrained nature [...]. The fact that there has been virtually no challenge to, or questioning of, widely held racial prejudices in China [...] means that they will continue to exercise a powerful influence."[38]

Revolution and war

The Chinese revolution of 1911 did, however, create the possibility of recasting relations with the Western powers and revising attitudes. The overthrow of the imperial system brought to the fore a disparate group of reformers – democratic republicans, socialists, Marxists, anarchist terrorist groups – movements which had their counterpart and inspiration in the West. They organized under a Revolutionary Alliance whose figurehead was Sun Yat-sen. If there were unifying threads, they were combined to express a sense of Chinese nationalism and an ambition to modernize the Chinese economy using Western technology. After the overthrow of the imperial administration, there was a brief interlude of elected government (chosen by an electorate of forty million property-owning and educated men) in China's only democratic election. A government was formed under the Kuomintang (KMT), a party born out of the Revolutionary Alliance.[39] That single election earned China, and the KMT, a somewhat tenuous claim to "democracy".

Within months, however, the democratic regime was subverted by a succession of military coups and rebellions led by regional warlords.[40] The weakened central government was, then, too preoccupied to offer effective resistance to a cynical agreement at the Treaty of Versailles, which handed the German concessions in China to Japan over weak Chinese and American objections. There was no acknowledgement that many Chinese had supported the war effort, mainly as labourers in France.

The Western powers had been shown to be duplicitous at China's expense – and this, in turn, led to the massive demonstrations of 4th May 1919, which gave a new impetus to nationalistic feeling. The May 4th Movement gave rise to an intellectual ferment – at least among students and the intelligentsia, who invited the likes of Albert Einstein, Bertrand Russell and Rabindranath Tagore to bring their ideas to China. Crucially, also, these events pricked the interest of Lenin, who saw conditions favourable to the creation of a Communist Party. It was launched initially among Chinese students in France, including Zhou Enlai and Deng Xiaoping, and clandestinely in China in July 1921 with Mao Zedong and its first leader, the "Chinese Lenin": Chen Duxiu.

The exhaustion induced by the First World War led to the disengagement of the Europeans from China, although British governments continued to press their two main concerns: the protection of British commercial interests (the UK had by far the largest stock of foreign investment in China, until overtaken by the Japanese in the early 1930s) and, for strategic reasons connected with the empire in India, the cause of Tibetan autonomy.

The two powers which now called the shots in China were the USA and Japan. In the case of the USA, despite the overt racial exclusiveness of its immigration policy and the self-interest of its businessmen, there was an element of idealism and a wish to do good. Much of that idealism was inspired by Christianity and the influence of missionaries: "Like the businessmen of today who dream of cracking the China market and selling to hundreds of millions of customers, missionary societies envisaged the day when they would 'plant a cross on every hill'."[41]

The Chinese figure who most appealed to the Americans was Chiang Kai-shek, the KMT leader who seemed best placed to unify China and who was willing to take on a growing Communist insurgency. Chiang enhanced his appeal by marrying a Christian and then converting himself.[42] At a more popular level, the Chinese novels of the Nobel Laureate Pearl Buck – drawing on her background as the daughter of missionaries – took a positive view of the Chinese, including the rural poor, into millions of American homes. The idea of the Chinese people as a "yellow peril" began to recede, replaced by a more sympathetic image.

The Japanese did not have to carry the baggage of the "White Man's Burden" but were able to concentrate single-mindedly on economic exploitation and territorial acquisition. They had colonized Korea and the formerly Chinese territory of Taiwan in the late nineteenth century, imposed favourable economic access rights in China in 1913 and acquired a foothold on the mainland after the First World War. Despite efforts to project themselves as less oppressive than the Westerners, it soon became clear that the Japanese version of empire was just as exploitative, if not more.

There was an underlying economic rationale in the form of an East Asian Co-prosperity Sphere, in which the Japanese exercised leadership and the Chinese were junior partners, supplying crude materials for Japanese manufacture: "Japan presented its proposal as a way of promoting Asian interests at the expense of the West; in reality it was an attempt to subjugate Asia in the interests of an imperial Japan."[43] Moreover, an economic and political crisis within Japan brought on by the Great Depression and by American tariffs led to the ascendancy of the military with its ambitions of imperial conquest overseas. In the wake of a contrived dispute (the Mukden Incident of 18th September 1931), Japan assumed control of Manchuria, renamed it Manchukuo and imposed a puppet "chief executive", the former Chinese emperor Puyi.

The 1930s witnessed a complex power struggle in China, with Chiang Kai-shek seeking to impose central government authority on a country pressured from the north by the Japanese, in parts of the countryside by Communist guerrillas and in many parts of the territory by regional barons or warlords pursuing their own agenda. The Communists appeared defeated at one point but embarked on the fabled Long March to relative safety. The balance of forces changed again when the Japanese launched outright war in 1937, resulting in such events as the Nanking atrocities, which radicalized Chinese opinion and left a legacy of anti-Japanese hatred to this day. The KMT and the Communists joined forces (in theory) against the Japanese.

Then the entry of the United States into the Second World War at the end of 1941 led to China being recognized as a "Great Power" by the USA and an important ally (with the USSR). The key factor for the Americans in the Pacific was that the Chinese kept fighting (unlike the British, who surrendered ignominiously in Singapore). The Chinese tied down an estimated 40% of the Japanese forces. The involvement of the United States on the side of the Chinese government was however limited in practical terms – loans rather than weapons or troops, although Roosevelt authorized the sale of a hundred fighter planes, with pilots to fly them: "Though he hymned the Nationalist struggle, Roosevelt was set against any commitment of ground troops to fight the Japanese in Asia. His 'Europe First' policy meant that there were not enough GIs to spare."[44]

Crucially, however, the temporarily suspended existential struggle between Communists and Nationalists was overlooked: "Looking further ahead, the President saw the Nationalists and Communists coming together as China emerged from the war as one of the Four Policemen of the post-war order alongside the USA, the USSR and Britain."[45] Under the Nationalists, China played a role in setting up the United Nations and its various protocols and institutions, though it also laid down a nationalist agenda in relation to the South China Sea and other territorial claims later continued by the Communists.

To sustain the illusion of Nationalist power, Roosevelt had to pretend that the Nationalists were stronger than they were and overlook the corruption and fundamentally undemocratic nature of the KMT (in the 1930s its leadership looked to Germany for inspiration and advice and had its own "blue shirts"). The illusion survived the war but, for the KMT regime, American help was too little and too late for its long-term survival. It was virtually bankrupt, with hyperinflation in the economy: its troops were exhausted and often press-ganged to fight. By contrast, the Communists were building up their military strength with the help of Soviet weapons and attracting political support – or acquiescence – as they advanced.

The ideological divide

The civil war which followed the defeat of the Japanese and led to the Communist victory was the beginning of a new phase, in which the West no longer saw China through the eyes of businessmen and missionaries, as a country to be exploited or converted – or, latterly, supported as a plucky ally. It now saw China through a new lens. China was on the other side in the Cold War with the Soviet Union.

Before and during the Civil War there had been little interaction with the Communists. Apart from sympathetic observers like Edgar Snow, the main contact was through American emissaries during the war trying to bring the Communists into play alongside the KMT. Roosevelt seems to have been persuaded that they were essentially rural reformers – and he contrasted them favourably with Chiang Kai-shek's corrupt regime. When Truman replaced Roosevelt, there was a less romantic view of China in general, but he declined to help the KMT financially, regarding them as "grafters and crooks [...] looking for handouts".[46]

But there was an increasingly influential China lobby, mainly in the Republican Party, building up ideological hostility to the Communists. They were helped by episodes like the killing of a group of American soldiers – which included John Birch, who became a martyr for anti-Communists in America. More fundamentally, the support for the Communists from the USSR when the Civil War raged in north China clearly placed the Chinese Communists on the wrong side of the Iron Curtain. The fact that Soviet support was qualified and was followed by the stripping of a vast amount of Chinese industrial assets – which created deep suspicion of the USSR in the Chinese leadership – was not appreciated in the USA at the time.

In the post-revolutionary inquests into "who lost China", it would be argued that more could have been done to save the KMT regime. But the capacity of the Americans to change the course of the Civil War was very limited. Truman was quite clear that nothing could be done, and washed his hands of China – including, seemingly, Taiwan.[47] Several Western countries – notably the Scandinavians – as well as East European and non-aligned countries like India, recognized Communist China. So did Britain – but China rejected British recognition, as there were still British diplomatic ties to Taiwan.

After consolidating power, Mao indicated that he was "leaning to one side",[48] and made his first-ever trip abroad in December 1949 to visit Stalin. But six months later the Korean War broke out, with a massive invasion by the Communist North, which came close to overwhelming the South. Initially there was no indication that China was involved, but this changed rapidly after an American-led UN force under General Douglas MacArthur drove back the Northern troops and made major inroads into the Northern side of the partition line. When Chinese troops – described as "volunteers" – joined the war on the side of the North Koreans, they drove back the international force, once again, to the partition line. Casualties were on a large scale: perhaps a million Chinese troops, with 160,000 Americans dead and seriously injured.

For a generation, perceptions on both camps were shaped by having fought on opposite sides in the Korean War. For the Chinese, the war was proof of the perfidy of Western imperialism, and it identified the United States as China's prime enemy.

Chinese troops' courage and endurance provided the regime with powerful propaganda at home, but also commanded some respect amongst Western adversaries, which had been absent for the last century and a half. That respect was however tempered by a revival of old prejudices about the Chinese putting little value on life.

The war also helped to fuel a wave of domestic anti-Communism choreographed by Senator Joseph McCarthy. In his vitriolic campaign, the "Red scare", his targets included leading officials in Democrat administrations who were allegedly involved in "twenty years of treason". Prominent among them were the wartime Chief of Staff and then Truman's Secretary of State, George Marshall (of the Marshall Plan), who had briefly been to China in a bid to forge cooperation against the Japanese.[49] The fact that the Roosevelt administration had toyed, however briefly, with the idea of helping the Chinese Communists in the war against Japan, was proof enough of "treason".

Cold War and isolation

For twenty years, China then retreated into isolation, and relations with the Western world were effectively put into cold storage. The single issue of Taiwan, which the USA had pledged to defend during the Korean War, and which the PRC was committed to reclaim, acted as a block on Chinese entry to the UN and other international fora. One of the practical consequences of the mutual estrangement and propagandist, long-range ideological exchanges was that little was known about life in Communist China. What Chang and Halliday called "The Unknown Story" remained largely hidden, and the horrors unseen: "Mao, who for decades held absolute power over the lives of one quarter of the world's population, was responsible for more than seventy million deaths in peacetime, more than any other twentieth-century leader."[50] The early waves of retribution and ideological purification resulted in mass killings – and they were, in turn, superseded by the calamitous Great Leap Forward: "Close to thirty-eight million people died of starvation and overwork in the Great Leap Forward and the famine, which lasted four years […]. This was the greatest famine in the twentieth century, and of all recorded human history. Mao knowingly starved and worked tens of millions of people to death."[51] It could have been worse. Mao went on record with the following claim: "We are prepared to sacrifice three hundred million Chinese [about half of China's population at the time] for the victory of the revolution."[52]

Mao's psychopathic tendencies and paranoia, and total lack of humanitarian concern, all fed off and fed a perception that China was under threat from the rest of the world. On one side, there was the unremittingly hostile United States, armed with nuclear weapons (which had been considered for use during the Korean War and were expected to be used in any new conflict, leading China to launch a vast programme of underground nuclear shelters). On the other side was another nuclear state, the USSR, whose relationship with China, despite the common ideological bonds, had become rather frayed. There had long been suspicions in China about Stalin's commitment to helping China, and then over the strings attached. Khrushchev's sudden, retrospective attack on Stalin weakened the ideological glue. And to add to China's sense of isolation, kindred revolutionary spirits, in Indonesia especially, were crushed.

From the outset of his regime, Mao had wanted nuclear weapons to rebalance power relationships with the USA (and later the USSR). China achieved and tested a nuclear weapon in 1964, which further disquieted its adversaries and neighbours, presenting them with the prospect of an H-bomb and delivery systems to come. The Americans were so alarmed that Presidents Kennedy and Johnson seriously considered sabotaging China's nuclear facilities and discussed the options with Khrushchev.

China's declared foreign-policy objective of support for revolutionary movements around the world heightened the sense of confrontation with the capitalist world. An estimated 7% of GDP was spent on revolutionary prospects, including such projects as the Tanzam railway in Tanzania. There was however little to show for this money.[53] Even when revolution succeeded, as in Vietnam, it was Soviet help which was more decisive and earned the credit.

As the Cultural Revolution gained momentum in the late 1960s, China faced upheaval at home and isolation abroad. Beneath the rhetoric, however, something new was stirring. The perceived threat from the Soviet Union, with the build-up of Soviet troops on the Chinese border, prompted the thought of playing the American card.[54] Moreover, under the newly elected American president, Richard Nixon, the idea of cultivating China as a counterweight to the Soviet Union began to gain traction. There were doubtless other motives on both sides. "In 1970, when it was inescapably clear that Maoism was getting nowhere in the world, [Mao] decided to invite Nixon to China. The motive was not to have a reconciliation with America, but to relaunch himself on the world stage."[55] For his part, Nixon had long-term vision, as well as tactical calculation: "We do not want eight hundred million people living in angry isolation. We want contact."[56] "In fifty years' time we shall be adversaries and we shall need to be able to talk to them"[57]

Out of isolation

It was a long way, yet, from outright hostility to the serious opening-up of China and economic engagement, which was to get under way a decade later. But there was little doubt of the profound psychological shock of the world seeing the fiercely anti-Communist Nixon and the ageing revolutionary leader in China together, in amicable – or at least business-like – conversation. The meeting inspired much hope and even an opera. Nixon himself described the visit as the "week that changed the world".[58] He received a welcome boost to his waning popularity. There was little of substance agreed to Nixon's frustration. But what was much more important was that the meeting happened, and it remains controversial. A recent suggestion from the Chinese that the fiftieth anniversary be celebrated was rejected by the Americans.

From the Chinese side, an overriding concern was not with the substance of the policy (which Mao apparently brushed aside as "detail"), but the choreography.[59] It was designed to confirm Mao's status as a revolutionary leader, and to signal that China was no longer subservient but a respected superpower in the making. In the diplomatic manoeuvring before the meeting, China was admitted to the UN and Taiwan thrown out on a narrow vote, which the USA quietly accepted, conceding one of the central objectives of Chinese foreign policy. In discussing the final communiqué, Kissinger advised that the Chinese should not waste time on commerce, "which could only be infinitesimal in terms of our total economy".[60]

America continued to see China mainly in geopolitical terms. The Nixon–Kissinger approach of treating China as part of a triangular balance of power with the USA and USSR was continued by their successors. When Jimmy Carter assumed the presidency with his own Kissinger (Brzezinski), he wished to pursue détente and nuclear-arms control with the USSR, but also normalize diplomatic relations with China, formally recognizing the PRC (which meant rescinding formal recognition of Taiwan as a separate entity). For its part, China became sufficiently alarmed by the growth of Soviet influence in Vietnam that, fearing encirclement, it invaded its neighbour (January 1979). Chinese troops suffered a military setback, but the intervention succeeded in persuading the Vietnamese to reduce the Soviet role.

The author of that intervention, Deng Xiaoping, was, however, engaged in a much bigger project: the economic transformation of China. In marked contrast to the nineteenth century, the opening of the Chinese economy did not occur because of external pressure. Rather, it was driven by modernizers within the Chinese leadership, following the death of Mao and the defeat of his "leftist" disciples. Deng was the prime mover, and this period is dominated by the ascent of Deng Xiaoping to de-facto leadership. From that position, he was able to pursue the adoption of an agenda focused on economic development and reform.[61] Deng and the reformers had assembled enough of a critical mass of political support by the end of 1978 to launch, at the (third) plenum of the (eleventh) Central Committee, a series of policy changes – "reform and opening-up" – which then provided the basis for more specific changes.

Deng was a pragmatist, unencumbered by ideological dogma: an attitude summarized in his catchphrase "it doesn't matter what the colour of the cat is, provided it catches mice". His pragmatism was reflected in a willingness to learn from capitalist countries. In October 1978 Deng had started his new modernization offensive with overtures to Japan, since he "knew that no country with the possible exception of the United States could be more helpful in its modernization with modern technology and effective management".[62] His problem was the hatred built up in China from memories of the past, reinforced by Chinese propaganda about the atrocities committed during the World War and the earlier conflict at the end of the nineteenth century.

Deng decided that the way to manage public opinion was to go to Japan in person – the first Chinese leader to do so for over two thousand years – and to go in a spirit of reconciliation. In Japan there was a remarkable – and televised – public outpouring of goodwill, coupled with apologies for the past. Political reconciliation paved the way for serious practical collaboration, involving technology transfer, investment and management training. Deng was disarmingly frank: "We are a backward country, and we need to learn from Japan."[63] Deng's approach – to be humble without being obsequious, and to be open to new ideas without surrendering Chinese interests – was the very opposite of that of his imperial predecessors, who combined arrogance and closed minds with weakness.

The Japanese visit served as a template for future dealings with capitalist countries – and it was a forerunner to a visit to the United States. A practical obstacle was the issue of recognition of the PRC and downgrading the status of Taiwan, but that was agreed before he went. Deng set off early in 1979. As with the Japanese visit, it was a great success: widely reported on Chinese as well as American TV. For the first time, the Chinese public was shown a positive view of American life. From the visit directly flowed more student and academic exchanges and expressions of investor interest. But the importance of the visit was primarily psychological, breaking through the mutual suspicion and hostility left over from the Maoist era. The Nixon visit to Mao had been personal diplomacy – this was popular diplomacy.

What was more specific, but also profoundly important for the long term, was when Deng raised the issue of "most-favoured nation" (MFN) status for trade, which would enable China to compete on an equal basis without facing discriminatory trade barriers. Deng predicted (in contrast to Kissinger's much more pessimistic dismissal) that trade with the mainland could soon expand tenfold if it were opened up. The USA agreed to Chinese requests. Deng's prediction was soon proved right, if conservative.

Learning from abroad

Much of Deng's reform agenda was domestic and had little to do with overseas relations. It involved creating the right incentives for peasant agriculture to raise food production and the incomes of the vast majority of the population, who lived in rural areas. But Deng could see that foreign ideas, technology, capital and trade would be important for modernization. This would require a change in China's attitude to the outside world and overseas attitudes to China. The fundamental change in Chinese attitudes to the outside world brought about under Deng stemmed from an underlying confidence in China's potential: he set the stage for a period in which the Chinese were willing to swallow their pride, admit their relative poverty and backwardness – with the implicit criticism of the Maoist past – and learn everything they could from abroad.

To gain maximum exposure to new ideas, Deng encouraged young Chinese to study abroad and Chinese generally to travel and welcome visitors. This represented a complete break with the carefully controlled exposure of the Maoist era – indeed of other Communist countries obsessed by the danger of "defectors". He accepted that there would be a "brain drain", and that some would prefer to make their homes overseas but believed that the costs of opening up were outweighed by the benefits. No doubt he was guided by his own experience as a young man in France and the USSR, learning from abroad but remaining a patriotic Chinese and a revolutionary.

There was then the question of which countries could offer best advice. On matters of technology and industrial management systems, it was clear that Japan and the USA (later Germany) were the best sources, although there was the tricky issue – especially with US companies – of the protection of their intellectual-property rights, which continues to be a problem today. As with other Asian countries seeking to modernize, notably Japan in earlier times, it is not always clear when "learning" becomes the "theft" of knowledge. On the issue of policy advice, the initial move was to study the lessons from "Reform Communism" in Yugoslavia and Hungary, but it was already becoming clear that they were not a success. A senior minister, Gu Mu, led a mission looking for ideas in Western European economies.

In 1980 the Chinese government decided that, instead of piecemeal engagement with Western countries, it should join the Washington-based Bretton Woods bodies, the IMF and the World Bank, meeting their exacting standards. The World Bank in particular combined policy advice with development aid (moreover, without ties to specific donor countries). The World Bank is often attacked for its supposed addiction to the "Washington Consensus" of free markets but was very active in China (as in India), working with economic planners and state enterprises on how to introduce more sophisticated macro- and micro-economic policy tools.

But the main learning process would take place via direct exposure to foreign business through investment and trade. Under a new law, in 1979, China lifted the ban on foreign investment, reversing three decades of nationalistic resistance to exploitative foreign capitalists. Residual suspicion meant that there was initially a strong preference for joint ventures rather than wholly owned foreign ventures, and for keeping foreigners out of sensitive sectors (as continues today and as is common in emerging economies). But the direction of travel was clearly indicated when, during the crucial plenum meeting, Coca-Cola announced the proposed opening of a bottling plant in Shanghai to sell its products in China, and an order was placed for three Boeing jumbo jets: two powerful signals that Western products were no longer taboo.[64]

In parallel with the liberalization of foreign investment, trade regulations were also relaxed, allowing market forces to operate rather more freely. It was not that China was an autarchic, closed economy (trade accounted for around 5% of GDP in 1978 compared to 7% in the USA). But trade was totally regulated by twelve state corporations to balance shortages and surpluses within the planning system. The system of central controls was to be dismantled bit by bit.

Deng's approach to opening China was also to experiment pragmatically: "Crossing the river while feeling the stones". One mechanism was to create a trial system through Special Economic Zones (SEZs). The idea was not completely new: from the mid-1970s, before Deng came to power, there had been areas set aside for exporting which avoided complex customs procedures. But Deng's SEZs, starting with the Shenzhen Special Economic Zone, followed by several others in Guangdong Province, then Fujian, were more ambitious. They tried out different approaches to the relaxation of controls to create an attractive business environment for investors, including those who wanted to use Chinese low-wage labour and imported raw materials as the basis for manufacturing exports. The SEZs were not, however, primarily a means to promote exports, but to provide "windows and bridges", so that foreigners could get a glimpse of what China could offer and the Chinese could sample new arrangements, especially the use of markets, to see what worked and what were the limits of political acceptability. They were laboratories for policy experiment.[65]

Foreign investment poured in, especially from the Chinese diaspora, and export growth was rapid. But there was initially some hostility among Deng's colleagues – who saw the SEZs as a modern incarnation of the nineteenth-century treaty ports – and others who saw them as undermining socialist planning. A cautious and highly influential reformer, Chen Yun, attacked the SEZs for creating corruption, as local officials exploited "black markets" arising from differential prices inside and outside the zones.[66] But by 1984 Deng felt confident enough to press ahead with more zones – now fourteen of them. The overall success of Deng's reforms in raising economic growth rates and living standards meant that opening the economy had political support in the Party. Success bred success.

It was a measure of Chinese self-confidence in dealing with Western countries and their increasingly positive view of China that Deng was able in 1984 to secure an amicable agreement with the British on the future of Hong Kong. Hong Kong's seizure in 1840 had been the event which had set in train decades of retreat in the face of Western countries' demands and was a symbol of that era of humiliation. The PLA could have taken over the colony at any time, since the colony was militarily indefensible. India and Indonesia, among other newly independent countries, had dealt with colonial enclaves in this way.

Even under Mao, however, the Chinese had found the colony useful as a bridge to the outside world and respected the terms of a lease agreement governing the New Territories on the mainland. But the lease expired in 1997, and the Chinese made it clear that they wanted the territory back – preferably in an orderly way. A straightforward takeover was an option that was seriously considered. But Deng could see the usefulness to his economic reforms of keeping Hong Kong's distinctive character as a financial centre. That led to an agreement to allow

Hong Kong fifty years after 1997 as a "Special Administrative Region" operating the "one country, two systems" principle. The agreement was seen as a success for Deng's pragmatism. But the rest of the world might have been less surprised and indignant in 2020, when the Chinese introduced draconian legislation to curb mass demonstrations, had they known that Deng had warned, back in the 1980s, that serious disturbances in the former colony would not be tolerated.[67]

The momentum behind the opening-up of China under Deng continued with spectacular growth rates and rapid expansion of trade and foreign investment. A GDP growth of 10% or more was recorded in the 1980s (though statistics were not wholly reliable), and an export growth of around 14% p.a. This signalled the emergence of a "Greater China", which included Hong Kong and Taiwan, with mutually reinforcing trade and investment links.[68] The Chinese government prepared the way for entry to the GATT (now WTO), which would guarantee MFN treatment throughout the international trading system: that meant replacing import controls by tariffs, a more transparent mechanism which was welcomed by Chinese reformers, since it was consistent with the introduction of domestic markets.

There were a few murmurings beginning to be heard about the impact of Chinese competition – especially among other Asian exporters, who were starting to feel the heat – but these voices did not gain much traction in the liberalizing mood of the time.[69] Crucially, there was also broad support from Carter's successor, Ronald Reagan, whose viscerally anti-Communist views were subordinated to the enthusiasm of American business for China and his own for capitalism in general (he observed that Deng "didn't seem like a Communist").[70] Reagan was particularly exercised about Taiwan and threats to its de-facto independence. But as long as that issue could be managed, all seemed set fair with Deng's model of engagement with the West, vindicated as much as his domestic reforms. Then... 1989 happened.

Saying no to democracy

Engagement between China and the West (and Japan) was essentially economic: it was about business and trade. Deng never wavered from his insistence that economic liberalization was separate from political liberalization. Whatever the radicalism of his economic policies, he did nothing to challenge the idea of China as a "party state" in which the Communist Party would remain firmly in control. The United States and other Western powers, even under someone as ideologically motivated as President Reagan, accepted this separation of economics and politics, and showed no inclination to challenge the internal political order in China (as opposed to the export of revolution and threats to Taiwan).

That understanding came under strain from two factors. The first was the move towards political liberalization – *glasnost* – in the USSR under Gorbachev. Deng was contemptuous (according to his son, he described Gorbachev as "an idiot").[71] But others, in China and the West, were noting that the political liberalization of Communism was now on the agenda. The second element was that, to use one of Deng's phrases, opening the windows had let in some flies. By the mid-1980s, forty million Chinese had TV, and growing numbers were taking advantage of the greater freedom to travel. New ideas started to percolate, which traditional Communists like Deng regarded as "bourgeois liberalism", but which had appeal to young people especially. In 1986 there was a wave of student protests, mainly over conditions in universities, but also voicing demands for democracy. One of Deng's leading reformers, and heir apparent, Hu Yaobang, was held responsible for the breakdown in discipline and sacked. But others in the leadership wanted to explore limited "political reform".

Deng's overwhelming preoccupation was making a success of the economic reforms. The road from success to hubris, however, is well trodden. In the late 1980s Deng (who had formally stepped aside from his Party roles in 1987) and his more radical colleagues thought it was time to sweep away price controls. These were a major obstacle to the creation of a market economy and blunted the incentives for business to supply more goods and services. The move, in 1988, led to soaring inflation (30% in Beijing) – at least in the short run.[72]

The emergence of serious inflation, along with growing corruption, job insecurity in state enterprises and visible inequalities, played into the arguments of more conservative reformers, led by Chen Yun. He had been concerned, from the outset of the reform programme, about excessive speed and the imbalances and distortions it would create, expressed in a debate between "builders and balancers". And there was a mounting list of wider concerns among parts of the general public, such as the widening economic disparities between different parts of the country and the many continuing controls governing everyday life: internal migration, family size and choice of occupation by students.

Public dissatisfaction was expressed in the form of protests and demonstrations – some of which, in central Beijing, could be characterized as pro-democracy, though bread-and-butter issues loomed large. The law-and-order situation deteriorated in cities across China, leading to a declaration of martial law and then open, violent conflict between protesters and the army – which, in turn, led to the suppression of the protests. Hundreds, if not thousands, died in the crackdown in June 1989. In relation to other bloody episodes of Chinese history, including those under Communists, the Tiananmen Square massacre (or "events", in official language) was not a major episode, but the fact that it was conducted in the full glare of global publicity made it one. It also stood in vivid contrast to the largely peaceful retreat of dictatorships in Eastern Europe in the face of democratic uprisings and the fall of the Berlin Wall a few months later. The picture of the lone figure in the square standing in front of a column of tanks became iconic – a symbol of individuals everywhere standing against tyranny and for the values of liberal democracy. It also cast China in a negative light abroad, which was to influence external perceptions for years to come.

The impact on China itself was more limited. Deng had had no qualms about ordering the crackdown, which was consistent with his overall set of beliefs about what he thought was necessary for China: crushing a politically inspired counter-revolutionary movement which was disrupting his programme of economic reform. He lost his leading economic reformer – Zhao Ziyang – whose equivocation in the face of the protests and support for "political reform" resulted in his downfall. But Deng identified another economic reformer to be his successor: Jiang Zemin, the Party leader in Shanghai – who, in turn, brought into leadership positions people like Zhu Rongji, who would instigate the deregulation of prices and take Deng's reforms to another level. There was a short period of economic slowdown caused by stabilization measures insisted upon by Deng's colleague Chen Yun, but Deng did not wait long before returning to the charge. In a couple of years, he performed – in an unofficial capacity – his last major contribution to public life. He visited South China at the beginning of 1992, urging a redoubling of economic reform, building on what had been achieved. Deng's underlying strategy – opening up the economy, keeping politics firmly under Party control – was reaffirmed and continued by his successors.

What was crucial – and fortunate for China's future relations with the West – was that the 1989 events occurred on the watch of Reagan's successor, George H.W. Bush. Bush had been US emissary to China in the mid-1970s, before becoming head of the CIA, and he had come to know Deng. They had struck up and maintained a personal friendship and line of communication. Bush fully understood Deng's position and sympathized with him. Bush also shared Nixon's long-term vision of good relationships with a developing, modernizing China, and didn't want them derailed by the backlash to Tiananmen Square. His position was uncomfortable, however, since the US Congress and other G7 countries (except Japan) were clamouring for tough sanctions. Bush felt he had no alternative but to go along with mild sanctions, such as suspending World Bank loans and cancelling agreed sales of military equipment. He sweetened the pill by writing a handwritten, apologetic letter to Deng, saying that notwithstanding the sanctions, he wanted to maintain good relationships.[73] He sent secret emissaries to keep lines of com-munications open, and in May 1990 he ensured that a renewal of MFN status for Chinese trade was approved without fuss. Deng acknowledged the gestures, and, in an orchestrated move, ensured that some political detainees were released.

Bush was an old-fashioned practitioner of personal diplo-macy and negotiation between states. This appeared to be out of place in a radically changed environment where the ideas of Western democratic capitalism seemed to be carrying all before them and Communist China looked like a relic of a bygone, discredited age. He was wise enough not to be carried away by rhetoric about the "end of history" – and suspected that China was unlikely to follow Soviet Communism to a sudden end. What Bush could not prevent, however, was the attempt in Western countries to introduce the concept of "human rights" and "democracy" into dealings with China over foreign and trade policy – though he knew that this would be a red rag to the Chinese bull.

In 1992 he had to run for re-election against someone who seemed more in tune with the new age. Bill Clinton campaigned on human rights, pointing the finger at the "tyrants" in Beijing in particular. The Democratic Party was however split between business-friendly legislators who represented firms eager to cash in on the China market and human-rights activists wanting to punish China for political repression. A compromise was reached: the once routine renewal of MFN status would become conditional on political conditions being met. China would be required to allow free emigration, bar exports of goods made with prison labour and "show progress" in releasing political prisoners and protecting Tibetan religious freedom. There was a furious reaction from American business – and a large group of them, led by Boeing, lobbied hard for MFN. Clinton's economic team, worried about unemployment – around 7% at that time – had little patience with the human-rights argu-ments. The author of the human-rights policy (Michael Lord) complained of "sabotage",[74] and there were allegations of a conspiracy, orchestrated by the Chinese.[75]

The Chinese were probably not involved in any conspiracy. But they were not just passive spectators. The belief that Deng had been right to see off attempts to push China down the Gorbachev road seemed vindicated by the disintegration of the USSR and its chaotic aftermath. Old resentments about Western condescension resurfaced with a vengeance. The new Chinese leader, Jiang Zemin, and his more conservative prime minister, Li Peng, who had never been persuaded of the wisdom of Deng's opening to the West, made it abundantly clear to Western visitors that China would not budge an inch in response to foreign demands for political change. A popular Chinese book at the time captured the growing hostility to Western demands. It was titled *China Can Say No* – an expression of Chinese nationalism which was considered too aggressive even by the regime, and therefore banned.[76]

Faced with concerted pressure from US business to drop provocative political demands of China, Clinton was persuaded to follow his strategist's maxim: "It's the economy, stupid."[77] He abandoned the idea of MFN conditionality. He advocated economic engagement with China: "President Clinton learnt hard lessons that continue to apply to China. It's tough, if not impossible, to get China to make changes that it views as opposed to its national interests, especially ones that might weaken the Communist Party's grip on power."[78]

For the next twenty-five years, until the advent of Donald Trump, it remained the consensus amongst Western decision-makers that economic engagement with China – ignoring political differences – was of strong mutual interest. There were, even at an early stage of Chinese reform, some tremors of nervousness over the pace of Chinese export growth: "In some OECD countries, especially those of Western Europe, where rising unemployment is an acute political and economic issue, there are serious concerns over competitive pressures from China."[79] These concerns were met with somewhat contradictory arguments – that the benefits of China's successful economy outweighed the costs, or that the competition was too small to worry about. Moreover, it was assumed that a bigger Chinese economy could be accommodated within the existing international system. And there was an assumption, usually implicit, that economic and social development must inevitably, in time, lead to political liberalization: a weakening of the Communist Party and a convergence of values and institutions with the West which would in turn reduce frictions. The debate about whether the growth and development of China are good not only for China but also for the world is central to arguments about the "new Cold War". And there has been a rapid reappraisal in recent years.

The big rethink

For the best part of a generation, there has been little questioning of the view that China's emergence from centuries of extreme poverty and hardship was not merely praiseworthy, but beneficial more generally. This benign view of China, which was reflected in public opinion in Western countries,[80] reached its high point in the wake of the financial crisis of 2008–9. A massive investment programme unleashed in China staved off recession at home and acted as a powerful stimulus to the rest of the world – indeed, the growth stimulus was sustained for most of the next decade.

Perceptions, as revealed by public-opinion surveys as well as official comments, then shifted strongly in a negative direction – from seeing China as the saviour of the world economy to seeing it as a dangerous and disruptive competitor; from regarding internal Chinese politics as irrelevant or broadly benign to perceiving an alarming ideological challenge; from acknowledging China's role as a "responsible stakeholder"[81] to denouncing it as an aggressive and bullying power. These abrupt changes owe something to President Trump and his belligerent "America First" economic nationalism, directed especially at China, and to the more systematic demonization of China by his Secretary of State Mike Pompeo and his team. There was a receptive audience for influential opinion formers, especially on the right of the Republican Party, who had long warned of the long-term political and security, as well as economic, threat to the USA from a resurgent Communist China and of the alleged complacency of those who had consistently underestimated the threat.[82]

Such warnings acquired more traction as it became clearer that President Xi was establishing a more authoritarian – and dictatorial – leadership in China; re-establishing internal political discipline around a strengthened Communist Party; and killing off any illusions in the West that China was on a path to liberal democracy. Moreover, his forceful projection internationally of his "China Dream" was seen as aggressive.[83] It departed from an unassertive, modest, self-effacing leadership style which Deng Xiaoping described as being to "hide your ambitions and disguise your claws"[84] A key turning point was when, in 2018, Xi removed term limits on his presidency, allowing him potentially to rule for life and formalizing what some have called a "Third Revolution" (after Mao and Deng).[85] The process of confirming President Xi's leadership for another decade (and potentially longer) was also the centrepiece of the 20th National Congress of the Chinese Communist Party in October 2022.

This more negative and confrontational approach to China (and by China) reflected in part the specific issues involved in competition between two superpowers – one established and seeking to uphold a wider international order, the other new and challenging. The fear of a more assertive China has been expressed by some of China's neighbours, notably Japan, at least on security issues. Europe has been slower to follow. In 2015, President Xi was welcomed to the UK and celebrated a "Golden Era" of bilateral relations. Shortly afterwards, however, the UK disengaged from close collaboration with Huawei on telecommunications, faced with US displeasure and sanctions. And the UK has now joined a military collaboration with the USA and Australia in the Pacific. The main continental European countries, especially Germany, have seen the relationship in almost entirely commercial – and positive – terms, but have increasingly joined in criticism of China and distanced themselves from closer collaboration, emphasizing "strategic competition".

Events in 2020 and beyond have given a new and negative twist to the Western perceptions of, and by, Xi's China. The prolonged disturbances in Hong Kong and the subsequent National Security Law and political repression in Hong Kong, which effectively ended the "one country, two systems" model, was one. Then the Covid pandemic led to recriminations against China, where it originated, aggravated by Trump's exploitation of the "China virus" for political ends. China's reputation was then restored by its effective, if draconian, zero-Covid policy (though its initial success in cutting deaths to negligible levels proved to be something of a Pyrrhic victory, as the Omicron variant swept China, with strict lockdowns causing great economic damage and hardship). A deeper and more insidious legacy of Covid is that it has seriously compromised face-to-face communication at leadership and popular level. Before the pandemic, 130 million or more Chinese travelled every year to do business, study or for tourism. Drastic impediments to travel since have increased isolation and reinforced negative stereotypes.

Since the election of President Biden, perceptions have become even more negative. He initiated his approach to China with frontal, public attacks on China's approach to human rights and an alleged "genocide" of Uyghurs in Xinjiang, followed by targeted sanctions which China has reciprocated. The administration's attacks on China have been expressed more coherently than by Trump – no longer stemming from occasional, unpredictable, hostile rhetoric and tweets based mainly on trade disputes, but as part of a comprehensive message treating China as a threat and, moreover, the "greatest threat". The Chinese threat is seen as economic, technological, political and military, and involves a long-term struggle between what are seen as two incompatible and rival systems from which there can only be a winner and a loser.

This current American perception of China – shared across an otherwise bitterly partisan Congress and by the wider American public – is that China plans to usurp the role of the USA as the dominant superpower and centre of what is currently a Western-based international order. And the answer to this perceived China threat is containment and the building up of a "coalition of the willing" among democracies prepared to "call out" and confront China on its aggressive posture and abuse of human rights. Biden has managed to assemble a coalition with the EU and Canada to criticize China on human rights. And a loose, embryonic, military grouping has been launched involving Japan and India as well as the USA and Australia.

China's perception of the West, as articulated by the leadership (of party and state) but widely shared, as far as can be judged, is that it is in terminal, long-term economic and political decline. China, by contrast, is an emerging economic, technological and financial superpower with a successful and stable system of governance. It does not consider itself as an enemy of the West: it is the West that has created an "imaginary enemy". But China demands respect and sees the West as trying to frustrate and undermine its rise, including by interfering in what it sees as its internal affairs as in Hong Kong, Xinjiang, Tibet and Taiwan. The Chinese view is that the United States cannot accept that it is no longer the sole superpower, and that lesser Western powers like Britain and Australia have a colonial mindset, seeking to impose their alien values. China will resist external pressure with the help of what President Xi calls "a great wall of steel". This "wall of steel" is taking the form of a rapid expansion of China's military capability, including technologically sophisticated hypersonic weapons and a build-up of its strategic nuclear deterrent. It also involves economic sanctions against countries – from Australia to Lithuania – which cross what the Chinese regard as "red lines" in foreign policy.

The Ukraine war has added to mutual suspicion and conflict with China. China has studiously avoided explicitly taking sides, in the company of a group of "neutral" countries including India, Pakistan, South Africa and other nations from Africa and the Middle East. But it has recently negotiated a comprehensive treaty, strengthening economic and security ties with Russia, and has been giving Russia tacit support albeit without openly breaching Western sanctions. The Ukraine war has also focused attention on China's declared long-term intention of incorporating Taiwan – if necessary, by force. The two cases are different: Taiwan is not an internationally recognized sovereign state, and the amphibious military challenges are an order of magnitude more serious than any faced by the Russian army. But the "strategic ambiguity" of American protection of the island is a source of continued uncertainty, and a Chinese attack is increasingly seen as a matter of "when" rather than "if".

The Ukraine war has also reinforced a trend which was already apparent: to question the merits of close economic interdependence where this might impinge on "security". The range of activities potentially affected is huge, but certainly concerns advanced semiconductors, rare minerals and metals, key infrastructure, medicines, energy and food production. China has already embarked on a "dual circulation" strategy to hedge against the risk of US sanctions, and the USA is actively decoupling in some sectors over and above the reduction in exposure to overseas supply chains, which is happening commercially in response to the disruption of the pandemic. Meanwhile, the Ukraine war has led to a perception that China and Russia are closely linked in strategic terms, opposed to the West and its Asian allies.

The result of this clash of perceptions and of interests is considerable geopolitical tension. But it coexists with close and seemingly growing economic integration through trade and investment, despite attempts at "decoupling". The countries of the G7 have committed themselves to a policy of "de-risking" rather than "decoupling", but it is far from clear what these concepts mean in practice; how they will be collectively implemented and monitored; and how the Chinese will respond. There is also a recognition of common interests in dealing with "international public goods", like the problem of climate change. During the COP 26 conference in Glasgow, the USA and China managed to agree to cooperate on the outlines of a zero-carbon agenda, despite non-communication in other areas. The outcome is what has been described as a "cold war" or a "hot peace" – a complex and unstable mixture of mutual suspicion and hostility combined with practical commercial and other cooperation.

My objective is to try to look through the changes in perception and to establish if they are justified and where they lead. I look first (Chapter 2) at China's status as an economic "superpower": what it means and whether the label is justified. I look at the very different assessments of the "bulls" and "bears" – from those who extrapolate the notion of China's past (relative and absolute) success to predict a future where China dominates the world economy to those who see deep structural problems which will derail it. Some believe we have already seen "peak China". I look then (Chapter 3) at the question of whether China's economic rise is benign or malign – or a mixture. I ask whether an international order built around essentially liberal ideas can include Chinese "state capitalism" or "socialism with 'Chinese characteristics". There is the linked issue of technological leadership – in fields like 5G and AI – and whether it is possible for a controlled system, closed to many competing ideas, to develop the creativity and innovation required to surpass the USA. And, if it does, where does that lead? (Chapter 4).

Then there is the difference of values and conflicting interpretations of "democracy", "human rights" and the "rule of law" (Chapter 5). If the Chinese system, rather than converging, diverges from that of the West, does it matter? It isn't altogether clear what China stands for outside its own internal system. So, if China then becomes a world power, even a hegemonic power, what does it want? I look at these questions by examining the different parts of the world where Chinese economic and political influence is becoming substantial (Chapter 6). And lastly, I look at the combination of competition and conflict, cooperation and confrontation, which is emerging or could emerge (Chapter 7). In looking at the future I try to avoid predictions but consider different scenarios. There are very different ways in which the current geopolitical conflict could play out, and there are very different outcomes possible for the Chinese economy, among many other uncertainties. I conclude by making a strong but unfashionable case for continued engagement with China, recognizing that there are things which make liberal democrats in the West very uncomfortable, but that the alternatives are worse.

Chapter 2

The New Economic Superpower

Size matters. The total of what a country produces or consumes defines its economic importance. It also establishes the potential for spending economic resources on military capacity or other ways of exercising power internationally. The debate around China, as economic threat or opportunity, starts from the reality that, after four decades of prodigious Chinese economic growth, there are now two economic "superpowers" (unless we treat the European Union as a single entity). There may be big differences in living standards and in the future trajectory of their development, but on the matter of size there seems little doubt: depending on how we measure it, China approaches the USA or has already surpassed it.

It is easy to see why the Americans are exercised by such convergence. China has over four times the population of the USA. It has achieved rough parity of size at roughly one quarter of America's per-capita production and living standards (roughly equivalent to Thailand). Averages conceal considerable differences, but if China were to get to roughly half American levels (currently equivalent to Romania), which does not seem a wildly implausible long-term objective, it will, by simple arithmetic logic, have an economy twice as big with all that that implies in terms of heft. That is a simplistic way of looking at the world, but very crudely it illustrates the recent and potential future shift in economic importance and the political response to it.

Size and growth

Arguments about economic size rest on estimates of relative GDP, which are not without controversy. They tell us nothing about the quality of the goods or services, about the wider quality of life or the stock of public or private assets and wealth or the stock of natural resources, human capital and labour supply, or the benefits of such intangibles as having a global currency. GDP statistics do not capture such factors as environmental pollution, as with China's poor air quality, which is estimated to have led to the premature deaths of thirty million people this century.[1] Comparisons are especially difficult when comparing different countries under different systems of government, at different levels of development and using different economic concepts, as with China and the West.

Comparison of overall GDP is, nonetheless, the best measure we have to hand of the economic size of countries – what they produce or the scale of their market. What the numbers tell us is that in 2020, according to the IMF, the 330 million people of the USA produced (in terms of value added) around $22 trillion of goods and services, while the 1.4 billion Chinese produced $17 trillion at the official exchange rate of approximately 7 yuan (or renminbi) to the dollar. That is the usual understanding of the pecking order of country size: that China is very much second to the USA, though a long way ahead of the next-biggest economies – Japan ($5.1 trillion), Germany ($4.2 trillion) and the UK ($3.1 trillion) – and roughly on a par with the whole EU.

But 7 yuan can buy a lot more in China than a dollar can buy in the USA. This has led to re-estimation of GDP levels to reflect true purchasing power. There is much debate over how to capture purchasing power in a meaningful way, since there are big variations by product, by region and over time. The measure used by the IMF in 2020 suggests that GDP corrected for purchasing-power differentials (the PPP) is, in China, close to $27 trillion, while the World Bank has a figure of $24 trillion. Both estimates place China ahead of the USA as number one in economic size. The third-biggest economy on a PPP basis is India ($10 trillion), and the UK falls from fifth to tenth.

These two sets of numbers are highly controversial, and there is no definitive right or wrong. There are different ways of looking at the same set of facts. A generation ago, it was clear to economists that there was a very big gap between official GDP at market exchange rates and a PPP-adjusted rate when it came to assessing China's economic size. There could be a multiple of as much as six.[2] The significance was that businesses and governments could be dealing with a country whose market and production capacity was equivalent to France (PPP measure) as opposed to Belgium. There has since been a substantial degree of economic integration of China into the world economy, and price levels have become closer, reducing the multiple to around two. But the difference is still considerable and cannot just be swept aside as some do: "But for all practical intents and purposes, including those of trade and commerce, savings and investment, defence and politics, market exchange rates matter more."[3] That is not the position of the World Bank and IMF when measuring economic size in a meaningful way, and I will follow their convention.

The conclusion, derived from the PPP measure, that China now has a bigger economy than the USA is reinforced by other analysis. Subramanian compiles a measure of "economic strength" based on a combination of the two alternative GDP measures together with its share of world trade and net exports of capital.[4] On his measure, China overtook the USA in 2020. Others would argue that China's "economic strength" is fatally undermined by the fact that, unlike the USA, it does not have a convertible currency used internationally.

There are also questions over whether Chinese economic figures can be trusted from the point of view of accuracy and honesty. There have long been doubts over the quality and meaning of Chinese economic data, though it has been greatly improved in recent years since China joined the IMF and World Bank.[5] Until recently, services were not regarded as productive, and were systematically understated, as was "imputed rent" for measuring housing income; there have been problems collecting data from millions of small farms and village industries; and it is difficult to estimate the amount of grain and other foodstuffs fed to animals rather than sold to human markets. GDP estimates vary depending on whether they are calculated by production or expenditure. One estimate of Chinese GDP suggests that official numbers may be under-estimated by a factor of 13% to 16% because of differences in accounting methods.[6]

As to honesty, ministers in the Maoist period asserted that "statistics are a weapon in the class struggle".[7] Whilst ideological zeal is no longer rewarded in quite the same way, it would be surprising if the habits of mind had entirely disappeared. That is especially true of sectors of the economy such as heavy industry, where specific planning targets still apply. Local and provincial administrations have an incentive to inflate numbers in order to impress their superiors. On the other hand, a generation of officials has been trained to produce numbers which are trusted by the IMF and the World Bank, and which meet their standards of reporting. The Central Bank is highly regarded for competence and integrity. If there is any temptation to cheat at a national level, it may also be to understate rather than overstate economic measures, since China has been anxious to avoid the loss of the concessions which come from being regarded as a developing economy in the World Bank and World Trade Organization. In any event, Chinese data is now crawled over in detail by commercial analysts as well as inter-governmental organizations, and any systematic upward or downward bias would surely have been found by now. A belief in the integrity of Chinese data has however been somewhat dented by the disappearance from publication of a lot of statistical series and by delays in the publication of GDP figures (when they seemed likely to be uncomfortable).

Comparisons over time are more difficult than at a single point in time, especially when long periods are involved.

Maddison has pieced together data over the last century.[8] He, in turn, draws on six centuries of agricultural-production data assembled by Perkins,[9] as well as attempts by Wu and by the US Congressional Office to make sense of the statistics of the pre-reform, revolutionary era.[10] He concludes that "official growth estimates for China are very weak".[11] That is true, even today, when annualized growth is presented with implausible precision and stability over time.

Such precision is because GDP figures perform a different function in the Chinese system from the West. In market economies, variations in GDP reflect what happened to production, expenditure and income, after the event. In China, growth rates are set in advance by the central planning system, which survives, in part, despite an era of market reform. The growth figures then determine what local officials must do to make the figures happen by pulling the levers at their disposal, such as the supply of credit and approval of projects. Since officials win favour and promotion by making happen the expansion envisaged by their superiors, the outcomes are likely to come close to the objective.[12] Those following the Chinese economy closely use real indicators like electricity consumption or rail transport movements to assess short-term trends. Plausible re-estimates of growth moreover suggest that the past actual trend rate may be 2% to 3% lower than claimed (i.e., 7.5% rather than 10%).[13]

The combination of the serious economic problems discussed below and Covid restrictions has forced the authorities to reduce their annual growth expectations to 5.5%, and the true figure will be less. Pessimists see a continuing decline to growth rates comparable to those of the USA or EU as China sinks into the mire of problems facing other middle-income countries. But a more optimistic story of continuing technological catch-up through the large manufacturing sector and the transfer of many of the remaining quarter of the workforce from agriculture to more productive roles is also plausible. I shall look at the evidence for these very different views.

The story of growth

The China inherited by Mao's successors was a very poor country, and the China inherited by the Communists even poorer. But it would be a mistake to imagine that both were drawing on a blank sheet of paper. Despite the chaos of the "cultural revolution" and the devastation of the Great Leap Forward, China's level of development at the beginning of the reform era was significantly higher than, say, India's in terms of industrialization, literacy and schooling, access to sanitation, life expectancy, large-scale irrigation and much else.[14] And despite the upheavals of war and domestic conflict, there had been patchy progress in the pre-revolutionary period, with some modernization of infrastructure and industry and with a near doubling of overall output between 1885 and the revolution.

A question long debated by historians is why Chinese civilization, which was in many respects more advanced technologically, in agriculture especially, than Britain and other Western countries at the beginning of the nineteenth century and before, failed to make the leap into the industrial revolution and economic "take-off" much earlier. Adam Smith had noted at the end of the eighteenth century that "China is a much richer country than any part of Europe".[15] There were well-developed markets, enterprising peasant farmers and a burgeoning merchant class. The popular explanation has long been that China stagnated because it was a closed society: the Chinese elite had closed minds, born of a sense of superiority, with little interest in trade or foreign ideas.

Whilst that was true, there are other explanations. These include the notion that China was caught in a "high-level equilibrium trap". Its expanding population had no outlet in the form of colonial settlement. Overpopulation dragged down living standards and the cost of labour to such an extent that there was no incentive to mechanize.[16] Then subsequent generations, under the imperial court and after, never had the cohesive leadership and stability to sustain the kind of modernization drive which was accomplished under the Emperor

Meiji in Japan. Other considerations may have included the fact that China had a highly centralized (as well as dysfunctional) state, whereas Europe had a significant number of separate and competing states, which fostered experimentation.

Whatever the reasons for China's failure to modernize, its share of the global economy shrank from just under 30% at the beginning of the nineteenth century, with 35% of the world's population, to around 6.5% with 20% of the world's population by the late 1970s. The reforms of Deng Xiaoping then dramatically unleashed rapid development, with the achievement of annual growth rates of 9% to 10%. The economic-policy changes have been thoroughly described elsewhere and do not require detailed repetition here. They included the liberalization of markets, the deregulation of prices and ownership reform, initially for agriculture, with de-facto property rights – such as long leases on land – extended across the economy, as well as the opening-up of the economy to trade and investment.[17]

It would be wrong, however, to see the reforms simply as a series of economic-policy changes. It was also a political revolution which entailed an overhaul of the role of the state to something closer to the developmental-state model of East Asia.[18] Decision-making was also radically decentralized to provincial level and to local government. Crucially, lending was devolved to local banking institutions, and their credit supply became more significant than that of central bodies.[19] Competence, or at least pragmatic decision-making – in delivering material improvements – replaced ideology as the main criterion of performance. The central objective of policy – and the basis of the legitimacy of the ruling Communist Party – became one of sustained, rapid growth leading to increased living standards, achieved without crises and shocks.

In the pre-reform period of 1970–78 the economy grew by around 5% p.a., with per-capita income growth of 3%. After the reforms, the recorded annual growth rate was, as already noted, 9% to 10%. Agricultural production growth accelerated from 2.7% p.a. in the pre-reform period to around 9% in the following twelve years, with a spectacular growth of cash crop production.

Agricultural production growth was the most direct result of the reforms, increasing farm incomes, lifting large numbers out of rural poverty and improving the quantity and variety of food. Productivity growth in farming also freed up labour from the land, creating a vast pool of labour for work in manufacturing and in cities. The share of agriculture in employment shrank from 70% before the reforms to 60% just over a decade later.

The rest of the world was more conscious of the impact of these reforms on trade. But China was growing its trade from a very low base: under 1% of world trade in 1978 and still only 1.6% a decade later but growing rapidly.[20] With more than 12% of world trade, China now leads the world, at least in trade in goods. There was also an explosion of inward foreign direct investment, rising to 7% of GDP by 1995, marking a very different pattern of development from other East Asian countries like Japan and Korea, which did not welcome FDI. And it was this integration of China into the supply chains of global companies, through foreign investment, which established China as an integral part of the process of globalization.

Agriculture leads the way

The story of how China moved from reclusive poverty to the status of an economic superpower is remarkable, and there is a vast literature describing and analysing it. In order to deal with the issues around China today, it is however necessary to review briefly how it got where it is.

It is helpful to see the growth take-off of China following Deng's reforms, and those of his successors, as passing through a series of stages when the impetus came from different sources. The first, over the first five or six years, was led by agriculture. As noted above, even in the pre-reform era, Chinese farmers were productive whenever political stability permitted, and were achieving a growth of production faster than the growth in population as a result of the expansion of irrigation and intensive use of fertilizers.[21]

But the key step in the reform process was the adoption of the Household Responsibility System (HRS), which restored the primacy of households over collective production teams. Peasant farmers were assigned collective land, initially for fifteen, then fifty years. They were required to deliver a quota of production to the state – but, beyond that, they were free to dispose of surpluses as they wished. The incentives had an electrifying effect on farmers' willingness to try new techniques, especially hybrid seeds and new crops, and there was a remarkable spurt of crop yields and output growth, with an annual average growth of agricultural production of 11.5% between 1978 and 1984, which subsided to a still impressive 6% growth for the rest of the decade.[22]

There was still much to do to liberate the productive potential of agriculture. The process was uneven, reflecting the political priorities and farming potential of different regions. Moreover, the process of liberalizing prices and reforming the system of procurement and marketing happened over a longer time frame and was somewhat haphazard, especially when there was strong resistance from urban consumers to removing price controls.[23]

Agriculture, nonetheless, made a major contribution to the success of the reforms in two ways, over and above the supply of food. First, the surge of farm incomes was accompanied by a big increase in household – as well as corporate – saving, providing capital for future investment. China's savings rate was already around 30%, and this surged to almost 40% by the end of the 1980s. Second, the growth of productivity in agriculture meant that there was a vast army of surplus labour to supply the needs of industry, especially the rapidly expanding exports based on labour-intensive manufactures.

Export and investment-led growth

The second phase in the growth story, lasting roughly from the mid-1980s until the global financial crisis of 2008, has been characterized as export-led – and specifically led by manufacturing exports. In fact, as elaborated below, the designation "export-led" is misleading, since it was investment alongside exports which together were the main driving force. Consumption grew in absolute terms with a growing economy, but its relative contribution was suppressed.

Export growth was important, since it enabled China to step up the import of technology in the form of capital goods. It also generated large-scale employment in labour-intensive activities. There was a very low export base. Before the 1970s China's exports had hovered around $2 billion a year, and the total grew to around $10 billion at the beginning of the reform period, still barely 1% of the world total. But after the reforms exports took off. By 1991, exports had reached $70 billion and surpassed those of Korea. Since then, for almost two decades, growth was around 20% p.a. in value and 15% p.a. in real terms.

Export growth came from two sources.[24] The first was a direct result of the incentives created in Special Economic Zones attracting inward investors, mostly from Hong Kong and the rest of the Chinese diaspora. By 1995, around 30% of exports were generated in this way. Another major source was the Township and Village Enterprises. These were originally part of the Maoist vision of rural industrialization. But entrepreneurs and enterprising local community leaders then took advantage of the first wave of reforms to create what were essentially small and medium-sized companies operating with minimal hire-and-fire and other regulation, weak social obligations and an absence of political interference.

TVEs operated in fiercely competitive markets with increasingly professional management and many moved into exports, either directly or by subcontracting to larger entities with overseas marketing outlets. In the first full decade of the reform era – 1980 to 1990 – TVEs had expanded from employing thirty to ninety-three million workers, surpassing state-owned enterprises as employers (seventy-three million). Purely private Chinese firms were growing rapidly too to service Chinese and foreign markets, though the borderline between private and collective was very blurred.

Exporters were able to benefit from very low-cost but productive labour. Large profit margins in turn generated a surplus for future investment. Western consumers were able to enjoy the benefits of cheap manufactures. Chinese workers at least had a job, though conditions were poor and pay meagre. The labour conditions enjoyed by migrant factory workers were particularly harsh.[25] The harshness was compounded by the fact that migrant workers had no settlement rights or welfare entitlements in the cities but were tied to their place of origin under the so-called "hukou" system – effectively a system of internal passports. Nonetheless, this model of development served to modernize China, and served the economic interests of the West (of which more in the next chapter).

This remarkable export-producing machine, which within a generation was to dominate world trade, wasn't just a product of cheap, compliant labour, but also of policy reform guided both by experiment and the demands of international markets. The reforms included: a phasing-out of administrative controls; removal of mandatory import and export prices; decentralization of national foreign-trade businesses – from twelve to several thousand; delicensing; tariff cuts; reduction of barriers to importing inputs for processing in China; and liberalization of conditions for foreign investment. Perhaps the most crucial step was, in 1994, the devaluation of the currency by around one third – from 5.8 yuan/renminbi to the dollar to 8.7, where the rate was held for a decade.

The consequence was not merely rapid export growth, but an export structure which became a textbook example of comparative advantage. China specialized to reflect its comparative advantage in those products requiring abundant labour to produce. The share of exports characterized as being "labour-intensive manufactures" rose from 31% in 1978 to 57% fifteen years later in 1993. Its imports were increasingly of capital-intensive manufactures (59% in 1978; 72% in 1993).[26]

The simple caricature of China as a source of clothes, shoes, wigs and toys produced competitively by mass production with cheap labour was, however, already becoming dated by the end of the 1980s, as China started exporting at scale telecom-munications kits, electrical appliances, office articles, watches and audio equipment in competition with more established exporters in Korea and Singapore. In 1991 high-tech industrial parks were also being established, including an Experimental Zone housing leading Chinese universities and research insti-tutes alongside investors who were required to have more than 30% of employees as graduates. This was to be the so-called Beijing Silicon Valley, soon to be replicated in thirty inland cities. The culture and objectives were very different from the coastal SEZs. China was becoming the workshop of the world but was already thinking several steps beyond the role of being a supplier of cheap and cheerful manufactured goods.[27]

Growth spread from islands of successful manufacturing across the country, absorbing more surplus labour into cities and urban-based services and manufactures. Per-capita incomes rose rapidly, doubling every decade. The numbers living in absolute poverty on an international, World Bank definition fell from more than 50% at the start of the reforms to less than 20% by the mid-1980s, and then to under 10% at the turn of the century. Whilst a substantial proportion of the returns from this growth represented profit margins for the producers, leading to high savings and investment in businesses, there was also a significant growth of consumer demand to create new markets for domestic industries.

Consumption, however, while it represented 50% of GDP up to 1990 and was growing rapidly in absolute terms, was shrinking as a share of the total. The share had shrunk to around 35% of GDP by the time of the next major phase in Chinese development after the global financial crisis. That fall is explained by the rapidly increasing share of investment (and net exports), which together grew from 25% to 50% of GDP.[28] China resembled post-war Japan and Korea (and Stalin's USSR) in squeezing consumption to finance investment.[29] In the case of China, much of that investment was ploughed into infrastructure and housing in the rapidly expanding cities. But a lot also went into inefficient and polluting heavy industry.

Indeed, such was the growing influence of domestic investment that it is somewhat misleading to talk about "export-led"
growth at all. The exports themselves drew in large quantities
of imported components and raw materials. If we look at net
exports, a more meaningful definition of the contribution
of trade to demand, it has been estimated that less than one
third of Chinese growth from 1990 was driven by net exports
as opposed to domestic demand in the form of investment.[30]

China was not overwhelmingly export-dependent in the
way post-war Germany and Japan had been, or the smaller
industrializing countries of Asia. But exports mattered not
just in growing the capacity to import capital goods and the
associated technology: exporting was a means of gaining
access to Western and Japanese markets and investors, and
furthered Chinese understanding of new ways of doing business. Learning was, after all, the original aim behind Deng's
reforms, and not just achieving a spurt of economic growth.

The sheer scale and growth of Chinese exports nonetheless
presented several problems. The first was a willingness by the
rest of the world to accommodate a major new economic competitor. I have described above the political battles in the USA
around "Most Favoured Nation" treatment at the beginning of
the Clinton administration. More broadly, there was nervousness about China's willingness or ability to follow international
rules. The process of admitting China to the World Trade
Organization – crucial to protect China from discriminatory
and arbitrary trade restrictions – took fifteen years from its
application to join in 1986, and the country was subject to the
most detailed and demanding list of conditions required of
any new member.[31] There was a lot of frustration, especially in
the USA, that China had since been selective in the reduction
of its trade barriers, but it was "crucial in promoting China's
integration into the global trading system".[32] This success also
exposed China to the risk of serious recession in its main export
markets and a collapse in demand, as it was to discover in 2008.

Another problem was that a serious imbalance began to
emerge in trade and current-account transactions. Initially that

was not an issue. Throughout the 1980s, China ran deficits in its external payments. Tariffs were cut to far lower levels than in other emerging economies like India and Brazil. But then, crucially, in 1994 the Chinese authorities fixed the value of the Chinese currency to the dollar at a low value designed to boost Chinese exports, much as Germany and Japan had done in an earlier period in history. In this way, exports benefited from greater price competitiveness and imports became more expensive for Chinese consumers. With the continued very rapid growth of exports, net exports – trade surpluses – rose from 2.1% of Chinese GDP in 2001 to 8.8% in 2007. China was thereby accumulating current-account surpluses of 9% to 10% by the time of the financial crisis.

A different way of looking at the same problem is to see it not as a facet of trade policy, but as a result of imbalances between savings and investment. China was accumulating savings at a higher rate than they could be absorbed in investment: the rate of savings had risen from 30% of GDP at the launching of reforms to almost 50% by the time of the financial crisis, and only about half of the increase was capable of being invested, despite the extraordinary level of investment taking place. This savings surplus was, in effect, exported. At the same time, the USA had a very large savings deficit, reflected in its "double deficits": a large budget and current-account deficit. Chinese savers financed that deficit by buying up US government bonds.

There was a mutual interest in maintaining the situation, since if the Chinese had offloaded their stock of dollar assets, they would have driven down their price (the value of the dollar) and devalued their own reserves. The USA was content that someone – in this case the Chinese – would finance its dearth of savings, enabling American consumers to absorb cheap imported Chinese-manufactured products (and, in the process, finance the US budget deficit by buying government bonds). Chinese foreign reserves, largely US Treasury notes and bills, grew rapidly. China sought to hedge against the over-dependence on holding US government debt and sought to diversify its overseas assets by encouraging overseas investment by Chinese companies under what was called a "going out" policy (which led to such high-profile acquisitions as Lenovo's buyout of IBM's PC business in 2005).

The symbiotic relationship between China and the USA was variously described as a "balance of financial terror" or, less emotionally, as Chinamerica or Chimerica.[33] Tolerance of imbalances depended however on an absence of nationalistic politicians exploiting such obvious targets as the dependence of the USA on Communist China and Chinese "currency manipulation" (or, from the Chinese viewpoint, poor Chinese savers financing self-indulgent American lifestyles and budget indiscipline). Such sentiments were indeed aired with growing annoyance in the US Congress, and China sought to appease the mounting hostility by allowing a gradual appreciation of its currency after 2005. It was too little, too late for the critics. Constant financial diplomacy between US and Chinese decision-makers kept the "balance of financial terror" from breaking down – just.

The vulnerability of both sides to a sudden shock and lack of market confidence was however then exposed by the financial crisis of 2008. China's realization that over-dependence on export growth exposed it to the consequences of a "crisis of capitalism" caused a sharp change of direction. But there was a deeper recognition that the whole economy had become seriously unbalanced; only a year before the crisis, Prime Minister Wen made a frank acknowledgement that "the biggest problem with China's economy is unstable, unbalanced, uncoordinated and unsustainable growth".[34] The financial crisis and China's response to it were to make those problems worse.

The investment binge and the hangover

The collapse of credit and global economic activity in the wake of the banking crisis in 2008 had dramatic effects in China. The sudden large fall of export orders caused large-scale job losses in the labour-intensive manufacturing export sector and those firms in the supply chain or dependent on spending from the workers in that sector. Millions of Chinese workers lost their jobs, many returning to their villages. More than a million or so of those left without work were graduating students – a particularly sensitive group after the Tiananmen "event".[35]

The authorities realized the necessity for prompt and decisive intervention and authorized a vast investment and current government-spending programme of 12.5% of GDP on top of existing investment plans. At a time when Gordon Brown was convening the G20 to agree a smaller coordinated stimulus package, the Chinese acted unilaterally and on a massive scale. A key element was the programme of high-speed trains (an extra 10,000 km to be built over five years), together with heavy discounts on the purchase of consumer durables and a roll-out of a national health service. That was just the beginning. The provinces came up with plans around six times as ambitious as those of the centre, involving local infrastructure, the financing of big property developments and heavy investment by public enterprises.[36]

The radicalism of the proposals did not just lie in the scale and speed of response, but in the way they were funded. The huge fiscal stimulus was to be financed by large-scale credit creation through state-owned and controlled banks or credit-creating mechanisms available to provincial and local government. The Chinese authorities thereby killed several birds with one stone. They revived the Chinese economy, which grew at 9% in both 2008 and 2009. Millions who had lost their jobs were quickly re-employed. Although much money was wasted on speculative building projects, unnecessary additions to industrial capacity, corruption and poorly designed projects, there were big, tangible improvements in infrastructure, the supply of housing, health and other services.

The authority of the Communist Party was undoubtedly, if only temporarily, enhanced. The stimulus also had global impacts: boosting commodity markets and the economies dependent on them, as well as capital goods exporters in the developed world. Together with the US Federal Reserve and the Obama stimulus package – and of greater importance than either – China lifted the world economy, gaining in prestige and self-confidence.

The warm economic glow from the stimulus package continued for several years, and the world economy recovered from the financial crisis with continuing help from Chinese growth, albeit that growth was gradually slowing. From mid to late 2015 it became clear however that the party was at an end, and a serious hangover was setting in. First, the stock market began to slide as a reaction to speculative over-optimism. Despite official attempts to stabilize it, the market continued to fall, losing half its value in six months. Second, in response to an IMF invitation to demonstrate the strength of the currency by moving to greater convertibility, exchange controls were relaxed. Far from demonstrating its strength, the currency fell sharply in value, dragged down by large-scale capital flight. A lot of rich Chinese judged that now was the time to get their money out of the country.

These two manifestations of the volatility of financial markets appear to have had a significant effect in reinforcing the more conservative instincts of President Xi, who had come to power in 2012 determined to clamp down on some of the excesses of a more liberalized economy, such as rampant corruption. He had already demonstrated considerable ambiguity on the issue of whether to liberalize markets further, building on earlier reforms, or whether to pause the reforms because of their negative side effects. The 2013 plenum of the Party had taken the significant step of defining markets as "necessary" – the strongest statement to date – and playing a "decisive role"; but then it also agreed that the role of the state was "commanding" (alongside a list of sixty concrete policy initiatives designed to deepen market reforms). There was a built-in contradiction between state restraint and market liberalization.[37]

The Chinese authorities did succeed in containing the 2015 crisis, stabilizing both domestic and foreign exchange markets, the latter with the reimposition of stronger capital controls. But it was clear that financial-market worries were symptoms of a deeper malaise. The Chinese economic miracle looked less impressive from close quarters. In particular, the imbalances in the economy, which Premier Wen and others had warned about years before, were no better – and arguably worse. China was still highly dependent on investment, and in particular property development, to drive growth. That mattered for two reasons. A lot of the investment was wasted – which meant more and more investment had to be poured in to get the same amount of growth. Magnus points out that it took, on average, 2 to 4 units of yuan to be invested in the period 1976–2006 to generate an additional yuan of output – but in the splurge of investment after the financial crisis, to 2015, it took 9 units of investment.[38] And because the investment was financed by an extraordinary burst of credit expansion, there was a legacy of debt on the balance sheets of the borrowing companies and bad loans as assets in the Chinese financial system.

Much of the lending took place through credit intermediaries operating outside the system of bank regulation and traditional banking institutions – the so-called "shadow banks". The lending was of questionable quality, and potentially unstable.[39] Roughly 40% of outstanding debt is now owed to these shadow banks. There was a lot of very ill-advised property speculation, by individuals and by big developers like Evergrande, with vast numbers of unsold flats overhanging the market – perhaps 20% of the total, today.[40] It was estimated that 60% of Chinese bank loans were tied to real estate.[41] Heavy industry had also enjoyed an investment boom, leaving a lot of spare capacity – more than 25% – in sectors like steel, oil refining and cement. The government has had a real dilemma: how to support demand to keep the economy growing in order to maintain and improve employment and living standards – and how, at the same time, to shift reliance from growth away from investment, simultaneously reducing exposure to property, flaky debt and unstable financial institutions through orderly deleveraging.

Pandemic and war: managing shocks

While China has been trying to deal with these long-term structural issues, there have been two major economic shocks, resulting from Covid and the Ukraine war. It isn't yet clear how these crises will play out, but they are an important test of resilience. Growth of 6% was reported in 2019, the pre-pandemic year, well down on the era of double-digit growth, but healthy enough were it not for the fact that the authorities appeared to have only one answer to any slowdown: to pump more credit into the economy. When the pandemic hit, China's strict lockdown, zero-Covid approach initially worked well to minimize both the disease and the economic impact. A fresh stimulus package – again, built around infrastructure and other investment, backed up by credit growth of 14% – was however launched in 2020 to offset the effects of the virus. At around 5% of GDP, the package was small compared with China's reaction to the financial crisis – and small compared to leading Western economies, which suggests caution about aggravating the underlying weaknesses. It was however sufficient to make China the only country of any importance to have grown in 2020, by around 2%,

China appeared to have escaped the worst of the Covid pandemic, and in 2021 was able to benefit from the world recovery through a big expansion of exports, up 30% over the previous year, resulting in a large trade surplus. Despite some interruption to production and disruption in power supplies, the economy grew well in excess of the 6% target: perhaps between 8% and 9%. In the early months of 2022, however, it became clear that there were serious problems ahead. The zero-Covid policy had failed to eliminate Covid. China remained very vulnerable, with a large percentage of older people not fully vaccinated. And draconian lockdown and quarantine arrangements were seriously impacting economic activity – initially in Hong Kong, then in Shanghai and other cities. The deterioration of the Covid position coincided with the Ukraine war, sanctions on Russia and the severe global impact on energy, food and other prices.

The official target growth rate of 5.5% was already scaled down reflecting the process of deleveraging in the property sector and stagnation there affecting almost as much as 30% of the economy on one measure.[42] The lockdown of Shanghai, a megacity of 25 million people which accounts for more than 10% of China's economy, and then other provincial cities directly affected overall Chinese growth, and in particular disrupted supply chains in the export sector. China's overseas customers have been given an additional incentive to diversify their sources of supply away from China. There were reports of foreign investors considering moving out of China because of Covid measures.

Restrictions on movement in quarantined areas also prevented migrant workers returning to work in the fields for seasonal harvests, disrupting food supplies. And the war interrupted imports of corn and barley on which China depends. One consequence has been a renewed emphasis on food self-sufficiency and stockpiling (it was estimated that China in early 2022 was already hoarding 70% of the world's maize stock, 60% of rice and 50% of wheat).

The combination of the supply shocks of the Ukraine war and the pandemic together with the slowdown induced by the deflation of the property bubble has created a worrying slowdown with side effects such as recorded youth unemployment of almost 20% (which understates the problem, since it excludes the rural youth and long-term unemployed). The high unemployment levels amongst young people coexists with much lower rates of overall unemployment (5.2%, April 2023), albeit with higher rates among over-50 migrant workers, who lack the education and skills to adapt. The existence of high unemployment among recent graduates is a source of particular concern and is blamed by the government on lack of flexibility and an unwillingness by young people to adjust to changing national priorities.

The sudden lifting of Covid restrictions created the potential for a rapid recovery in 2023, with an official forecast of 5% growth over the year. But the early indications were that recovery was disappointingly slow, with poor growth reported for consumer spending, corporate revenue, output and business investment.

A stimulus is required to revive flagging growth, but the authorities' freedom of manoeuvre is limited. China has low inflation (around 1% p.a. in early 2023), which should permit the use of low interest rates, but China cannot allow interest rates to fall too far behind the USA, for fear of precipitating a sharp fall in the exchange rate and capital flight, underlining the reliance on fiscal policy to keep the economy expanding.[43] The use of fiscal stimulus rather than credit growth to keep the economy going runs up against the limits of government borrowing to offset the long, deflationary consequences of a collapse of property and land prices. Real estate and related spending accounts for around a third of government revenue. The fall in land prices has brought local authorities (and whole provinces) to the brink of bankruptcy. The government's priority is to control fiscal risk, which eliminates the scope for expansive fiscal stimulus. Indeed, the old model of using big bursts of public investment, national and local, to sustain rapid economic growth is now broken.

Deeper problems: is China running out of steam?

Over and above the economic challenges created by the pandemic and the Ukraine war, deeper problems remain. One question is whether the weaknesses exposed in 2015 and recognized in broad terms almost a decade earlier actually being dealt with or merely brushed over. The more pessimistic analysts believe that the debt problem and underlying economic weaknesses are unresolved, representing "red flags" which constitute a threat to China's continuing rise.[44] The problem is essentially not technical, but political: to stabilize financially, China's growth needs to slow because of the earlier reliance for growth on debt-based investment, especially in property. But slower growth risks political instability, as employment and living standards fail to meet expectations.

There may be, also, deep-rooted structural issues, such as a falling labour force and ageing population, and a set of challenges called the "middle-income trap". These lead to some basic questions about the future. Has the Chinese economy run out of steam? Have we passed "peak China"? Is China trapped as a middle-income country unable to grow further, or will it go on to catch up with the West in living standards? And has President Xi's political dominance and emphasis on restoring Party control made these problems more difficult to resolve?

There have long been two contrasting views of China's future: those of pessimists and optimists – bears and bulls. Although there have been specific reasons for arguing that China faces insurmountable problems, they come back to the same basic point: doubts that a country under the control of the Communist Party can reform a state-dominated economy, making it adapt to market forces and adjust to the demands of increasingly sophisticated technologies and consumers. There is the challenge, acknowledged but unaddressed, of how to achieve structural change away from over-dependence on debt-financed, low-productivity capital investment. The fate of the Soviet Union, which failed in its economic restructuring – perestroika – is evidence for the pessimists.

But the culture of the Chinese Communist Party is unique and complex and has evolved greatly from Mao to Deng and his successors, and now to Xi.[45] The degree of pragmatism of Chinese reformers and their willingness to use market forces and a form of capitalism are on a different scale of radicalism from anything seen in the Soviet Union or even its reform-minded satellites (even taking into account President Xi's greater scepticism about the private sector and markets). There are those who would argue that a state without democratic accountability and openness to challenging ideas and dissent can never succeed in the long run; others that what really matters is government effectiveness and public trust. On both points modern China scores much better.

There is an additional form of scepticism which is not ideologically based but draws on the experience of a significant number of countries which have become stuck in a "middle-income trap". The idea comes from empirical observation, in particular the work of World Bank economists, who have tried to explain why countries fail to make the jump from developing to developed status.[46] The evidence suggests that with a few significant exceptions – most notably Korea, Chile and Poland – there are not many developing countries that have made the full journey from low-income to high-income status. There is a group of states with per-capita incomes from $1,000 to $12,000 (2011 prices), formed of countries in Latin America, the Middle East (Turkey), South-East Asia (the Philippines), Eastern Europe and South Africa, who have run into seemingly unmanageable problems resulting in a serious economic slowdown.[47] For some reason, they have been unable to develop economies characterized by innovation and higher productivity from a more educated labour force rather than capital accumulation (investment), or high-value rather than low-labour-cost exports.

The concept does not have secure theoretical foundations, and it remains controversial. And for a vast country like China its meaning is unclear, since big regional differences mean that some provinces are already well beyond the middle-income trap even in terms of nominal (rather than PPP) GDP per capita: Guangdong, Fujian, Zhejiang and Jiangsu, and the metropolitan areas of Beijing, Shanghai and Tianjin. Nonetheless, Prime Minister Li warned explicitly about the dangers of the middle-income trap, and the finance minister put the risk back in 2016 at around 50–50. It is now plausible to argue that China has, overall, passed the high-income threshold. But it could still fail to realize its potential.[48] I turn to specific reasons advanced for the pessimism.

The demographic dividend expires

Much of China's growth in recent years has been powered by surplus rural labour. China has, so far in its development, been a textbook example – as were Japan, Korea and Taiwan before it – of rapid growth underpinned by large-scale movement from low-productivity agriculture to higher-productivity urban and industrial sectors – the so-called "Lewis Model", after the theory that was first set out by the Nobel Laureate W. Arthur Lewis.[49] I have already described above aspects of this model, but a key part of it is access to surplus labour. Wages are kept low, so there are large profit margins, which are mostly saved and ploughed into investment, leading to business expansion. If labour costs remain low, this model of expansion can continue – and, indeed, develops a "virtuous circle" of success. But China is now said to have passed the "Lewis Turning Point" – the end of rural surplus labour.[50] The turning point, it is argued, has been brought about by a combination of very rapid economic growth and a low birth rate, the legacy of the "one-child" policy. But what a "turning point" means for China is rather unclear: there are still just under three hundred million Chinese peasant farmers, between a quarter and a third of the labour force, employed, full time or part time, in low-productivity agriculture.

The overall working population is currently estimated to be just under 900 million. It has been falling from a peak of 940 million in 2012, and on current trends will fall by another 100 million by 2035. Such aggregates are somewhat misleading, however, since China does not have an integrated labour market with free population movement. Movement from villages to the cities has been governed by the hukou system, which has restricted social-welfare benefits payable to migrant families and tied the families of migrant workers to their home districts. An estimated 278 million people were, in 2015, officially recognized migrant workers.[51] Despite some relaxation of the rules around migration to the cities, there has been plenty of evidence of growing labour shortages among the remaining third of the labour force – that is, the formally employed, who are neither migrant workers nor peasant farmers. Hukou reform potentially frees up a large potential urban labour force.

A key factor in the shrinkage in overall numbers is the very low birth rate, resulting from the "one-child" policy introduced in 1979. Until recently, the general view among policymakers in China, shared by many Western "experts" on development, was that China had a "population problem": too many people. Chinese poverty has long been explained in these Malthusian terms. The Chinese government's response was drastic: the "one-child" policy, with some coercion in the form of fines or pressure on women to have abortions or undergo sterilization, to discourage large families. The policy has, if anything, been too successful, and has reduced fertility (the average number of children born to a woman of child-bearing age) to a level far below the level required to maintain a stable population. The Chinese fertility rate is estimated to be as low as 1.3, as against 2.1 required for replacement of the population, and is now below that of Japan (though official estimates are higher: 1.5 to 1.7). The global average is 2.4 (2019), as opposed to 3.5 in the 1950s.

China's population is now falling, having peaked at 1.41 billion in 2021. At the same time, older people are living longer, with an estimated life expectancy of 77 (79 for men; 75 for women) – very similar to the USA (79) or the UK (78). Therefore, the population is potentially shrinking and ageing at the same time, with growing numbers of elderly dependants supported by a falling labour force. That has led to the fear of China "becoming old before it becomes rich", with an elderly population trapped with low pensions and an inability to work, and dependent on a single offspring for support beyond meagre state provision. Among the consequences is a tendency to save for old age rather than spend, depressing consumption levels.

To stabilize the demographic trends, the government has relaxed the "one-child" rule (to "two-child" in 2015; now three), but this appears to have made little difference, and there was a further sharp fall in births during the pandemic. A generation is emerging which rejects the idea of breeding at the request of the state – what has been called "voting with the womb"[52] – and is more preoccupied with the problems of living in crowded accommodation and its cost, and the opportunities for career development. Government promises of better maternity benefits and childcare and stronger employment rights for women may or may not be realized. The shortage of children is however already causing important social changes, such as greater acceptance of unmarried mothers, of gay couples adopting children and higher valuation of baby girls. Another approach to boosting the labour force being mooted by government is postponing the retirement age from 54 to 65 in stages – necessary but unpopular. Ideas such as retraining older workers and banning age discrimination are also gaining ground.

Why should a declining labour force affect growth potential? There is an obvious arithmetic point that GDP growth is not growth in GDP per capita, and it is the latter but not the former which is the aim of policy: rising living standards, not "economic size" for its own sake. Indeed, Japan may already be a country where the perceived ill of economic stagnation and decline is experienced as rising living standards. For China, if the aim is to achieve Western living standards, the singular pursuit of very high growth rates is only partly relevant. What is also needed is a recognition that the next stage in China's development is the achievement of rapid productivity growth accompanied by higher wages. The World Bank calculates that "total factor productivity", or TFP (growth explained not by labour supply or capital investment, but by improved efficiency), has been just over 1% p.a. in the last decade, a third of the previous three decades.[53] The IMF also notes a fall in the last decade over the previous decade.[54] But the Conference Board calculated it at 3% p.a. growth between 2015 and 2019, at a time when the same measure was falling in high-income countries.[55] A consensus view is that TFP is now low and declining.

The regime is aware of the challenge and published in 2020 a thirty-two-point plan to improve productivity. A key driver of productivity is education and skill. The 2020 census showed that there were 218 million graduates, a doubling over a decade, but still far below the levels of developed economies, where up to half of the population is college-educated. Adults in China have an average of ten years' education as against 11.5 in high-income countries,[56] though children now entering the school system can expect thirteen years of schooling. The population is also becoming more urban (to 64% from under 50% a decade ago) and more concentrated in the productive coastal belt. A key challenge is what Rozelle and Hell have identified as a vast, mainly rural, underclass.[57] They argue that this underclass is of roughly 800 million people, either rural or migrant workers with rural hukou, only 11% of whom have high-school education; 75% of all babies, moreover, are born into this class. The restrictions of the hukou system mean that they are educated in poor-quality rural schools rather than the high-pressure, competitive institutions enjoyed by the urban middle class. Part of the authorities' response to the bigger productivity challenge is to create clusters of big cities which workers will find it easier to access and which will have the benefit of 5G mobile networks and better transport connections. A large part of the anticipated productivity improvement comes from moving the agricultural labour force into the cities. Farming still accounts for 23% of employed (2021), 20% more than in rich countries.

There is some evidence – from wage trends – that a shift to higher pay is already beginning to happen. The National Bureau of Statistics estimates of annual real-wage growth averages have been around 10%, ahead of GDP growth, which suggests that, overall, workers are now sharing the proceeds of growth. There are also numerous reports of labour unrest and wildcat strikes as workers push for better pay and conditions and try to exploit localized scarcities of labour. Not all labour unrest, however, is caused by labour realizing its growing value. As the economy has slowed over recent years, many firms have struggled financially and have tried to manage their cash flow by paying wages late, leading to a growing recourse to strike action by the labour force. The authorities have identified in principle with worker grievances, while suppressing anything which threatens serious disorder.

A rational economic response to a declining labour force and growing labour scarcity is to automate. The process of automation is gathering pace in Chinese manufacturing. According to the International Federation of Robotics, China has around 800,000 robots, a third of all the robots in the world. This quantity works out at 100 robots per 10,000 industrial workers – around half of US levels, but catching up fast. But as Deng understood when he first saw production lines in Japan, more is involved than installing machinery: it is the management systems behind the machinery and the software which determine whether automation is efficient. The government has ambitious programmes to give companies good advice and improve software for manufacturing. That takes us to the issue of economic reform. But interwoven with the issue of long-term economic productivity is the more immediate question of debt.

Debt and the property bubble

I have described above the mechanism by which, especially in response to the financial crisis of 2008 and the Covid crisis of the last two years, the authorities kept the economy going: investment, financed by credit to Chinese firms to build infrastructure or housing. There have long been warnings about debt levels from international organizations such as the IMF and the Bank of International Settlements, and their concerns were echoed by the Chinese Central Bank and President Xi himself, warning of the dangers of financial instability. Yet debt grew inexorably, by an estimated annual average of far more than 20% since 2008.[58]

There is some dispute over the numbers. A lot of the debt of Chinese corporates is hidden in the obscure accounts of the "shadow banks", specifically created to avoid regulatory scrutiny. The very crude overall aggregates for debt in the economy (corporates, households, financial sector and government) has China with a debt-to-GDP ratio of around 260% at the end of the first quarter of 2020, according to the Central Bank, while the International Institute of Finance (IIF) in Washington had a figure of 335% at the end of 2020. I will use IFF data from here on.

At first sight the Chinese figures are not exceptional. The global total at that time was 363% (for the USA 383%, the UK 500% and Japan 663%). In the case of China, anxiety has stemmed from the rapid growth and concentration in corporate debt.

If we look at the various components of debt, China's household debt as a percentage of GDP (around 60% at the end of 2020) is very close to the global average and well below that of the UK (88%) – but it is increasing rapidly. Government debt is relatively low (63%) compared to the global average (105%), let alone heavy public-sector debtors like Japan (257%). The financial sector is also well below average in terms of debt (48% versus a global average of 90%). The concern centres on one item in particular: corporate debt at 160%, as against a global average of 95% and lower levels in the USA and UK (around 78% each).

So why is this a problem? Comparative experience suggests that "credit growth is a powerful predictor of financial crises".[59] This generality seems to fit the Chinese experience: "China's credit boom is one of the largest and longest in history. Historical experience of 'safe' credit booms of such magnitude and speed are few, and far from comforting."[60] Much of this debt was incurred to support property speculation in China's highly distorted and corrupted property and land markets and is therefore vulnerable to a painful property-market correction. In the housing market, where there is already an estimated 20% of unoccupied homes, the fifteen million homes a year which were being built by developers until recently – largely for speculative purposes rather than for owner occupation – were adding to the glut as economic growth and population growth fell. And where there was investment in real activities, in state enterprises, it was often – as noted above – in poor-quality projects and cannot be serviced or repaid in the longer term. I will return later to the issue of how the reform of state enterprises is seeking to address this problem.

It is the speculative bubble in property and the enormous amount of investment channelled into the housing market which has fuelled the argument of the debt pessimists. We have got to a point where a sharp economic downturn potentially leads to a crash in asset prices which makes a large chunk of this outstanding corporate debt worthless. There could then be a financial crisis which could be one of two kinds. First, a cascade of bad-debt default could lead to the collapse of major institutions, as occurred in the USA and UK in 2008 and could happen in China if "shadow banks" which finance much of the property investment drag down other systemically important banks. Alternatively, if the default is contained, there could be a long period of stagnation, as in Japan after 1990, with "debt deflation", as financial institutions concentrate on rebuilding their balance sheets and writing down bad debt rather than lending to support the economy.[61]

It is the sheer scale of the property sector which makes either of these scenarios so potentially lethal for the Chinese economy. There are so many linkages between property and other sectors of the economy that it is difficult to be precise about the boundaries. But Rogoff and Yang estimate that it accounts for 29% of Chinese GDP,[62] up from 20% in 2010 and 10% at the turn of the century (by contrast, the UK figure is around 20% and that of both USA and Germany 15%, calculated on the same basis). Economists at the Asian Development Bank have suggested that the Chinese figure is a more modest 15%,[63] and Goldman Sachs economists have estimated 23%.[64] The property sector is big however calculated and Martin Wolf's response to those seeking to minimize the problem is that it is the sheer scale and growth of leverage, much of it of poor-quality loans, which puts China in a uniquely risky position.[65]

China's leaders, from the president down, and its technocrats (especially in the Central Bank) have been aware of the seriousness of the problem. For President Xi, the wild excesses of the property sector embodied everything he disliked about the model of development China had been pursuing: rampant corruption, financial instability, rewards for the undeserving super-rich. His dictum that "houses are for living in, not to speculate in" was a warning shot across the bows of property developers. The technocrats had already been refining the tools required to bring the sector under control with a growing battery of financial regulation. The Central Bank had developed a complex array of credit priorities and controls in what would be called "macro-prudential" policy in Western economies.[66] Property markets are, consequently, regulated both from the demand side (30% minimum deposits for mortgage borrowers and a ban on borrowing for second homes) and in terms of credit supply (home loans no more than 70% of lenders' assets). A toughening of policy was signalled at the March 2021 meeting of the National People's Congress, when there was discussion of how to manage financial "bubbles". There followed the publication of a series of "red lines" for developers: strict control on the amount of permissible debt in relation to assets, cash and equity.

The aim was to create a "controlled explosion" – to deflate the property bubble in a managed way and to force developers to deleverage. They would no longer be able to borrow more to service their debt obligations. If necessary, the biggest developers could be allowed to go bust and be forcibly dismembered and restructured following the precedent of Anbang, the insurer, Huarong, a specialist in managing bad debt (whose corrupt chairman was executed) and the developer HNA.

At the time of writing, it was unclear whether the "controlled explosion" would achieve its objectives. But some of the casualties of the detonation were becoming apparent. The biggest developer, Evergrande, was forced into technical default on its bonds, while others – Modern Land, Shimao, Sinic – were reporting difficulties. Indeed, the whole industry appeared to be at risk, like a collapsing, speculative Ponzi scheme. There has been a sharp fall in developers' bond prices both in Chinese and offshore markets. In a desperate search for liquidity, firms have tried to tap new markets such as commercial paper and unorthodox shadow banking as with LGCVs (Local Government

Commercial Vehicles), threatening wider contagion. House sales have fallen sharply, followed by house and land prices. The fall in house prices has hit household spending, since housing accounts for 80% of household assets by value. The fall in land prices has had a drastic impact on local government, for whom land sales account for around 30% of their revenue. And the property crisis has rippled through the whole economy, undermining consumer confidence and dragging down sectors linked to property sales.

The authorities are painfully aware of an acute policy dilemma: the need to stop speculative excesses leading to house price "bubbles" which so affront President Xi's idea of "common prosperity"; but also to recognize that the property sector is crucial to growth and too big to fail. In November 2022, when evidence emerged of a 20% fall in investment in the sector, year on year, and a fall in housing sales of a third, the government reversed policy. It removed tough restrictions on lending, relaxed "red lines" on thirty leading firms and intro-duced sixteen new measures, including credit lines, for "good quality" developers. There was also a public recognition that the problem was not simply one of allowing developers enough liquidity to put their finances on a secure footing, but also to sort out the finances of local government. Local financing vehicles – which finance developers and enable infrastructure projects to proceed – have accumulated around $10 trillion in debt, much of it bad. Many local authorities have been effec-tively bankrupted, and, moreover, are unable to continue to use land sales as a source of revenue. A restructuring of this local debt and finding new revenue sources (like local property tax) is urgent.

The authorities appear confident that a controlled process will prevent a Western-style bank collapse, and it is heading off political trouble by ensuring that priority is given to protest-ing home buyers who have made advanced purchases, at the expense of other creditors and shareholders. Some genuinely constructive reforms are being undertaken, like experiments with property taxation to widen local-government revenues and dampen speculation, but they are still on a trial phase.

CHAPTER 2

The authorities ultimately have the powers to control the banking system and utilize the vast stock of foreign as well as domestic assets (little Chinese debt is to overseas creditors in any event). They can also make use of the scope for fiscal expansion or converting private into government debt (since public debt is low). The last point is crucial. Many troubled institutions are ultimately owned by the state, and their corporate debt is, in effect, sovereign debt. China is very far from having a sovereign-debt problem, with a low ratio of (gross) national debt to GDP and large official asset holdings in foreign currency.

Warnings about China's company debt have been so loud and persistent – and yet unrealized – that there is a sense of "crying wolf". Thomas Orlik describes China as "the bubble that never pops".[67] But even if the risks may have been overstated, there is a degree of consensus amongst China optimists and pessimists that it is not plausible to expect a continued expansion of corporate debt on the scale seen hitherto. The Chinese authorities appear to concur. How far and fast China can continue to expand and move to more sustainable debt levels depends on the extent of wider economic reform. And that depends on the ability of the president and the Communist Party apparatus to make reform happen.

Can China reform? Markets and "Common Prosperity"

Reform is a popular word in China, though it is often unclear what it means. In economic policy it will often mean the greater use of markets, but also the opposite: regulation to deal with instability or modernization in the form of more efficient state monopolies and the adoption of "national champions", especially in high-tech industries. The common thread is productivity to maintain growth.

Reform presents a practical problem: how to neutralize or circumvent those vested interests in the public and private sector who are potential losers from being exposed to the disciplines of the market, greater transparency or tougher regulation – and how to do it while maintaining effective Party control.

For some, however, the problem is ideological. They believe that China under its present rulers cannot succeed. This is the conclusion of Acemoglu and Robinson, authors of the book *Why Nations Fail*,[68] which has become a seminal statement of the reasons why only liberal democracies can prosper economically. To succeed, they argue, countries need institutions which facilitate innovation and "creative destruction". These qualities can only emerge under political and economic freedom. Countries cannot thrive under institutions which are economically or politically "extractive" – which in China's case is represented by a powerful state accountable to the Communist Party. In short, they cannot succeed under authoritarian government. Time will tell if that view is correct: that in due course China will go the same way as the Soviet Union. But it sits a little uncomfortably, as it sometimes does, with the idea that China is a threat because the state is so competent that it will win the race to adopt the latest technologies and, in the end, rule the world.

The current Xi administration seems determined to confound the critics and to prove that economic reform and political liberalization are quite distinct. It has become unambiguously more authoritarian. But it has also supported economic reform and has improved the business environment in some respects. When President Xi came to power, he identified financial excesses – high leverage and undisciplined lending – as priority problems. His administration responded by strengthening bank regulators, reining in off-balance-sheet lending, promoting debt-equity swaps, strengthening capital requirements, writing off bad debt and allowing insolvent firms to close by improving insolvency procedures (legal bankruptcies have risen by a factor of five in the last few years). In order to help firms raise capital in more transparent ways, there is now a bigger and better-regulated corporate-bond market and stronger and better-regulated stock markets (after the meltdown in 2015).

Another dimension of the president's approach to reform is his crackdown on corruption. At the start of his period in office he warned that unchecked corruption would "damn the Party and the country", because it was "utterly destructive politically, shocking people to the core".[69] For him, the conundrum was that economic growth was necessary to sustain Party legitimacy but was leading to extreme corruption which undermined that legitimacy. He could have added that development orthodoxy links improved economic performance to reduced corruption.[70]

How serious is corruption in China? And how much does it matter? There is no easy answer to the first question, since there is no consensus on metrics. The Corruption Perception Index used by Transparency International currently ranks China at number 78 out of 180 countries – just behind Romania, South Africa and Ghana in overall honesty, but ahead of India, Brazil and Turkey, and well ahead of kleptocracies like Russia or the Congo.[71] Its ranking in 2020 was pretty much as it was when President Xi launched his clean-up eight years earlier. But one of the most thorough pieces of analysis of corruption in China comes to a more positive conclusion by unbundling the corruption phenomenon.[72] The author concludes that because the most prevalent form of corruption in China is "speed money" – bribing contacts to speed up decisions – rather than "grand theft", corruption does little to impede growth, though it undoubtedly adds to the problem of misallocated resources.

Because of the corruption crackdown, in 2013 alone (Xi's first full year in office) 182,000 Party members were investigated over corruption allegations – a tenfold increase over the previous year. The number disciplined rose to over 600,000 in 2018. Corruption is however a nebulous term that can be applied to many transactions and individuals. Accusations of corruption have also been used to destroy political opponents – like Xi's erstwhile rival Bo Xilai – and silence critics in the business community. It is a moot point as to whether the business environment has improved more from the reduction of corruption than it has deteriorated from the weakening of property rights as out-of-favour businesspeople have had their assets seized or devalued.

One metric of the overall business environment is the World Bank's survey of the "ease of doing business".[73] The survey was however caught up in controversy with accusations, vehemently denied by the Bank, that pressure had been exerted by senior Bank staff on the authors of the report to give China a good review. In its 2019 report, covering the year before the pandemic, the World Bank designates China as one of the top ten most improved countries, with simplified bureaucratic procedures, enhanced legal protections and smooth insolvency proceedings. China now ranks well ahead of other emerging markets like Brazil, Mexico and India – mainly because of superior logistics, the quality of labour, tax rates and reduced corruption, bad though it is. And it even ranks ahead of some developed countries: Japan, France and Italy. Whether or not the ranking is flattering, the survey clearly shows that the general direction of travel is to liberalize markets and improve the treatment of intellectual-property rights. All of that suggests some willingness and capacity to reform in ways which are meaningful to business.

There has been a cross-cutting theme in Chinese policy in the form of the president's "common prosperity". The slogan, first used in a speech in 2016, has been interpreted in very different ways: from a reassertion of Communist values, hostile to the private sector, to a mildly social-democratic course adjustment. The phrases used by the president to clarify the concept include attacks on "social ills" like gambling, private tutoring and fandom, the "reckless expansion of capital", used to refer to construction especially, "excessively high incomes", "unacceptable inequality", abuse of worker and consumer rights and "conflicts of interest" ("crony capitalism").

Among the main targets for public criticism and regulatory intervention have been the big Internet giants. They have been the subject of strong anti-trust action, involving fines from the State Administration for Market Regulation, financial regulatory intervention from the Central Bank and action on data security from the Cyberspace Administration. Specific targets have included Jack Ma's companies, especially the fintech company Ant; Pony Ma's Tencent, with its big Internet gambling interests; Pinduoduo, an agriculture-focused Internet platform; Meituan, a food-delivery platform; and DiDi, a car-hailing platform like Uber. They have all faced big fines for a variety of regulatory breaches, and have made large "voluntary" donations to good causes associated with "Common Prosperity". All have suffered big losses of value in their internationally listed shares. The private, profit-making tutoring sector has been almost wiped out.

Critics of Xi's policies argue that it is damaging to be taking aim at precisely those companies which are best placed to generate productivity growth and innovation. Also, it is a disincentive to entrepreneurs in general to be told that success and billionaire status will put you in the crosshairs of hostile officials. You risk the fate of the high-profile entrepreneur, Sun Dawu, sentenced to eighteen years in prison for "provoking trouble" – or you run the risk of having a big slice of your wealth wiped out at a stroke. The mood has undoubtedly changed since Deng proclaimed that "to get rich is glorious": now, getting rich is potentially dangerous. There are nonetheless entrepreneurs who are still becoming seriously rich by managing to keep party officials onside, or who have business strategies which the party likes: Zeng Yuqun, for example, whose CATL makes batteries for electric-vehicle makers, or Peter Ma, who is pressing, through the holdings of his insurance company Ping An in HSBC, to split the bank and force it to move its main operations to China.

It is wrong to characterize "common prosperity" as "anti-business". A more sympathetic interpretation is that the government needed to act in the interests of long-term political stability. In fact, the number of dollar billionaires in China has risen from an estimated 89 in 2010 to 1058 in 2020. In many cases, fortunes have been based on "crony" relations with officials, especially in sectors like construction and property, banking, casinos, raw materials and defence. Such behaviour brings the government as well as business into disrepute. A parallel can be drawn between China today and the "Progressive Era" in the United States, when trust-busting was at the fore of policies to curb the excesses of the Wild West.[74] The regime could also say that Internet platform companies are being reined in elsewhere – through the European Commission and the US competition authorities – though action there is less peremptory than in China and is governed by legal process.

President Xi has been walking a fine line between his socialist commitment to Common Prosperity (with the belief that political stability requires economic stability and a sense of fairness) and an understanding that entrepreneurs drive growth and rising living standards. Xi's new deputy, Li Qiang, a former mayor of Shanghai, has been tasked with ensuring that Common Prosperity is compatible with "a new era for entrepreneurs" and with reassurance to foreign investors that they are "not guests, but family". The pro-business rhetoric must be balanced against more intrusive regulation and the use of 1% "golden shares" to ensure that business moves in the direction favoured by the Communist Party and the President. At the heart of Common Prosperity is a shifting balance between growth and Party control.

Consumption and inequality

A key test of China's progress in reform is how fast and how far it can progress in shifting the drivers of growth from investment and net exports to consumption. There has been a very slight increase in the share of household consumption in GDP from a low of 34.6% in 2010, the peak of the investment boom after the global financial crisis, to 37.8% in 2020. But international (World Bank) comparisons of the share of household consumption in GDP suggest that China is still well below the average of 130 countries (63%), and even the most frugal among them, such as Germany (53%)[7]or South Korea (49%).

The reason for this frugality is the extraordinary concentration of resources on investment including property development. The share of investment (gross, fixed, capital investment) in China has declined slightly from 46.5% of GDP at the peak earlier in the decade to 43%, but China is still in a league of its own. According to World Bank comparisons, the global average is 25%, with 21% in OECD countries and 29% in middle-income countries. Korea, which has preceded China as a high-investment/high-growth economy, has an investment ratio of 30% – still one of the highest in the world.

The same phenomenon can be seen in a different way by looking at the labour (employee) share of income (as opposed to the share of profit and interest in national income). The labour share fell from 51.4% in 1995 to 43.7% in 2008, and then increased to 46.5% in 2014. The numbers are strikingly different from those elsewhere. In the OECD economies, the labour share is much higher, even though it has been declining, from 66.6% in 1990 to 61.7% in 2015.[75] There is a certain irony in the fact that the labour share – often used in Marxist analysis to demonstrate the degree of exploitation of workers by capitalists – is much lower in China than in the capitalist world. The government is aware of the awkward contrast, and has set the objective of boosting the labour share as part of Common Prosperity.

It is commonly argued that one of the key factors behind low levels of consumption is inequality. Higher-income groups tend to save a higher proportion of their income, though in China poor families also have an incentive to make substantial precautionary savings because of insecurity due to lack of public health and pension provision.[76] A major survey of the data concluded: "China has moved from being a moderately unequal country in 1990 to being one of the most unequal countries."[77] The evidence basis for that claim is the change in the Gini coefficient of income distribution (the coefficient is 0 if income is equally distributed, 100 if one individual accrues all the income). The authors calculate a deterioration of the Gini index from 35 in 1990 to 50 in 2013 – at which time the Latin American average was 45 and the OECD average was 30. Since then, inequality has undoubtedly diminished, thanks in part to government action in creating a rudimentary system of social insurance. The most recent World Bank comparative figures suggest that China is more equal than extreme cases such as South Africa and Brazil – or the United States – but is still much more unequal than OECD countries, including Asian states like South Korea.

The government's priority was not, until recently, reducing inequality, but the absolute reduction in poverty – and, in that respect, it has been strikingly successful. Whilst the income share of the top 10% of the population grew from 26% to 42% between 1980 and 2008, the incomes of the bottom 10% still grew by 60% over the same period.[78] The proportion of Chinese in absolute poverty (on World Bank definitions) fell from 90% to under 10% in the reform period. Extreme poverty is now largely restricted to a few remote, isolated areas, and President Xi now claims that those pockets have been eliminated.

What lay behind the big increase in income inequality? There is a well-established trend in development, the so-called Kuznets curve, which suggests that inequality invariably grows during development before declining later.[79] The process of urbanization is a key factor, since higher incomes in cities are both a cause and an effect of urbanization. According to census data, China's urban population grew from 23% to 51% over the period 1985 to 2010, and to 64% in 2020. There was a parallel trend in migration from the poorer interior to more affluent coastal areas, and some analysts judge that regional differences are the main source of inequality.[80] Others argue that this is largely a misunderstanding based on counting people where they are registered rather than where they live.[81] If the population of coastal areas includes the poorer migrant workers who have come from inland areas, and are still registered there, the issue of regional inequality appears less serious.

There is however an important sense in which the hukou system is a barrier to reducing inequality. Because entitlements are linked to the place of registration rather than residence, few children of migrant families are allowed admission to the free high-quality state schools in the big cities. They must pay fees in the cities or attend poor-quality schools in the towns and villages where they are registered. As a result, they rarely qualify for admission to universities – especially the more prestigious ones. An estimated 75% of urban children with urban hukou go to universities, but only 15% from rural areas. The government has shown awareness of the problem by imposing tough regulatory requirements on home-tutoring companies which make money by helping those who can afford it to cram for competitive examinations to enter elite institutions. It has, however, been less willing to tackle the hukou system itself.

But if China's growth is to make the transformation from being investment-based to consumption-based, a reduction in inequality is important. The government has recognized that inequality must be reduced, and that objective was given priority in the 2016–20 Plan. The most straightforward action is using tax and public spending. But the use of taxation and public spending to level up or down is made much more difficult in China by the fact that the central government's tax base is very small, as a result of the radical decentralization that was part of the reform process. Taxes collected by central government account for only around 10% of GDP, as is also the case in big federations like the USA and India. Action depends on efforts at provincial level (as demonstrated by, say, Kerala in India and California in the USA). Lack of activity at local level in China is one of the main factors behind the neglect of education in poor rural areas, which appears to be storing up serious long-term problems.[82]

Despite the fiscal constraints, the government has prioritized the creation of a "safety net" in the form of social insurance to provide universal health care and a basic pension. As mentioned above, worries about lack of health-care provision and the need to pay for services have been one of the main reasons for high saving rates even amongst poor families. As part of the stimulus package in 2008–9, there was an ambitious health-insurance programme. Since then, public spending on (near) universal health care has been quadrupled, and much has been done to improve delivery of health services.[83] But they remain poor by the standards of rich countries. Indeed, one reason for the zero-Covid policy was the belief that services could not cope with a wave of infections.

Free movement within China is also key to successful economic reform. The government set the objective of transferring a hundred million people to cities under the 2016–20 Plan. It has also claimed to be liberalizing the hukou system so that the rural population could migrate to the cities without losing the right to pay into and draw on social security. There is however some scepticism as to whether this initiative will get much beyond the announcement stage, since the system of control is important not just to regulate flows of people into the cities, but to maintain social and political control. Taken overall, the authorities recognize that, to deal with the problem of "under-consumption", inequalities matter. But the focus of policy and "Common Prosperity" is the middle-class urban consumer.

The coming of the Chinese "middle-class" consumer

The transition to a more consumer-based society also requires an infrastructure of retailing, payments and credit. Despite income inequality, China has developed a vast and highly sophisticated retail sector. The Chinese "middle class", roughly comprising the 180 million or so who live at or beyond Western living standards – though some use figures of 300 to 400 million – has grown by an estimated ten times over the last decade. The consequence is a retail sector now believed to be the largest on the planet, 20% of the world total, which has overtaken the USA from a position of being one quarter its size ten years ago.[84] Sustained economic growth, supplemented by continued urbanization and the widening of the "middle class", will expand it further. Such is China's scale that even the rich elite can generate their own market: an estimated half of all luxury-goods sales in the world are in China.

What is distinctive about Chinese retail, apart from its scale, is the degree of development of digital business through e-commerce, mobile payments and "social commerce" (the integration of social-media platforms with e-commerce).[85] Unlike Western countries, which have had to adapt a legacy

of high streets, shopping malls and supermarkets to new ways
of shopping, the big Chinese retailers (Alibaba, JD.com and
Pinduoduo) have built up digital businesses from scratch.

The starting point is that there are far more Chinese who
are connected by the Internet than in any other country. Size
matters. By the end of 2020, there was an estimated 65%
Internet penetration (a billion individuals) compared to 90%
penetration in the USA (288 million) – well over three times
the number in absolute terms (the closest in absolute numbers
is India, which has an estimated penetration of around 40%:
700 million people). China has a big advantage, therefore, in
the size of its digital home market – which also has scope for
considerable further growth in numbers of users.

China has got ahead qualitatively as well as quantitatively.
E-commerce is further advanced than elsewhere and growing rapidly (China has an estimated 20% annual growth in
e-commerce). The figures are approximate and rapidly changing, with a massive growth due to the pandemic, but McKinsey
data in 2021 suggested that about 27% of Chinese retail sales
by value were by e-commerce, as against 20 % in the USA.
Only the UK, with a 24% share, comes close. The overall
Chinese e-commerce market (which is far bigger than retail)
on one estimate is around $2'8 trillion, more than the USA
and Europe combined. A key factor in the growth and scale
of e-commerce in China is the ease of payments: not just
contactless, but increasingly performed through mobile apps.
Over 50% of Chinese are estimated to have made payments by
mobile phone as against 20% in the USA. An estimated 80% of
all e-commerce is mobile led, making use of mobile "wallets".

The significance of mobile use for commerce is that China is
also pioneering "social commerce" – an estimated 12% of retail
sales. The techniques of social media such as live streaming are
being used to make shopping easier, better informed and more
pleasurable. As a result of the interaction between social-media
operations like WeChat and online retailers like Alibaba, there
is what the Chinese call "new retail" – as if Amazon, PayPal
and Instagram were to make a combined offer. Moreover, the

broadening of the online retail offer is accompanied by greater competition from companies like Pinduoduo and Meituan, as well as more aggressive anti-trust policies (directed against Tencent and Alibaba, which have been accused of selling below cost). The attempt by the government to regulate more closely all the leading Internet-platform companies does not – yet – seem to have affected the overall retail offer.

The combination of factors described above has several implications for the wider economy. One is that consumption is being made easier and more attractive for those who have access to digital communication – most of the population and a growing number. This cannot but help to shift the balance of the economy away from over-reliance on investment. A second factor is that the growth is not merely in volume, but through productivity improvements. This manifests itself in the form of price discounting, pushing down prices. The behaviour of Chinese middle-class consumers in driving productivity growth through the digital economy will feed through into higher living standards – though these are the living standards of the already connected and well-off rather than "left-behind" communities and individuals.

Nonetheless, the rapid development of a consuming middle class is an answer to those who see in China another Soviet Union in the making. There is an enormous contrast between modern China and the Soviet-era world of queues, rationing, low-quality clothes, shoddy consumer durables, poor service and abacus-based payments systems. China is becoming a consumer economy in a way that is recognizable in the West (and Japan and Korea). On a purchasing-power basis, Chinese GDP per head – a rough proxy for living standards – is, at just over $20,000, a bit less than Thailand or Mexico, half the level of South Korea ($45,000) and a third of US levels ($67,000). But as noted above, hundreds of millions of residents in richer provinces are living and consuming at well above the average.

Apart from the retail sector, consumer-durables manufacture, distribution and servicing is a vast area for expansion and employment. A good example is the car industry. Given space constraints and population densities, it seems improbable that China could ever reach – or be allowed to reach – the car-ownership rate of the USA (around 850 per 1,000 people). But the current rate of car ownership of around 200 vehicles per 1,000 people already gives China the biggest car fleet in the world (275 million vehicles, slightly more than the USA), and could plausibly rise to Japanese levels (650 per 1,000) – or, at least, South Korean (475). The Chinese car market overtook that of the USA several years ago (25 million sold in 2017 as against 17 million), and after a sharp recession with Covid restrictions is again growing rapidly.

A new Chinese economy is emerging which is consumer- and service-based, replacing the old industrial economy of steel and cement – albeit some provinces, notably in the north-east, are more "old" than "new". When the reform process started, industry accounted for almost 50% of the economy, agriculture 30% and services 20% (bearing in mind the tendency to understate the value of services). According to the most recent figures, industry's share has shrunk to 38%, agriculture's to 8%. Services have expanded to 54%. For big urban areas, the shift is even more pronounced – for Shanghai and Beijing, more than 70% of the economy is based on services. Among the younger generation there is also a significantly higher propensity to consume, no doubt since there is less financial insecurity, but also because, through travel or use of social media, there is more familiarity with consumer brands, including global brands.

The switch from heavy industry and big infrastructure projects to consumer goods and consumer-based services as the main driving force in the economy has now acquired a substantial momentum. Demand and supply feed off each other, and migration to the cities continues. But big structural changes will not happen through serendipity alone, if vested interests seek to block change or divert resources, not least Party officials insisting on control. Much depends on the success of the Chinese model of "state capitalism" in reforming a strong state sector while permitting the private sector to grow.

State capitalism and reform of the public sector

I noted earlier the profound disagreements between observers on such an apparently straightforward factual matter as the size of the Chinese economy. There are similar disagreements on the relative importance of the private and the state sectors. One approach is to take official categories at something like their face value – in which case around 60% of GDP, 70% of investment, 90% of exports and 90% of employment can be traced back to the private sector. These figures lead some to conclude that, if we deal with concrete reality rather than official jargon about "socialism", China is unambiguously a capitalist economy, since it is the private sector that drives growth.[86] But many companies that are theoretically private are in fact offshoots of state entities, national or local. And so much of the economy is subject to state direction through control of credit, labour and land that there can hardly be said to be a level playing field between the public and the private sectors.[87] Ringen makes an educated guess of a 50–50 economy.[88]

But Western mixed economies could also be said to be 50–50, and they are very different. So what do we call China? I use the phrase "state capitalist" – a mixture of state enterprises dominating the "commanding heights" of the economy, but operating within some market disciplines, and a thriving entrepreneurial private sector which is required to accept nonetheless the key role for the state under the control of the Party. There are contradictions within that formula, and a shifting balance between the various elements. Different language has been used to describe this hybrid system – not just "state capitalism", but "market socialism" or "socialism with Chinese characteristics".

In the four decades since Deng initiated market reforms, the balance shifted towards a bigger role for the private sector, though there are many blurred boundaries: some "private" activity is subject to close state control, and some "state" activity involves companies mimicking capitalist enterprises. President Xi has reasserted state and Party control in crucial areas. A key influence on his thinking seems to have been the 2015 stock-market panic and the unplanned devaluation of the currency due to capital flight. His behaviour since has tended to emphasize the importance of state control in the interests of stability. One of his biographers has written of a "backlash" against freewheeling capitalism.[89] Another analyst has written of a generally more dirigiste approach to government.[90]

So where does the balance lie now? And how serious is the problem of unreformed state enterprises? There has long been a tension between allowing them freedom to operate commercially and accepting the painful consequences of company failure in competitive markets, with the major employment implications that would follow. There has also been a tension between allowing commercially minded managers to make decisions in the interests of individual enterprises and the wider national – or Party – agenda.

The most recent moves have been to strengthen central and Party control. At the beginning of 2020, there was a clear message that state firms are "subject to the will of the people" and accountable to the Party, as well as regulators or courts – though, theoretically, regulators and courts are to serve the Party, so there should be no contradiction. Party committees embedded in firms take precedence over directors.[91] Potentially, this could set back the work to improve governance and decision-making, though it could also be a warning to bosses of big "zombie" companies that they are not acting quickly enough to carry out earlier instructions that "we must ruthlessly bring down the knife".[92]

The reform of state enterprises with the overall aim of making them more efficient has been carried out in fits and starts since the process started seriously in the late 1990s.[93] Employment in state-owned enterprises fell from 70 million in 1997 to 37 million in 2005 through a mixture of privatization and rationalization. Much of this rather brutal contraction occurred during the Premiership of Zhu Rongji, whose uncompromising commitment to market reform is now regarded with mixed feelings, especially in parts of the country which were devastated by mass redundancies and the loss of the "iron rice bowl" of job security and social security. In any event, the process went into reverse with the massive expansion of investment that took place after 2008, much of it in state-owned enterprises. There was a subsequent deterioration in state-owned enterprises' return on assets. There was also a big increase in the number of loss-making companies, and the emergence of spare capacity once the economy slowed and credit was reined in. Subsequently, the government has talked tough and insisted on tighter financial discipline, usually without being willing to confront politically dangerous mass layoffs.

At the start of his period of leadership, President Xi put forward ideas for creating a "Temasek model", based on Singapore's system of managing a portfolio of shareholdings at arm's length. But this has given way to an earlier system of centralized control through SASAC, the ministry responsible for state assets. Under SASAC, which was originally set up in 2003 to provide a coordinated approach to public-sector management, there has been a major effort to amalgamate some of the thousands of state-owned entities into around a hundred holding companies. An example of this is the rationalization of several rail rolling-stock companies into one group. Underlying the policy is a belief that big is good. In practice, however, such amalgamations provided a means of reallocating staff and redistributing losses rather than facing the difficult decision to lay off large numbers of workers in sectors, like steel, where there is serious excess capacity. For example, the public announcement in 2016 that 100,000 workers would be laid off by a state-owned steel enterprise in the north-east – regarded as an indication of government seriousness – was dealt with by redeployment rather than downsizing.

The president trumpets the virtues of the public sector in speeches heavy with ideological language, but the earlier reforms have not been reversed. The 70% of state-owned enterprises that were privatized or part-privatized remain so. The biggest companies have continued to acquire listings in major overseas capital markets, as part of the "opening up" strategy, so that foreign institutional investors would exert pressure to improve governance with external audits and the appointment of independent non-executive directors. That process has however been curbed somewhat, partly reflecting Chinese government concerns over data leaks – with DiDi having to delist from the NYSE – and partly because of American resistance to the spread of Chinese-owned companies into the USA.

Another discipline on public sector companies has been through Chinese capital markets. Company borrowing has been increasingly via corporate bonds, which exposes loans to the greater transparency of domestic as well as foreign capital markets (although bond markets in China are still underdeveloped and lack effective credit rating). CEOs have also been given performance-based contracts with dividend targets rather than crude output metrics. But, at the same time, executives are expected to observe Party discipline, exercised through Party committees which have been embedded in companies and which may require them to take decisions about investment, personnel and other commercial matters that may clash with their commercial judgement and their financial obligations.

The contradictions in these policies started to unravel in 2020, when several ailing state companies defaulted on their domestic debts, mainly corporate bonds, having been abandoned by their parent companies or their local-government creditors – and, ultimately, central government. Companies in the $4 trillion corporate-bond market (part of a bigger $14 trillion market for bonds) were seemingly left to sink or swim. The most significant was Yongcheng Coal & Electricity Holding, until recently one of the most prestigious and biggest state companies and part of a bigger company, Henan Energy & Chemical Industry Group. By allowing Yongcheng to default, the authorities triggered a tightening of the corporate-bond market, with higher costs of borrowing and reduced availability of credit. This will in turn flush out – and drag down – other weak companies. Among other casualties of bond-market transparency has been Tsinghua Unigroup, a smallish maker of microchips, which is being allowed to fail despite being part of a government priority sector. The crackdown on the property bubble has also involved letting very big companies like Evergrande default on bond payments. Xi Jinping's advisers have continued to insist that the discipline of the corporate-bond market in policing business failure must be strengthened.

For all the ambiguous signals about Party versus profit, the market is being allowed the last word, though it is not clear what massive employers like Yongcheng are then required to do when they have been exposed as insolvent. Government messaging about state-enterprise reform remains confused and contradictory. There is a belief in the transparency of capital markets and the dangers of moral hazard, but not if the result is painful collapse. State-owned enterprises must observe budget discipline – but the discipline is "soft".[94] If there are hard financial disciplines, they are experienced in the private sector, from which will come the growth in productivity required to raise living standards.

How private is private enterprise?

The other side of Chinese "state capitalism" is that, while state enterprise is subject to market disciplines, private enterprise is subject to political disciplines. But the degree of political interference is largely a function of company size. Big business must look over its shoulder at the politicians – and that is true also in the West, albeit in a more pluralistic political context. For smaller and more numerous private companies, however, business is business, and operates in China's often wild, unregulated and ferociously competitive markets. There may be as many as ten million private firms, mostly microbusinesses. Politics intrudes only in the sense that a pervasive feature of the business culture is the importance of "connections" – informal networks and contacts that are essential for getting credit, obtaining permission for local development, acquiring land rights and inducing local officials to turn a blind eye to breaches of regulation.

But one important qualification to the description of much of Chinese business as operating in a wild, unregulated environment is that the Chinese state is putting in place a system of "corporate social credit". Under it, numerous regulatory requirements governing, among other factors, tax compliance, product quality, prices, licensing and credit records are being monitored on massive databases. This is occurring in parallel with a similar system for individuals. Seen optimistically, such a system will reduce fraud, ensure compliance with environmental and other standards and replace "influence" and "connections" in decision-making with objective scoring. Western critics, however, see the makings of an Orwellian nightmare of total state surveillance and control.

More generally, business is still subject to the preferences of the Party and government functionaries who impose taxes and make laws and regulations. But, as noted above, the overall business environment – as measured through the World Bank "ease of doing business" indices – has, in general, improved in China, with a greater degree of legal clarity over fraud, insolvency and intellectual property, and more closely regulated credit markets. At least on these indices, China is an easier place in which to start and operate a business than a lot of countries we would regard as "capitalist".

It is a different story for big business – the companies which are now quoted on the main Chinese and global stock markets, many of which are major multinational companies. Over 160 of the world's most valuable 1,000 firms are now Chinese, and the top 100 among them were valued (in June 2021, before the recent crackdown on internet companies) at around $9 trillion, roughly comparable to the top 100 European companies, though much lower than the $26 trillion for the top 100 American listed companies. The list of Fortune 500 companies now has more Chinese companies (143) than American (133). Most of these originate with charismatic and widely admired entrepreneurs like Jack Ma, founder of Alibaba and his digital-payments company Ant, which, until its recent reining-in by Chinese regulators, was planning the world's largest share flotation; Ren Zhengfei of Huawei; Pony Ma, CEO of Tencent and owner of WeChat; Zhang Yiming of ByteDance (owner of TikTok); Wang Chuanfu of BYD, the electric car maker; Robin Li and Eric Xu of Baidu, the leading AI company; Li Shufu of Geely (owner of Volvo); and Rong Yiren, the founder of CITIC (China International Trust and Investment Corporation).

These companies vary greatly in their business organization, overseas exposure and closeness to the regime, but they mostly resemble big Western enterprises that have evolved rapidly from private to public companies and retain the personality, and often the control, of their founders. The attitude of the authorities towards them is ambiguous. There is some pride at the global success of Chinese companies. But the super-rich are regarded at home with some suspicion and have been told to contribute more to society.

In a Forbes survey of the top Chinese tycoons at the end of 2021, the richest was Zhong Shanshan of the Nongfu Spring (mineral water) company, who was worth $66 billion. He was closely followed by Zhang Yiming, the owner of TikTok ($59 billion), Robin Zeng of the battery company CATL ($51 billion), Ma Huateng, aka Pony Ma ($49 billion, a fall of over $10 billion over the year), and Jack Ma ($41 billion, also a fall of $10 billion). Many of these entrepreneurs became very rich with apparent official approval. But there are definite limits. Few business leaders would dare to criticize the regime in public, and those who have found themselves facing criminal charges leading to imprisonment or worse. One retired property tycoon, Ren Zhiqiang, was sentenced to eighteen years for "corruption" after publishing an essay describing President Xi as a "clown". The chairman of Huarong Asset Management, a big company with a focus on distressed-debt management, was executed for abuse of power in financial markets (and bigamy).

The Internet giants have seen their owners subject to tighter controls, and Jack Ma, formerly an internationally celebrated "thought leader", now has a much lower profile. Many businesses err on the safe side by publishing in their annual reports eulogies of President Xi and other signals of loyalty to Party and state. Successful, leading entrepreneurs are often card-carrying members of the Chinese Communist Party. Beyond that, publicly traded companies have Party committees which require that "Party discussions are prerequisites for major investment decisions".[95]

As with Western companies, there is greater freedom from domestic restrictions, including political pressure, by going global. When Chinese companies went global and listed in New York or other prestigious markets, listing directly helped the companies gain access to capital from sophisticated capital markets, and was a spur to improving governance systems and management. It was also seen as a way of circumventing Chinese currency controls and Chinese regulation, though that may be less of an issue with the emergence of the "stock connect" system, which directly links mainland stocks to the Hong Kong market, where there is a deep pool of capital and full convertibility. But the authorities have now cooled on overseas listing, because it opens gaps in the system of regulation, especially of "big tech" and, in any event, the USA is seeking to exclude Chinese companies which fail to meet strong audit standards and are not transparent.

Even the biggest and most prestigious entrepreneurs can get the balance of political risk and opportunity wrong and find themselves in trouble with the authorities. As referred to earlier, the most significant has been the decision of Jack Ma to pull Ant's $37 billion IPO – the largest in history anywhere – at the very last moment, after intervention from Chinese financial regulators. And his company is now subject to tighter regulation. The motives behind the intervention are still being debated. Ma is, after all, one of the most respected and successful Internet entrepreneurs.[96] One view is crudely political: that Jack Ma had become too big for his boots and needed to be cut down to size. The university that he founded had become an alternative source of ideas, and influence, to the Chinese Communist Party (CCP). He had also, undoubtedly, ruffled feathers by making public criticism of financial regulation. Since the president himself had argued strongly for tight regulation to ensure systemic stability, and equated such stability with "national security", Ma's remarks were dangerously close to a personal criticism of President Xi's leadership.

It also seems likely that there were genuine concerns on the regulatory front. Ant – through its payments operation (Alipay) – has an estimated one billion customers and handled $16 trillion in transactions in 2019 (twenty-five times more than PayPal). The business has evolved from electronic payments to providing credit: peer-to-peer lending. Whilst such decentralized credit has the potential to stimulate the economy and ease start-ups, it has also been prone to irresponsible, aggressive and sometimes crooked lending – in the West no less than in China. Ant has been using its payments platform to become a major player in the consumer-credit market, as well as emerging as a major asset-management company (along with running the world's biggest money market fund). Crucially, for regulators, it was effectively operating as a large bank but without a banking license or banking supervision. Regulators everywhere are seeking to control such activity in the interest of systemic stability, and it is unsurprising that the Chinese authorities want to do the same. This interpretation of the intervention is consistent with what has happened since: new draft rules for online microlending, which specify a higher percentage of loans (30%) on Ant's own balance sheet. And Ant must raise more capital. The consumer-lending part of Ant's business is licensed and will be ring-fenced in a unit directly under the control of regulators.

The fate of Jack Ma and his businesses is a cautionary tale of what happens to businessmen who openly challenge government regulation and imply criticism of the President. His trillion-dollar business empire lost more than half its value; he lost control of his companies and was, in effect, exiled to Japan. He did not however go to jail like some less famous tycoons, and has been partially rehabilitated by being invited back to China to advertise the government's pro-business credentials, despite being much reduced in wealth and status.

Jack Ma is not alone: there has been a wider reining-back of the big tech companies, which (as in the West) are being criticized for excessive power and monopolistic practices. After the criticism of Jack Ma and Ant, all the leading Chinese tech companies were summoned to appear before the Central Bank and reprimanded for anti-competitive behaviour and abusive practices more generally. Several of the companies have since faced large fines, and pressure on them is growing. Taken as a whole, the internet companies had roughly a trillion dollars wiped off their shares valuation as a result of the crackdown.

The ambiguous benefits of Chinese big tech

It is not wholly surprising that the big tech companies and their founders have come under attack, whether they have also caused political offence or not. Their counterparts in the West have also acquired considerable influence, as well as attracting criticism. In China's party state, however, where any threat to the Communist Party's monopoly of power is resisted, these entities are considered particularly problematic.

But they are also indispensable. They are the backbone of the modern services sector and drivers of consumption, both of which are essential to economic restructuring and balanced growth. They reduce dependence on foreign firms and technologies in highly sensitive sectors involving the transmission of information. They have, through the development of fintech, provided an alternative to inefficient and badly run banks and other credit institutions. They have also been until recently a source of prestige and "soft power" overseas.

Crucially, however, the companies are harvesting vast amounts of data, which the state wishes to see used to develop a clear national narrative and its policy priorities, as well as to strengthen surveillance capability. And it has no wish to see the development of competing centres of power. The government is making it clear that it will inflict financial costs on the tech companies if this is necessary to assert its control. For example, the government forced DiDi to postpone its New York IPO while security agencies and regulators probed its mapping system and prevented the use of some DiDi apps. The IPO has been switched to Hong Kong, and DiDi's share price was badly hit.

There may be other motives too. The Chinese authorities are known to want to use state institutions to pioneer innovative developments in financial markets using Artificial Intelligence(AI) and "Big Data" (the collection and ordering of masses of data so that it can be used by AI) . The Central Bank has launched a crypto currency. Such innovations are potentially beneficial to the public, if they increase efficiency in credit markets and identify risk or malpractice. But there is a reluctance to devolve such experiments to privately owned digital platforms. The authorities are reluctant to allow complex algorithms needed for frontier "fintech" technologies to remain solely under the control to a handful of businessmen, however respected – though the price of state control is the risk of losing the flair which Jack Ma and his fellow entrepreneurs have brought.

And that, in turn, leads to the way in which Chinese big business and the state are becoming entangled. China has an explicit industrial strategy aimed at developing critical technologies. There are "national champions" in core technologies where the interests of the company and the state overlap. In this sense, China is not greatly different from Korea, Singapore, Japan, France and Israel (and arguably the USA), which have supported their own "national champions" in order to get a competitive advantage in new technologies. But China's capacity to mobilize resources on a sustained, long-term basis and to command adherence to a national plan is on a different level from most competitor countries.

We can see the "national champion" model at work with several leading Chinese companies. Huawei has performed this role in telecommunications, attracting the hostility of the US government. We do not need to accept propagandist arguments that Huawei is involved in spying or is actively working against the interests of host countries to acknowledge that it is not wholly independent of the Chinese state. In the same way, China's push to match the USA in AI technology is not limited to government laboratories but involves promoting the leading digital-platform companies. China has produced some remarkable entrepreneurs and fine companies, but they are also expected to be "patriotic" and play their role in China Inc., reflecting the regime's emphasis on technological and energy self-sufficiency.

State involvement in private business also operates at one remove. The Chinese state takes "golden shares" stakes in big companies. And the state can operate through financial intermediaries. There are around 1,000 government-directed and government-supported funds in private equity and venture capital. These are often in competition with private funds, though they are less concerned with maximizing investor returns than wider social and political objectives – including political compliance.

Whilst the role of the state should not be underestimated, we should not underrate either the entrepreneurial energy and business acumen which has led to so many world-class companies emerging in China. Even in the face of sanctions abroad and regulatory interventions at home, China's leading companies have shown a remarkable capacity to adapt and become successful multinational companies. There is around $130 billion in overseas investment by Chinese companies. TikTok is managing to overtake Facebook in the social-media business through a slicker offering, and its parent company Byte-Dance, by headquartering in Singapore, has been able to avoid further American pressure. Other companies have used astute localization or have gone for large numbers of small takeovers to avoid the controversy of megadeals. Numerous new companies are emerging.

State capitalism: the Chinese model

"State capitalism" is a good way to describe such a system in which state enterprise is being forced to compete in the open markets and private enterprise is never fully released from the long arm of the state. The balance and boundaries of public and private sectors are not fixed, and we could be experiencing a fundamental, long-term shift to tighter political control over larger private firms. The crackdown on the big tech companies has resulted, as noted above, in a sharp reduction in their valuation in international markets: the combined share index for Chinese tech companies listed in the USA fell by two thirds after the regulatory tightening of controls on Jack Ma's Alipay, the blocking of DiDi's IPO, the criticism and censuring of other tech companies, the drastic action against the private-tutoring industry and hints of tougher regulation to come as with online gaming, online health care and gig-economy companies.

Overseas analysts and investors have been left wondering what all of this means for investment in Chinese companies and for China's general sense of direction. It seems very unlikely that these are random policy initiatives by sectoral regulators without approval from above. It also seems unlikely that the regime will jeopardize the overall economic performance and the living standards on which its legitimacy depends. And it seems unlikely that China will turn its back on overseas investment so soon after opening the financial-services sector – though policymakers may well have been only too happy to see a cooling of the massive inflow of "hot" money earlier in 2021 which might have destabilized monetary and exchange-rate policies.

A consensus view is that President Xi was seeking to make clear to the country's leading businesspeople that the Party – and he personally – are in charge and do not tolerate alternative power centres. Businessmen can become rich but are there to serve China's wider interests as defined by the Party. Xi has not suddenly become anti-business or anti-reform or anti-globalization. His intentions have been clear for a long time, albeit expressed in rather opaque ideological jargon: "No matter how we reform and open up, we should always adhere to the socialist road with Chinese characteristics – [which is] socialism, not any other -ism."[97] But why now and in this form? The "socialist road" can best be seen as Chinese party jargon for what in the West would be regarded as normal public-sector interventions. Authorities in the EU, among others, are using fines and tougher regulation to curb the growing power of big tech. The Chinese private-tutoring industry was undoubtedly catering to an increasingly unpopular educational elite, which is being attacked in other countries through "positive discrimination" or curbs on private-sector privileges. Online gambling is being seen as an addictive "opium" everywhere. Requiring gig-economy companies to pay social insurance to protect their employees follows Western initiatives on insecure work. What differentiates Chinese regulatory intervention is that whereas in the West there is usually a long and complex process of lobbying, press campaigns and compromise in the legislative stage, in China regulatory change is likely to be sudden, uncompromising and not open to legal challenge.

But there is also a new thread running through the various regulatory interventions: data and data security. In Europe and the USA there is a fierce debate as to whether data is owned by the individual, the company which collects data or – in some instances – the state. China has a similar internal debate, which has produced the Data Protection Law and the new Personal Information and Protection Law. Unsurprisingly, the concerns of the state (and party) loom larger in China. That is in part about internal security and partly about making sure that the data companies concentrate on national priorities like AI and robotics.

But the new element is the deepening "cold war" with the USA and the West. Just as the Trump administration became obsessed by worries that TikTok chatter between teenagers might finish up in Beijing data-collection centres, the Chinese are also becoming obsessed by leakages of data through foreign stock markets and foreign entities in general. Data is the raw material of the modern economy, and data security is becoming the major obstacle to economic interdependence.

Rampant China or Peak China

The book has reviewed a variety of challenges which are giving rise to greater pessimism about the Chinese economy: the government's ambiguous attitude to big business; the problems of the property sector and their ramifications for the government's fiscal stability and the viability of local government; the deeper problems of the "middle-income trap"; most seriously, the premature decline and ageing of the population. These factors have combined to produce a more negative view of China's growth potential. A recent consensus was that China would continue to grow relative to the USA or the EU and inevitably become the pre-eminent economy (and military) power, overtaking the USA in terms of GDP at market exchange rates as well as on a purchasing-power parity basis.[98]

Now a much more downbeat view is emerging that we have reached "Peak China" and that China may never surpass the USA in market size.[99] The numerical basis of the argument is that productivity growth will not sufficiently offset the effect of falling labour supply. If the Chinese authorities continue to frustrate the potential of Chinese high-tech firms and American sanctions further erode China's growth sectors, then (total-factor) productivity growth could be halved from a currently projected 5%. At the same time, just as China's growth capacity may be overestimated, that of the USA may be underestimated. They might continue at roughly the same level for decades.

Chapter 3

*Is Chinese Economic Success
Good for the World?*

It should be obvious that China's growth and its integration with the world economy are in the wider international interest. One of the few areas of economics on which there is general agreement is the global value of more trade and international exchange. The post-war international economic order points to the overall value of openness. From the urgings of Lord Macaulay two centuries ago to the advice of Western governments, agencies and business in recent decades, a unifying theme has been the desirability for China, and the world, to increase its openness to trade and investment. China has done much to follow that advice, with spectacular consequences for its growth. What has followed is the improvement of incomes and living conditions for hundreds of millions in China.

Western consumers have also benefited from being able to buy a wide range of goods of growing quality and sophistication. And many people elsewhere have had their living standards enhanced as the growth of China has fed through into commodity markets. There is a rough rule of thumb that China "consumes half of everything". It accounts for roughly 75% of iron ore and 60% of steel consumed in the world; around 60% of refined copper and aluminium; around 60% of coal and 20% of oil; 20% to 30% of many foodstuffs, including vegetable oils, rice and wheat. Commodity exporters in South America, Africa and Australia have boomed on the back of Chinese growth.

It is possible to put figures on the contribution of China to global growth. From 2001, when China joined the World Trade Organization, until 2008, the year of the global financial crisis,

China accounted for 24% of global growth, by virtue of its size and pace of development. From 2010, when China injected a major stimulus into the world economy, until the pandemic in 2020, China's contribution to world growth was just short of one third.[1] Such growth accounting is a rather mechanical way of quantifying China's share of world growth. But China also *drove* world growth, which was higher as a consequence.

The slowing of Chinese growth, with the attempted rebalancing away from investment and exports, has however reduced the link between Chinese and global growth. The contribution of China in the period 2016–19 was estimated at 35%, but fell to 25% since.[2] The share of exports in GDP has fallen from 35% in 2010 to around 20%. And the harsh, uncompromising Covid lockdown further disrupted supply chains and weakened China's links to the world economy. Shanghai suffered especially, and Shanghai alone accounts for 3% of GDP and more than 10% of China's trade. The "cold war" environment, sanctions and the war in Ukraine are also challenging the assumptions on which China's integration into the world economy were based. A process of decoupling of China and by China is taking place, though political rhetoric is yet to be reflected in trade numbers. The world of economic "globalization", which China joined and was encouraged to join, is no longer seen in the West as inevitable or even desirable.

A *variety of sceptics*

It is now becoming commonplace to see China's economic success portrayed as a problem for the rest of the world (and, conversely, its slowdown, economic problems and "decoupling" seen as a source of relief). This negativity comes from different sources and is due to various reasons. There are those who broadly share the positive story about China's growth and its impact but are concerned about the country's non-compliance with some of the international rules which it has signed up to. There is a more extreme version of this viewpoint which sees

China, because of its "state capitalism", as a "cuckoo in the nest" that threatens to undermine the whole market-based global system. But these concerns have been expressed about other economies outside the Western orbit, such as Japan and then South Korea, and in both cases the answer was seen in terms of more engagement and integration. Countries like India, Brazil, Mexico and Turkey present comparable challenges, albeit on a smaller scale.

There are others who accept the broad arguments about the positive economic impact of China but assert that other concerns are more important: "human rights", "security" or "the environment". I shall return to "human rights" issues later but suffice it to say that differences in values should not preclude closer economic integration – otherwise there would be little of it. It is also now clear that China is not easily seduced into changing its political system by economic success – and it is unlikely (or even less likely) to be coerced into changing by economic "decoupling".

In the same way, it is not at all clear that environmentalism is at odds with China's economic success and integration with the rest of the world. Its most polluting heavy industries are, in fact, a legacy of a period of autarchic "self-reliance". There is a growing awareness in "globalized" China of the imperative of "sustainable development" and a declared willingness to engage in cooperative work to deal with problems of the "global commons", like climate change. So far, this awareness may not have progressed far, but it is hard to believe that a conscious decoupling would encourage Chinese decision-makers to think more about their obligations to the "global commons".

Security: the dominant concern

"Security" concerns are more awkward to deal with and difficult to quantify in any trade-off with economic factors.[3] And security issues are now coming to dominate relations with

China – not just military, intelligence and cyber-security concerns, narrowly defined, but what is called "economic security".

But what does "economic security" mean? The first and most obvious context is when equipment or technology is being sold to a potential military adversary or the obverse: when there is a dependence on supplies from a potential adversary. That sounds straightforward, but isn't: we cannot tell long in advance who the adversaries might be. Nor is it obvious how to treat "dual-use" goods which can be used for both peaceful and military purposes. There is a wide range of goods which could be considered "risky". The USA has deemed the supply of advanced semiconductor "chips" to China to be a security risk because they might be used to develop new AI systems. But AI is not inherently dangerous and has many peaceful new applications; nor is it clear how "advanced" the "chips" need to be to be "risky".

Data is at the heart of current preoccupations around economic security. The Chinese themselves have a zero-tolerance approach to data imports which breach their strict censorship and to foreign companies' use of data which could involve "spying", and the rules on both have been tightened. The USA insists that Chinese companies involved in telecommunications, or which use surveillance technology, must be a threat to security and the net has widened to include social-media companies like TikTok. The security arguments may be tenuous, but few politicians want to be accused or carelessness or naivety in national-security matters.

Then there are the traditional arguments about energy and food security, when energy producers and farmers will argue for protection against import competition on "national security" grounds. These have become live concerns again in the current "cold war" environment, with China in particular preoccupied with its vulnerability. It should be possible to quantify risks and costs and the ease of switching supplies, but in a world dominated by security concerns "self-reliance" becomes an end in itself. The arguments around "security of supply", "de-risking" and "dependence" are considered in more detail below, but now centre on rare but critical raw materials.

Another concept which has been introduced under the rubric of "security" is "critical infrastructure" and the supposed security risks attached to foreign ownership, especially when the foreigners are from unfriendly countries. Candidates include ports, airlines and airports, water systems, pipelines, railways, power generation and distribution, telecommunication and broadcast networks. It isn't always obvious what damage a foreign entity can do through part or whole ownership of assets, or what motive they would have to commit sabotage. Emotions play a big part; a Chinese minority shareholder in a nuclear-power company probably presents minimal risk, but can be made to seem like a James Bond villain.

Security concerns are now being invoked in a wide range of economic activities. China has the world's largest fishing fleet, with 10,000 or more vessels operating around the world. The fishing fleet is accused of illegal fishing, environmental and labour abuses, depleting stocks of threatened species and much else – but now, crucially, of posing a security threat: seen as kind of maritime militia.

The overarching concern is that growing economic links with China make us more insecure, because we become more dependent on a dictatorial government that does not wish us well. But that argument cuts both ways. China becomes less secure as its economy becomes more reliant on the supply chains of Western multinational companies or Middle Eastern oil. Those who argue for "decoupling" on the grounds of security need to consider whether China would be easier to deal with if it was more self-reliant. Indeed, China is now set on a course of greater self-reliance in advanced technology, energy and food in a process of mutual decoupling which is reinforcing competition and suspicion on both sides.

There are "security of supply" issues in relation to some raw materials – notably oil – and technologies, but they affect China as much if not more than China's trade partners. There are, for example, specific "security of supply" issues in relation to the "green" economy, in which China is a big player, as in battery development and renewable energy more generally. The

White House review of critical supply chains (8th June 2021) identified Chinese dominance in the supply chains for some "rare earths" (which China has made use of in trade disputes with Japan earlier in the decade) and, to some degree, for lithium, nickel and cobalt. In the case of cobalt, 60% of supplies come from the Congo (DRC), where Chinese companies have a major role in mining and in the control of long-term supply contracts. I shall deal with the "security" issues below, but sometimes "security" is deployed as an argument rather carelessly in relation to China, and often boils down to a sense of alarm in the West that the country is not just economically successful, but too successful.

These security concerns in relation to China and the willingness to accept economic costs to address them are also a source of considerable debate and discord amongst Western allies, and even within the US administration. Jake Sullivan, the National Security Adviser, has defined a new "Washington Consensus" in which security considerations take precedence over the earlier belief in the primacy of economic benefit: no more of Clinton's "It' the economy, stupid". But the Treasury Secretary, Janet Yellen, argues for "a healthy economic engagement which benefits both countries", and that decoupling would be "disastrous". Whether this is a genuine disagreement isn't clear. In any event, an attempt has been made to bridge the differences with a new formula: "de-risking, not decoupling".

"De-risking" is essentially a qualification to the general proposition that economic globalization, including China's role in it, is good for the world. Many of the arguments for economic "decoupling" from China, which have become the orthodoxy in US politics, start from a different premise: they do not accept that there are significant overall economic benefits at all. China is sometimes treated as a subset of a general hostility to economic globalization based on the belief that any advantages are swamped by the negative impact of the "unfair" distribution of costs and benefits. Costs are assumed to fall onto workers in developed economies and the "exploited" working class in China itself; benefits accrue mainly to multinational capital and "elites", whose ill-gotten gains are sequestered in their boltholes in tax havens.[4]

There is a different but often overlapping anti-globalization argument from the populist right of the political spectrum, rather than from the left: that the world operates on "zero-sum" principles. Gains for one country are at the expense of another. There is a narrow version of this argument centred on bilateral trade deficits – mercantilism – which was popular with President Trump. But there is a broader version which sees international relations as a contest for supremacy: "America First" or "China First". Competition is between countries – not, as in economic textbooks, between firms. Between the two "superpowers" there is essentially a winner and a loser: both can't be winners.

There are influential writers and political figures who see this contest for supremacy in broader and deeper terms: as a clash of civilizations. The main threat to "Western civilization" and its values of "liberal democracy" is no longer seen as Soviet Communism or Islam, but China. The influential Michael Pillsbury sees this conflict as a long-standing struggle only now coming to a climax.[5] Economic success matters, in this context, not as a source of welfare and improved living standards, but as a means of acquiring dominance in technology, military capability and political influence. Some reach back into ancient history to predict that conflict is an inevitable outcome of such a contest, even if the "war" is currently cold rather than hot.[6] Such thinking also has its counterpart in China, but its main significance at present is that many in China now see the West, and especially the USA, as attempting to block China's rise through economic warfare.[7]

To summarize, for those of us who share a broadly liberal approach to trade and economic integration generally, there are no serious economic arguments for excluding China, while the non-economic arguments being advanced for decoupling carry a serious economic cost. China's economic rise should be welcomed.

Gains from trade

The argument that China's economic rise benefits the rest of the world stems in large part from trade. So what are the facts? Based on 2020 data (which was affected negatively by Covid restrictions), China was the world's biggest exporter of goods by some way: $2.7 trillion compared to $2.1 trillion for the USA and $1.7 trillion for Germany (out of a world trade figure of around $19 trillion). China's share of world trade was 13% as against just under 1% at the start of the reform process in 1978 and 2% a quarter of a century ago. In terms of imports, the US imports more, $2.4 trillion, compared to $2.1 trillion for China and $1.1 trillion for Germany. Overall, China conducts more trade in goods– $4.6 trillion – as against $4.2 trillion for the USA and $2.7 trillion for Germany. The USA has a large deficit on trade in goods – $1 trillion – while China and Germany have large surpluses: China's is larger in absolute terms, but proportionately smaller (in relation to trade) than Germany's.

The position is very different for services trade. US services exports were $0.83 trillion and imports $0.58 trillion; China's $0.23 trillion and $0.53 trillion respectively; and Germany's $0.35 trillion and $0.37 trillion. China has a large and growing deficit on services – much of it in the form of "travel and tourism", some of which is believed to be disguised capital flight – Chinese nationals evading exchange controls through their overseas travel.

Aggregate data is only part of the story. The make-up also matters. The commodity composition of trade is now very different from what it was a generation ago. Then, China was an exporter of low-skill, labour-intensive manufactures (clothing, footwear and toys) and an importer of raw materials and capital goods. China was a textbook case of specialization by comparative advantage. Those features haven't wholly disappeared: clothing is still a significant export (5.6% of the total), and there is a substantial share of raw materials in the value of imports, including oil (17%), metal ores (around 10%) and foodstuffs such as soya. But both imports and exports are now dominated by manufactures from higher technology sectors.

Now Chinese trade is intra-industry rather than inter-industry. 44% of Chinese exports consist of electrical items and equipment, or other machinery including computers; the same two categories account for 33% of imports. China exported $102 billion of integrated circuits but imported $313 billion of the same group of products. There is a similar pattern of exporting and importing mobile-phone devices, computers and their components, optical equipment and related items, vehicles and parts. This pattern of intra-industry trade is the product of complex supply chains produced by companies like Apple. In many ways, this is a particularly (and mutually) advantageous form of trade. But such dependence on Chinese high-tech products has been one of the factors leading to a call, especially in the USA, for "decoupling".[8] By the same token, China is also dependent on overseas suppliers, and has reacted to threats of "decoupling" by embarking on its own version of decoupling called "dual circulation".[9]

A further complicating factor is that the trade data can be very misleading. The very complex specialization within supply chains can lead to a lot of double or treble counting, as the trade data records the value of shipments rather than the value added. And a lot of the value recorded represents intangibles – royalty payments for intellectual property, licensing and consultancy fees charged within companies. The recorded value may be chosen by corporate accountants to minimize tax liabilities. Chinese exports of iPhones, for example, incorporate US-made chips and components from Taiwan, Japan or South Korea, sometimes paid for within a company, sometimes at arm's length. It is estimated that Chinese imports and exports may be overstated by a factor of 30%, and US imports and exports by a factor of 20%.[10] And that excludes the distortion created by the separate recording of imports and exports to and from Hong Kong, much of which involves trade with the mainland.

Despite all the uncertainties over data, basic economic principles tell us that the sheer volume of trade with China, within industries or between them, creates considerable benefits for the world economy. China's emergence as a major exporter of low-cost manufactures was an example of comparative advantage at work, and the West benefited considerably in economic terms. There are issues, however, in respect of primary commodity trade, where China is a major and sometimes dominant source of demand. How Chinese demand translates into higher prices as well as higher volumes for commodity exporters will depend on the elasticity of supply and of demand in other countries. China has been a major and growing influence in some commodity markets and, since 2010, has replaced the USA as the biggest influence on commodity markets in general.[11] As noted above, China is a dominant consumer of many metals, foodstuffs and energy.

There are some markets where China is a significant exporter and a price-setter. These are markets where China, able to extract monopoly profits or coerce purchasers in other ways, can act as a near-monopoly supplier. Concern has been expressed about China's role in the market for "rare earth" metals, which are of major importance in electronics or metallurgy.[12] There are seventeen "rare earth" metals, which include Neodymium, Europium, Cerium – all important in iPhone manufacture – and Lanthanum, used in electric vehicles. China has an estimated 35% of the world's rare-earth deposits. But as a result of a long-standing policy of prioritizing rare-earth mining and processing, China has been producing 85% of rare-earth oxides and 90% of metals, alloys and permanent magnets. Of US imports of rare earths, 80% come from China. For Japan and Korea the share is around 50%. But after a big price spike in 2011, caused by Chinese export quota restrictions and threats to use rare earths in trade "warfare" with Japan and the USA, there has been a rapid process of diversification taking place among China's customers. Therefore, the issue is less pressing, but it has been a reminder that trade with China can migrate from the purely economic to the highly political.

The bizarre economics of bilateral deficits

The questioning of the benefits of trade with China is often based on the notion that it is "unfair" (to everyone else). Prominent among the complaints are those concerning bilateral trade deficits. In a world of complex, interlocking supply chains, such measures are largely meaningless. But even if the measurement could be made more precise, it is difficult to see how the information could be useful. For a given level of demand, cutting or ending trade with one supplier would result in a switch to other suppliers. Without addressing the structural imbalances which have led to an excess of demand spilling over into imports, attempts to balance trade with one country would simply unbalance trade with other countries.

Despite those considerations, President Trump made bilateral imbalances the centrepiece of his trade policy, especially with China. The CEO of one company, looking for locations to place plants which would not be affected by US tariffs, noted that "the President only targeted nations that ran big bilateral trade surpluses".[13] Trump's particular grievance was about the large imbalance on trade in goods with China. In 2019, US exports of goods to China were valued at $106 billion and imports $452 billion, resulting in a deficit of $346 billion. The USA had a surplus of $37 billion on services trade. The resultant current-account deficit of £309 billion is then used to explain a loss of domestic production and jobs. But it makes little sense to see US–China trade in isolation – let alone to set targets to reduce bilateral imbalances, since the USA has deficits with each of its major trade partners: Mexico, Canada, Japan and Germany as well as China.

There are some parallels with a debate which was taking place in Europe two hundred and fifty years ago. The prevailing orthodoxy, then, was that running deficits on trade was economically damaging, since imbalances resulted in an export of gold. So, imports had to be restricted and exports promoted. This "mercantilist" view was demolished by Adam Smith, who set out the case for free trade, including the simple point that the importing country has the advantage of being able to consume more. The modern equivalent of mercantilist thinking, which Trump echoed, is that US deficits are paid for not by the export of gold, but by issuing IOUs in the form of US Treasury bills that are held by China (and other "surplus" economies) as foreign-exchange reserves. This stock of liabilities has been said to give China leverage over the USA (though the Chinese could say that the USA is uniquely privileged in being able to live far beyond its means, and that the USA has leverage over China, since it could choose to devalue its currency and the value of Chinese assets). Long before China was seen as a problem, other countries railed against what was called the "exorbitant privilege" enjoyed by the USA as a result of having the world's dominant currency. The fact that China has almost all ($3.2 trillion) of its foreign reserves in dollars reflects Chinese rather than American vulnerability – certainly the Chinese see it that way.

It is more meaningful, in a world where capital is (mostly) free to move, to think of imbalances as being due to big differences between countries' inclination to save and invest. If a country saves more than it can productively invest, as has been the case in China, the surplus savings must go somewhere – and, in practice and in a globally integrated world, they flow overseas. A corollary of the savings surplus is that there is a glut of production over what is consumed, and this is exported as a trade surplus (arithmetically, the trade surplus should equate to the export of capital). As I discussed in the previous chapter, China accumulated in the early years of the century large surpluses of savings even when there were high rates of investment. These surpluses spilt over into trade surpluses, amounting to as much as 10% of production, offset by the export of capital in the form of dollar assets forming China's foreign-exchange reserves.

However, even if such imbalances are seen as nullifying the benefits of trade, the imbalance has been substantially reduced in the last decade. The overall Chinese current-account deficit shrank to around 1% to 1.5% of GDP, as against 9% to 10% of a decade ago (although 2022 figures suggest a modest increase to around 2.0% of GDP, mainly because of Covid effects). Chinese surpluses are in any event proportionately small compared to those of Germany (5% of its GDP), Switzerland (7.5%) or Singapore (18%).

It is rational that, as global capital markets open up, rich countries should deploy surplus savings in poorer countries where, basic principles suggest, returns on investment should be higher, since capital is scarce.[14] The Chinese experience, in recent years, has however been the opposite: it exports savings to richer countries (which are probably under-reported because of leakage through exchange controls). But if there is any ground for complaint, it is from poorer Chinese, who should have been consuming more rather than saving and exporting their savings to finance tax cuts and undisciplined spending in the English-speaking world.

There is another worry about imbalances: that, at times when the world economy is depressed and interest rates are low, the export of savings by "surplus" economies adds to the problem of surplus savings and potentially deepens the slump.[15] But, as noted above, China – unlike, say, Germany – no longer has large structural surpluses. And far from legitimizing trade warfare based on bilateral trade deficits, the problem is best dealt with through a more coordinated and cooperative approach to global economic management via the IMF and the G20 group of countries including China.

The currency weapon and convertibility

Whilst economic imbalances between China and its trading partners have deflected attention from the trade benefits of economic integration, the imbalances themselves are not immutable, and one of the factors bearing most strongly on both trade and capital flows is the exchange rate. If the Chinese currency appreciates against the rest of the world, this doesn't just make its exports less competitive and imports more so but raises domestic consumption (because imports are cheaper). One of the complaints made against China is the allegation that the exchange rate has been manipulated downwards to promote exports and trade surpluses rather than upwards to help boost consumption.

In the 1990s and 2000s, there was undoubtedly a good basis for arguing that China was, indeed, a "currency manipulator". In 1994, there was a big devaluation, and the currency was pegged at the rate of 8.3 yuan (or renminbi) to the dollar for over a decade, with predictable results in terms of boosting exports and discouraging consumption (adding to the excess of domestic savings). The currency was thought to be under-valued by around 30% (more if currencies are to be aligned on the basis of purchasing-power parity). The US Treasury, in its biannual report on currency manipulation, highlighted the complaint, which was made at the time by industries like steel and furniture.[16]

After 2005, and for the following decade, the People's Bank of China allowed the currency to appreciate gradually, and there was also relatively high inflation (compared to the main trade partners), so in real terms the value of the currency rose strongly, by 60% against the dollar.[17] The policy was a major factor in rebalancing the economy, to reduce savings surpluses and current-account surpluses. Complaints about "currency manipulation" disappeared – for a while. The fact that the yuan maintained and increased its value consistently over time also boosted its status as an international currency, and in 2015 it overtook the yen in terms of usage for payments (albeit only accounting for around 3% of transactions). There was suffi-cient confidence in China's currency for the IMF to incorporate the renminbi into the basket of reserve currencies, and the IMF encouraged further moves to currency convertibility. This was seen as a step towards a long-term aim: to make the Chinese currency a global one alongside the US dollar.

Would it matter and be a problem for the rest of the world if China did acquire a global currency of the same standing as the yen, sterling or the euro – as well as, obviously, the US dollar? It would enable China to borrow more freely in its own currency. It would also enable China more easily to withstand economic sanctions, should it come to that. The use of Western sanctions against Russia, involving the freezing of Russian foreign reserves held in dollars, has moreover given that theoretical worry some real substance. Were military hostilities to break out over, say, Taiwan, the Chinese fear is that their reserves could be seized in a like manner.

But any concerns that China might achieve full convertibility, let alone replace the dollar, now seem remote. The moves to greater convertibility were unfortunately timed, since at the end of 2015 there was large-scale capital flight caused by a combination of a loss of confidence in China's economic management and a plunging stock market, as well as people taking advantage of the new freedoms to take money out of the country. Reserves fell by around a trillion dollars to just over $3 trillion. The currency fell sharply in value by more than 10% to 7.1 yuan to the dollar. The currency was then stabilized, in part by reintroducing exchange controls and reversing the moves to convertibility. Since then, the yuan has been attached to a basket of twenty-four currencies and has stabilized in real terms against the basket.

Recent experience has shown the difficulties of managing the transition to a more open and liberal economy in China. Indeed, it has been argued that without comprehensive liberalization – political and economic – China will not be able to make the transition. Whether or not that is correct, partial liberalization will have unintended side effects. Removing import barriers and exchange controls will push the exchange rate down, raising the cry of "currency manipulation" from trade partners. The practical consequence of China's inability, for the moment, to reconcile these factors is that exchange controls will stay for the foreseeable future in order to stop a serious slide of the currency. Nonetheless, in June 2021, the strengthening of the Chinese currency against the dollar led to the relaxation of capital controls, allowing Chinese savers to invest more outside China. But evidence of the weakness of post-pandemic recovery has led to currency decline (a 6% devaluation against the dollar in May 2023, year on year).

Whilst keeping exchange controls in place is a sign of weakness, it is also clear that China can no longer, reasonably, be accused of currency manipulation. There is also an understanding among policy-makers that the old crude arguments for promoting exports by devaluing the currency have to be weighed against the fact that China's trade is now made up of complex supply chains, and devaluation is no longer an effective means of achieving competitive advantage.[18] For these reasons, the argument that the benefits of trade are nullified by large systemic "surpluses" on trade and current account, and by "currency manipulation", no longer have any serious credibility.

Alarm has however been expressed about a new currency "threat" arising from China being the first major country to introduce a digital currency (the eCNY) through the Central Bank. The currency is being used domestically for financial transactions, displacing mobile-currency providers, and as an asset. Some commentators are warning that China could "mint the currency of the future".[19] However, having a digital domestic currency does not obviously translate into global monetary dominance. The Chinese renminbi has a very minor role in international payments (3%), or as a store of value in foreign reserves (2.5%), for very good reasons. Chinese capital controls and limits on convertibility slow down currency transactions and eliminate whatever advantages digitization may bring. Yet the Chinese authorities, in particular the Central Bank, have learnt some of the lessons of the currency crisis in 2015, making cross-border transactions in digital currencies easier and carefully relaxing its controls on capital flows in order to rebuild confidence.

The Ukraine war and the sanctions which have followed have reopened the whole issue of whether the dollar hegemony can continue and whether in the long term a Chinese-based system could emerge as a serious competitor. At present, the US dollar has all the necessary qualifications for a global currency: a stable store of value, ease of transactions and reliability as a unit of account. In the short run there is little threat to its status. But there are straws in the wind suggesting that the dollar's long-term future is less secure. Since the turn of the century, its share of Central Bank reserves, globally, has slid from 70% to 60%. The nervousness generated by the impounding of Russian reserves has led some countries to look for alternatives: Saudi Arabia, for example, has expressed a wish to conduct its China trade in renminbi. The hitherto rock-solid reputation of the USA for political and financial stability, and as a bastion of the rule of law, has taken a knock with Trump's refusal to accept election results and the Federal Reserve's inefficacy in fighting inflation.

There is a very plausible scenario of a fragmenting global economic system in which the Chinese currency plays a bigger role, especially if the technology around the digital currency evolves to make it easily accessible for transactions. After the launch of the eCNY in May 2022, there was a rapid growth in digital "wallets" to 260 million users (though interest has since peaked). In principle, the eCNY could also be used for foreign transactions, which would be difficult to block.

If the eCNY could be internationalized, it would address a specific problem around cross-border payment. One of the key elements in the sanctions imposed on Russia has been restriction on access to the SWIFT system operating out of Brussels, which conducted $140 trillion of transactions last year and has a virtual monopoly on handling payments (around 90%). The Chinese have been conscious for some time that they are vulnerable to the same sanctions if relations with Western countries deteriorate. They have established a parallel system, CIPS, with payments in renminbi, operating in a hundred countries, and accounting, so far, for 5% of global transactions. If the "cold war" gets colder, China is developing a system which would enable it to function and service a China-dominated part of a fragmenting world while retaining its system of capital controls.

The rising tide of protectionism

When President Trump left office, there were some hopes that the USA would return to its role as a champion of an open, liberal economic system. That hasn't happened. The Biden administration has continued the protectionist trade policies of its predecessor, albeit without the obsession with bilateral deficits or the appetite for "winning trade wars". There is a continued atmosphere of distrust and scepticism about the benefits of trade with China. In the world of Trump populism, "scepticism" was an understatement. The former president repeatedly referred to America's experience as the economic equivalent of "rape".[20] There are two influential lines of argument which have been used to bolster these accusations in economic terms: one is the impact of China's trade on workers' jobs and incomes in Western countries; the other is the accusation of "cheating" as a result of having a "state capitalist" system with a very uneven competitive playing field.

As to the first, there has long been a popular argument in industrial countries that their workers are "unfairly" exposed to competition from "cheap labour" or "sweated labour" driving down wages and threatening jobs.[21] There is a vast economic literature on the theory and practice of developed countries' opening their markets to the exports of newly industrializing countries, including China. The consensus has been that the overall economic benefits, to consumers and the wider economy, comfortably exceed the undoubted costs of adjustment for displaced workers; that import competition is in most cases less of a factor than productivity-raising technological change in displacing labour from labour-intensive industries; and that policy should concentrate on helping achieve smooth structural adjustment through retraining or compensation schemes for regions hurt by trade.[22]

Some influential studies have however been less sanguine. Autor, Hanson and Dorn drew attention specifically to Chinese competition, and attribute to it the loss of 1.5 million manufacturing jobs between 1990 and 2007 in the USA (which they later increased to 2.4 million in manufacturing and services between 1999 and 2011).[23] Their main conclusion, however, does not relate to the aggregate numbers (which take no account of offsetting factors in the economy), but to the localized impacts. Some communities were devastated, while most others weren't affected or benefited. And those whose jobs were displaced, by and large, lacked college education and did not have the skills to adapt. The data is historical, and it is possible that many of the jobs would have gone anyway because of technological change. And, moreover, the authors "think the world is better off with China in the WTO, and that policy makers should have provided the spending necessary to help regions hurt by trade".[24]

Nonetheless, the findings gave powerful ammunition to those pushing for restrictions on Chinese imports. There are provisions within existing multilateral trade agreements in the WTO to act against "surges" of imports and against "dumping" where prices are artificially held below cost through "loss-leading" export strategies to build up market share or through subsidization. But in practice it has been difficult for the USA and other aggrieved countries to prove "damage" from surges or to gather evidence of dumping – or there has not been the necessary political will to launch and sustain cases. And the motivation to pick a fight with China may have been undermined by the realization that the affected industries accounted for only a small part of China's trade.

The other main argument employed by those who are sceptical of the merits of close economic integration with China is that, as a "state capitalist" economy, China does not play by the rules of a market economy but engages in "unfair" forms of intervention at the expense of Western business competitors. That matters for the wider arguments about trade policy, since it has traditionally been business (and those reflecting the wider and more diffuse interests of consumers) whose voice has prevailed over labour unions and politicians representing areas most affected by import competition. If businesses investing in China also feel threatened or cheated by Chinese "state capitalism", then a powerful voice for openness is lost.

The importance of this change of emphasis is that, since the 1990s, "trade policy" has been less about the traditional problems of import competition and more about the equitable treatment of foreign investors and their intellectual property. This reflects the reality of "globalization" as something much deeper than "arm's length" trade and is proving to be a more potent source of conflict and scepticism about the economic benefits of engagement with China than trade narrowly defined. In any event, both China and the USA have become much more concerned about "security" and "strategic competition", and business preoccupations have become secondary.

China and the treatment of foreign capital

There is something of a gulf between the current rhetoric around foreign companies in China, which centres on discrimination, bullying and theft, and the survey data, which suggests that China is a relatively attractive destination compared to most emerging markets and some developed countries. Moreover, multinational companies are doubling down on their Chinese investments, and foreign direct investment into China has been growing rapidly. China's stock of foreign investment is worth around $1.8 trillion according to UNCTAD, having grown from $590 billion in 2010. It currently accounts for roughly 15% of annual FDI, the second largest after the USA, and there was 20% growth in 2021. A survey by the American Chamber of Commerce reported that 60% of American companies increased their investment in China in 2021, up 30% on the previous year. Enthusiasm cooled in 2022 because of Covid restrictions, not because of a negative business environment in general. There are however now growing reports that geopolitics is inhibiting investment.

As noted in the previous chapter, the World Bank survey of "the ease of doing business" ranked China virtually on the same level as Japan, ahead of France and Italy, and way ahead of most emerging markets. The story does not tally closely with the popular narrative on China under President Xi, which is supposedly reverting to pre-reform, anti-business, behaviour. However, the survey was said to be subject to political manipulation, following a big improvement in China's rating, and there was criticism of the responsible World Bank official, its then Chief Executive, Kristalina Georgieva, now Managing Director of the IMF (who vehemently denies malpractice). The survey has been discontinued.

Despite the large stock and growth of FDI in China there are several specific complaints, though most of the unhappiness is related to one factor: the Chinese hunger for acquiring new technology. A crucial issue for foreign investors with valuable brands or copyright or unexpired patents is the theft of intellectual property by partner companies, competitors or pirates. The Trump administration complained of hundreds of billions of "thefts" from US companies either based in China or following infiltration by Chinese hackers or "spies" in the USA. IP however is an issue not just for foreign investors, but for Chinese companies which have now developed valuable intellectual-property assets of their own. IP theft is one of the features of the "Wild East" business environment which President Xi has been trying to curb by establishing more powerful IP courts. It appears that more prosecutions are being made, and that the courts increasingly find for victims of theft, including foreign companies. Moreover, China pays large sums for legitimate acquisition of technology: around 8.5% of all cross-border payments for IP. The World Bank specifically noted improvements in this area, as well as continued problems.

A second related concern has been the use of joint-venture structures to force the transfer of technology. The Chinese claim to be relaxing the demands on foreign joint-venture partners, and they may or may not be. But it is surely not a surprise that a host government tries to extract the best deal it can from inward investors: most governments do so, with varying degrees of skill and forcefulness. Moreover, the Chinese have been genuinely mystified that this has become an issue, since the idea of joint-venture structures was encouraged by Western governments and business as a way of introducing China to foreign investment. Some companies, like Rolls-Royce, were worried about Chinese technology demands and walked away; others embraced the idea, fully aware of the implications. In other cases, as with commercial aircraft, the Chinese have been able to acquire technology by acting as suppliers and sub-contractors to leading Western companies like Boeing and Airbus, which were happy enough to secure the sales in the first place (though in the case of aviation the Chinese have not been very successful in using their new knowledge).

A third complaint, and one more easily demonstrated, is that China bars foreign investors from sensitive sectors which are open to Chinese companies elsewhere. The most obvious case is the exclusion of American data and social-media companies: Facebook, Google, Twitter, WhatsApp, Instagram, YouTube. In some cases, there is a barrier to foreign ownership in the sector. In others there is the barrier thrown up by censorship of incoming data through the so-called Great Firewall. The Chinese would say that the companies were free to come but chose not to comply with Chinese regulation on the flows of information, which would necessitate duplicate databases, cloud servers and software. In any event, the position is not totally clear-cut in that some technology companies like Apple or Microsoft's LinkedIn have seemed to operate successfully in China (though LinkedIn's offering has had to be scaled back for "compliance reasons"). Apple's position as the world's most valuable company was built in part on using China as both a base for production and as a big market for its products.

There is also a wider point that success or failure in China may have less to do with Chinese government policy and discrimination against foreigners and more with managing local relationships, the attractiveness of products, the depth and length of commitment, the response to competition and business models adapted to Chinese conditions. Western business-school studies have shown that the main reasons for failure are business- rather than policy-related.[25] The big tech corporations, for example, face competition from Chinese companies which did not just have comparable technology and scale but were very familiar with the idiosyncratic demands of Chinese customers: Amazon from Alibaba; eBay from Taobao; Airbnb from Tujia; Uber from DiDi; Google from Baidu. Some of the Western companies, such as Google, haven't given up, and have been trying to build businesses in China.

Foreign enterprises do face restrictions on overseas hiring and local content and can face all manner of interventions to favour domestic competitors. But the position varies greatly from sector to sector. In advanced-technology sectors foreign companies are usually well received and given favourable treatment, including exemption from red tape, but can also face issues with local partners and pressure to transfer proprietary technology. In the luxury-goods area, including motor vehicles, foreign companies are welcome and compete on a generally level playing field. The big German car companies for example derive a substantial share of their revenues and profits from China, in the case of VW around a third of sales and half of profits (though Chinese EV competition is becoming serious).

The sheer volume of inward investment in China suggests that foreign investors can operate in China despite the obstacles. There are some ways in which foreign companies, particularly those which have invested in Special Economic Zones, have benefited from tax reliefs, lower tax rates or other privileges not generally available in the rest of China. There are plenty of Western companies that pronounce themselves satisfied, or more, with their operations in China: car companies (VW, BMW, JLR, GM, Ford); fast-moving consumer-goods brands; energy (Shell); some high-tech companies (Qualcomm, Apple); and professional services, as in accounting and audit.

Recently China has further opened previously closed areas of financial services, such as asset management, investment banking and life insurance (some companies, like AIG and Allianz, are long established). Companies like BlackRock, JP Morgan and Goldman Sachs have long operated without much success in China, but are now allowed to have fully owned and controlled subsidiaries and are planning a big expansion.

The Chinese see substantial benefit from having a significant presence from the likes of Goldman Sachs and BlackRock. Not only do they bring substantial financial expertise and institutional investment in their wake, but they are also seen as "adults in the room" when it comes to American policy on trade with China.

All that said, there are those who argue that a combination of US hostility to China and President Xi's crackdown on certain business sectors as part of his "Common Prosperity" drive have, together, created a totally new and less friendly environment for foreign investors. President Xi's ministers and advisers publicly welcome inward investors, but the welcome is in sharp contrast to painful experience with Chinese regulators. Recent negative signals have been: police raids on consultants – Bain, Mintz, Capvision – which pay an important role in due diligence and investment appraisal; record fines on Deloitte; the banning of Micron from infrastructure activities (in retaliation for harsh G7 words at the Hiroshima summit); retaliatory sanctions against Lockheed Martin and Rayethon. New anti-espionage laws increase the risks around the handling of personal data. New laws also sanction companies which comply with US sanctions, forcing them to choose between the superpowers. There is a growing worry among investors more generally that what has happened in Russia – with a forced disinvestment following sanctions – could happen in China should US–China relations deteriorate further. In addition, the spread of ESG among investors has led to a targeting of companies which have operations in Xinjiang or China more generally. Adidas was a recent case, following its sponsorship of the Beijing Winter Olympics.

Some foreign investors continue to do very well in China. Louis Vuitton and Dior have jumped into the top-ten most valuable companies in the world on the back of China's luxury market. The big German car companies appear to be doubling down on their Chinese investments. Pharmaceutical companies like AstraZeneca and Pfizer are expanding to take advantage of the big demand from China's growing population of elderly.

What may however be happening is that major foreign investors committed to China, like Apple, are diversifying their supply chains somewhat (in that case to India), while others are adopting "asset-light" businesses in China or developing split corporate structures which unable them to operate separately in China and the West if conditions deteriorate.

Two-way flows: portfolio investment

In addition to direct investment, Chinese stock markets are now a major attraction for portfolio investment. With 4,000 listed companies and, after the market crash of 2015, better regulation in the interests of shareholders, Western fund managers are investing heavily in Chinese stocks. With 15% of the world economy but only 5% by value of world equity markets, the potential is obvious. Moreover, market movements in China are not closely correlated with those in the West, providing balance to portfolios. There has recently been a surge in investment in Chinese stocks and bonds which offer high yield. Chinese shares are also becoming more attractive as liquid assets, as it becomes easier to get money out to a fully convertible currency via "stock connect" with Hong Kong. And conservative macroeconomic management provides stability. Blackrock, J.P. Morgan and other asset managers are expanding, with improved access to take advantage of these opportunities. At the same time, the nervousness around a deteriorating geopolitical environment inevitably affects investors. ESG investors may not look kindly on Chinese investments. The US government might well try to ban Americans from investing in Chinese companies which have a military link or can be associated with human-rights abuses. Indeed a Biden executive order took effect in August 2021 barring American companies from investing in 59 Chinese groups, including Huawei and SMIC, on security grounds. The order also stops US investment in funds which have holdings of companies involved in Chinese security and military work.

An alternative route for foreign investors is to acquire shares in Chinese companies listed on foreign exchanges. In the United States alone, Chinese companies have had a capitalization of over $1 trillion, and there have been rapidly growing numbers of Chinese companies listed abroad. The attractions for the company are obvious: easy access to equity and bond finance in competitive financial markets, reputational benefit from a New York listing and some detachment from Chinese regulation. At the same time, investors have been able to circumvent the restrictions on foreign ownership in China. It is precisely those private motivations which have led both the US and Chinese authorities, for opposite reasons, to want to restrict these money flows.

Following legislation by Congress – the Holding Foreign Companies Accountable Act – the US Securities and Exchange Commission is now demanding disclosure of more accounting and audit data than some Chinese companies have been willing to provide, threatening the delisting for some of the leading Chinese companies. There is also concern over the governance of some Chinese companies, including political appointments to boards – that is in addition to those blacklisted on security grounds. In some cases, the Chinese authorities themselves have intervened to block foreign listings. The issue came to a head when DiDi ignored warnings that it needed Chinese approval, since there were data issues. DiDi was eventually delisted from the NYSE. With both US and Chinese authorities curbing the listing of Chinese companies, albeit for different reasons, the globalization of Chinese business is threatened with a major step backwards. On the audit issue, the Chinese have partially backed down and agreed that more audit data can be provided to meet US needs. Some Chinese companies are switching to US or Singaporean auditors to meet US audit standards. Whether this will prove enough to reopen portfolio investment – which has largely stalled – remains to be seen.

A form of portfolio investment which has hitherto attracted little attention is that of Chinese, state-backed investors in Western private-equity markets. Leading private-equity firms like Blackstone, Carlyle, Permira, Bridgepoint and CVC Capital Partners have utilized such funding alongside sovereign wealth funds. The Chinese Investment Corporation and the State Administration of Foreign Assets, both backed by the Chinese state, have deployed around a quarter of their combined assets (roughly $2.5 trillion) in this way. As a result, the Chinese institutions have small individual holdings in large numbers of Western companies. It is entirely rational for a savings-surplus country to use resources in this way and for private-equity companies to deploy them as they have. But for conspiracy-minded Western security "hawks" this is another example of the insidious infiltration of the Chinese Communist Party.

Also, there are still significant areas of dispute involving foreign companies in China and their Chinese competitors, especially in technology sectors, and these have fed into wider disputes around trade. The question then is whether disputes should be resolved through bilateral negotiation, unilateral action, multilateral rules or some combination of the three.

Dispute resolution and the WTO

The problem of how to incorporate big emerging economies into the system of global rules and dispute settlement is not unique to China and has been repeatedly confronted in the evolution of the General Agreement on Tariffs and Trade, GATT (now WTO). The process of absorbing Japan and South Korea into the world economy involved similar challenges. Other Socialist countries – Yugoslavia, Poland, Romania – were admitted while they were still non-market economies. India and Brazil are among many economies with "state capitalist" characteristics. Moreover, China had been already subject to demanding conditionality during its admission to the WTO in 2001.

The Chinese first registered their intention of becoming a fully-fledged member of the GATT back in 1986, and it took fifteen years of difficult negotiation to secure admission.[26] Two problems in particular dogged the negotiations: one was the prevalence of state-owned enterprises (SOEs), with evidence of the widespread use of subsidization or cross-subsidization. The other was the issue of transfer of technology, with accusations of infringements of property rights and discriminatory treatment of investors.

A form of words was agreed at the time to secure China's admission, in WTO legal language, and China agreed to slash tariffs, quotas, subsidies and other non-tariff barriers. In return China obtained "Most Favoured Nation" status, which guaranteed that there could be no discrimination against China by WTO member states. This removed the threat of losing access to the USA on the annual whim of Congress. At the time, retiring President Clinton and newly elected George W. Bush were only too happy to have responsibility for managing trade disputes with China transferred to a multilateral body.

A latent, unresolved, question remained unanswered. Should China be required to become a fully-fledged market economy – no longer "socialist with Chinese characteristics" – and, in effect, agree to change its system of government? Or should the WTO be changed to reflect the fact that the world trading system has as its largest participant a country which is different in character from its founder members led by the USA and UK? Western governments argue (and tend to assume) that China – and other emerging economies – must converge towards standards which they have established. Their frustration that China is slow or reluctant to comply was brought to a head in the WTO by a formal complaint from the EU in 2018 that China is in breach of its obligations in respect of foreign investors and technology transfer. There had already been a series of specific disagreements with China over its decision to increase tariffs on cars, contrary to its agreement on accession, and its failure to deliver the promised opening-up of banking, telecommunications and electronic payments. There is also evidence that subsidization has increased, not decreased.[27]

There are some commentators who argue that it is both right and more realistic to reform the WTO to accommodate China and other emerging economies.[28] Others believe that the same end can be achieved through legal draftsmanship.[29] One of the arguments for keeping negotiations with China within the WTO framework has been that, at least, there is a mutually agreed enforcement mechanism. President Obama used it in a dispute over tyres, where the WTO accession agreement allowed automatic levy of penalties for Chinese infractions of the rules.

The arguments are complicated by the fact that China is itself seeking "market-economy status" (MES) – indeed, it was promised that this status would take effect, automatically, fifteen years after China acceded to the WTO in 2016. The status matters, because it affects the way action can be taken in relation to alleged subsidization of exports or selling at below cost (dumping). If a country is officially a "market economy", it can claim that its domestic prices can be assumed to be set by the market rather than by government; if it is not, it is easier for an aggrieved importing country to bring evidence of dumping based on international price comparisons.

The EU and the USA are seeking to block China's MES application on the basis that it isn't a market economy on reasonable definitions. But by doing so they undermine China's legitimate entitlement to MES and the legal authority of the WTO itself. Two alternatives then open up: one is to use negotiation with China under WTO rules to improve access to Chinese markets, and to find ways to make anti-dumping and other action more effective. The other, chosen by President Trump, is to ignore the WTO altogether and to fight a bilateral trade "war". With Trump's departure, we are now in a position to assess the strengths and weaknesses of that approach.

Trump's trade war

There has been a long history of bilateral negotiations over trade between the USA and China from the original move to normalize relations in the 1970s to President Clinton's fraught negotiations over MFN and human rights, to annual MFN renewal and, lastly, over the terms of WTO accession. Under President Trump, there was a challenge to the consensus of the previous four decades that economic integration with China was broadly beneficial, despite specific complaints. His view that the USA had been "raped" by China was based on several interrelated grievances: bilateral trade deficits, "currency manipulation", job losses and the "uneven playing field" facing Western firms in competition with Chinese state-backed enterprises (including several specific, inherited disputes such as data-storage requirements in China and access barriers facing foreign makers of electric vehicles, computer networks and other equipment). As noted earlier, several of these complaints had little substance.

What Trump did have was the ideological support of those who saw competition with China as an existential challenge. These included his adviser Peter Navarro, co-author of the much-quoted *Death by China*.[30] But for Trump China was only one of several problems created by globalization and the "globalists". Trade wars would be fought on several fronts, including with Germany and the EU: he claimed that "Europe treats us worse than China".[31] Mexico, Japan and Vietnam were among other offenders. These adversaries, identified primarily by the size of the bilateral trade deficit, would be fought by America alone, not through what Trump regarded as a discredited global body, the WTO.

Trump had several distinctive views which cut across a straightforwardly protectionist narrative. First, he was driven by confidence in his own ability to use trade warfare to get "great deals". As the author of *The Art of the Deal*, Trump would use his negotiating skills, proving that "trade wars are good and easy to win".[32] On this basis, it would be possible to turn relations with China round to be beneficial to the USA. A second belief was enthusiasm for tariffs: denying the evidence that the cost fell on American consumers and was, instead, a levy borne by foreigners.[33] The focus on tariffs also shifted attention away from the non-tariff issues, which were central to the concerns of American business. And, thirdly, Trump's main metric for economic success was the stock exchange: any trade negotiations had to be conducted in ways that boosted stock values.

Trump's intentions were advertised long before he came to office. He was a strong advocate of high tariffs on Japanese exports in the late 1980s. When he first toyed with the idea of a presidential run in 2011, he advocated 25% tariffs on Chinese products and, when he joined the 2016 campaign in earnest, he planned to reverse the "greatest theft in the history of the world" with 45% tariffs.[34] The Chinese were well prepared for hostilities. But the first move was friendly: a personal visit by President Xi to Florida, leading to the establishment of a US–China Comprehensive Economic Dialogue incorporating trade negotiations.

At the outset, mobilizing for trade war proved more complex than Trump had imagined. He needed Chinese help over North Korea. He was preoccupied with trade problems with Mexico and NAFTA. He was being given strong advice not to compromise the economy – and the stock market. The Treasury Department acknowledged that China could not be labelled a "currency manipulator". The Chinese initiated trade talks by making seemingly generous offers, under the new Economic Dialogue, to buy more beef, allow Visa and Mastercard to operate in China and reduce steel capacity. Trump's team were divided on how to respond, and more generally on tactics and strategy. Trump himself seemed flattered by the attention he received on reciprocal visits with President Xi.

A decisive change came with the appointment, as trade negotiator, of Robert Lighthizer, who advised that the USA should make a decisive legal break with the multilateral WTO approach to trade disputes. He argued that, instead, the US administration should take unilateral action under dormant powers (Section 301 of the 1974 Trade Act). Using the powers of Section 301, the administration could act as prosecutor, judge and jury in deciding whether China or other countries were using trade practices that are "unjustifiable, and burden or restrict US commerce". This was to provide the template for two years of fraught negotiations and escalating conflict over trade with China. The concrete form of the complaint on Chinese practices was a report, in March 2018, which sought to quantify in detail the loss to US companies from "forced" technology transfer. An estimate was made of a cost of $60 billion a year from cyber espionage, theft or the misuse of joint ventures, regulatory reviews, anti-trust investigations and other action.[35]

Trump reformulated the complaint in his own terms, demanding an immediate reduction of $100 billion in the bilateral deficit, and warned of tariffs if the demand was not met. The Chinese threatened to retaliate, and Trump threatened tariff escalation if China did retaliate. Months of public and private sparring followed, along with preparation for trade conflict should the threats materialize. In May 2018 an American negotiating team went to Beijing with a long list of demands: reducing the bilateral deficit by $200 billion, ending all pressure to transfer technology and much else, including a demand that China not retaliate. The Chinese treated the demands as humiliating and rejected them, while offering a few sweeteners including access for more Hollywood films. Trump in turn offered to ease restrictions on the telecom company ZTE, which had fallen foul of US sanctions because of its business in Iran. But neither gesture could halt the juggernaut of tariff warfare.

The Chinese tried to forestall higher tariffs by offering to buy $100 billion more of imports from the USA. But a tariff of 25% on $50 billions of Chinese goods still went ahead, and China retaliated with 25% tariffs on American goods, mainly agricultural. Trump prepared, in turn, a new round of tariffs. It soon became clear that both sides were suffering damage: in the USA from higher prices to consumers and fewer farm exports; in China from a slowdown in exports and loss of manufacturing jobs. But there was no inclination on either side to compromise on what were seen as fundamentals. The Americans set in train preparations to raise tariffs on a further $200 billions of Chinese imports: tariffs would, then, cover 80% of imports from China. The Chinese responded with threats of tariffs on $60 billions of additional US imports, but as a goodwill gesture they also undertook to buy more and promised to deal with a variety of other US grievances. But their gesture was well short of what was being demanded, and the Chinese also insisted that US tariffs be withdrawn before they would consider further concessions.

The trade war reached a new pitch of intensity in May 2019, when the long-threatened US tariffs took effect, at a higher rate and on more products. At the same time, action was taken to cut the supply of key components to Huawei, China's most successful technology company, which had long been a target of the China "hawks". The costs of escalation were also becoming more apparent to both sides. It was estimated by Chinese sources that five million jobs had been lost in Chinese export industries over a year, and there was a potential exodus of US investors. US studies showed that the damage from Chinese tariffs on the USA was sufficiently well targeted as to hit Trump-voting areas disproportionately very hard.[36] Another study suggested that Chinese tariffs were costing the average US household $1,500 a year.[37] The US economy was slowing as a result of the trade war – and, crucially for Trump, the Dow Jones slumped. Despite a face-to-face meeting between the presidents, the conflict rumbled on with threats from the USA and unconvincing offers from China.

By the end of 2019, there was a serious appetite for a cessation of hostilities – a truce – leading to a "Phase 1" trade agreement. The USA withdrew some tariffs but left most in place. China agreed to buy more American foodstuffs. China gave no meaningful ground on the legal and regulatory changes demanded but made promises on intellectual property and other technology issues. Both sides predictably claimed victory, but one author, well disposed to what Trump was doing, concluded that "little had been accomplished by early 2020, measured by the complaints in the Section 301 report and the demands the US made of China".[38] The conflict had however set in train a process of disengagement, or decoupling, that has not ended with Trump's war. The US Strategic Competition Act will accelerate the process with forced disengagement from supply-chain products such as rare earths and semiconductors. The Chinese, for their part, adopted a new economic strategy of "dual circulation" to make China less vulnerable to pressure in future conflicts.

Neither side was aware at the time of two key developments that would radically reshape relations with China. The first was Covid, which had the effect of poisoning attitudes to China in the West. The second was the defeat of Donald Trump. The Biden administration does not disagree fundamentally with Trump's protectionist approach to trade, but it places greater reliance on multilateral cooperation with allies. I will now turn to how US allies in Asia and Europe see China's economy, and how they are dealing with its growth and success.

The multilateral approach

China's economic relations with its Asia-Pacific neighbours vary enormously and also have strong political overtones. The variations reflect differences in size, system of government and level of development. Taken as a whole, the region undoubtedly benefits significantly from the growth of China and the demand it generates, and there are very effective business networks within "Greater China" and with Japan and South Korea. But there is nervousness about being dominated.

The heterogeneity of the region probably explains why there has been little progress in trade liberalization through regional agreements of the kind seen in Europe and North America – with the partial exception of ASEAN in South-East Asia. Such trade liberalization as had occurred has been unilateral or through global WTO auspices. One regional concept which gained traction was led by the Obama administration, to create a Trans-Pacific Partnership (TPP). It sought to bring together East and South-East Asia, the Pacific Anglosphere and the main countries of the Latin American Pacific.

A group of eleven countries launched the TPP with the aim of breaking down tariff and other trade barriers in the region. It was founded on the principles of "open regionalism"; other countries were welcome, and existing arrangements were incorporated. Crucially, China was not included – though neither were South Korea, Taiwan, Indonesia or Malaysia. Its leading proponents – the USA and Japan – saw the group as a potential mechanism for developing global standards which were not Chinese, as well as giving an impetus to trade liberalization, which had largely stalled in the WTO.

The TPP suffered a near-fatal blow when newly elected president Donald Trump withdrew the United States from it. It has been rebooted as a Comprehensive and Progressive Agreement for Trans-Pacific Partnership (CPTPP), and it is trying to make progress without the USA. Ironically, China has seen the benefits of the organization even if the USA has not. It has applied to join (as has Taiwan), and it is difficult to see how it would be excluded. The CPTPP has, in any event, been partially upstaged by an alternative grouping which already includes China, the Regional Comprehensive Economic Partnership (RCEP). The fifteen members of RCEP embrace all of Asia, including the ten South-East Asian members of ASEAN, South Korea, Australia and New Zealand, but none from North or South America (or India, which declined to sign). It has agreed some liberalization of tariff and non-tariff barriers, together with a common approach to IP and trade-related investment rules. To add to the spaghetti soup of Asia-Pacific economic arrangements, the USA has launched the Indo-Pacific Economic Framework (IPEF). Within a week of being launched, fourteen countries – from Fiji to India – had applied to join, though it offers its members very little additional market access in the USA. It remains to be seen how the CPTPP, IPEF and RCEP will interact with each other and with various bilateral agreements. But crucially, China wants to be at the centre of Asian trade liberalization and rulemaking and the USA, for domestic protectionist reasons, has opted out.

The European Union has also sought improved access for its companies in China and has reached an agreement specifically on the treatment of investment. It is designed to remedy complaints about "forced" technology transfer and other Chinese practices. Issues like subsidies and procurement rules are being pursued separately through the WTO. The draft agreement has

been criticized for undermining the incoming Biden administration's attempts to have a coordinated approach that also
considers human-rights considerations.[39] For its part, the EU
has claimed that new access conditions, helping EU firms in
the automotive sector and cloud computing, among other
industries, simply bring the EU to the level agreed in the US
Phase 1 "truce". Tactics and detail apart, however, the EU
no longer regards China as a "normal" trade and investment
partner, but as a "strategic competitor" – and, even if trade
negotiators find common ground, the European Parliament is
threatening to block the agreement on human-rights grounds.

The focus of trade negotiations with China is likely, with
President Biden, to shift back from bilateral to regional and
multilateral fora, but in a more hostile environment. Delinking is
becoming a cumulative process. American sanctions over human
rights and Hong Kong are being legally reinforced under the
Biden administration on top of "security of supply" measures
related to supply-chain resilience and disengagement from companies with links to the Chinese armed forces. But China has
its own long-standing preoccupation with "security of supply",
and its security consciousness is being strengthened by American
action and geopolitical tension more generally. China has already
embarked on a "dual circulation" policy of strengthening self-
reliance and is now introducing measures to be taken against
companies in China which comply with US or EU sanctions.
Companies are in effect being forced to choose between the
Chinese and the US (with some other Western) markets. The
perception of China as a competitor or systemic rival, rather
than a partner, now dominates thinking in the Western world.

How far could decoupling and sanctions go?

The deterioration in relations between the USA and China is
generating its own dynamic. The US Chips and Science Act
simultaneously makes the USA less dependent on importing
high-end semiconductors (at a cost estimated by Goldman Sachs

at 45% higher than imports from Taiwan) and also makes it more difficult for China to access the most advanced "chips". China, in turn, has reinforced its plans to make itself self-sufficient and independent of the West (also at great cost). The decoupling then has knock-on effects and added costs for third parties like Korea and Japan, which had hitherto straddled the US–China divide. A similar process is underway for other technologies considered sensitive, and there is a commercial process of supply-chain diversification also, which has taken China's share of US manufactures from Asia from 70% in 2013 to 50% in 2023 (so far). The possibility now arises that the kind of sanctions regime being applied against Russia would be applied against China should China invade Taiwan or make a major breach in the Russian sanctions, or otherwise arouse the ire of American Congressmen. China is no stranger to the use of coercive sanctions, having itself deployed tariff and non-tariff measures against Australia and other countries. Both sides in the new "cold war" are calculating the costs of a potential deep split, and what it means in the short and long term. In this lose-lose world, a question both sides are asking is: who has leverage?

China and the USA have lived with one potential flashpoint for decades: the accumulation of dollar reserves by China, which has given China the potential ability to sell off the reserves precipitating a dollar crisis – but at the cost of devaluing its own assets. Currently, two thirds of China's reserves are invested in US government dollar securities: $3.2 trillion. In the application of Russian sanctions, the USA has, in effect, seized control of Russia's much smaller reserves. And by blocking Russian access to the payment-clearance system and to the use of other Western banks, it has made it impossible for them to dump their dollar reserves. There is now the risk that a similar technique might be deployed against China. Given time, China can diversify its assets and develop a parallel clearance system for transactions. Now that the risk has been advertised, it may well do both, widening the split in the world economy into two competing systems.

If the US and its allies resorted to the confiscation of Chinese property as is happening with Russian state and oligarch assets,

China could retaliate in kind. There are an estimated $3.2 trillion of foreign direct investment in China, and another $2.2 trillion of portfolio investment.[40] These sums are, however, together more than twice the sum of Chinese investment abroad – around $2.2 trillion.[41] putting Western interests at greater risk. In addition, any damage from blocking the business of the four leading Chinese banks has wider repercussions, since they are amongst the thirty systemically important banks whose difficulties would be transmitted to the Western financial system.

The degree of trade interdependence is such that sanctions would hurt the West as much as China, or more. We have already seen that Trump tariffs inflicted costs mainly on the USA. Furthermore, Chinese-sourced components account for a third of US and UK imports of parts and components, 25% in the EU, 45% in Japan. Adjustment to exclude Chinese products in a trade war would be painful and difficult, especially for companies which export to as well as import from China. Many countries trade more with China than the USA, and might opt to preserve their Chinese trade if forced to choose. That is true for countries in the Middle East, Latin America and Africa, which export raw materials to China. The sanctions regime might be highly targeted, but China could target back, as it has done in disputes with the USA and Australia. Overall, it is far from clear that a regime of sanctions against China would work or work without inflicting great costs on the sanctioning countries.

Awareness of these costs is one factor slowing the process of decoupling. There are, for example, difficulties in getting allies to comply. In Germany, Japan and Korea there has been strong resistance from companies which export to China, are embedded in Chinese supply chains and may judge that, in the long run, China is still a good bet. Arguments about the speed and scale of decoupling now wages in many company boardrooms.

The main battleground in this process of "decoupling" – or, to use the less provocative European formulation, "de-risking" – is technology. And to this I now turn.

Chapter 4

The Technology Race

Whether we choose to regard it as a race or a competition or a war, the dispute between China and the USA and its allies is essentially about technology. There is a concern in the West that China, on the back of its economic success, is fast catching up in terms of new foundation technologies. And beyond the concern is a fear about what China might do if it establishes technological superiority. It was clear, in Trump's "trade war", that apart from his own idiosyncratic obsession with tariffs and bilateral deficits, the real issue in the confrontation was technology: the allegations of Chinese intellectual-property theft, forced technology transfer and subsidization of China's technology champions. And the most significant event in that trade war was a parallel set of measures to exclude Huawei and other Chinese technology companies from the USA and other Western countries, including the UK.

Why does technological competition matter? First, technological capacity has a strong bearing on military strength. China is not, at least in global terms, a serious military competitor to the USA. But military factors were advanced as the main reason for concern by a US Congressional Commission in its warning that that China is on track to surpass the USA as an AI superpower.[1] Security interests extend more widely than weaponry, to encompass cyber security and espionage, as with a recently reported hack by a Chinese group of Microsoft Exchange's email servers used by defence companies.[2] The Chinese also claim to be worried about breaches of data security, as with Tesla cars and other Western operations in China which use sophisticated software and data storage, and which could involve compiling data on Chinese nationals. The action of Chinese regulators to block an IPO in New York by DiDi was supposedly prompted by concerns over DiDi's non-compliance with rules on data security. It is very difficult to know exactly how to strike the balance between free data exchange and data security, but there seems to be a drift towards worrying more about espionage risk over economic benefit in relation to China (as well as by the Chinese authorities themselves in relation to their own tech companies).

There are also undoubted "first mover" economic advantages from having a technological lead for the individuals, companies or countries involved: income from royalties or from enjoying a temporary monopoly, or the ability to set international standards which competitors have no choice but to follow, as in telecommunications or renewable energy.

And thirdly, technology matters for the political sustainability of regimes: the advances in systems of control – censorship or surveillance – are a factor of particular importance in China, with the development of an Internet system which controls sensitive information flows but enhances personal choice in other ways.

The arguments about technological competition are complicated by the fact that there are also important respects in which technology is a public good: when it serves global environmental goals; vaccine development and other health advances; improved communication systems; the dissemination of basic scientific knowledge about the universe and life.

And, arguably, the most important role of technology is raising living standards by increasing productivity and, through trade and investment, spreading those benefits internationally to poorer countries. So, competition and cooperation often go together and also represent a source of tension in joint ventures or collaborative projects, as with Chinese companies and individuals.

Why technology matters for growth and development

China's main concern in recent decades has been to use technology to promote growth and development. That reflects an understanding of economic theories of growth and development which have given technology pride of place. Schumpeter saw technological progress as the key driver for economic growth and was willing to sacrifice competition for monopoly where it led to innovation.[3] Proponents of "new growth theory" have stressed the value of policies which engender a climate supportive of innovation: education, learning and risk-taking.[4] Others have stressed the importance of institutions, among them a regime protecting intellectual-property rights.[5]

There is, however, at the heart of technology policy, a contradiction which has often resurfaced since Britain led the world in technological innovation in manufacturing, with the steam engine and the mechanization of textiles manufacture. On the one hand there is the interest of the inventor or innovator in protecting their intellectual property (IP) by creating a temporary monopoly and the public interest in encouraging invention by creating a secure legal framework around intellectual-property rights. On the other hand, there is the interest of consumers and competing individuals and firms who want to see the benefits of the new ideas spread as widely and quickly as possible through the opening-up of access to the technology. There is no right or wrong, but an issue of balance.[6]

Arguments about that balance can become toxic when they relate to national governments acting for their firms, as is now the case with China and Western competitors, and more generally with countries at different stages of technological development. The merits of stronger and weaker IP regimes will vary according to the level of economic development and have been promoted by different countries at the same time and the same country at different times.[7] IP also matters more in some industries: patents are especially valuable for pharmaceuticals for example.

Since arguments around IP and China are usually couched in angry and ideological terms, it is useful to start with a brief review of how attitudes to IP have evolved and how China fits within that context. When Alexander Hamilton was envisaging the early industrialization of America at the end of the eighteenth century, he was faced with a Britain so obsessed with protecting its monopoly of technological knowledge that the emigration of artisans from the UK and the export of machinery were both banned.[8] He did not accept that the USA should be permanently restricted to an agrarian economy – hewing wood and drawing water. Textile technology was obtained from an escaping British artisan, and the first mill was built in 1791. To a significant degree, the economic take-off of the United States was based on theft.[9]

A century later there was a new upstart, Japan, seeking, after the Meiji restoration, to modernize using Western technology.[10] The established industrial countries – mainly Britain, France, Germany – sought to protect their technological lead by creating an international legal framework to reinforce IP rights: the Paris Convention (1883) for patents and the Berne Convention (1886) for copyright (the USA at that stage was both poacher and gamekeeper).[11]

Japan adapted to the new rules by creating its own patent system (JPS), based on the assumption that it would be a technology importer, while it gave protection to Japanese businesses making only slight modifications to foreign technology. Japan benefited greatly from its weak IP regime, until in 1975 it felt sufficiently developed to adopt a stronger system.[12] South Korea had a similar journey.[13] It was initially an acquirer of foreign technology by fair (and at times foul) means, until challenged by the threat of US trade sanctions. It responded, like Japan, by introducing IP laws which favoured importation but created legal protection for minor adaptation. Taiwan also made the trip from nil to weak to strong IP as it developed. What is undoubtedly the case is that getting access to technology was a critical factor in the "Asian miracle".[14] China is no different from its Asian antecedents, except in scale and the speed with which it is moving from technology acquirer to technology developer.

China: the journey from technology follower to leader

There are undoubted similarities between China and these other Asian economies, though China's vastness and complexity, and its authoritarian politics, make it very different, as does its history.[15] There was a distant time when China's advanced agricultural and industrial technology far exceeded in sophistication and extent anything available in the Western world.[16] But centuries of stagnation and isolation then left China far behind. Attempts in the early years of the Republic to modernize the country technologically spluttered to a halt as China descended into chaotic politics, civil war and Communist revolution. Attempts to modernize and reform under Deng mark the point at which modern China made serious efforts to catch up technologically. Deng was quite clear that China was at that stage technologically backward and learning from foreigners was at the heart of his project, to be achieved through overseas study and exchanges, promoting inward investment and joint ventures. His Western interlocutors endorsed and encouraged his approach.

For much of the reform period, Chinese development and rapid growth was based on rapid capital accumulation for infrastructure and industry alongside rapid export growth. By the turn of the century, there started to be more attention to developing a capacity for innovation and an awareness that future growth would have to come from technologically driven productivity improvements.[17] After 1998, the so-called "Project 985" put a lot of resources into universities and research institutions to boost underlying science research and technological capability. In 2006 the government launched its "National Medium- and Long-Term Plan for the Development of Science and Technology", designed to promote "indigenous innovation" in advanced manufacturing. It identified sixteen huge programmes for research and development (R&D), and money was poured into such areas as integrated circuits, communications equipment, high-speed broadband and synthetic materials.

There is much debate on the value of the results from all the resources put into scientific development in China, but little doubt as to the scale of the effort. In 1991 R&D accounted for 0.7% of GDP, and in 2013 the share had risen to 2% of GDP. In the period between 2004 and 2013 alone, R&D outlays quintupled. By 2010 China had already overtaken the USA in the number of STEM (Science, Technology, Engineering and Maths) doctorates, and while there are legitimate questions over the quality of some of the qualifications, the fact that so many were snapped up to work in the USA suggests that their employers valued them. There are similar doubts over the explosion of published research papers, but growing numbers were being published in internationally cited papers based on peer review. In terms of commercial value, the Chinese venture-capital industry, by 2008, was already the second biggest in the world, and was fuelling the growth of large numbers of high-tech start-ups.[18]

A big change of gear occurred in 2015. This was the year when the worries about the direction of Chinese economic development – debt, over-investment, waste of resources – came to a head with the run on the currency and on inflated equity prices. It was also the year of the publication of 'Made in China 2025', a ten-year strategy for industrial development. Where it broke new ground was in looking well beyond the China market. It set ambitious targets for achieving a share of the world market (for its chosen markets, 40% by 2020 and 70% by 2025). It set out plans for global leadership in AI, robotics, next-generation IT, advanced manufacturing, electric cars and biomedicine – all areas where China was still some way behind.

There were two sets of negative reactions of an opposite kind. Foreign business leaders felt threatened. The EU Chamber of Commerce in China complained that China was, in effect, "telling companies round the world that their market share would be reduced".[19] The United States Chamber of Commerce gave a similar reaction. The Trump administration used the report as a major piece of evidence for its central argument that "Beijing intended to replace the United States as the global economic leader and had to be stopped".[20] Its own report cited 'Made in China 2025' more than a hundred times to make the point that the plans could only be realized by heavy subsidization and by stealing technology.

Chinese critics, more familiar with the way Chinese planning and industry policy operated, downplayed the significance of the report. The outspoken former finance minister Lou Jiwei was temporarily demoted for saying publicly that the plan "wasted public money",[21] and another leading Chinese economist was equally scathing: "Basically every department came up with its pet projects. But there was no real action strategy."[22] 'Made in China 2025' was essentially a motivational tool for domestic consumption. But it scared foreigners – a good example of how perceptions can drive policy rather than substance. A detailed study carried out at the Hong Kong University of Science and Technology concludes that: "Investment is driven by profitability and private entrepreneurship, not by government policies. The findings negate foreign concerns that the Chinese state, via industrial policies like 'Made in China 2025', is creating national state-owned technology leaders."[23]

Whether in response to domestic or foreign critics or both, the plan was quietly buried and replaced, in November 2019, with a new industrial strategy which said much the same, less provocatively. The new Five-Year Plan, published in March at the 2021 National People's Congress, contained the same list of manufacturing priorities from robotics to electric vehicles. It also set out the frontier technologies deemed vital to national security and development, with more focus on those areas of technology which are potentially subject to US sanctions ("stranglehold technologies"), especially semiconductor design, but also other specialist areas of advanced manufacturing. The deteriorating geopolitical context, aggravated by the Ukraine war and the demonstrated willingness of Western countries to use far-reaching economic sanctions, has further laid stress on the objective of self-reliance.

Overseas analysts struggle to differentiate hype and hope from carefully calibrated plans when judging threats. An example of this confusion has been the adoption of 'China Standards 2035', which sets out in a very assertive way China's ambition to be a major force in global industry-standard-setting bodies. It has followed words with action. The International Telecommunication Union has been buried in more than 800 technical papers to be reviewed by technical committees, more than from the USA, Europe and Japan combined. Most of the papers being reviewed by the International Electrotechnical Commission are from China. More predictably, the global 3GPP standards body for 5G receives more submissions from Huawei than any other company.

This attempt to colonize the standards world causes some alarm.[24] But those familiar with the workings of these bodies say that the Chinese contribution is quantity, not quality: hype and public relations. Moreover, the Chinese appear not to understand the way the system works: industry-led, not government-led; rules-based; consensus-based; voluntary; designed to achieve interoperability for consumers, not to promote one brand or company.[25] The wide range of perceptions of China's self-promotion prompts wider questions about the actual level of technological development.

Where is China in terms of technology leadership?

There has been a tendency among some commentators, as above, to downplay the level of Chinese technological development and to dismiss the claims of those overstating China's achievements and the fears of competitors. It is not easy to judge these assessments in aggregate, since the position is changing rapidly and varies considerably from one sector to another. But there are two recurring themes. The first is that innovation in complex ecosystems requires decentralized and entrepreneurial decision-making. This is not obviously compatible with China's centralized system, which relies on the motivation of middle-level state bureaucrats. But China is not quite the centralized system depicted – certainly not like the former USSR. Indeed, as I noted earlier, many of China's recent economic-management problems have stemmed from a high level of decentralization when it comes to investment decisions, and the funding base of central government is weak.

The second source of scepticism is that Chinese "innovation" is based on little more than copying and making minor adaptations, reflecting the weakness of the IP protection system. But like Japan before it, "once following a model of 'copying', China has slowly shifted into a model of domestic innovation: effectively the country has 'leapfrogged' other technologically advanced countries".[26] The massive increase in patents and the recent emphasis on IP enforcement via specialist courts suggest serious change. In a review of China's innovation policy, Sheehan dismisses attacks on China based on IP theft as out of date and complacent, based on a failure to distinguish stealing from learning.[27] China has learnt much from joint ventures, venture-capital investment in Silicon Valley and genuine scientific collaboration without the need to steal technology.

There are several reasons to be positive about China's capacity to innovate. The country has a highly entrepreneurial business culture, especially among the Chinese diaspora, who have invested heavily in the motherland. And there is also a determined party state with long-term commitment to modernization. The combination of the two has proved very effective in promoting technological leadership across a wide range of sectors.

Specifically, there is a high level of resources being ploughed into R&D. At the turn of the century, the governments of both China and the USA were spending just under 1% of GDP on R&D (when China was a much smaller economy). By 2018, the US Federal Government's commitment had fallen to around 0.75% of GDP while the Chinese had jumped to 2% of GDP[28] – more than double that of the USA in absolute as well as relative terms, since the Chinese economy was by then so much bigger. However, this is a measure of government support, not of national commitment. The World Bank rankings of R&D intensity suggest that if we include privately financed R&D,

the USA was close to the top of the global league table, with 3% of GDP, while China was at 2.5% of GDP.

The US National Science Board calculates that, on a PPP basis, the USA accounted for 25% of global R&D and China 23%. The figures relate to 2017, and China has probably now closed that gap.[29] There is also an issue of quality. Almost all Chinese R&D is funded by the government, although 75% is spent by the Chinese private sector. But three quarters of American R&D is privately funded, and arguably subject to stricter standards of "value for money". Also, a higher share in the USA – 17% against 6% – is basic research dealing with fundamentals rather than small adaptations. But the growth of spending is significantly higher in China, with an estimated 17% real growth in R&D spending in the last decade, compared to 4.5% for the USA. Both countries are growing their R&D spending at roughly twice the speed of their economies, and China's economy has, until recently, been growing faster.

Secondly, the quantity of scientific and technological manpower is on a much bigger scale than in the USA or anywhere else. China has tripled its number of universities in a decade to over 3,000, hosting more than forty million students. It is creating the biggest pool of STEM graduates and postgraduates in the world by far. In 2016 China produced 1.75 million science and engineering first-degree graduates as against 800,000 in the USA. For doctoral students, both countries were producing around 30,000 in science and engineering.[30]

Of course, quantity is not quality. Just as more soldiers do not make a more effective army, more scientists do not mean better science. China has a recent history of undermining scientific excellence. In the 1970s, during the Cultural Revolution, any pretence at serious higher education was abandoned in the chaos. After Deng assumed power, however, an early priority was the re-establishment of academic research and teaching, albeit the starting point was low.

In recent years, some Chinese universities have acquired a reputation for excellence. Critics argue however that, although several mainland, as well as Hong Kong, universities are now cited in the lists of leading global universities, mainly on the strength of research, there are lower levels of academic freedom.[31] That may be more of an issue in the humanities than STEM, where a level of quality control is maintained by the policy of encouraging Chinese students to study abroad. Because the USA is more open – about a third of science and engineering professionals are of overseas origin, and half of postgraduates – it sets global standards. China doesn't – yet.

But in areas where there is a mission to succeed China is achieving exceptional standards of quality. In AI, for example, with the Thousand Talents programme a large cadre of very advanced post-doctoral students is being established, with a minimum qualification of an overseas Ph.D. and proof of entrepreneurial flair. The programme is sufficiently substantial to be considered a major threat to the USA, which alleges that the US-trained Ph.D. graduates are taking sensitive material back to China[32] (though a review of the recent US crackdown on overseas scientists suggests that there was "overreaction", leading to racial stereotyping of Chinese and a counterproductive disruption of mutually beneficial research).[33]

A further strength of Chinese technological development derives from the very high savings rate, which has created a large pool of capital for investment. Many high-net-worth individuals are looking for high-risk, high-reward investment opportunities, leading to angel networks and a big venture-capital market. By 2008, the Chinese venture-capital market was already the second biggest in the world, and in 2018 it was bigger in scale than the US equivalent, with over half the venture capital available globally.[34] It was described as "one of the most dynamic VC markets in the world, with both domestic and leading global investors".[35] The Chinese VC industry, mainly of state-owned financial institutions, may however be less adventurous than others in its support for start-ups, as opposed to later-stage investments. And the market also dried up in 2019 during the Covid crisis.[36]

Nonetheless, the scale and sophistication of the VC industry provide important support for Chinese expansion of its technology firms. And the VC institutions cannot be seen in isolation from the wider ecosystem designed to support innovators – government-funded innovation parks and incubators, part of a so-called Sparking Programme involving income-tax breaks for start-ups and those who finance start-ups.[37] There are continuing deficiencies in what the government calls the "innovation state", such as the underdeveloped status of IP rights, where China is roughly where Japan was in the '60s and South Korea was in the '80s. But this deficiency is recognized, and recent reforms have been designed to address it.

In addition, scale matters. Even allowing for some inefficiency and uneven quality, the scale of R&D, the scientific and engineering labour force and the availability of risk capital already put China close to parity with the USA. One unambiguous advantage is the size of the home market, providing economies of scale and rapid growth of sales of new products. By the earlier part of the last decade, China was already the world's largest market for cars, smartphones, computers, household appliances and machine tools, and for the many firms using the Internet.

There is another advantage enjoyed by Chinese innovators: "process knowledge". Dan Wang describes the way that Chinese manufacturers can process knowledge rapidly and at scale and develop high-quality supply chains which can produce goods better and more efficiently than competitors.[38] Companies like Apple, GE and Tesla have harnessed this capability, which is why China is essential to them and they are so essential to China (and why the costs of decoupling are so high). While the US may well surpass China in scientific innovation, China has developed a capability in advanced manufacturing that will be difficult to match.

One aspect of scale relevant to China's future growth is the availability of data. Chinese data is superabundant, due to the magnitude of the e-commerce platforms and lack of privacy restrictions on its use. There has been a battle going on between state agencies and the big-data companies over how much the companies should share their data with the state. It appears that the companies have been reluctant to hand over to the state access to their data stores and have not been pressed to do so. But the recent crackdown on tech companies over regulatory lapses has made it clear where power lies. In practice, the state could obtain commercially owned data if it chose to. There are, in addition, two hundred million cameras in use in public spaces, many for innocuous and worthwhile purposes, like traffic management, but also providing the basis for a surveillance system which would not be tolerated in Western societies. Overall, the vastness of China's supply of raw material for the new data-based industries like AI gives its firms a significant advantage.

The Chinese potential for data gathering is leading some in the West to invoke "security" concerns over what appear to be – and probably are – innocuous or useful activities. An example is the "smart cities" technology which Chinese companies have been marketing around the world. Some British cities like Bournemouth have been reconsidering the technology after security concerns were raised. The supposed risks include the monitoring of individual Bournemouth residents by Chinese agencies, access to sensitive data on individuals and the potential use of "kill switches" to destroy critical infrastructure. The National Cyber Security Centre has highlighted risks in general, though there is no evidence of these threats materializing, and the dangers to Bournemouth seem improbable. But in a world where Western governments and companies are struggling to define the limits of data protection, Chinese involvement is a complication some would rather do without.

Putting these factors together, it seems abundantly clear that those who have sought to minimize China's technological achievements and potential are simply wrong. As the head of the UK's technical intelligence and cyber agency put it: "We tell ourselves that western liberal democracy is the key to creativity in technology, but it turns out that a centralized command economy can do innovation pretty well."[39] There is some evidence from patent filings at the European Patent

Office and the Intellectual Property Organization that Chinese firms are catching up fast in terms of output as well as input.

A new innovation model

What baffles some Western observers is that the government's attacks on tech companies under the slogan of Common Prosperity appear to be at odds with China's quest for technological parity or dominance. A more sympathetic interpretation is that the emphasis has changed to counter what the government considers to be a "disorderly allocation of capital" and to reflect the new emphasis on self-reliance and security concerns. There is to be a shift from consumer facing "soft tech", in which the Internet giants excelled and greatly profited – Tencent, Ant and Alibaba, Didi, Meituan and Pinduoduo – to "hard tech" or "deep tech", which involves investing heavily in the key new foundation technologies: semiconductors, artificial intelligence, industrial software, big data, robotics and clean energy.

This redirection of resources requires a deeper change, involving large numbers of technology incubators based in provincial cities inland from the coastal areas where much of China's development has been based hitherto. The established tech companies are encouraged to redeploy their resources, but the emphasis will be on large numbers of "little giants". These are rapidly growing new companies approved of by the authorities and drawing their capital from government-supported private equity and venture-capital funds and new stock exchanges catering to high-tech, medium-sized companies.

The existing platform companies such as Alibaba and Tencent are in effect being blocked from profitable areas of expansion – fintech, online tutoring, video games, news gathering – and pushed into state-sponsored activities such as cloud computing, which are already very competitive. Attempts to diversify abroad meet growing suspicion in China and abroad. Unlike their Western equivalents in the platform economy, their innovative, entrepreneurial energy is being stifled.

Critics see this new approach as a recipe for massive waste and underachievement. But recent history suggests that China should never be underestimated. The fact that some earlier state-led technology campaigns flopped does not mean that they will in future. There are already several substantial sectors where Chinese firms are already dominant players globally and are innovating. One is high-speed trains. The original technology came from Japan and Western Europe, but the Chinese have taken it to a new level, operating at a unique scale, precision and speed of installation. Another sector is e-commerce, where China is by far the largest market, and one where Chinese firms have innovated through the integration of online retailing with social media and cashless payments, a process which does not seem – yet – to have been disrupted by the regulatory action against the leading firms. Others can be added to the list: high-voltage transmission, drones and renewables – especially solar power and electric vehicles.[40] Beneath these applications lie foundation technologies in telecommunications, semiconductors, Big Data and AI – and this is where technological competition and conflict are now most acute.

Telecommunications and the rise of Huawei

The most important issue in the technology "war" between China and the USA, so far, has been Huawei and its role in future 5G development. There are essentially two ways of looking at the matter, which essentially reflect the standpoint of the company and its supporters on the one hand and that of those in the USA and some its allies on the other. The former view is that what is at stake is a form of commercial protectionism: Huawei has out-competed its rivals, mainly American, with innovative technology, achieving market leadership, and the USA simply cannot accept that a Chinese company should succeed to this extent. The counter view is that commercial concerns are secondary, and that Huawei is acting for the Chinese government to carry out espionage and establish political control over a technology fundamental to our future. There are more balanced opinions, heard in Europe, which contain elements of both: Huawei has got where it is through genuine competitiveness, bringing value to its customers, but there is a security risk, potentially, in future.

These different perceptions are reflected in different inter-pretations of how the company evolved in the mid-1980s, when it was established by Ren Zhengfei as a state-owned importer of telecoms equipment for the domestic market. Isabel Hilton stresses the links with Ren's former colleagues in the army (the PLA), the support from the Chinese government through loans and Huawei's adoption as a "national champion" favoured with big military contracts and equipped with "deep pockets that were hard to account for in its existing commer-cial operations".[41] Dennis Wang points out, by contrast, that many companies in the West, as well as in China, have been founded and led by former middle-level military officers; that it is standard practice in business everywhere to make use of government contacts; and that the real story behind Huawei's rise was its ability "to survive in harshly competitive Chinese markets, where hundreds of similar companies existed, but Huawei thrived".[42] Hilton stresses its early beginnings based on reverse engineering – "low-level piracy" – and subsequent state patronage, while Wang emphasizes relentless hard work and the creativity of its R&D.

Douglas Fuller's in-depth study of the sector suggests that Huawei's initial success was because it kept well clear of the embrace of the state, unlike its Chinese competitors, Julong and Datang, which remained dependent on government pro-curement and the patronage of state banks and never flour-ished. Huawei's business model was outward-looking, to world markets, as soon as possible. The company ploughed back exceptional amounts into its R&D, and established an attrac-tive working environment for scientists, building up to 10,000 Ph.D. graduates.[43]

Huawei's big breakthrough occurred in 1997, when it launched a Chinese 2G telecommunications GSM (Global

System for Mobile Communications) based on European stand-ards. Having established the necessary international standard, Huawei set out to compete with the likes of Ericsson, Nokia and Marconi, which at that stage were well ahead. And within a short time it had driven out of business the last of those with alleged price-cutting below cost. Within a few years, Huawei was the dominant firm in the global industry, but its rapid rise was contested from the outset, initially by the president of Cisco in 2003, when he claimed that Huawei received an annual subsidy from the government (which Huawei denied, inviting KPMG to do a full audit of its accounts). Lawsuits followed in the USA, alleging all manner of IP infringements, and have continued to this day, backed up by press campaigns alleging spying and "theft". All this occurred long before Trump appeared on the scene.

Despite strong competition and – in the USA – political opposition, Huawei became, with 3G and then 4G technology, the world's leading provider of telecommunications equipment, with base stations in 180 countries. Its global revenue overtook Nokia's in 2014, when both had a market share of 24%, and Huawei has since grown to a share of 28% (2019), while Nokia has declined to 16%.[44] Over the same period, Ericsson's share declined from 17% to 14% and Cisco's from 8% to 7%. The other significant provider is the Chinese company ZTE, which has grown its share from 8% to 10%, despite facing sanctions in the USA because of its business in Iran. Huawei was also poised to lead the move to 5G, having acquired the largest number of patents ahead of Nokia and Samsung (with ZTE fifth in the rankings, and another Chinese company also in the top 10).[45] There is little doubt that Huawei's leadership in the industry is due to intense R&D investment, as well as the economies of scale of its global operation. Wang estimates that it is around two years ahead of its rivals in 5G.[46]

The significance of 5G is that it is not just an incremental technology, but potentially transformative, because of advances in three key respects. The first is speed, increasing by up to 1,000 the data which can be processed and by up to a hundred the speed of even the worst connection, and enabling data transfers to take place on a wholly different scale and with much more processing in the "cloud". A second feature is much lower latency – the time lag between messages being sent and received – thus allowing much more precision. And, thirdly, there is to be a big cut in the energy cost of operating systems. The practical consequences of 5G's potential are so far only speculative but include big advances in driverless cars; remote surgery; the development of the "Internet of Things", with much greater connectivity between devices; a big step forward in automation; and opening up other fields of technological advance such as AI and Big Data.

The all-pervasive and uncertain consequences of 5G are a major reason why ownership of the technology is so contentious. Quite apart from any issues connected with Chinese politics, Huawei has established a strong proprietary grip on the technology. It is ironic that after all the attacks on Chinese companies (and the early Huawei) for "stealing" technology, Huawei is now the gamekeeper of new, innovative technology, rather than the poacher. It has close to 100,000 patents or patent applications protecting its technology, many essential for 5G.[47] It is willing to use the courts to protect them. The potency of IP protection is further reinforced by the ability of dominant firms to set industry standards. Initially the telecommunications sector was divided between the European GSM, adopted by Huawei and much of the world, and the American and Russian CDMA. The US initiative failed to get support from telecoms users and died, and out of its failure emerged a combined global standard, 3GPP. The system of common standards has survived the political rift, and Huawei is the industry leader in 3GPP. But with the emergence of geopolitical conflict now overshadowing the industry, there are moves to create a digital "iron curtain", with a new split in technical standards and the governance around them: one set to be used by Qualcomm and US allies, the other for Huawei and whichever country remains aligned to its systems.

Trump targets Huawei

In 2018 President Trump moved to ban the use of Huawei in the USA as part of the trade dispute with China and a wider campaign to curb China's development of new technologies (250 Chinese companies have been targeted) . His own instinct was to use the company as a bargaining chip, but his national-security advisers insisted that a purely economic and commercial approach would be "like Reagan and Thatcher saying 'Let the KGB build our computer systems, because they are offering us such a great discount'".[48] "Hawks" in the Congress and in the administration have continued to insist that the challenge of Huawei is one of national security over and above the concerns of the competitor companies.

The charge that Huawei has been "spying" has a straightforward political appeal and is difficult to prove one way or the other. There is little evidence beyond rather vague assertions, such as that of the former chair of Google that "information from Huawei routers has ultimately ended up in hands that would appear to be the [Chinese] state. However that happened, we are sure it happened."[49] Indeed, although there have been numerous uses of judicial and administrative powers to disrupt the company in the USA in support of the civil cases brought by rival companies, there has never been any suggestion of enough evidence to substantiate criminal espionage charges.

Although there is no clear proof that Huawei has ever tried to create a "back door" into Western networks, and although Huawei insists, plausibly, that it would be wholly counter-productive to its own interests to do so, the core of the security concern is that it might. The argument is that the Ministry of State Security does have the capability, and that Huawei could, theoretically, be compelled under China's 2017 intelligence law to cooperate with its government in any overseas espionage operation. It is well understood in the West that there are links between intelligence agencies and "friendly" companies, so it would be surprising – indeed, highly improbable – if such connections did not exist in China in relation to Huawei.

A critical issue is how independent Huawei is in China. Chinese commercial law and rules around corporate governance are not as securely embedded as those in the West, but increasing importance is attached to formal status. Huawei claims to be worker-owned and to have employee representation and shareholdings. There seems little doubt that the 180,000 workers do benefit from profit-sharing and limited participation in the company. But ultimate ownership and control is opaque, and critics continue to insist that the idea of employee control is a myth.[50] The implication is that the state is the ultimate arbiter through Mr Ren, the founder, and the various Party committees within the company.

Whatever the justification, Huawei has been effectively banned from the USA, and there is now severe pressure on the company's global operations as a result of sanctions. The USA has imposed restrictions on the supply of advanced semiconductors from the USA and on the machines and the software required to make them. Huawei's main 5G-equipment business, creating telecommunications infrastructure, and its smartphones both depend heavily on US components, and the USA has identified a vulnerability in China's failure so far to develop its own capacity in the whole area of advanced microcircuits (chips) and the semiconductors used for making them.

US sanctions are designed to undermine Huawei's ability to supply global 5G telecommunications networks, but there is also a parallel effort to cut demand, particularly in Europe. While Huawei can rely on China's considerable home market for sales, 60% of its revenue comes from overseas, and more than thirty countries have already signed its 5G contracts. The issues facing governments in countries pondering the future role of Huawei are several. Do they share the concerns of US security agencies about potential threats to national security from having a Chinese infrastructure provider? Even if they don't, do they wish to defy the USA? How much do they weigh the advantage of using Huawei in terms of cost and early access to the new generation of 5G technologies against the risks of trying to work with a company subject to US sanctions?

The UK has had a complex and changing relationship with Huawei, reflecting an evolving approach to the questions above. In 2003 Huawei outbid Marconi for a contract to supply British Telecom with equipment to modernize the industry's fixed and mobile infrastructure. Any security objections were ignored, equivocal or too late. When security risks were identified, they were managed through a monitoring facility – the Huawei Cyber Security Evaluation Centre (HCSEC) – and, until a critical report in 2018, there were no reports of compliance failings. There has never been any serious suggestion that Huawei was seeking a "back door" into sensitive intelligence networks.

Confronted with a decision on whether to let Huawei participate in 5G networks, the British government's initial reaction was to allow the company into "peripheral" parts of the network, like base stations and antennae, but to exclude it from the "core" involving data storage and processing. The decision was made in spite of US threats to stop intelligence-sharing. The government was influenced by warnings from Vodafone and other users of the infrastructure that a ban would push up costs and delay 5G innovation by several years, along with assurances from security advisors that safeguards were adequate.[51] But faced with the US ban on component exports the security judgement was changed, since the UK would then depend on "untrusted" Chinese-made components. The earlier decision was reversed, and a commitment was made to remove Huawei from existing networks at considerable cost.

Other countries have excluded Huawei or chosen one of its rivals: Canada, Sweden, Japan, India, Singapore, France, Portugal, Denmark and Australia. Major countries in the Global South have however resisted pressure to drop Huawei: Saudi Arabia, Indonesia and Brazil. The main Western opposition to a ban on Huawei comes from the German government, motivated by the interests of German telecoms providers – Deutsche Telekom has a close relationship with Huawei – and German exporters to China, especially the car industry.[52] There was some political opposition in Germany to Merkel's pragmatism on China, and there is wider European interest in Nokia (despite its financial difficulties), Ericsson and US firms such as Qualcomm working together to provide an alternative to Huawei. It may be that the problems will be eased by the development of new open-source technology, OpenRAN, which has been used in Japan. But the likelihood is of further moves to split the global 5G telecommunications infrastructure and, potentially, its standards between a Chinese variant and one or more others.

The success of any Chinese variant depends on whether Huawei can survive the imposition of American sanctions. It suffered severe damage initially with a fall in consumer-goods sales of 50% and in overall revenue of 30%. Unable to obtain the necessary specialist "chips" for its smartphones and its network equipment, it was forced to draw on its falling stocks. Large government subsidies protected its profitability, enabling R&D to continue apace. It has apparently succeeded in replacing many of the banned US exports and redesigned its circuit boards. It has even ventured into the development of high-specification machines to manufacture "chips". But it has a long-term survival strategy concentrating on the China market for consumer goods and moving into software development, which doesn't require American chips. And it is seeking to keep one step ahead of Western competitors by doubling down on research on 6G. Survival and successful development beyond that will however depend on China's ability to produce its own semiconductors with high specification.

Semiconductors: the new technological battleground

One of China's main vulnerabilities is its high level of dependence on imported semiconductors – currently valued at more than imported oil – and its failure, so far, to develop its own despite a large amount of money being thrown at the sector. Wang estimates that when the bans became effective in 2019 barely 16% of the semiconductors used in China were made there, and only half of those by Chinese companies (many were made by the Taiwanese company TSMC).[53]

The challenge for China is not merely a quantitative one of ramping up production, but a qualitative one of making the machines that etch the surface of silicon wafers, applying microscopically thin layers of chemicals and carrying out testing on the products. At present only a handful of firms in the world can make the chips with the right specifications, and a smaller number, mostly American, make the equipment to carry out the manufacture. At present, China faces American restrictions on obtaining American chips with the right specification and the USA and its allies persuaded Holland to refuse an export license for the equipment to make advanced chips in China. The Chinese government is, in response, mobilizing financial and human resources for what is a complex project demanding considerable expertise.[54]

So far, the history of China's efforts to produce globally competitive firms capable of designing and manufacturing specialized and complex integrated circuits is not a happy one – characterized by failure, scandal and waste. Fuller's study of the semiconductor sector is a long story of failed state-backed enterprises. The successes are what he calls "hybrids" using the skills and capital of the Chinese diaspora.[55] There are only a few companies that are believed to have the necessary competence, and on them now falls the burden of making China's supply of chips: Taiwanese-owned TSMC; SMIC, which follows the Taiwan model and makes extensive use of overseas partnerships and overseas Chinese staff; and the Huawei subsidiary HiSilicon, which produces exclusively for the parent company.

There is a difference between the challenges presented by design and manufacture. Design depends on highly innovative firms. For the most sophisticated chip designs China is precariously dependent on the licensed technology of British-based but Japanese-owned Arm (through a subsidiary in China which, until the intervention of the Chinese authorities, came under the control of a break-away management team). In October 2022, Arm refused a request (from Alibaba) to export a cutting-edge design because of US restrictions, and the Chinese are pressing Arm to defy US pressure. In terms of manufacturing, the problem is that for the most sophisticated products there are now only two companies in the world capable of producing at the necessary level of quality and quantity: Samsung in South Korea and TSMC in Taiwan (and with a Chinese offshoot). The Koreans are being dragged into the "chips" war with pressure from the USA to stop exporting advanced chips to China and pressure from China in the form of inducements to lure away key engineers and researchers. TSMC is the world's leading producer. It has an 85% market share for the smallest, most efficient microcircuits on which Apple, Alibaba and other tech companies depend.

Both the American and Chinese governments are nervous about being so reliant on a single supplier in a very sensitive and politically exposed place. (if hostilities were to break out between China and Taiwan, the world's leading producer is in the middle of the battlefield.) The nervousness has been accentuated by experience of an overall global semiconductor shortage which has disrupted production in the car industry among others. The US and Chinese (as well as European) governments have been pressing TSMC to guarantee supplies in the short run and to offshore production to their respective countries in the longer run by establishing new foundries. The company itself appears to be maintaining neutrality and resisting pressure to build capacity overseas for "security" reasons, driving up costs.

The Chinese hope that, within a few years of a nationally driven mission to overcome this bottleneck, Chinese designers and manufacturers, backed by large amounts of government money, will solve the challenges, and a more self-reliant Chinese semiconductor and chip-making industry will emerge, no longer dependent on global supply chains.[56] Some breakthroughs have occurred. It was reported in summer 2022 that SMIC had made a 7-nanometer chip, putting it only one or two generations behind the industry leaders. Vast resources are being deployed to build on this advance in a race joined by the USA, the EU, Japan and India, and currently led by firms in Taiwan and South Korea. It is a big leap of faith.

The divided Internet and separate development

In telecommunications and semiconductors, external pressures are forcing China into greater self-reliance and away from global standards. There are also strong internal pressures within China to pursue separate development. When the early Internet was first used in China, there was great enthusiasm among users for the ability to tap into global information systems. It soon became clear to the authorities that, to repeat Deng's metaphor, "too many flies were getting in through the open window". In the year 2000, a Chinese engineer, Fang Binxing, developed what was initially known as the "Golden Shield", later the "Great Firewall", a system to identify, intercept and block unwelcome information. Shortly after, Google ceased to be available, after the company declined to engage in self-censorship.

Initially, the system operated with some subtlety. Recognizing the practical problems of trying to censor trillions of data flows, the system offered "porous censorship". Instead of trying to block access to large areas of data, the authorities made it difficult by burying search results or introducing distracting information. They operated by creating "friction, not fear".[57] A typical technique was "flooding" – hiring a lot of students to create a deluge of irrelevant material to frustrate users searching for data abroad in sensitive areas. In addition, there was the possibility of VPNs (Virtual Private Networks) providing an encrypted tunnel to gain access to otherwise inaccessible networks, but these were bothersome to create and few in number.

The system in many ways worked well. Politically, millions of people were able to let off steam, airing their frustrations about daily life and local problems through popular "microblogs" (on Sina Weibo). VPNs provided a line of communication to the outside world for businesses, scientists and other scholars who needed it. And, crucially, the emergence of a Chinese Internet offered a protective shield, enabling the emergence of the big e-commerce companies – Baidu, Tencent, Alibaba, recently joined by Meituan, JD.com, Bilibili and Pinduoduo – which have come to dominate the China market and are now serious international companies able to offer an alternative to the likes of Google, Amazon, Facebook and YouTube, and operate on the same scale.

The advent of President Xi moved the story on.[58] Still too many flies getting in! New guidelines on content were issued in 2013. There was big investment in upgrades to make monitoring and censorship more effective. In 2015 the "Great Cannon" was developed to filter more precisely and adjust incoming material. Foreign content shrank. The Sina Weibo system of microblogging also shrivelled. VPN users were harassed, and in some cases imprisoned. The underlying objective set out by President Xi at the World Internet Conference in 2015 was that "we should respect the right of individual countries to independently endorse their own path of cyber development" – internet sovereignty.[59] The clampdown has been reinforced by restrictions requiring companies to make their data available and – of particular concern to foreign companies – disclosing source codes. AI is being used along with thousands of highly trained operatives to make the censorship system more effective, quicker and less intrusive.

Paradoxically, despite the controls and censorship, Internet use within the Firewall is spreading, and often more sophisticated than in the West. The Internet is also being more widely used for permitted purposes: search, social networking, online videos and, above all, e-commerce. Internet users grew from 573 million in 2012 to just over a billion at the beginning of 2022. This paradox exposes a dilemma at the heart of the China-net. There is the government's political imperative of maintaining effective Party control through widening systems of Internet censorship – but, at the same time, the Internet is crucial to the growing economy.

The China-net is also being used for a massive experiment in social control through a "social credit" system which rewards or punishes good or bad behaviour in matters such as personal indebtedness or compliance with traffic regulations. It is seen by critics as an extreme and all-embracing system of intrusion – and may become so, but it is currently fragmented and semi-privatized.

The direction of travel is clear, however: the accumulation of data and tighter state control over its use. A blizzard of new legislation, including laws on personal privacy and data security, tightens control especially over anything (broadly) defined to involve national security and public order. New rules require tech firms to write code for algorithms which produce content that the government likes and screen out material outside approved values. Data cannot be taken out of the country without express permission, and data-rich foreign companies operating in China, like Apple, Microsoft and Tesla, are having to establish local data centres and accept responsibility for self-censorship.

How then to reconcile tighter control with commercial innovation? Elizabeth Economy concludes that China is paying a heavy price for its "Internet sovereignty".[60] So much sand has been thrown into the machinery that Internet speeds are among the world's slowest (though big efforts are being made to improve efficiency). Foreign and domestic investors are being deterred by the data-control measures, and extra costs are being imposed (offset in part by the "privatization" of the censorship operation – companies are paid to employ more than two million people in a "cyber army" for this purpose). Most seriously, innovation is being affected by, for example, the inability of scientific researchers to access Google Scholar. That raises the question of how far the separate development of the Internet and the schism opening in 5G will go. Another line of attack on interconnectedness has come from US initiatives to curb successful Chinese Internet companies operating in the West.

The decision of the Trump administration to outlaw Huawei had a security rationale, even if the security arguments are debatable. The use of national security to justify a ban on a couple of popular apps was altogether more frivolous, though the objective – to inflict a serious blow on Chinese Internet companies – was serious and calculated. Potentially more far-reaching was the executive order in 2020 effectively stopping Google and Apple from stocking WeChat, an app with 19 million users in the USA and especially popular with the Chinese diaspora. WeChat is owned by one of the Chinese Internet giants, Tencent. Whilst the vast majority of Tencent's one billion plus users are in China, and whilst its gaming business was to be spared, it could have been a big blow to the company, which was trying to diversify out of China. In the event, US courts stopped the administration's action.

Even more difficult to understand was the attempted ban on the popular app TikTok, which showcases creative talent and provides teenage entertainment.[61] Apart from being Chinese-owned – by the company ByteDance – its main offence seems to have been to show videos lampooning President Trump. TikTok was used by young people who block-booked seats at a Trump rally and didn't show up, damaging the start of his presidential campaign. It also competes successfully with a Facebook app, Reels. A survey by the Pew Research Center has found that 67% of American teenagers used TikTok as against 32% for Facebook. It is also becoming the most popular Internet domain, replacing google.com. The justification for the proposed ban – that the company could, in theory, be forced to hand over American personal data to the Chinese authorities – provoked the counter from the company that they would be happy to store data under a transparent system in the USA. They already store international data in the USA, Singapore and Ireland. ByteDance has also itself shifted its global operations to a Singapore base to avoid being caught in geopolitical rows. But TikTok's critics haven't given up. Several governments have banned its use by public servants, and the US state of Montana has led a drive by Republican states to have TikTok banned altogether. In one important respect, United States policy is reinforcing the "split internet". It has been systematically excluding Chinese companies, including the cable manufacturing company HMN Tech (a merger of Huawei and Hengtong), from involvement in the laying of undersea fibre-optic cables wherever possible. A *Financial Times* survey (13th June 2023) showed that US government intervention – the Clean Network initiative – blocked a contract between China Mobile, Amazon and Meta for a 12,000 km cable between California and Hong Kong (which had already been laid), and other cable projects involving the World Bank prevented Chinese companies from bidding. The aim of the intervention is to prevent data leakage from US sources to China. In effect, the global Internet is being physically segregated.

The significance of these interventions, as well as the case of Huawei, is to make it difficult for Chinese companies to straddle the Chinese and American systems. Other highly successful enterprises, like the videoconferencing company Zoom, are having to structure their business in order to avoid falling foul of the demands of one or other jurisdiction. The process of separation is self-fulfilling. China's superiority in 5G, which has led to its exclusion from the USA and its allies, is providing the ingredients – high speed and bandwidth – to enable China to pursue a separate Metaverse.[62] In this way the Internet is being irrevocably split into two different worlds.

AI and the frontier technologies of data and computing

Stephen Hawking described AI (artificial intelligence) as potentially "the biggest event in human history" (he added: "It might also be the last"). In essence, it is a form of computer engineering allowing machines to perform human-like cognitive functions, continually adapting and learning to make better decisions – potentially, like electricity, permeating all aspects of the economy and our private lives. The vast potential implications for economies and societies and for specific applications like weapons and medicine have been described elsewhere.[63] What is relevant here is that only two countries, the USA and China, have the infrastructure and research capacity to build an industry at scale based on AI technology.

Chinese commentary tends to stress the country's ambition, but acknowledges that it is some years behind the USA.[64] But some influential non-Chinese observers believe China is on a trajectory to emerge ahead within a decade – though there are different indicators and dimensions to this particular race.[65] Part of the reason for taking the Chinese challenge seriously is that they do so themselves, with the president himself setting timelines for achieving targets, establishing measurable performance indicators and naming the five "national champions" who will lead on commercial applications: Baidu, Tencent, Alibaba, iFlytek and SenseTime. albeit that there are enormous numbers of Chinese companies with AI pretentions springing up around the country in local incubators. Chinese ambitions involve tripling the revenue of AI companies within four years. The former software chief at the Pentagon judged that China was headed for dominance in AI and that to call it a "near peer adversary" was to greatly underestimate Beijing.[66]

China appears to be matching or surpassing US efforts to establish a strong knowledge base, with the largest number of cited peer-reviewed scientific papers on AI in 2021 in all categories except the top 1% with "breakthrough" contributions.[67] Chinese entries are dominating international competitions for AI-based developments in speech and facial recognition and drones. The largest number of the most valuable international venture-capital investments in AI start-ups are in Chinese firms. China has three times as many computer scientists as the USA, and the numbers of those with internationally recognized overseas qualifications under the Thousand Talents programme are growing fast. In 2019 there were an estimated 219 supercomputers, as against 116 in the USA. Chinese companies and government are not inhibited or delayed by the same ethical concerns. Crucially, Chinese dominance of new product markets in fintech and payments, combined with the absence of inhibitions on data use and surveillance, means that there is a vast supply of the industry's raw material: data. The business model of the giant new Chinese Internet-based companies makes them ideally placed to facilitate the rapid introduction of AI applications.[68]

There are good reasons, however, not to overestimate the extent of Chinese advance. In the foundation models which lie behind generative AI, American companies are thought to be two to three years ahead. GPT-4 (which lies behind Chat GPT) has a computing power many times that of Chinese ERNIE. China's apparent advantage in data availability is nullified by the way generative AI can use unstructured data from the Web, most of which is in English and very little in Chinese, though Chinese companies are thought to be working around the problem through language translation machines. Many of the techniques needed in advanced AI can be obtained from open sources, moreover. China has a different problem in managing the release of generative-AI products to the public, since China has a strict set of rules around permissible content. The draft regulatory framework for AI contains many features advocated by the West, but also a requirement to "reflect the core values of Socialism". These restrictions may not be helpful for innovation.

Another serious, urgent problem, as we have seen, is the supply of advanced semiconductors for the new AI chips, required for AI-enabled devices and programmes. As discussed above, China has struggled to develop its own production for some years, and now the US export boycott creates further obstacles. There has been nervousness in China about the fate of Arm, the British-based semiconductor design company, whose IP is used in 95% of Chinese-made chips. Were Arm acquired by a US-owned company, it would put it within range of US sanctions if these were to be applied extraterritorially to the UK or if its HQ was to move to the USA. The immediate risk has receded after a Nvidia bid failed.

The USA also has some deeper-rooted advantages: the global English-speaking talent pool, the "brightest and the best", feeding Silicon Valley (especially if immigration restrictions were lifted); the strengths of its leading "platforms"; dominant operating systems (Android and Apple); and a continued lead in original "breakthrough" technologies. To be set against that is China's combination of numerous hungry entrepreneurs selectively backed by the resources of the Chinese state and vast quantities of raw data.

Much of the attention in the technology race between the USA and China is centred on the interconnected technologies around 5G, AI and Big Data. A related technology, to advance the systems around data storage and security, is blockchain, which has been given top-level political backing.[69] It is not a coincidence that an official crypto currency has been launched with Chinese government support. Research at the Stimson Center has described China as "a significant player" in testing blockchain applications, and as a "rapid adopter" of block-chain in fields such as medicine, finance, energy and supply chains.[70] Chinese firms had 59,000 blockchain patents in 2019, ahead of any other country. To the annoyance and frustration of the authorities, Chinese innovators are even using blockchain applications to outwit the censorship system.

One area of work where Chinese technologists are experimenting is quantum computing and communications, with the Micius space probe testing the possibilities for creating secure encryption for long-distance messaging. Supported explicitly by President Xi, China has established a well-funded laboratory to act as a hub for quantum research, and US defence researchers have argued that China is now sufficiently advanced in quantum technology surrounding encryption that it could well put the USA at a defence disadvantage.[71]

Chinese technology: cooperation, competition, containment

There are other areas of "frontier technologies" where external evaluations of China's progress range from the awestruck to the totally dismissive, and where there are radically different views as to how China's achievements and failures should be treated. A recent internal Chinese paper from Peking University's Institute of International and Strategic Studies, which briefly appeared on the Internet, frankly acknowledged that China was far behind in some important areas and was nowhere near being self-sufficient. These include, as above, semiconductors and computer operating systems. They also include civil aviation. Years of attempting to reverse-engineer or otherwise learn from Boeing and Airbus achieved little (though a Chinese airliner has now appeared).

Despite a heavy dependence on imported food, China has not succeeded in making big strides in agrochemicals because of a reluctance, as in the EU, to trust genetic modification. The most embarrassing and costly failure has been in vaccine development. China has produced its own Covid vaccines, which have given some weak protection. But these vaccines have proved inadequate in the face of the highly transmissible Omicron variant. Great economic damage and much harm is being done by a reluctance to supplement Chinese vaccines with the stronger Western varieties. Covid exposed the folly of trying to be technologically self-sufficient in everything.

That conclusion, in turn, raises the question of how far overseas commercial, academic and government bodies should collaborate with their Chinese opposite numbers in those areas where China is, so far, not at the scientific and technological cutting edge. There are currently many areas of emerging applied science where we see an uneasy mix of collaboration between Chinese and overseas researchers, competition and confrontation: the many branches of biotechnology, from gene-editing and personalized medicine to cancer detection and artificial photosynthesis; new materials like graphene; nuclear fusion; space exploration and research; new renewables technology.

The question which arises in many of these fields is how much technological development is a public good, meriting cooperation, and how much is crucial to national advantage in terms of security and military ascendancy. The assumption behind much of the argument driving technological competition with China is that, as with trade, we are operating within a "zero-sum game": any Chinese success must be at the expense of the USA and its allies. But most advances in science and technology have little to do with "security", even widely defined. There has been a great deal of collaboration between Western and Chinese scientists and technologists. Such collaboration has recently been inhibited by visa limitations and closer surveillance of Chinese scientists in the USA. There have been cases of theft of intellectual property and what could be described as "spying", but there is little to suggest that they are common. And recent, leading scientific journals like *Nature*, *Scientific American* and *The Lancet* have concluded that restrictions are disproportionate and damaging to Western economies.[72] Chinese researchers have shared more "high impact" scientific research (but less of advanced technology) than US equivalents.

One area ripe for both cooperation and beneficial competition between firms is pharmaceuticals and health technology in general. China's pharmaceutical industry is now among the leading ones in the world. As with India's industry, the emphasis on generics and over-the-counter drugs brings down the cost of health care in China and globally. Nevertheless, some Republican politicians have been trying to make the case that the USA has become over-dependent on Chinese drugs, to the extent of 80% of drug supply and 97% of antibiotics.[73] Other analyses, including by the regulator, the FDA, show the claims to be a wild exaggeration, and one study concluded that US dependence on Chinese drugs was of the order of 18% for active ingredients and 9% for antibiotics. Moreover, China imports finished products from the USA.[74] As for medical research in general, there is scope for cooperation in many areas where neither security nor commercial concerns are pre-eminent.

Another sector which illustrates both the opportunities and the risks is space exploration and research. China's space programme has landed craft on Mars and on the dark side of the moon. It has assembled a space station. It has started exploring for extra-terrestrial intelligence with a large radio telescope. Its enterprises have large numbers of commercial satellites in orbit. It has launched a satellite-based navigation system, BeiDou, to rival GPS. There is clearly an element of national pride involved in a "space race" – NASA spent roughly

$23 billion in 2020, and the Chinese equivalent spent around $10 billion. And there is also a genuine defence concern about China's "counter-space" capacity – the ability to shoot down satellites needed for key infrastructure.[75] But there is also common interest in sharing knowledge about the universe, in exploration and in developing rules around such issues as space junk. At present, however, there is an effective bar on space collaboration by the USA, and also the beginning of intense long-term competition in space – through the Artemis project – to rival China.

Green technologies: cooperation and competition

Nowhere are there more obviously common interests than in the adoption of "green" technologies to combat climate change. Here is, pre-eminently, a "public good". However, even here, the language of confrontation and competition tends to dominate. Chinese activity is portrayed as a threat, as with "leadership" in "green" technologies. The US Secretary of State has warned that America has "fallen behind" in the "green" economy: "If we cannot lead the renewable-energy revolution, America will miss the chance to shape the world's climate future in a way that reflects our interests and values, and will lose out on countless jobs for the American people."[76] There appears to be alarm that Chinese companies hold a third of the world's renewable-energy patents; are the largest producers of solar panels, wind turbines, batteries and electric vehicles; and have five out of six of the largest solar-panel manufacturers.

China seems to be well ahead of the field in building a dominant position in solar power through the technologies involved in solar cells, assembling solar panels and developing efficient manufacturing techniques which have given Chinese firms a big cost advantage. By contrast, Chinese producers seem to be some way behind European wind-turbine makers like Siemens and Vesta, and depend on protective tariffs.

But why should Chinese development in these fields be a "threat"? On the contrary, the faster China can reduce its coal-burning and overall carbon emissions, the better for all of us. And, if China can export relatively low-cost renewable-energy equipment and systems to the rest of the world, this will speed up the deployment of carbon-reducing technologies everywhere. Such progress will, furthermore, diminish the geopolitical tensions around competition for oil and gas supplies, especially in the conflict zones of the Middle East.

There is also growing Chinese competition in the market for electric vehicles. Tesla is the global market leader, producing 1.3 million vehicles in 2022, 20% of which were manufactured in China. There has been a proliferation of Chinese companies engaged in fierce competition to be "the next Tesla". The Chinese government has been an active supporter (and funder) of the industry, and there is a rapid build-up of charging infrastructure and battery-swapping infrastructure – also, battery development through the leading company BYD. Another Chinese battery company (CATL) has emerged very quickly to become the world's largest (and most valuable). The rapid growth of Chinese battery development and EV production is transforming the global car industry. China is already the biggest producer of EVs: 6.5 million in 2022 as against 3 million in the EU and 2 million in the USA. Production is, currently, for the Chinese market, the biggest, where a third of new vehicles are EV or plug-in hybrids. Second, the EV advance in China is being led by Chinese companies (plus Tesla). These companies, led by BYD, are now poised to attack world markets and to build on China's existing dominance in batteries and car parts. By contrast, the big Western car companies which have done well in China with internal-combustion vehicles are losing market share.

The new Chinese companies arguably inject competition which is beneficial to consumers and spreads the externalities from low-carbon technology. They also sit at the centre of geopolitical rivalries and anxieties. CATL's success reflects the entrepreneurial achievements of its founder, Zeng Yuqun, but it is also one of the success stories of the industrial policy of the Chinese government, which is a (small) shareholder (alongside Warren Buffett, who was an early backer). The dominance of CATL and BYD in batteries has also created a supply chain of raw materials dominated by Chinese companies. These companies account for an estimated 70–80% of lithium supplies (though there are other abundant supplies in Chile and other ways of extracting the material being pursued by Bill Gates). Chinese companies also have substantial control over other metal supplies, as with cobalt, through investment in the Congo. The dilemma facing those trying to balance environmental, commercial and security factors was recently illustrated when Elon Musk's Tesla opted for iron-based batteries in his electric vehicles using a technology favoured by Chinese producers.

If geopolitics and security concerns dominate, there will be a less accommodating approach to the Chinese EV industry. There will be strong resistance to a big Chinese export drive for vehicles and pressure to cut the Chinese dominance in batteries and car components. But if security-driven policy prevails, it will raise costs and prices and slow the transition to zero carbon in transport.

Conclusions

China has been designated a "strategic competitor" by the USA and the EU largely as a result of some of its companies and scientists achieving high levels of performance in advanced technologies. The sense that this is a "threat" is couched in terms of "security": defence applications; cyber security; espionage; theft. But there is perhaps a deeper fear: that for the first time since the Industrial Revolution a non-Western power has emerged with actual or potential superiority in the technologies which shape our way of life (with the possible qualification of a brief period in the late 1980s when Japan was talked of in similar terms).

Running through the analysis I have sketched out above, there are two caricatures of Chinese technological development which circulate widely and form the mental maps of decision-makers elsewhere. One is the rather dismissive view that with the exception of a handful of world-class, highly innovative, world-leading companies like Huawei, China's technological development is overrated: more input than output; adaptive rather than innovative; seriously behind in "breakthrough" technologies; vulnerable to disruption of key inputs like semi-conductors; with a deficient system of protecting IP; and with a very large cadre of very talented individuals hamstrung by state interference and starved of necessary information by censorship of the Internet.

The alternative view is that China has already reached or passed American, European and Japanese levels of develop-ment across a wide range of key technologies; has unbeatable advantages in terms of scale of markets, size and quality of talent pools and availability of the most important raw mate-rial, data; has proved to be capable of producing research and innovative products and processes of the highest quality; has a supportive government capable of thinking strategically, taking a long-term view and deploying vast resources in support of R&D; and has numerous entrepreneurial companies of native or overseas ethnic Chinese who are capable of competing on merit in international markets.

Both views cannot be right, though we are dealing with a country of massive size and complexity, where elements of both stories may be dominant. Whichever interpretation is correct, however, will determine the outcome of the current attempt by the USA and its allies to exclude Huawei and other companies and to cripple their supply chains. It is very possible that the move will succeed and set back Chinese development in the affected sectors by some years, perhaps indefinitely. It is also possible that it will spur Chinese innovation in sectors where it has fallen behind – as with the design and fabrication of advanced semiconductors – creating even more formidable competition within a short period of time.

There is also growing evidence that Huawei may just be the first of many examples of attempts to decouple from Chinese technology because of "security" fears. The reason is that, increasingly, trade is digital and involves exchanges of data. Lack of confidence in Chinese data security or fear of espionage is being given as a reason for stopping British local councils using Chinese technology for "smart cities" and for intervening to block any Chinese software that bypasses Apple privacy rules.[77] If current trends continue, with growing numbers of technology exports and imports being blocked, the inevitable outcome is a bifurcation of global technology relating to data (or possibly trifurcation, if US and EU data rules cannot be reconciled).

Relations between China and major Western countries can be seen as on a spectrum from cooperation to competition to conflict. There are currently elements of all three: cooperation in many relatively uncontroversial areas of research and on shared problems like understanding the Covid-19 genome; competition (now elevated to "strategic competition") in the USA and EU in areas with – loosely defined – "security" implications; and outright conflict as we see over Huawei. All three may continue in different areas, though there is clearly a move taking place along the spectrum away from cooperation and towards conflict. Conflict originates in geopolitics and the values which underpin it, to which I now turn.

Chapter 5

China and Ideological Competition

Hostility to modern China and its model of government is not simply based on worries about economic and technological competition, or even its military potential, but the fact that it presents a different set of values. China rejects Western ideas of "liberal democracy" and the "rule of law" and has a different interpretation of "human rights". The problem is not just that China is different – Western states coexist comfortably with feudal monarchies and have alliances with dictatorships of various kinds. And there are also some important values in common: a belief in scientific rationality and in material progress – values not universally shared, especially by theologically inspired and populist regimes. The Western concern is that China is on track to be a superpower – perhaps the global hegemonic power, certainly a regional leader – without subscribing to the values of the existing order. Martin Jacques describes the challenge of this rising "civilization-state" to the Western global order as "existential".[1]

Within the broader debate about relationships between China and the West, there are the challenges presented by the current regime under President Xi. The period under Mao from the revolution until his death in 1978 differed greatly from that of Deng and his successors – a time of opening, rapid growth and radical economic reform. President Xi has in turn changed China with more emphasis on stability, Party discipline and ideology at home, as well as increased assertiveness abroad. This increased assertiveness, strengthened by a belief that the West, and the United States in particular, is in terminal decline, has led to growing geopolitical confrontation and the use of economic sanctions against (and by) China. And that in turn has strengthened autarchic economic policies. Xi has, furthermore, declared his intention to continue in power beyond term limits, which creates uncertainty over the long-term political future of China.

Beliefs and values

For much of the post-war era, there was ideological competition between the West and the Soviet Union and its allies, which was decisively won by the West with the largely peaceful collapse of the Soviet empire – the so-called "end of history". It could be argued – and some in the West believe this – that China is basically just a new variant of the Communist one-party state subscribing to the principles of Marxist-Leninism, and that it will, in due course, come to the same end as the Soviet Union.

But this may well be wishful thinking, because there are some profound differences. First, China, unlike the USSR, has adopted many of the features of a successful capitalist economy. "Socialism with Chinese characteristics" is full of contradictions which President Xi is currently wrestling with in his Common Prosperity policy. But modern China is not contesting the value of markets and the importance of successful private entrepreneurs for wealth creation. Moreover, its success to date with its model of "state capitalism" leads China to see competition with the West primarily in economic and technological terms, rather than through an "arms race". It is not, like the USSR, "Upper Volta with rockets".

Further, China is not seeking to export revolution (at least since the days of Mao Zedong). President Xi set out his approach before he became leader: "First, China does not export revolution; second, it does not export famine and poverty; and third, it does not mess with you. What else is there to say?"[2] Maybe there isn't anything else to say. But there is a reasonable question as to what a potential superpower stands for beyond managing its own business and that of its neighbourhood.

There is a value system built around "Confucianism", which was rejected by Maoists as elitist, but is now being rehabilitated for its emphasis on discipline and deference to authority. Beyond that, it isn't at all clear what that means other than a general belief in the importance of stability, order and hierarchy – and it certainly doesn't seem very exportable beyond the mixed experience of Confucius Institutes (of which more below). Similarly with Xi Jinping Thought, which has become a pervasive feature of Chinese life and essential study for those eager to stay on the right side of the regime. But it does not translate easily into messages with universal meaning like Mao's revolutionary one-liners or Deng's colourful and pithy metaphors explaining the virtues of pragmatism and common sense.

To take the regime at face value, the CCP has a Marxist-Leninist ideology, and the current president, unlike his post-Mao predecessors, seems to attach importance to ideology and, conceivably, believes in it. Shortly after Xi came to power, the Communist Party Central Committee issued an uncompromisingly ideological statement, Document 9, detailing the "Seven Nos": constitutional democracy, universal values, civil society, neoliberalism, a "free" press; historical "nihilism" (attacking the Party's record) and questioning the role of socialism. There is some parallel between Chinese "state capitalism" and the model which Lenin developed under the New Economic Policy, though that brief experiment was in a far less sophisticated economy.[3] Although ideology matters, a more straightforward depiction of the CCP is that its fundamental aim is simply to perpetuate its rule in the same way that other revolutionary or liberation movements have attempted to do.[4]

Arguably the most successful self-perpetuating party state is Singapore, though there is at least some element of democratic choice in Singapore and the scale is totally different – the CCP, by contrast, has a mass membership of 90 million. But what the two have in common, crucially, is that the ruling party justifies indefinite rule based on its performance in delivering economic growth and stability (as well as a sense of national pride and accomplishment). What makes China unique – or almost: Vietnam follows a similar path – is that its ability to deliver economic results, and stability, is explicitly separated from Western ideas of democracy and the "rule of law".

Why China rejects Western democracy

Since his election, President Biden has chosen to make a dividing line with China over a commitment to multi-party democracy. To this end, he invited to G7 meetings the governments of Australia, South Africa, Brazil, South Korea and India, and has continued to champion "democracy versus autocracy". By contrast, China's experience of Western-style democracy is very limited indeed. In well over 2,000 years of Chinese civilization there has been but one brief and unsatisfactory period of democratic government, in 1921. There was a contested general election on a qualified and male franchise, which led to a few months under a parliamentary system before intervention by warlords and civil war. Yet there has been an expectation in the West that, with modernization and development, China would evolve towards democratic government. There has been a sense of disappointment, even betrayal, that this hasn't happened. The decision of President Xi to abolish term limits on his period of office crystallized that disappointment.[5] From being an authoritarian regime with some checks and balances, China took a step towards becoming uncompromisingly dictatorial.

"Democracy" is a widely used concept which most governments seek to own in their own way (including China). If, however, we take the Freedom House definition – though it represents a partial and Western perspective – China clearly does not belong to the "consolidated democracies" or even "partial democracies" which allow contested multi-party elections. On their overall scoring, China gets 10 out of 100, which is below such outlaw states as Russia, Belarus or Iran – on a par with Sudan, Yemen, the CAR and Cuba, and above only a dozen of 210 countries including Syria, Eritrea, North Korea and Saudi Arabia.[6] From a Chinese standpoint, however, such metrics totally fail to capture the value of personal freedoms which exist outside the narrower definitions of political "freedom": overseas travel as tourists or students; the freedoms which come from a greater choice of goods and services and the elimination of poverty; the (qualified) freedom to protest locally; and, in President Xi's period, relaxation of rules around family size, urban migration and establishment of businesses.

But on the narrower definition of political freedom and democracy, one of the constant themes of comment from Western leaders is that China could and should progress, through modernization, to a Western model of democracy, even though nothing Chinese leaders have said has encouraged that expectation. Hilary Clinton is quoted as reflecting the sense of inevitability that one-party rule must end: the Chinese are "trying to stop history, which is a fool's errand. They cannot do it. But they are going to hold it off as long as possible."[7]

Deng, as the instigator of the post-1978 economic reforms, never gave any encouragement to multi-party democracy, and was totally unapologetic for having given the necessary orders to crush the demonstrations in Tiananmen Square in 1989. As Kissinger put it, "Deng clung to one-party rule not so much because he revelled in the perquisites of power, but because he believed the alternative was anarchy."[8] His three successors have been equally uncompromising defenders of one-party rule for the same reason. The rationale for one-party, authoritarian government may be self-serving, but it is deeply rooted in a craving for stability.

Several factors lie behind it. First there is the long history of China in which every case of loss of central political control has led to disorder and thence to all manner of disasters, from mass starvation to civil war. The convulsions of the nineteenth century, such as the Taiping Rebellion, and the disasters of the twentieth – occupation, civil war and the Cultural Revolution – explain the fact that "in Chinese political culture, the biggest fear is of chaos"[9] – "knowledge of this history is a given for elite leaders, and they are sensitive to any notion of instability and the threat this brings".[10]

Secondly, there is a more specific and recent reason for the hardening of resistance to Western democratization: the collapse of the USSR, leading not just to the end of party rule, but to the break-up of the country and continuing violent conflict. Deng warned against Gorbachev's folly – as he saw it – and was proved right.[11] Experience of the "Arab Spring" has reinforced those negative conclusions: the descent into civil war in Syria, Yemen and Libya; the upsurge in religious fundamentalism, until suppressed, in Egypt, Algeria and elsewhere. There was a great deal of soul-searching in China about the collapse of Soviet Communism in particular. The main conclusion was clear: political liberalization and the relaxation of party discipline and control are a recipe for chaos.

Thirdly, and most recently, the crisis in American democracy created by President Trump and his refusal to accept the clear result of a democratic election (and wider lapses into the politics of populism) is not just the source of some cynical humour in the Chinese elite, but confirmation of their faith in the Chinese way. Other democratic "mistakes", like Brexit and the fact that Trump-style politics is far from dead, reinforce that judgement – the collapse of "democratic" Afghanistan too.

And finally, there is the belief that strong dictatorial government is the only way to "get things done", especially in countries as big and complex as China. There is nothing specifically Chinese or "socialist" about that belief. The promise that "the trains will run on time" has a long pedigree. And in some cases, as with the Park military regime in South Korea, it has been demonstrably successful (by contrast with messier models of democratic government as in, for example, India). China's ruthless and initially effective response to the pandemic added force to that conviction, though the failure of the zero-Covid policy to contain the spread of the disease, the reluctance to use foreign vaccines and the vast human and economic cost of severe lockdowns undermined the regime's reputation for competence.

A more challenging question than why China hasn't adopted multi-party democracy and national elections is why all forms of political reform appear to have ground to a halt. Before

President Xi, there was a great deal of experimentation, freeing up political choice inside and outside the Party. In 1998, there was a law mandating village-level elections with a choice of candidates for decision-making roles. An estimated three million such "democratic" votes took place. And they still do, in theory. But to the extent to which it is possible to follow trends in hundreds of thousands of Chinese villages, external reports suggest that the role of elected committees is being downgraded in favour of appointed Party officials.[12]

President Hu also introduced "intra-Party" debate, holding office bearers to account for their actions. Indeed, the lack of checks and balances within the small group of top decision-makers is a crucial issue, and largely unaddressed. American democracy may have produced a Trump, but the Chinese one-party state produced a Mao. President Xi is not a Mao – though Western critics sometimes portray him as one – but he has created a model which is potentially unstable. He seems to have established a system of government reportedly built around informal committees of loyal supporters, most of which he chairs. Rule by a Chairman of Everything, even if he is very capable, is not sustainable.

Kerry Brown's assessment is that "both these initiatives [i.e. in local choice and accountability at the centre] have largely ceased [...]. The Party is now about unity and discipline."[13] There has been, nonetheless, a good deal of low-level protest, which has been tolerated if it is not directed against central government. Scholars have reported tens or even hundreds of thousands of incidents a year over land rights and local corruption, and numerous complaints against officialdom. Much of that has continued into the Xi era, with an estimated 74,000 episodes between 2013 and 2016.[14] Localized protests – advertised on social media – have continued despite the hardening approach of the government to disorder. One trigger point was the default by property companies on their obligation to deliver completed homes to those who had bought upfront. There were demonstrations and office occupations across China. They worked: the government has instructed the companies to give priority to complete and deliver stalled developments. There have also been widespread strikes directed at companies which, because of their financial problems, have paid wages late or not at all, or have failed to honour contracts around severance. There were riots at the Foxconn factory in Zhengzhou, which supplies Apple phones, and unrest at Meituan, a big food-delivery company in the "gig" economy. Strikes and demonstrations can get results, but the official response has been to criminalize protests and petitions. Rather, the emphasis has shifted to tighter surveillance of the population through closer oversight of social media and behaviour monitoring through facial-recognition technology, ubiquitous cameras and a "grid management" system operated at neighbourhood level, overseen by local Party officials. Such surveillance identifies potential "troublemakers", but also helps to understand social trends and grievances, so that the Party can be ahead of the curve, solving problems before they become serious. The wider significance is the use of technology to cement the Party's role. It may even be useful in making the Party more popular.[15] However, Xi has been concerned with a bigger political project than how best to accommodate dissent.

A fundamental change in the Xi era is the consolidation and perpetuation of his personal rule. Xi has carried out several far-reaching purges of rivals and enemies: in 2012 of Bo Xilai and high-ranking military and security personnel; in 2015 of top security officials and police; and continually of provincial and military officials deemed to be unsafe or disloyal. All of this contrasts with the attitude of his predecessors after Deng put in place a system of planned succession to refresh the leadership and reduce the risk of another tyrant in the style of Mao. The model worked well until Xi extended his term beyond the scheduled 2022 date of transition. Xi now faces the problem of all dictatorial leaders: there is never a right time to retire. The number of mortal enemies – side-lined or imprisoned – grows, with the prospect of retribution and revenge. He now finds himself in the company of leaders in Turkey, Rwanda, Russia and Uganda and elsewhere who may once have been energetic and innovative – even popular – "strongmen", but now cling to power. He has created a model providing short-term certainty and stability, but long-term uncertainty and instability. And his grip on power is tightening, either to ensure survival or to deliver his promised goals.

The Xi revolution

There is now a large literature on President Xi's significance – about his Thought and actions.[16] Almost all analysts agree that, whether his influence has been for the good or ill, it is profoundly significant, to the extent of representing a break with the past perhaps as important as that represented by the Communist revolution after 1949 and the Deng revolution after 1978.[17] His central mission has been to continue the work of his predecessors to make China a strong, respected, confident and prosperous country. A crucial means to that national end is the Communist Party. His distinctive contribution has been to reform and reinstate the Party to the centre of national life. The aim has been to build unity through acceptance of a common ideology and a bigger, more intrusive role for the state, through the Party. The Party has recovered political discipline, as defined by a more powerful central leadership, and the Party has been required to develop a sense of service – fighting corruption or monitoring Covid and enforcing lockdowns– rather than simply enjoying the exercise of power.

The party over which Xi presides is a massive organization with a membership of more than 90 million. Despite the size, it is exclusive, with a careful vetting and admission policy. No doubt ideological conformity and knowledge of Xi Thought are important qualifications, and no doubt also there are many thugs, bullies and snoops. But the party is also the country's meritocratic elite. Ambitious students and graduates see it as a conveyer belt to career advancement – and over half the members are graduates. Private entrepreneurs join to establish their bona fides with regulators and local officials. There is reported to be a substantial queue of people waiting to join.

A common mistake of many China critics has been to equate the concentration of power in the hands of Xi and the Communist Party with a restoration of Maoist revolutionary Communism. Far from it, his "China Dream" set out in 2013 was about control and discipline, not chaos and upheaval. It also involved raising living standards to a point where they were comparable to those of developed countries. Measured by GDP per capita, living standards were set to double between 2012 and 2020, and there was to be an emphasis too on collective well-being: a cleaner environment, better welfare provision and stronger national defence. As Brown put it: "The China Dream was building a bourgeois China – a place where the middle classes were king."[18] But the emphasis was also on social, collective well-being rather than individualism.

To realize the China Dream required a deepening of the reforms set in train by Deng – and, to this end, the 2013 Party plenum decreed those markets were "necessary" for reform. But at the same time, it was necessary to deal with one of the main negative by-products of introducing markets into a country with fuzzy boundaries between private and state: corruption. If there is one defining characteristic of the Xi years, it has been the massive and sustained attack on corruption – individual enrichment by party officials and administrators at all levels, which had become commonplace under his predecessors. The numbers of Party cadres disciplined for corruption rose steadily from slightly more than 100,000 a year in 2011 to over 600,000 in 2018.[19] Many have been prosecuted and imprisoned. And since corruption was all-pervasive, the choice of whom to prosecute also had a lot to do with political scores being settled, enemies being marginalized, and potential rivals being removed from circulation. The victims of this puritanical purge conspicuously did not include members of Xi's family, around whom swirled some ugly rumours (and haven't taken in the wife of the last premier, Mrs "Granny" Wen, whose corrupt influence-peddling was the subject of a recent book.[20]

In an earlier chapter, I described the economic significance of the anti-corruption drive and the counter-intuitive research which suggested that corruption "Chinese-style" did the economy as much good as harm.[21] The anti-corruption drive has, however, also served an important political purpose in strengthening the purged Party's role in national life – as an upholder of austere standards and values in a world where openness and uncontrolled markets were undermining the party's legitimacy in the eyes of the public. Not just Party apparatchiks, but businesspeople must be subject to these standards – hence the demand for tighter supervision by the Party of private firms. In the early months of Xi's third term, when official speeches were designed to reassure private business, there was, nonetheless, an intense crackdown on corruption in business. A former chair of the Bank of China came under investigation; the founder of the investment bank China Renaissance was detained; numerous firms were investigated; others slashed bosses' pay and bonuses to win favour.

At the heart of the Xi project (at least at an early stage, before geopolitics has got in the way) has been the management of the tension between a more open, market-based entrepreneurial economy and the need for stability, order and consistency, which only a powerful, disciplined Party can provide. Xi's "Four Comprehensives", set out in 2016, reflect this tension: the search for a prosperous economy; deepening reforms (other than political reform); improved Party governance (that is, more discipline); and embedding legal rules to govern individual and corporate behaviour. The last of these is critical.

The rule of law and Chinese rights

The concept of legality in Xi's China – Xi's insistence on "rule by law" – is something which clearly distinguishes the Chinese leader not just from Western ideas of law, but from his predecessors, Mao and Deng. The Western world prides itself on the "rule of law", a system in which no one is above the law and which restrains arbitrary action by those in power – where the judiciary and judicial processes are independent of government and political interference. In practice there are different legal systems within that framework and varying degrees of legal independence. The American judiciary is highly politicized (but still enables the president to be put on trial).

In Communist-ruled states, there has always been an awkward fit between high-minded, abstract constitutional principles and the rules that form the basis of the legal system and their implementation by judges and officials, whose role is to serve the interests of the state and Party (which in practice are the same). In China's case, there is continuity with the imperial system, in which the emperor was above the law and the task of the judiciary was to ensure that rules emanating from the imperial court were implemented efficiently. Now the Party is the imperial court – the Party chief is the emperor.[22]

Maoist China was chaotic and allowed the arbitrary exercise of power by Party officials acting in Mao's name. Post-Mao, great efforts were made to codify the legal system and make it more professional and less erratic. In 1982 a constitution was created incorporating the idea of legal rights for individuals. But there was a yawning gap between the constitution and what individuals encountered in the courts. Corruption and the arbitrary exercise of power by local officials meant that the concept of a "fair trial" was as elusive as ever.

One of Xi's central objectives was to remove the arbitrariness of the legal system – to establish a system of "rule by law" with consistent outcomes and with courts and trained judges operating according to clear principles.[23] But faced with a contest between these principles and the authority of the Communist Party, Xi has been absolutely clear that the authority of the Party must be upheld. The crackdown on human-rights lawyers in 2015 and the use of the courts to crush dissent are clear evidence that "rule by law" does not extend legal protection into politically controversial areas.[24] Nonetheless, there are grounds for believing that for millions of citizens whose interest in the law is not "political", but involves neighbour disputes, property rights and the enforcement of laws governing consumer and environmental protection, there is some redress in the courts.[25]

Xi's reforms try to address one of the central claims of China's critics: that it is simply not possible to have a successful, prosperous, developed economy without the "rule of law". Secure property rights, they argue, are essential and cannot exist within a system where ultimate authority is vested in a party rather than a legal system with an independent judiciary to enforce it. It is striking that Xi's priorities have included strengthening both aspects of this seeming contradiction: a flourishing system of commercial law with stronger property (including intellectual property) rights, but systematic repression of a range of "human rights" which clash with Party values and authority.

Living with contradictions

It isn't yet clear whether the contradiction between more dictatorial politics and freer economics can succeed. The problem of legality is one difficulty. Another is freedom of information. Proponents of Western capitalism argue that the complexity of information systems is not consistent with Party control over information flows and ideas. Invention and innovation require creativity, questioning and challenge – all inimical to a controlled system. But again, China's most recent successes have centred on its Internet businesses, which have been at the frontier of innovation. The national political leadership has simultaneously recognized the unavoidable necessity of billionaire owners while seeking – as with Jack Ma – to prevent them exerting independent influence over decision-making. More generally, the Xi method is on the one hand to maintain a business-friendly environment, but also to extend the control of the Party and the state over business or, at least, big business through politically approved "national champions" and tighter regulation.

Critics of Xi's rule argue however that he has crossed a Rubicon – that he can no longer be seen as pragmatically balancing internal stability and discipline against advance within a market economy, and that he is now obsessed by control and the consolidation of power.[26] This may be because he sees a narrow window of opportunity to head off China's internal threats, to counter "security" threats and to exploit the weaknesses of the West.[27] A version of that argument is that Xi has failed to carry through necessary economic reform and is battening down the hatches to manage the political fall-out.[28] The way in which the economy was sacrificed in the lockdowns of spring 2022 to sustain the zero-Covid policy suggests that political control trumps economics where the two appear to collide. Party control in the interests of "national security" and self-reliance is also the dominant force in the recent "cold war" with the USA.

A further and related argument from the critics is that the essence of successful market economies is decentralization. It is simply not possible for a centralized decision-making machine, let alone one powerful individual, to be efficient. Decisions are not made in a timely fashion; accurate but inconvenient information is suppressed; minions are frightened of the power above and of speaking truth to power, and so have no incentive to report accurately or make controversial, risky decisions. All of this tends to contradict the belief that centralized autocratic systems are good at "getting things done". Both the positive and the negative were features of the Chinese response to the pandemic. A cover-up and damaging delay were followed by a decisive and well-coordinated, if ruthless, response which was highly effective and resulted in less economic and public-health damage than in the more freewheeling Western countries. But hubris set in, and Xi's credibility took a bad hit from the spread of the Omicron variant, his refusal to allow in foreign vaccines and the economic damage from extreme lockdown measures. It is difficult to assess Chinese public opinion, but anecdote suggests that the urban middle class, the backbone of the regime, which initially credited him with leading a successful strategy, were angered by the leader's misjudgements and aloofness. The long-term consequences are difficult to judge.

CHAPTER 5

It may be that the critical factor for successful governance is something other than formal institutional arrangements: trust. The most successful responses to the pandemic were in democratic and capitalist countries with, apparently, higher levels of trust in fellow citizens: Korea, Japan, Taiwan, Germany and Scandinavia. Trust matters for business too, inspiring worker commitment and consumer loyalty, and a willingness to undertake transactions. At first sight, China does not belong in the company of high-trust countries. Experience of corruption and a politicized court system, lack of secure land rights, memories of the Cultural Revolution and famine, rich people seeking boltholes in San Francisco or London – none of these inspire trust. But survey data suggest the opposite. The main international study of trust levels is the Edelman Index, and while there must be scepticism about the measurement of such an elusive concept and the truthfulness of answers in more controlled societies, China emerges consistently as the country with high levels of overall trust – and trust specifically in government[29]

Putting aside scepticism about the numbers, it is more than possible that Xi's project is based on the insight that what really matters for long-term economic success as well as political stability is trust in the Party and government. And it can be sustained through building a reputation for effectiveness and stability, even at the cost of short-term inefficiency and fear. Ringen argues that far from gradually evolving a more liberal form of authoritarianism in the wake of economic success, it may be that it will navigate the challenges of a more advanced but more slow-growing economy with a very skilfully managed dictatorship which is "relentless, determined and unforgiving", and reinforced by ideological stiffening.[30]

One might add that it would have to be extremely skilful repression to persuade 130 million Chinese a year to continue to return home voluntarily from their overseas travel as students or tourists. Unlike the USSR, East Germany and now North Korea, China is not a prison – or, at least, it is a very open prison. Until Covid, at least, a variety of factors outweighed the negatives of living in a dictatorial system, including family ties at home and the hostility and racial prejudice encountered abroad. Post Covid, travel freedoms have returned on a smaller scale (and with restrictions for officials).

A more conventional and optimistic view is that the Chinese system will eventually yield to the need for political reform. Brown's view is that the centenary of the founding of the Chinese Communist Party was an occasion for celebration of the current model, but subsequently reform might well emerge.[31] Others write of the "broad and deep currents" of support among ordinary people for reform.[32] We have seen, in East Asia, pluralistic systems of government emerging from dictatorship in South Korea and Taiwan, and they seem to work well, but partly because they enjoy a high level of cohesion in the face of a threatening dictatorial neighbour. China is very different from these and it is difficult to disagree with Saich's assessment that "there is no reason to expect China to follow its East Asian neighbours [...] and develop into a robust democracy".[33] Another model is available, such as that in Singapore, where there is prosperity with indefinite one-party rule alongside limited choice and controlled dissent – but that is in a very small state which owed much to one visionary man.

The Chinese Communist Party as a "global public good"

But let us suppose that harsh dictatorship or liberal political reform fail to resolve the various contradictions that have emerged from economic development in a one-party Communist state. Suppose that the regime fails. What might follow? Alternatives include the very real possibility that if the Chinese system of government were to be unsuccessful, the outcome could be chaotic. The regime has an obvious self-serving reason for warning of the risk. But such considerations underlie one of the more intriguing and counter-intuitive arguments in circulation: that Xi's strengthened and dictatorial Communist Party regime is not merely good for China, but good for the world. This is an argument being made by people who are not remotely sympathetic to dictatorship or to Communism as a political and economic system.[34]

The first point follows from the argument above: that the health of China's economy matters for the world economy – and if the current regime is a necessary condition for keeping it healthy, then so be it. That assumes, of course, that the regime can manage the very big domestic economic challenges described in previous chapters which include the crisis in the property market and the structural problems associated with rapid ageing and population decline. And it assumes that an economically stronger China will want to play a constructive role in global economic governance. That is probably a reasonable assumption, though in the face of growing geopolitical tensions and sanctions there are strong pressures to turn inward and become more self-reliant. It is unlikely in any event that the Western world is capable of compartmentalizing issues in this way – trading and investing enthusiastically while putting human-rights and security issues in a separate box. But perhaps it must learn to if China and the West are to coexist. The doctrine of "de-risking, not decoupling" is an emerging example of such an endeavour.

A second point is that any alternative regime might well be worse for the world. The reason for believing it might be is the strong current of nationalism in Chinese society expressed as resentment for past injury or grievances, or as triumphalism about recent achievements. Jacques describes the outpourings of extreme Chinese racism and xenophobia which have bubbled to the surface in recent years until suppressed by the authorities.[35] There have been nasty incidents of racism directed, for example, at African students in China. The regime undoubtedly uses and exploits nationalism, and the China Dream is a nationalistic vision. But it also controls expressions of extreme nationalism and, arguably, keeps a lid on them.

It is difficult to pose a counter-factual alternative to the present regime, since we have no idea how an alternative would come about or how it would function. Mahbubani asks us to consider the prospect not of a calm and cerebral Chinese Obama (or Biden), but of a much more belligerent, imperialistic, aggressive – and unpredictable – leader. Cynics would say that that is what we now have. But Xi has been careful to pay lip service, at least, to multilateral cooperation. And modern China is way different from, say, imperial Japan in the 1930s. The main experience we have had of a democratic transition from Communist Party rule in a big multinational state was of Russia, leading to Putin and the various ethno-nationalisms of the former Soviet republics, and the horrors of the Ukraine war. One of the most important, quiet success stories of the ending of the Cold War was the collusion of the Yeltsin government with the West to make safe the Soviet nuclear armoury and to prevent proliferation to the Ukraine, Kazakhstan and unofficial groups. A Chinese transition might be a lot messier. And we know from the experience of Iraq, Libya and elsewhere quite how messy a change can be from dictatorship to failed state.

Then Mahbubani argues that the Chinese leadership is, whatever its failings, rational and calculating, and guided by factual evidence. It is therefore able to understand the case for collective international action of shared problems – climate change, pandemics and economic coordination. It isn't necessary to romanticize Chinese behaviour in its adoption of climate-change targets or its belated sharing of Covid genome data to picture a world where China simply refuses to cooperate (indeed, the current "cold war" is giving us a taste of Chinese non-cooperation). Nor, as a dictatorial one-party state, does it have to respond to the kinds of populist opposition experienced in the USA, India and elsewhere when it comes to making necessary but difficult decisions.

And, lastly, there is no sign of China wanting to export revolution or convert the world to Xi's Thought – whatever that might be. Maoist China did support revolutionary movements in South-East Asia (notably among the ethnic Chinese in Malaya and Indonesia) and India, albeit without success.

In the one genuine revolutionary success story, Vietnam, the Vietnamese are at pains to stress that Chinese help was a great deal less useful than that of the Soviet Union. Mao's China also lent its name to parties of almost comical incompetence and irrelevance elsewhere. By contrast, modern China has worked with established regimes of all ideological stripes and makes "non-interference" and "sovereignty" central tenets of its foreign policy. Western critics point to the extreme sensitivity in response to any endeavour by foreign governments to meet the Dalai Lama or to befriend Taiwan. And there are serious Chinese attempts to spread influence through Confucius Institutes and overseas operations of its state TV channel (CGTV), to which I shall return later. But these initiatives fall a long way short of getting the workers of the world to unite behind socialism with Chinese characteristics.

Such reassuring arguments fail one crucial test, however: sustainability. President Xi, like his three predecessors – Deng, Jiang and Hu – might be totally rational, but there is a lack of clarity in the governance of modern China over succession and over the operation of checks and balances within the tight leadership group around Xi. That matters for the world. The world, however, has very little influence on what happens in Chinese politics. Whether the regime is good or bad, more or less dictatorial, better or worse at economic management, is largely beyond the control of the outside world. A belief in peaceful, externally supported regime change and a repetition of the (initially) orderly aspects of Soviet experience is a dangerous fantasy.[36]

For the moment, what is most striking about the current state of the ideological conflict between the West and China is that it hasn't been taking place within Western countries, but on the peripheries of China itself: Hong Kong, Xinjiang and Taiwan. In each case, "territorial integrity" and the imposition of order take precedence over self-determination and freedom of expression.

The return of Hong Kong

Hong Kong's history relates back to the nineteenth-century Opium Wars and the surrender of the island to a punitive Britain. The future of Hong Kong Island was however only viable with a hinterland providing water supply and other resources, which was secured by means of a 150-year lease on the New Territories. The lease expired in 1997. The Chinese made it clear that they wanted the territory back, and they could very easily have acquired it at the expiry of the lease. Other Asian countries used force to acquire colonial enclaves – India in Goa for example – with far less legal basis. It is clear from the record of negotiations between the British government and the Chinese in 1984 on a Framework Agreement for the transfer of sovereignty that the Chinese side considered annexation. But they opted for a consensual arrangement with the British. There would be a fifty-year transition during which the territory would enjoy "a high degree of autonomy" within a "special administrative region", operating under a so-called "Basic Law" acting as a form of constitution under Chinese law. The principle of "one country, two systems" was adopted.

The motives of Deng, who negotiated the transfer arrangements, were not difficult to fathom. The formula provided a precedent for the smooth, non-violent recovery of other "lost" territories, Macau and then Taiwan. It provided opportunities for China to benefit from the continued functioning of Asia's largest financial centre. And, for Deng, there was the attraction of using Hong Kong as part of his experiments in liberalization, in particular the adjacent area around Shenzhen. But it was equally clear that there was potential for misunderstanding. Deng had explained in the negotiations that serious disorder would not be tolerated: "China would still allow people in Hong Kong to criticize the Communist Party, but if they should turn their words into action, opposing the mainland under the pretext of democracy, then Beijing would have to 'intervene'."[37] Many Hong Kong residents regarded the freedom to demonstrate as part of their promised autonomy, but the Chinese insisted on "stability".

The Basic Law promised, as an "ultimate aim", the use of universal suffrage to choose a legislature (LegCo) and a chief executive. Such choice was never available under colonial rule, though a process of democratization started in the 1980s and was accelerated under Governor Chris Patten, so that there was a directly or indirectly elected LegCo in 1995. The Chinese made it clear that they did not agree with these moves, though they were prepared to "consider" the idea of elections in 2007 as part of a wider series of experiments with direct voting, accepting a modest expansion of the franchise. After 2010, the LegCo had direct elections for thirty-five of its seventy members, while the remainder were chosen from "functional constituencies", mainly representing traditional business interests, but five of whom were nominees of elected councillors. Under this hybrid system, the LegCo retained most representatives sympathetic to the mainland. More generally, the concept of "two systems" was interpreted differently – in the Chinese case as not infringing on their sovereignty and as an expression of "harmonious differences".[38]

The misunderstandings – if such they were – surfaced in the form of mass demonstrations in 2014, when the Chinese made it clear that the chief executive would after all be appointed, not elected, and the LegCo would retain a restricted franchise (which "pro-democracy" politicians rejected). But a crisis point was reached in 2019, when the chief executive Carrie Lam introduced legislation on extradition which many Hong Kong residents feared would facilitate extradition to the mainland. Massive protests followed. She had clearly misjudged the public mood and agreed to withdraw the proposals.

But the protests continued on a massive scale. Many demonstrators were not reconciled to joining the PRC in 2047. Some were demanding "independence" for Hong Kong, though that was never remotely a prospect, and appears from surveys to have had little public support. There were others motivated by long-standing local problems, like the shortage and cost of housing.[39] Most of the demonstrators were peaceful. Some (highlighted by the authorities) were violent, with protesters using Molotov cocktails and longbows against the police and vandalizing public buildings, including the LegCo. There were also violent counter-demonstrations. There were rumours of agents provocateurs seeking to provoke a Chinese crackdown or provide a pretext for it. Local opinion polling suggested that the public was roughly equally divided between approval and disapproval of the demonstrators, and a large number were apolitical and had no strong view.[40]

What were the authorities to do? The dilemma was acute. To allow continuing mass demonstrations and violence was to tolerate "chaos" and the breakdown of order. The Chinese were keenly aware that, whatever the censorship of the Great Firewall, information on the disturbances would be available across China, advertising the seeming impotence of the government in the face of mass protest. Or they could crush the protests, in clear breach of the "two systems" principle. They might have been expected to use force. Many authoritarian and some democratic regimes have done so. The Basic Law provided for the deployment of 6,000 troops in an emergency. The PRC was perhaps mindful of the international reaction to Tiananmen Square. Instead, they invoked a draconian National Security Law, which has specified severe prison sentences for a wide variety of offences: subversion, sedition, terrorism and collusion with foreign powers. It is also applied "extraterritorially" to people outside China and Hong Kong. Politicians, including moderate and strictly non-violent figures, and a leading newspaper proprietor (Jimmy Lai) have been sentenced to jail terms. Thousands have been detained in what is called a "white terror".

There was a strong overseas reaction to the steady stream of arrests. The USA removed the trading privileges which previously applied separately to Hong Kong and imposed personal sanctions on named individuals such as the chief executive. The UK offered a route to citizenship for refugees from the territory with British overseas passports and many thousands have emigrated to the UK.

Most of the overseas government condemnations have centred on two issues: democracy and the "rule of law". As to the first, there never was a democracy under British colonial rule, though a semi-democratic hybrid system was created late in the day. Before the recent local elections, political participation was low, but there was a free press and vigorous political debate. Following the crackdown, it has been announced that future LegCo elections will be contested only by candidates vetted for "patriotism" and with a reduced number of freely elected seats. In Hong Kong, public criticism of China has been muted. Any expectations – which were always unrealistic – that Hong Kong might accommodate a Western-style democracy have been firmly squashed.

Pessimism has also been expressed about the future of Hong Kong's valued independent legal system. Critics of China suggest that it is inevitable that courts will become politicized. President Xi's views on "rule by law" as opposed to the "rule of law" are often quoted: "China must never follow the path of Western constitutionalism: separation of powers or judicial independence."[41] The worry expressed in the business community is that politicization could start to affect rulings in commercial disputes where one of the parties has close PRC connections or could involve the suppression of critical business journalism on issues like political risk.

The key is the future of the membership of the Final Court of Appeal, currently dominated by overseas judges. Were they to leave, one of the main pillars of the Hong Kong system and its appeal to expatriate business would be removed. So far, the Chinese have been at pains to keep the system of commercial law separate from the new Security Law. Nonetheless, two senior British judges withdrew at the request of the Lord Chancellor in the UK. Others have chosen to stay. Lord Sumption, one of those judges and a former member of the UK Supreme Court, stated that "the Chinese and Hong Kong governments have done nothing to interfere with the independence of the judiciary".[42]

The long-term implications of the new National Security Law are not yet clear. A lot depends on the response of the business community, which is divided between relief at the termination of disorder and concern that the Security Law could gradually affect business operations. There has been survey evidence that some foreign-owned companies, of which 1,500 have regional headquarters in the city, envisage a shift of operations overseas. Nonetheless, major business transactions like large IPOs continue to happen. 2020 was an extraordinarily successful year for the finance sector, with an upsurge in Western institutional investors seeking to acquire Chinese stocks through the "stock connect" link to the mainland and a parallel growth in Chinese mutual funds looking outward. Other preoccupations, such as the rough treatment of expatriates under quarantine rules, and the Covid restrictions in general, have badly damaged Hong Kong's appeal. Indeed Singapore is reportedly enjoying a big influx of Chinese private wealth and expatriate business from Hong Kong.

The Chinese authorities may care less about Hong Kong than they did, as Shanghai has replaced Hong Kong as China's main financial centre, though Hong Kong, unlike Shanghai, has the unique facility of enabling Chinese companies to raise funds abroad through a centre with a fully convertible currency. Some argue that this segregation of political and commercial is not sustainable. Isabel Hilton argues that China can no longer play the role it envisages in the world economy, which involves internationalizing its currency, without free capital flows and open information. The crackdown in Hong Kong takes it in the opposite direction.[43]

The ethnic periphery

China has, until recently, escaped too much scrutiny of its approach to race, ethnicity and the politics of identity. But it now finds itself accused of "genocide" in respect of the predominantly Muslim population of Uyghurs in Xinjiang on top of a long-standing charge of suppressing the identity of Tibetans, with serious abuses of human rights.

Long before the Communist revolution, China's rulers were confronted with the problem of distinct ethnic minorities who were a tiny proportion of the population but occupied a large part of the land area. Jacques in particular identifies "cultural racism" as a feature of Chinese history over 3,000 years.[44] But Bill Hayton argues that the concept of China as we know it today is much more recent, and stems from an intellectual movement which occurred in the wake of the establishment of a republic a century ago.[45] After the foundation of the republic, the emphasis was on the Chinese race as a singular entity and the assimilation of minorities to customs and practices of the Han Chinese. Such habits of mind have clearly continued, though under the Communists there was formal recognition of 56 minority ethnicities, mostly weak, but with three in particular – the Tibetans, Uyghurs and Mongols – considered worthy of "autonomous" status. All harboured secessionist movements, which at earlier times of weak Chinese central government had led to periods of de-facto independence, notably in Tibet before 1951 and Xinjiang (as East Turkestan) in 1933.

China under the Communists has been firmly committed to maintaining its "territorial integrity" ahead of "self-determination" for its ethnic minorities. In that respect it has been no different from other historically new, multi-ethnic states like India, Turkey, Indonesia or Nigeria, which have used force to suppress secessionist movements. Chinese leaders look with horror at the break-up of the USSR and Yugoslavia (and they could add Ethiopia and Sudan), which have dissolved violently and chaotically amid ethnic conflicts. In the case of Xinjiang, its value as part of China has been enhanced by its being the country's main source of oil and gas. It is also a key staging post on the "New Silk Road" to Central Asia and has seen intensive economic development of the cities and infrastructure. Tibet's importance has a lot to do with its abundant high-quality water supply, seen as crucial to a country with per-capita availability one quarter the global average, and much of it polluted.

In order to cement the regions' integration with China, settlement has been encouraged by Han Chinese, who now account for well over a half of the Xinjiang population (from 10% in 1949) and are close to half in Tibet.[46] As in other countries where demographic facts on the ground have been changed in this way by settlers, there has been a strong reaction from the indigenous population – riots and repressive countermeasures. Hundreds were killed in race riots in both 2009 and 2014.[47] What has given particular virulence to the Uyghur situation is that the Uyghurs are not merely ethnically different and Turkic-speaking, but Muslim. Islamic terrorists from the Uyghur community were alleged to be behind a series of terrorist attacks in 2014 – called "China's 9/11" – which was the pretext for a "deradicalization" programme.

That programme led to large-scale internment of Uyghurs in camps supposedly for "re-education" accompanied by work, allegedly forced. The Chinese sought to justify it on security grounds: there were plausible reports of several thousand Uyghurs in ISIS camps in Syria.[48] Justification of the crackdown on counter-terrorism grounds attracted support from more than fifty countries in the UN, some of them majority-Muslim, and may have been a factor in gaining President Trump's initial endorsement.

The allegation that China has engaged in "genocide" has raised the stakes, politically and legally. There is no serious suggestion that, in its narrow literal sense of large-scale ethnic killing, genocide has taken place. There has, however, clearly been large-scale abuse of human rights, though there are many other countries of which that could be said. The charge against China is the systematic attempt to stamp out the Uyghurs' identity, language and religious faith, including coercive application to Uyghurs of China's harsh birth-control policy. The UN Genocide Convention, to which China is a signatory, includes "'measures intended to prevent births' with the aim to 'destroy, in whole or part' a national, ethnic, racial or religious group".[49] But what are the facts?

Nothing could be calculated to arouse greater anger on both sides of the current "cold war" with China than the assertion of

the outgoing Trump administration – endorsed by its successor
and governments of the EU, UK and Canada – that the PRC
has "committed genocide against the predominantly Muslim
Uyghurs and other members of ethnic and religious minority
groups in Xinjiang".[50] The accusation is probably the most
damaging that can be made of any regime in terms of human
rights, and the fact that it has been taken seriously by bodies
like the Holocaust Memorial Trust, putting it on the same
level as the Nazi Holocaust, the Rwandan genocide and the
Cambodian "killing fields", makes it an issue of exceptional
sensitivity.

There is a debate between lawyers as to what constitutes
"genocide" in terms of the relevant UN Convention, and
whether the evidence supports the accusation. Suffice it to
say that lawyers in the US State Department appear not to
have been persuaded of the case being promoted by their
political head.[51] But what of the evidence itself? Some serious
academics and analysts have endorsed the factual evidence.[52]
It is very unfortunate that one of the more comprehensive and
plausible critical reviews of the evidence has been devalued by
the unwillingness of the authors to identify themselves, fearing
professional retribution.[53]

One of the main sources used in the framing of the accusations against China is an article by Adrian Zenz which
extrapolated from several local reports to conclude that
around a million people – 10% of the Uyghur population –
had been interned in what the Chinese called "re-education"
camps.[54]

That material has been widely used to imply that a million people are in these camps. But as *The Economist* (which
declined to endorse the "genocide" claim despite being very
critical of China's record on human rights) pointed out, the
only evidence is of large numbers passing through the camps.[55]
The original Zenz article on which so much argumentation
has been based referred to internees being held only for short
periods: four to twenty days (the latter for the more intran-
sigent). No doubt "re-education" and "vocational training"

– Chinese-style – was not a pleasant experience and may have been brutal for people the Chinese regarded as hard-core. But it was a long way from mass indefinite detention in "concentration camps".

The "re-education" camps may, in any event, have closed at the end of 2019, and the accusations have now shifted to "forced labour" schemes.[56] There has long been concern throughout China about the working conditions of more than 250 million migrant workers in the country.[57] They lack the entitlements of urban workers under the hukou system and can also be subject to bullying employers. The Chinese government facilitates the movement of migrant workers around China and can reasonably be criticized for failure to support workers' rights. But even the studies seeking to demonstrate "forced labour" in Xinjiang (which have led to campaigns directed at firms which invest there) have been rather more cautious than the subsequent headlines, writing of the "risk" or "possibility" of coercion.

It is critical to the "genocide" case that there was not just harsh treatment in these camps, but that there was an "intent to destroy" an ethnic group. And the key piece of evidence was that there was "forced sterilization" of women. Again, the main source is Adrian Zenz.[58]

There is no reason to disbelieve the accounts given or to minimize the impact on the women concerned. What is in serious doubt is whether these practices have anything to do with ethnic minorities and the Uyghurs in particular. China's one-child policy has been associated with a degree of coercion: not merely fines on "offenders", but pressure on women to have abortions or be sterilized. In fact, the Uyghurs and other groups were long exempted from the policy, which applied to Han Chinese women – and that would explain why the 2010 population census shows almost 20% of women in Xinjiang as having three or more children, with the population of Xinjiang increasing in relative terms. The national policy was subsequently applied to Uyghurs and other minorities, which is when the cases of coercion occurred. The birth rate appears, as a result, to have dropped sharply in Xinjiang. In any event, the national policy has been abandoned in stages, and there is now a three-child policy throughout China.

A further element in the genocide claim is that the Chinese are pursuing "Sinicization" of religion and have a vision of what has been translated either as the "Chinese nation" or "Chinese race" (*Zhonghua minzu*). The implication is that the Chinese are trying to assimilate the non-Han minorities. Assimilation runs counter to our ideas of multiculturalism, but would be more readily understood in, say, Portugal or France. There is, moreover, as referred to elsewhere in the book, a Chinese approach to race which long pre-dates the Communists and is experienced at a popular level in ways which might be regarded as "racist" in a Western context. But it is a big leap to say that "Sinicization" is an "intent to destroy a people" – the current definition of "genocide".

For the ruling Communist Party, the main challenge posed by the ethnic periphery, in Tibet as well as in Xinjiang, is the threat of "separatism". Xi has said: "We must severely crack down on ethnic separatist activities and persist in the anti-separatist struggle with both cultural and military forces."[59] That is not the kind of language that would be employed in Western countries faced with separatist groups – like Catalonia. But it is not greatly different from the approach of states trying to exert the principle of "territorial integrity" over "self-determination": Sri Lanka, India, Pakistan, Indonesia, Nigeria and Turkey, for example. Again, a long way from an "intent to destroy a people".

There is moreover plenty of evidence to suggest that the Chinese government has been primarily motivated by security concerns. A team from the University of Missouri has documented in detail the CCP's change of internal security policy in Xinjiang as it evolved to prevent terrorism diffusing into China via radicalized, transnational Uyghur networks, particularly those with links to terrorist groups in South-East Asia and the Middle East.[60] Brutal counter-insurgency measures are not justified by terrorism, and may indeed be counterproductive – as could be said of the West's activities in Iraq and

Afghanistan, and with rendition and Guantanamo Bay (or in relation to British policy in Northern Ireland). But there was a credible threat of terrorism in China. The East Turkestan Islamic Movement – linked in turn to the Turkestan Islamic Party – was listed as a terrorist organization by the USA until 2020, on the basis that it was funded and supported by Al-Qaeda. Israeli intelligence is said to have identified 3,000 Uyghur fighters in Syria. The Missouri team, after looking at this evidence, concludes: "Our analysis suggests that those who seek to alter China's treatment of its Uyghur citizens may be more effective if they approach that behaviour as grounded in counter-terrorism policy, rather than framing objections on human-rights grounds."[61]

The facts will continue to be contested. But the accusation has become a powerful weapon in a growing propaganda war with China. In March 2021, Western governments – the USA, Canada, the EU and the UK – collectively imposed sanctions in the form of travel bans on named Chinese individuals involved in the Uyghur internment and human-rights abuse (as opposed to "genocide"). China promptly retaliated with its own sanctions on European officials, MPs, MEPs and academics (including Adrian Zenz). It is not clear where this tit-for-tat argument will lead. The Biden administration has, unlike its predecessor, chosen to work in a coalition which is much stronger. But the coalition excludes any non-Western country, even Japan.

A key development has however been the highly critical report of the UN Human Rights Commissioner, the former President of Chile, Michelle Bachelet, which is the nearest we can get to a politically independent assessment of the human-rights situation in Xinjiang. Its condemnation of "crimes against humanity" has, arguably, done far more damage to China's reputation than Western criticism. It has amplified a wider confrontation in which universal values – "human rights" – are one of the bones of contention. That brings into question the effectiveness of China's "soft power" initiatives.

Discourse power and Wolf Warriors

The combination of the pandemic, the Hong Kong situation and the Uyghur issue has given China a terrible press – at least in the Western world. Favourability ratings, which were high earlier in the decade, have plummeted, so that narratives about a "new Cold War" now chime with Western public opinion. That raises the question of what happened to the idea of "telling the China story better" – a major theme of the early Xi years. There was a shift, first seen at the 2012 National People's Congress, to move beyond the earlier "Five Principles of Peaceful Coexistence" – that is, non-intervention – or the self-effacing style advocated by Deng and to be more assertive: to advertise the Chinese economic renaissance, the "peaceful rising" in contrast to the "century of humiliation", and China's aspiration to be seen as a responsible world leader. The new doctrine was to be called "Great Power Diplomacy with Chinese Characteristics".[62] Out of that grew what has come to be dubbed "discourse diplomacy" or "the international right to speak".

The concept of "soft power", which is the use of economic and cultural attributes to influence international opinion, has become a commonly declared instrument of Chinese foreign policy,[63] and is essentially what "discourse diplomacy" is about. Unfortunately, there is little consensus on how to gauge its effectiveness. One approach is to try to measure national brand value by analogy with corporate brands. The main index has China as eighth of 100 countries in 2021, having fallen from fifth a year earlier (the USA fell from first to sixth at the end of the Trump presidency). Germany, Japan and the UK score highest.[64] Another index, clearly measuring something else, has China at No. 27 out of thirty countries.[65] An academic study of the effectiveness of China's "discourse diplomacy" judges that China has been very successful in projecting "the China story" to the Chinese diaspora and expatriates in Mandarin-language communications, but very unsuccessful in Western media.[66]

To counter the West's negative perceptions, the Chinese regime has promoted a wide variety of initiatives under the framework of a United Front organization in Beijing, ranging from supporting overseas think tanks sympathetic to China to an expansion of the Chinese broadcaster (CGTN) – recently expelled from Britain for "bias" – and the promotion of an English-language newspaper, *Global Times*, which presents the official Chinese view of the world in trenchant terms. None of this is particularly surprising and is not fundamentally different from the techniques employed by Western governments, usually with more subtlety and effectiveness. After all, the USA has its Peace Corps as well as the CIA, "dark ops" and "black propaganda", as well as the many more wholesome aspects of its "soft power". Similarly, the UK, France and other powers.

One device was the promotion of Confucius Institutes, of which there around 1,000 – mainly in the USA, Japan and South Korea, and with several in the UK, mostly partnered with colleges and other institutions in the host country. They were launched back in 2004 and have become a vehicle for promoting the Chinese language (to around 100 million learners) and Chinese culture (Chinese medicine and dance, for example). Because the Chinese government stands behind the organization – Hanban – which runs the network, there have been objections that CIs are not innocent replicas of the British Council or the Alliance Française, but propaganda vehicles which compromise academic freedom when they are located on campuses.[67] Some of the complaints are extreme, and may be motivated by anti-Chinese sentiment, but the large number of contracts terminated and projects blocked in different countries have badly damaged the brand.[68]

One of the main ways to spread influence has been to build up a presence in international organizations. China has been, historically, seriously under-represented, but is now systematically, in Xi's words, "taking an active part in leading the reform of the global governance system"[69] and ensuring that leadership positions reflect China's growing importance. China has taken the top posts in the FAO, the International Civil Aviation Organization and the International

Telecommunication Union (important for standard-setting), and occupies strategically important roles elsewhere – for example as a member of the five-member panel which selects UN rapporteurs on human rights.[70] President Trump withdrew the USA from the WHO, claiming it was "very China-centric" – and the Chinese were indeed highly influential, especially after carefully timed donations, and even more so after the USA left. It is difficult to quarrel with the Chinese argument that they should be represented more equitably and play a bigger leadership role in UN agencies, the WTO, the World Bank and the IMF (and pay subscriptions to match). They clearly intend to do so and are.

Perhaps the result of frustration at the reputational damage and loss of "soft power" in recent years, a new phenomenon is the emergence of very aggressive and sometimes abusive government spokesmen and diplomats – the "Wolf Warriors" (named after popular Rambo-style Chinese film characters). They have populated Twitter, which is used for trolling and spreading disinformation and conspiracy theories, sometimes seemingly working with Russian collaboration. This could be seen as part of a more aggressive and assertive approach in general but may also reflect an attempt by a new superpower to develop a range of "soft" and "hard" power instruments to deal with different countries. In particular, the geopolitical decisions opened up by the Ukraine war have shown that while China's reputation in the "Global West" has suffered badly, it has remained strong in Africa, Latin America and the Middle East: the "Global South". To these external relationships I now turn.

Chapter 6

The Many Varieties of Relationships with China

China's relations with the rest of the world are now often portrayed in binary terms – China versus the West – and in the primary colours of economic and military power, further sharpened by ideological difference. That is because China is invariably seen through the prism of US–China relations. Much of the analysis above is framed in these terms. The Trump era encouraged the idea that we are dealing with quite a simple game: like draughts, it has two players and moves quickly to a conclusion, with one country devouring the other's pieces in decisive wins. Those who hark back to the Cold War would cite the more complex game of chess, with opposing alliances, each with pieces of different significance, carefully planning for openings to secure a winning advantage. The Chinese view of the world is closer to the game of Go, with many more potential moves than chess and more gradations of gain and loss. That is closer to how we should see China's external relations: a complex web of relationships revolving around different objectives together with subtle variations of "soft" and "hard" power.

China looks outwards

China is on the way to becoming a "superpower" in economic terms, and as such will exercise a great deal of influence regionally and globally. But to what end? As discussed in the last chapter, ideology matters for the current Chinese regime, but it is not easily exportable. It isn't clear what view of the world China is trying to project under its current leader. Maoist China was, at least in theory, about a competing universal idea: revolutionary Communism. Deng's China was for economic growth and development within China's one-party state. There was no apparent interest in global power politics and a modest, self-effacing style reflected in his mantra of China "keeping its head low and biding its time".[1] Now that Xi's China has expanded beyond that in ambition and assertiveness, what is the goal? The official aim is "modernization of socialism with Chinese characteristics for the new era" – a statement of such depth of meaning and yet such opaqueness as to be virtually meaningless outside the parameters of Chinese language and politics.[2]

Various things can be said about what this more assertive China is about. First, it isn't so much to do with Communism as with the perpetuation of the power of the Chinese Communist Party. The distinction may seem obvious, but, especially in the ideologically polarized world of US politics, there are still people engaged in a struggle with something called "Communism". They are unlikely to find it in "state capitalist" China, despite the proliferation of Marxist-Leninist jargon.

Secondly, the regime and (to the extent it can be assessed) Chinese public opinion is very nationalistic, even by the standards of a world where nationalism appears to be enjoying a renaissance in reaction to an era of global integration.[3] There is evidence of strongly patriotic support for the regime among young people – not just in China, but among those who have travelled and studied overseas.[4] But it is a particular form of nationalism, reflecting China's being a civilization rather than a narrowly territorial nation and, moreover, with a sense of identity shared with the Chinese diaspora. Phrases like "rejuvenate the Chinese people" and "shared community of common identity" appear frequently and reflect the sense of pride that China is now, at last, restored to being a great power.

And thirdly, China is no longer, as in Deng's time, content to be a humble "learner", but is self-confident and expects to be taken seriously and to have a say in global affairs, as a reflection of its importance. A country whose powerful president has visited more than seventy nations, and who has invested in relations with the varied likes of Britain, Venezuela, Djibouti, Kenya, Hungary, Italy, Fiji, the United Arab Emirates and Kazakhstan could hardly be described as a "hermit state", like North Korea.

China scholars and commentators are divided as to whether modern China is aggressive or merely assertive of its newly found status as a successful major power – expansionist in respect of territory and resources or more concerned with exercising influence and being treated with respect. The discussion as to whether today's China is a "threat" has been essentially about economics and technology and the influence which derives from those, though there is a military dimension. But before examining in detail the nature of specific threats, it is important to look at the change in the framework of geopolitical thinking which has taken place within the last few years: a hardening consensus of US attitudes towards containment of China and China's response.

The US–China Cold War

There has been a tacit understanding since the Second World War around the idea of an international order led by the United States and its allies, which set the framework of rules around trade and finance and wider international dealings. Whether this understanding was based on an alliance against a common enemy (the Soviet Union) or a set of shared values was debatable, but after the collapse of the Soviet Union it was assumed to be based on the superiority of "liberal democracy". The result was a period of "globalization" with a focus on raising living standards generally and bringing "emerging countries" into a more integrated world economy. China was a major participant and beneficiary, and a key event, practically and symbolically, was joining the World Trade Organization in

2001. The fact that China had a different and more repressive political system did not initially matter, as long as China accepted US leadership of the global order and the United States did not interfere with China's internal politics. The assumptions behind this world have however crumbled.

First, China's economic growth has defied expectations and led to a shift in the power balance. China's emergence as an economic superpower, without adopting Western political norms, has clearly shocked the United States, even though it may have been inevitable.[5] It has led to a fear of being overtaken and a questioning of the value of an open economy which has helped to facilitate China's rise.

Second, within the USA especially, there has been a convergence of views towards a more hostile view of China. Business groups, hitherto a powerful lobby for engagement with China, have had mixed experiences in and with China. Traditional anti-China Republican "hawks" have made common cause with libertarians who have become more sceptical of the value of free financial flows and free trade because of the "security" dimension. And American liberals on the left have joined the consensus, affronted by human-rights abuses and reflecting long-standing concerns of trade unionists about the merits of free trade. The new consensus is summarized by a Biden adviser as "blunting Chinese power".[6]

Third, there is a shift in opinion in a wider group of countries which are apprehensive about the rise of China for different reasons, but primarily to do with the exercise of political, and potentially military, power in the Asia-Pacific region. The USA has been able to assemble a loose alliance of countries which feel militarily threatened, some of which also subscribe to democratic as opposed to autocratic values. More distant allies as in Europe have also come to question the benefits of economic links with China and worry about the clash of values.

There has been in China, too, a hardening of attitudes within the regime, and perhaps more widely, around several mutually reinforcing themes. One is that there is a "plot against China" – not just that a hostile West is trying to prevent China's economic rise, but that it is actively trying to destabilize the country politically in areas China considers to be internal: Tibet, Xinjiang, Hong Kong, Taiwan.[7] It isn't just the Chinese who worry about attempts to make ideology and arguments about values a dividing line. Henry Kissinger argues that ideology should not be the main issue, "unless we are prepared to make regime change the principal goal of our policy".[8]

Coinciding with a defensive reaction to what is seen as a "threat" from the USA and its allies, there is the self-confidence which comes from economic and technological achievement and the judgement that the West, more generally, is in a state of decline and weakness. The near collapse of the financial system in the crisis of 2008–9, the ignominious withdrawal by the Biden administration from Afghanistan, the failure of successive interventions in the Middle East, the political crisis in the USA, with Trump's attempted coup and continued influence, Brexit in Europe – all fed the declinist narrative.

The combination of negative US and Chinese perceptions and realities have become cumulative: a deepening digital divide; decoupling on both sides; the growth of security and economic alliances aimed at confrontation and deterrence. Beckley makes the argument that a new world order is being created based around confrontation with China, with the forces of "liberal democracy" (and a few unsavoury allies) lined up against China and its autocratic allies (Russia, Iran, etc.).[9] In pursuit of this goal, all manner of ad-hoc alliances is forming under US leadership around security, data exchange and advanced-technology cooperation. There is an "inner" group built around the AUKUS alliance of Australia, the UK and USA, and a so-called Quad of the USA, India, Japan and Australia, sometimes portrayed as an embryonic Asia-Pacific NATO, together with looser or overlapping groupings. What is however striking about these alliances is that they are primarily about military security and have little to offer in terms of market access or money (though the recently launched Indo-Pacific Economic Framework designs to restore the balance). By contrast the Chinese have been building up economic alliances through the Belt and Road Initiative and trade.

This alliance formation largely matches the pessimism of geopoliticians since the time of ancient Greece, who see an inevitable conflict between rising and declining superpowers.[10] There can only be one hegemonic power, and China is trying to usurp the position of the USA. The inevitable outcome – on this view of the world – is that economic competition with China will inevitably degenerate into military conflict, which is why we need to look at the military balance.

Is China a military threat?

I have discussed above the pessimistic geopolitical theories about the consequences of the rise of a new superpower, which predict that this will inevitably lead to war. The conflict between the West and the USSR almost did but became a peaceful "cold war". Chinese nationalism contains, for some, the ingredients for a new conflict – cold and hot.

China has live memories of bitter wars with its neighbour Japan and in Korea; border clashes with India and the former USSR; and a limited war with Vietnam in 1978–79, its last. But warriors do not loom large in China's gallery of heroes: there is no Napoleon or Caesar, or even a Marshal Zhukov or a General Patton. Pride is reserved mainly for the guerrilla predecessors of the People's Liberation Army, whose achievements are not greatly relevant to modern high-tech warfare. Deng regarded defence spending as a distraction from development and cut it. The main use of the army was maintaining order in China. Since the advent of President Xi, who chairs the Military Commission – which oversees the armed forces – more attention has been paid to improvements in military capability. His declared ambition is that China should have a "world-class force" by 2049.[11] As with many of President Xi's declared ambitions, there is much ambiguity and a sizeable gap between promise and performance.

There is certainly a lot more defence spending nowadays, and, in nominal terms, its growth is over 10%. China's rapidly growing economy has provided more resources. As far as can be measured, however, those devoted to the military are close to NATO target levels in relation to the economy. The most recent figures suggest that China is spending just under 2% of GDP on defence – about the same level as the UK and France, and substantially less than the USA (3.4%) and Russia (3.7%).[12] At market exchange rates, this currently equates to around 40% of US spending. But because of purchasing-power differences, the same spending will pay for more soldiers (though not for equipment bought at world prices).

Corrected in this way, China's defence budget may be roughly 75% of US levels (while Indian defence spending is 40% of US levels and Russia's is 30%). That is not enough to catch up with the USA, let alone overtake it. Moreover, much of this spending is to replace ancient equipment – 1950s tanks and outdated aircraft. The RAND Corporation judges that even after recent modernization only around 70% of the fleet and aircraft is "modern".[13] Furthermore, much of President Xi's modernizing and streamlining of the forces has been concerned with such issues as purging them of corruption and ensuring that they can actually perform after almost half a century without combat experience of the kind achieved by the USA in Iraq and Afghanistan.[14] And it seems to be the case that more is spent on internal than external security.

In any event, quantity is not quality, though the US Department of Défense points to some significant changes and advances.[15] The main shift of emphasis has been for China to build up its navy. China now has three aircraft carriers, but that number is dwarfed by the 20 of the USA. It has 59 submarines, some of them nuclear-powered, compared to 67 for the USA, and an overall fleet of 87 warships against 112 for the USA. Seen in regional terms, China is now ahead of India and Japan in naval capacity (with respectively 28 and 49 warships and 16 and 20 submarines), though sceptics point out that meaningful assessment requires more than crude numbers: many Chinese vessels are modest coastguard vessels.

There are also areas where Chinese technological sophistication appears to be developing apace. There are advanced air-defence warning systems and stealth aircraft (allegedly using stolen designs), a fleet of anti-ship ballistic missiles and the latest cyber-warfare techniques (which have allegedly been deployed in attacks on commercial targets). The fact that China can send a successful mission to the dark side of the moon and develop its own GPS system suggests at least a potential for high-technology warfare (though Russia's space achievements were not a good predictor of its field capabilities in Ukraine). The main area of contention and uncertainty is in the development of AI technology and its military applications. A recent two-year study for the US Congress warned that "China is already an AI peer, and it is technically more advanced in some applications. Within the next decade China could surpass the USA as the world's AI superpower [...] and is already training AI algorithms in military games designed around real-world scenarios."[16]

China also has around 300 nuclear warheads and the means to deliver them intercontinentally. Whilst this is much less than the US arsenal of around 3800 warheads (1,800 deployed), it was seen until recently as a more than effective deterrent. There have however recently been reports of a big expansion in the number of nuclear silos in response to the deteriorating geopolitical situation – though these could be part of a "shell game" to confuse adversaries. Pentagon assessments are that China could have 700–1000 warheads by 2030.

What has caused serious alarm in US military circles is the successful testing of Hypersonic Glide Vehicles, which combine potentially very high speed with manoeuvrability to hit anywhere in the USA evading radar and missile defences. At the same time, China appears to have upgraded its nuclear posture from a defensive "no first use" to "launch on warning". One interpretation put on these advances in nuclear capability is that they would deter the USA from resorting to nuclear weapons in any conflict over, say, Taiwan.

Pulling the threads together, there is a consensus among defence analysts that China is, yet, nowhere near being a military superpower, though its military technology is advancing fast. Some strategists believe that military conflict is however inevitable, and argue for early military confrontation to establish US credibility and to negotiate a "decent peace" – an approach sardonically described as "give war a chance".[17]

There is however no global, as opposed to regional, projection of military power and no serious progress, yet, towards having one. China does have a military base in Djibouti, which was justified on the basis that China needed to safeguard its shipping routes from pirates and required a base from which to protect its expatriates in the region, as with the airlift of 30,000 Chinese nationals from Libya. The Chinese have been scoping and negotiating others. There have been press stories of a potential base in Equatorial Guinea[18] and the diplomatic cultivation of the Solomon Islands and other Pacific territories like Vanuatu, Kiribati and Tonga could have military undertones (China has also been building bases on unoccupied islets in the South China Sea). But the USA has around 600 overseas bases, of which around 300 are in Asia – mainly in Japan, South Korea and Guam.[19] There are a few UN peacekeepers in Africa, and China provides more funding for UN peacekeeping than any other major country – perhaps to gain some battlefield experience short of war.[20] But it does have the aspiration and a growing ability to be a regional hegemon and to win conflicts around its borders. That reflects China's declared "core" objectives.

The first of these is to stop Taiwan becoming independent (to "defeat anyone attempting to separate Taiwan from China"), and perhaps to seize outlying islands. RAND judges the odds of China winning a conventional war over Taiwan as about 50:50, but the odds are shifting in China's favour, and Taiwan relies crucially on a US defence guarantee whose limits are not totally clear.[21] A second core objective is to take possession of disputed islands, which include those also claimed by Japan (the Senkaku, or Diaoyu Islands), leading Japan to conclude that China is "Japan's greatest national security threat".[22] Others concern areas that China considers its rightful borders, notably with India. But neither of these is of the same importance as Taiwan.

War risks: Taiwan and the disputed islands

There is one clear case where China consistently threatens military intervention: Taiwan. But since Taiwan is not legally recognized internationally as a separate state other than by a handful of countries, that is "aggression" of a rather unusual kind. Nonetheless, both China and the USA repeatedly warn of war if "red lines" are crossed. Russia's invasion of Ukraine has demonstrated the potential and the hazards of using military force to solve territorial issues. It may be that the Ukraine War has not affected China's approach to Taiwan, but it has raised awareness elsewhere of war risks. For that reason, Taiwan has become pivotal to future relationships between China and its neighbours, and the Global West, and I shall explore scenarios for the future below. Every Chinese leader since the revolution has seen the full eventual restoration of Taiwan to China as a fundamental principle and duty, and President Xi has followed his predecessors in making a "red line" of the issue. China's claim is based on long historical Chinese dominance, and more recently on the "theft" of Taiwan by Japan in the war of 1894–95, when China was at its weakest. In practice, there is a high degree of pragmatism: theory and practice diverge. Ever since the Nixon–Kissinger reconciliation in 1972, the USA has accepted that there is "one China", and later that Taiwan should be stripped of its recognition as an independent country. But Taiwan should continue and enjoy protection as a separate entity: de-facto but not de-jure independence. China has been pragmatic too, welcoming Taiwanese investors and two-way tourism, and deploying the formula "one country, two systems" to explain the anomalous status quo. China's Anti-Secession Law defines what can be accommodated within the concept of "two systems" – and, so far, Taiwan hasn't crossed the line. President

Biden's National Security Adviser, Jake Sullivan, has gone so far as to describe the maintenance of the peace as "the greatest unclaimed success story in the history of US–China relations".[23]

China has now coexisted with Taiwan for over seventy years, and there are twenty-seven years left before a promised final resolution of the issue. But there is a growing sense of urgency because of various destabilizing elements. Taiwan is now a flourishing multi-party democracy. The ruling party, the DPP, is a member of the Liberal International, and its supporters do not have a strong Chinese identity, unlike the former ruling party, the KMT, which traces its roots to those nationalists who survived the civil war. The DPP flirts with the idea of declaring independence, and its confidence has grown with the highly successful management of the Covid pandemic on the island. There is a growing sense of Taiwanese identity in most of the population, especially the young: 60% identify as Taiwanese, not Chinese. The effective termination of the "one country, two systems" formula in Hong Kong may have persuaded some Taiwanese that they need to clear the ambiguity over their own status. The powerful Taiwan lobby in the US Congress may encourage them to take risks by formally declaring independence and seeking recognition. The former US National Security Advisor, John Bolton, has urged that the "one-China policy should be revisited".[24] There is a danger that Taiwanese politicians or the US administration will cross the threshold which China regards as sufficiently provocative to justify an armed assertion of Chinese sovereignty. The current US security guarantees for Taiwan are becoming less ambiguous.

And on the Chinese side there are those who regard the current ambiguity as a sign of weakness, and feel a stronger China needs to be patient no longer. There are indications that President Xi has a sense of personal responsibility for achieving reunification, which implies a shorter time horizon than the century (2048), previously assumed to be the deadline. Xi is seventy years old (in June 2023). For his part, president Biden has hardened the American position from "strategic ambiguity" by repeatedly affirming that the US will defend Taiwan if it is attacked.

The Chinese however show no sign of preparing the massive logistical operation which would be required for an amphibious landing, invasion and occupation of a well-defended island. General Miley, chairman of the US Joint Chiefs of Staff, told the Senate (20th June 2021) that invasion was a "low-probability" event. Rather, the Chinese have engaged in incursions into Taiwanese airspace – more to intimidate than to invade.

When the US House Speaker, Nancy Pelosi, led a Congressional delegation to Taiwan in August 2022, the Chinese incursions reached a new level of intensity and the response suggested that, if provoked, China would seek to isolate Taiwan rather than engage in a frontal assault. What is also uncertain and undoubtedly dangerous is the significant possibility that China would occupy outlying islands close to the mainland, which would be difficult for Taiwan to defend even with US support. Another option for the Chinese would be to launch cyber attacks which could cripple Taiwanese infrastructure, but avoid the use of armaments. The borderline between peace and war would be intentionally indistinct, to exploit the remaining ambiguity in the US defence guarantee.

A new factor relates to the attempt by the USA to restrict China's technological ambitions by withholding advanced semiconductors and the equipment to manufacture them. One complication, as we have already seen, is that one of the very few manufacturing installations in the world is on Taiwan, and the company involved – TSMC – has a Chinese subsidiary which makes semiconductors for China as well as the USA, and 90% of the world's most advanced semiconductors. The United States has also woken up to its own high level of dependence on a Taiwanese operation and the risk that, were China to become involved in military conflict over Taiwan, a foundry on which both China and the USA – and the world economy – depend is in the middle of a potential battlefield.[25] The USA and the EU are developing their own capacity – which, in Chinese eyes, may make the island less valuable as a strategic asset to defend.

The Ukraine war has brought the risk of a Chinese attack on Taiwan into sharper focus. Had the Russian invasion been successful in meeting little resistance and little effective opposition from the West, this might have been interpreted as a green light for China to complete the business of unification through invasion. However, the invasion was a military disaster, and a combination of Ukrainian morale and good organization allied to Western weapons and severe financial sanctions on Russia have been highly effective in reversing the Russian attack. If the Chinese were planning a frontal attack on Taiwan (as opposed to more subtle tactics like occupying surrounding islands or a naval blockade), they will have had cause to think again. The Ukraine has also revealed a powerful armoury of potential US sanctions, including those affecting the payments system, which would be painful and difficult for China.

The existence of Taiwan as a separate entity is one of the many complicating factors in the set of territorial and maritime disputes in the South China Sea, which is another potential *casus belli* involving China. It was the pre-Communist KMT regime in China that produced the "nine-dash line", which is part of the legal basis for China's claim to the many islands in the South China Sea, hundreds of miles from China and overlapping the exclusive economic zones of other countries in the region. China buttresses the rather flimsy case around the "nine-dash line" with additional arguments for occupancy of the Spratly and Paracel Islands, the Scarborough Shoal and other islets, citing long historical "ownership".[26] There are eight separate disputes, seven involving China and various combinations of five other countries: Brunei, Malaysia, the Philippines, Vietnam and – to the extent that it is separate – Taiwan.[27]

The legal issues are complex, but one question – whether some of the Spratly Islands were habitable (as China claimed) or not (as claimed by the Philippines) was decisively resolved by an international tribunal against China.[28] China has refused to accept the ruling but invokes the Law of the Sea in other respects and continues with a policy (started by Vietnam) of reclaiming land to make the islands usable for military installations. The potential embarrassment to China of being in the legal wrong is offset by the fact that the USA isn't even a signatory of the Law of the Sea Convention (UNCLOS) and does not consider itself bound by international law on the matter.

Behind the legal disputes are matters of economic substance (and military concern where some islets have been converted into military bases). China claims that its territorial and military activities in the South China Sea are explained by a wider economic interest in protecting sea lanes, for the good reason that 80% of its energy imports and a third of the world's maritime trade pass through the South China Sea. There is however an unresolved dispute over the meaning of "innocent passage", and there is patrolling by the US Navy in defence of one version of the principle. And there are real risks of an accidental clash or misunderstanding by warships claiming to protect freedom of passage.

Apart from arguments over passage, there are thought to be large reserves of oil and gas which the neighbouring states, especially China, Vietnam and the Philippines, are trying to exploit. But there are widely different estimates of the scale of the oil fields, and the economic value of offshore exploration is now in some doubt for decarbonizing economies. The appetite, however, is such that China and the Philippines have agreed to a joint exploration in an area whose ownership they dispute. The emphasis on resources reminds us that, so far at least, China's main areas of interest and overseas expansionary activity have been economic rather than military. And the overarching concept which President Xi has used to frame China's overseas economic strategy has been the Belt and Road.

The Belt and Road

The Belt and Road Initiative (BRI) is one of President Xi's distinctive contributions. The phraseology is strange to Western ears, not least because the Road refers to the sea and the Belt to the land. The concept is a reconstruction in modern infrastructure of the Silk Roads, which once served as transport routes for China's trade by sea across the Indian Ocean and by land across the Eurasian land mass.[29] The plan is massive in scale and ambition: huge infrastructure projects in seventy countries to be completed by 2049. Large spending figures have been bandied about, such as $1 trillion over a decade, but actual commitments are elusive.

The BRI could be described as "globalization with Chinese characteristics" – two in particular: the emphasis on infrastructure (the main of five pillars of BRI), reflecting China's particular competence in large scale, rapidly completed infrastructure projects, and the choice of routes indicating priorities dictated by Chinese geography. President Xi felt that the BRI was sufficiently central to his thinking to have it enshrined in the national constitution in 2017.[30]

In order to put the BRI into a global context, the OECD estimates that there will be an estimated $5 trillion global shortfall in infrastructure investment by 2030.[31] Studies evaluating the BRI believe that it could have been getting out annually around $50 billion in loans earlier in the last decade, which is a tenth of the global investment deficit, were it to be sustained. But the programme has been sharply reined back in the face of borrowers' debt-servicing problems, implementation problems and the prioritization of domestic projects.[32] There is now a tilt to a "Digital Silk Road" and a "Health Silk Road", which do not involve the same heavy spending.

Nonetheless, some of the BRI landmark projects are already close to realization or have been completed.[33] Around 15,000 trains a year have been expected to take goods to and from China all the way to and from Duisburg in Germany (more quickly but more expensively than by sea). But its routing via Russia has become problematic after the Ukraine War. The China–Pakistan Economic Corridor, the biggest BRI project, has been mired in controversy in Pakistan, but nonetheless already incorporates a land route to the Chinese-built port of Gwadar. There is a road from Kunming in China to Bangkok. The Chinese-built Greek port of Piraeus is well on the way to becoming the leading Mediterranean container hub. New railways run from Djibouti to Addis Ababa and from

Mombasa to Nairobi. Other big projects, such as the railway line from China to Singapore, or roads and rail through Myanmar to the coast, have made some progress in construction, but are stalled for political reasons. As a result of BRI, there is now a considerable network of pipelines, roads and railways, ports, power grids and factories.

The projects are financed through loans, mainly through two Chinese state banks (the China Development Bank and the Export–Import Bank). This is not "free money" – indeed, the cost of debt service can be problematic for borrowers. But for recipients it has provided access to large-scale funding which might otherwise not be available for projects considered too ambitious or risky by more conservative lenders. The main Western aid agencies now do very little lending for physical infrastructure, and the alternative is expensive private funding. The Chinese are also at great pains to point out that there are no "geopolitical" strings attached (though some recipients, like Pakistan, appear to have accepted such linkage). The loans, furthermore, are free from the explicit conditionality now associated with the World Bank and other official funders – including uncomfortable demands around "governance" or "environmental-impact assessment". And being public-sector-led, the BRI does not involve having to fall back on US-style trade and investment agreements to protect private property, which are politically difficult in some countries. Not least, OECD norms, and US/UK legislation, around overseas corruption are not applied.

One of the positive by-products of the BRI has been the establishment of the Asian Infrastructure Investment Bank: AIIB. It has long been a source of frustration for the Chinese that their attempts to play a major role in the leading multilateral economic institutions, commensurate with their economic weight, were frustrated by being confined to a much smaller shareholding than the USA (in the World Bank and IMF) and Japan (in the Asian Development Bank). So, China decided to set up a development bank of its own. It promoted the AIIB, seemingly in competition with the World Bank and the Japanese-led Asian Development Bank and facing strong opposition by the USA.

Perhaps to China's own surprise, some Western countries, led by the UK, joined from the outset, and Asian countries not particularly well disposed to China have also joined: India, Australia and South Korea. The AIIB does not see itself as Chinese, let alone as a BRI bank, and, so far, it has operated in a genuinely multilateral spirit, with operational independence and good standards of governance (in fact, its disbursements under BRI projects are probably no more than $2 billion a year).

It is clear, however, that the Chinese motives behind BRI have been more complex and less disinterested than simply enhancing development and connectivity.[34] The USA was hostile from the outset, seeing the BRI (and the AIIB) as a direct challenge to its own influence in Asia. Despite denials from Beijing, there clearly was a geopolitical rationale: locking in relationships of dependence with weaker states which could give political support when needed; supporting infrastructure with military potential, as in Djibouti, Pakistan and Sri Lanka; seeking diversity in energy supplies, notably from Central Asia rather than the Middle East. Intensive development along the routes to Central Asia and the various transport hubs along the way were also seen as helping to bind remote and troubled areas like Xinjiang more closely to China.

There was also an economic logic to this: investment and export opportunities for Chinese firms and banks; creating a market for products with surplus capacity such as steel; stimulating development in China's poorer regions; boosting the use of renminbi for settling transactions; improving access to diverse supplies of raw materials. Cynics would see similarities with nineteenth-century imperialism, about which Lenin and Hobson wrote. The most obvious parallels are the hunt for markets that can absorb spare industrial capacity left by the under-consumption of capitalist economies, the domination of weak but resource-rich countries to guarantee supplies of raw materials, the building of infrastructure to reinforce patterns of dependence and exploitative returns on capital.[35] Such cynicism has been well aired in some recipient countries.

The starting point in any evaluation of the BRI is to note the extreme vagueness of its objectives and the opaqueness of its procedures.[36] The Chinese do not themselves appear to monitor progress systematically; projects are not appraised ex-ante or ex-post in the manner of most development agencies; there are no clear or consistent procedures for procurement and bidding. The BRI covers projects that started before the BRI launch and excludes some conspicuous failures within it. The number of countries considered to be involved varies greatly from around sixty to over twice that number. One consistent theme is that there have been some seriously bad projects which have left the borrowing countries with "white elephants" and a legacy of debt – and the Chinese lending institutions with bad debt to write off: on one estimate, $100 billion (out of flows of somewhere between $50–100 billion a year).[37]

Legacy debt has proved to be a major problem. Of 68 countries thought to have received BRI money in one major US study, 23 were debt-distressed – and that was in 2018, before the pandemic aggravated the problem of debt.[38] Six of the top recipients of Chinese development finance in the period 2013–15 were considered high-risk borrowers (Venezuela, Pakistan, Argentina, Ethiopia, Sudan, Zimbabwe), as against only two large borrowers from the World Bank, while the overall loan portfolio was 20% riskier than for the World Bank.[39] Furthermore, China is not a member of the Paris Club, which has a procedure for negotiating debt relief (though it joined the G20 moratorium on debt service – DSSI – in 2020.). Some critics have suggested that China is deliberately trying to trap countries into debt, though a Brookings survey concluded: "We find it hard to find evidence of debt-trap diplomacy."[40] A Chatham House study also came to the conclusion that the "debt trap" was a myth.[41] Indeed, borrowers have become more skilled at negotiating better terms or renegotiating, much as they have with Western lenders. There are some accounts of Chinese lenders being tough with defaulting debtors by, inter alia, seizing their assets, but research has suggested that there is, in fact, a lot of debt relief: $5.7 billion by 2022 as against

$4.5 billion under the Paris Club.[42] Some research has suggested that much of the debt is under-reported and far larger than generally believed, with forty countries having Chinese debt amounting to over 10% of GDP.[43] The Chinese response to growing debt-service problems has been similar to Western creditors: rescheduling together with a cut-back in new loans.

Debt burdens are one reason why political reaction in some host countries has turned sour. Democratic elections have brought to power governments which campaigned against BRI projects while in opposition and are more hostile than their predecessors: Malaysia, Myanmar, Sri Lanka, Pakistan and the Maldives, for example. In Malaysia, Mahathir Mohamad called BRI "a new version of colonialism", but he was later, in office, more supportive. Other countries reverted to more pro-Chinese sentiment, or have entangled China in complex local power struggles – including, as in Pakistan, Myanmar, Sri Lanka and Thailand, the relations between civilian parties and the armed forces. American spokesmen like Mike Pompeo used these negative experiences to warn off other countries from the BRI.[44] There is however, now, a recognition by the Biden administration that it is pointless and probably counterproductive to criticize the BRI if there is no Western offer to compete with it. It has therefore launched an alternative to BRI: Build Back a Better World (B3W). The EU has put forward an EU Global Gateway with similar aims. It is not clear yet how either will be implemented and financed – indeed, if they will even get off the ground and provide new money. There is, moreover, one part of the world where BRI is still expanding and is, broadly, well received: Africa.

China's love affair with Africa

China's large-scale involvement in Africa preceded the BRI and reflects twenty years of coordinated effort. Indeed, over a decade ago, there was already a lively controversy over the motives and impacts of rapidly growing trade, investment, labour flows and political linkages with Africa.[45] Was China a development partner, competitor or colonizer?[46] Since then, there has been a steady build-up of trade, investment, aid and migrant labour. Trade data is not easily interpreted, since the values of African exports reflect fluctuating commodity prices, especially oil, and since export and import data don't fully match. But with about 13% of overall trade by value (2019), China is now Africa's largest trade partner. It runs a significant surplus (around $110 billions of exports as against $80 billion imported). Nigeria is the biggest market (mainly manufactures), and Angola the biggest exporter (oil).[47] By comparison, US trade with Africa is around a fifth of Chinese trade by value.

The Chinese economic footprint is deeper than for trade alone.[48] Crucially, China has financed through its leading banks a surge in big infrastructure projects. China accounted for more than 30% of projects worth over $50 million in 2020 up from 13% in 2013, with the Western share shrinking from 37% to 12% in that time.[49] Over the period 2007–20 Chinese banks had funded $23 billion of development projects in Africa as against $9 billion from all other sources.[50] China became the "lender of first resort".[51]

Annual direct investment fluctuates, but has been consistently around $3 billion in recent years, and there appear to be around 10,000 Chinese companies active in Africa, with hundreds of billions of assets. China's aid flows are almost certainly now larger than from France, the other major donor, having risen rapidly to $3 billion in 2015 and, after a dip, continued at that level: $3.1 billion in 2019. China has attractions as an aid donor, making less onerous demands around "governance" and social and environmental impact.[52] The French in particular have appreciated the popularity of Chinese projects and are actively collaborating. Overall, Africa accounts for 45% of Chinese aid, though the definitions do not fully correspond to those of the OECD and the boundaries between aid and state banks' commercial lending is unclear (annual lending peaked at just under $30 billion in 2016 and fell back to $7.6 billion in 2019.[53] Much of Chinese aid and bank lending has gone into physical infrastructure: electricity, telecommunications and transport. And there are bodies on the ground: around 185,000 Chinese workers on construction sites, in factories and plantations (albeit down from 250,000 in 2015). There were also 80,000 African students at Chinese universities in 2019, the second-largest number after France.

A political framework unifies these economic and social interactions: FOCAC – the Forum on China–Africa Cooperation, comprising more than fifty countries – supported by regular high-level visits and political initiatives around Covid and suspended debt service (albeit that a financing pledge has been cut by a third, reflecting difficulties over debt servicing). It is a measure of Chinese political influence that only three small African countries out of 56 continue to recognize Taiwan (Burkina Faso, São Tomé and Swaziland). Some commentators have argued that the economic ties are less important than the political – that China's objective is the building of alliances and social networks which will help it claim its rightful place in the international system.[54] But, inexorably, China is being drawn into local conflicts – it has several thousand troops in Africa, mostly in peacekeeping missions – and it has been faced with the need to protect thousands of its nationals in conflict zones, as happened in Libya, when almost 40,000 Chinese had to be evacuated, and, more recently, in Sudan. China has made a major commercial and political commitment to Ethiopia, now beset by civil war.

If goodwill and influence are the aim, China is by no means getting all its own way. There is a vigorous debate between what are called the "Panda Huggers" and the "Dragon Slayers". Parts of the Chinese narrative are appealing: a shared experience of exploitative Western powers; "south-to-south" trade; opportunities for "win-win"; "non-interference" and respect for national "sovereignty".[55] Pew surveys of public opinion suggest that Africans regard China positively: 70% in Nigeria versus 17% unfavourable; 58% favourable in Kenya versus 25%; 46% versus 35% in South Africa.[56] Only in Russia does China enjoy such esteem. But there has been serious friction over Chinese workers displacing locals and being seen as colonial settlers;[57] bad behaviour by Chinese companies; Chinese import competition (in Nigeria); political interference (in Zambia in 2012, for example); the propping up of unpopular dictators (Sudan, Zimbabwe); and the creation of patterns of trade and investment characterized as "neocolonial". So far China appears, on balance, to be winning the argument that it is a positive force rather than predatory and neocolonial, but the reality is complex and multilayered.

So, what general lessons can be learnt about China's twenty years of deep involvement in Africa? First, China is clearly taking a global, not a regional, view rewarded with political alliances among the 56 countries in the continent which will support it in global fora. The political dimension has grown under Xi.[58] Secondly, it is taking a long-term strategic view that Africa will grow in importance based on its demography – an expanding and young population – with growing commercial opportunities presented by its rapid urbanization and expanding middle class. This is a different calculation from the pessimism about Africa across much of the Western world and the disinvestment by Western companies. But in one key sense Africa matters for the same reason that it has long mattered to Western governments and companies: its wealth of resources.

The growth of resource dependency and diplomacy

China's involvement with Africa can be seen as part of a bigger picture of dependency for growth on imported raw materials, oil and metals especially. Levi and Economy trace much of China's behaviour in Africa, Latin America and the Middle East, as well as Central and South-East Asia, to this vulnerability, and the need to minimize it.[59] The key commodity is oil. Seventy-five per cent of China's crude oil is imported, because production – 4.9 million barrels per day in 2019 – has fallen in recent years, whilst consumption – 14.5 million barrels per day in 2019 – has risen rapidly with economic growth. With imports of 10.1 million barrels per day in 2019 and 10.9 million barrels per day in 2020, China is by far the world's largest oil importer (23% of world imports in 2019; 13% for the USA; 10% India; 7% Japan).[60] In an environment of oversupply and weak prices, this dependence may not seem problematic, but market conditions could change significantly, as they have in the past. There is also the wider energy-policy context. Oil is only 20% of China's total energy consumption, and gas 8%. Coal dominates the power mix, with 58%.[61] Coal does not pose major problems of supply, but it is central to China's energy generation and creates problems of pollution and greenhouse-gas emissions. Now that China is taking its excessive energy use and carbon emissions more seriously, there is an incentive to utilize less carbon-intensive fuels, notably natural gas.

While there remains a major dependency on oil and gas imports, the Chinese response has been to diversify sources and to use BRI and other tools of "soft" diplomacy to maintain good, or at least stable, relations with the main suppliers. In 2019 the main suppliers of crude were Saudi Arabia (16%), Russia (15.5%) and Iraq (13.5%), but with significant amounts from Angola, Brazil, Oman, Kuwait, the UAE, Iran, Congo (Brazzaville), Libya and Venezuela. There is a similar dependence on imports of natural gas: two thirds as liquefied natural gas (LNG), mainly from Australia, and the rest as pipeline gas from Central Asia, especially Turkmenistan.

A Middle East Player

The dependence on the Middle East for around half the total of oil imports has drawn China into the region's politics and complex security issues. Given the reality of Saudi Arabia's close relations with the USA, especially in arms supply, it is difficult to see how relations with China could be more than transactional and based around oil sales. There is however a more secretive dimension. It is believed that, in the mid-1980s, the Saudis sought and obtained from China medium-range ballistic missiles to match the armoury of Iraq and Israel. The USA refused to supply them, and subsequently demanded withdrawal of the Chinese substitutes, but the Saudis refused to comply. Their continuing relevance is captured in reports that there may be a rocket-engine facility in Saudi supplied by China, and parallel reports that China is helping Saudi Arabia enrich uranium: both stories hinting at China helping Saudi Arabia keep open the option of nuclear weapons.[62]

A less secret piece of relationship-building came in 2016 with the announcement of a "comprehensive partnership". China rather than the USA is now Saudi Arabia's main customer for oil, and China is the biggest supplier of advanced technology, with Huawei's 5G network being used in the new city of Neom, a pet project of the Crown Prince. China also supplied advanced drones and has none of the conditionality attached to such products by the West. The policy of mutual non-interference was underlined in 2019 with a visit of Crown Prince Mohammed bin Salman to Beijing, during which he conspicuously declined to criticize the treatment of Muslims in Xinjiang and the Chinese omitted to mention the killing of the Saudi journalist Jamal Khashoggi. As a follow-up to the visit, China has assisted in dealing with the Covid outbreak. Relations are expected to improve further as the Saudis hedge against a distancing by their traditional ally, the USA. Quite how far the Saudis would go in their hedging became apparent when in the aftermath of the Russian invasion of Ukraine the Saudis announced their intention to accept renminbi payments for their oil instead of dollars.

Other Gulf states, like the UAE, Oman and Bahrain have developed closer relations with China for similar reasons. Iraq has also welcomed large-scale Chinese investments. The Chinese have not only managed to cultivate their main oil suppliers: their diplomacy has allowed them simultaneously to embark on an ambitious "twenty-five-year partnership" with neighbouring Iran. In this way, China achieves more energy security for itself and provides an escape route for

Iranian oil from US sanctions. The United States is reported to be threatening retribution in respect of this breach of its Iran sanctions, which could bring it into direct conflict with China. And to underline the seriousness of the Iran partnership, there were joint military exercises in the Indian Ocean with Iranian and Russian warships. But what is remarkable is that China has managed to maintain business-like relations with Saudi Arabia and the Gulf states while working closely with Iran (it has good relations with Israel too, although the USA has put pressure on Israel to block Chinese investment in infrastructure and security-related industries). The culmination of China's Middle East diplomacy has been mediation between Saudi Arabia and Iran to produce a formal agreement which stabilizes their fraught bilateral relationship. Western sceptics doubt that the agreement has much depth, but nonetheless the optics of the negotiation and agreement boosted China's aspiration to be a force in global diplomacy under President Xi's Global Security Initiative.

Resource diplomacy and Latin America

Another region where China has managed, so far, to secure good relations with major commodity suppliers and to build political influence is Latin America. Latin America is a significant supplier of oil (Brazil, Venezuela), metals (Brazil, Peru and Chile) and foodstuffs (Argentina, Brazil), and a substantial market for Chinese manufactures. Bilateral trade has soared from $12 billion in 2010 to $495 billion in 2022, and now accounts for 18% of Latin American trade. China is now the largest or second-largest trade partner for nearly all countries in the region. Brazil now has twice the value of trade with China ($100 billion in 2019) as with the United States, and Brazil accounts for half of all Chinese investment in the region. China also gave Brazil an opportunity to play a global role in the BRICS group of emerging countries (Brazil, Russia, India, China and South Africa), challenging the established international order dominated by the USA.[63] The economic relationship is not straightforward, however: while Brazilian farmers and miners welcome access to the China market, manufacturers – as in the rest of Latin America – struggle to compete with Chinese products, and have been demanding anti-dumping action. Overall, however, export interests dominate – China accounts for 30% of Brazil's physical exports (up from 20% five years ago): soya beans, beef, crude oil and iron ore. When China wanted to show displeasure with the Brazilian government, there was a two-month ban on beef imports to China.

The displeasure owed a lot to the idiosyncratic politics of President Bolsonaro, a populist who has followed President Trump in being highly critical of China, especially over Covid. His supporters denounced his own more pragmatic ministers as "secret Communists".[64] Bolsonaro was however a temporary departure from the norm of amicable relations with China, and President Lula has restored the earlier goodwill. China is also well regarded in Brazil, with 51% of Brazilians having a favourable view and 27% unfavourable (before the Covid pandemic). The balance of opinion is similar elsewhere: 50% to 22% in Mexico; 47% to 24% in Argentina.

China's involvement in Argentina also hints at a strategic as well as purely commercial interest. There is an advanced space-tracking telescope. China also loudly supports Argentina's claim to the Malvinas/Falklands. Were Britain to become seriously annoying in the Asia-Pacific region, China could bolster Argentina's military capacity threatening the islands. There is also a strategic interest in Communist Cuba, where China has a signals monitoring station which alarms the Americans (although the Americans have several of their own around China).

The wider Latin American connections have been reinforced by bank lending, Covid-vaccine diplomacy and BRI projects which are available to twenty countries in the region. This engagement has occasionally backfired. Venezuela, despite large credits from China – an estimated £67 billion since 2007 – has become a failed state from which China cannot obtain oil in any volume. Venezuela is also a serious credit risk for Chinese banks, which have almost half their loan exposure in Latin America put in jeopardy and are unlikely to see much by way of repayment. It is being suggested that China is seeking to disengage from a "lose-lose" commitment. Venezuela is however a small part of a much bigger economic and political picture. The picture has, moreover, changed with the growing importance of key metals like lithium, which are abundant in Chile and Argentina, where Chinese companies are active.

As in Africa and the Middle East, China has won a lot of friends by sticking to business rather than moralizing about human rights and democracy. A Chinese virtual summit of Latin American and Caribbean leaders in December 2021 concluded with a three-year action plan; by contrast a 2022 Summit of the Americas in Los Angeles revealed deep disagreements between the USA and, among others, Mexico and Argentina. The United States has also shown no inclination to compete with China in providing BRI-type finance or offering more liberal access to the US market.

Russia: a "friendship without limits"

The Ukraine war has cast a big shadow over international relations and the world economy. It has posed an exceptional challenge to China, which had just concluded a major and comprehensive agreement with Russia, amid protestations of undying friendship, with strong personal commitment from Presidents Xi and Putin. The Russian leader does not however appear to have tipped off the Chinese about the invasion, and China has since been improvising a response which reflects its substantial commercial interests in both countries as well as the wider geopolitical picture. There is officially declared neutrality in voting in the UN, rhetorical support for Russia's arguments (and in particular the complaint about NATO expansion) and a great deal of care to avoid being caught in Western sanctions.

The earlier history of relations between China and Russia (and the USSR) has been dominated by geopolitics and security issues: Mao's early dealings with Stalin; Soviet support for the Communist revolution; tacit understanding over the Korean War; cooperation with, then alienation from, the USSR, leading to China's "Nixon moment"; a border war and a proxy war in Indochina; China's alarm over Gorbachev's "folly". Economics didn't come into it but have played an increasingly important role.

Economically, there is a neat fit. Even before the war and Russia's need to secure oil sales with Western markets closing, Russia's struggling economy depended heavily on exports of oil and gas to generate tax revenue and foreign-exchange earnings. China has been anxious to reduce its dependence on imports of oil from the Middle East (and gas from Australia). Russia was close to displacing Saudi Arabia as China's main source of imported oil. If current plans come to fruition, Gazprom could triple gas exports to China and meet half of China's gas demand – and that objective has acquired a real urgency, from the Russian side, with the EU seeking to minimize its dependence on Russia.

The long-term mutuality of economic interests is clear. China is willing and able to develop physical infrastructure as part of the BRI; Russia needs help to finance and construct the infrastructure to fulfil its commitment to realize the single market of the Eurasian Economic Union (Russia, Belarus, Kazakhstan, Armenia, Kyrgyzstan). China is now a major partner in developing the Yamal LNG facility and the SIBUR petrochemical complex in the Russian Far East. The main constraint is not money or willingness on the Chinese side, but the inefficiency and corruption which characterize big projects in Russia. There are however reports that China has dragged its heels over the terms of a gas pipeline from Yamal to China which Russia is desperate to build as a new source of export revenue. Despite personal appeals from President Putin, the project has been stalled, which may suggest that Xi is anxious not to be too close to Putin, or that China is using its greater leverage to squeeze better terms from the Russians.

There is, indeed, an awkward imbalance: this is not a marriage of equals.[65] China's economy is six times bigger ($24 trillion to $4 trillion GDP on a PPP basis, on IMF 2020 data). Russia's trade with China, $110 billion in 2019, accounted for 15% of its total trade (the EU accounted for 35%), but is less than 1% of China's. There is an opposite imbalance in military terms, with Russia having a vast arsenal of nuclear weapons and providing 70% of China's imports of arms by value, its only export to China of any significance apart from oil and gas. The war has increased Russia's dependence on China. It has also opened new opportunities for Chinese firms in the field of telecommunications, where there is no longer any Western competition to Huawei or ZHE, and in the energy sector, where Chinese firms are well placed to acquire the assets of Western oil and gas companies as they disengage from Russia.

Despite the imbalances, the mood music around the relationship has been increasingly positive. There have been joint military exercises. China and Russia have supported each other politically in areas of contention with the USA, such as Syria, Iran and Venezuela, and in international fora, notably the UN. Long-standing suspicions in Russia of potential Chinese migration over the Asian frontiers and underlying racial and cultural prejudices seem to have been eased. Before the pandemic, two million Chinese visited Russia in 2019 as tourists. The Pew surveys of public opinion showed that China had the highest favourability rating in the world in Russia (71% against 18% negative). When Russia closed its borders to Chinese in the early stages of the pandemic and there were reports of attacks on ethnic Chinese, the Chinese authorities did not react (in contrast to, say, the Chinese response to smaller irritants from Australia).

Even before the Ukraine war, it was difficult to see how Russia could be co-opted to the Western side. President Biden's meeting with Putin in Geneva on 16th June 2021 was interpreted as the first step in normalizing US relations with Russia, with the long-term objective of weakening the Russia–China axis, but that prospect has disappeared now. It is possible, however, that relations between Russia and China could sour. They have before. One factor could be competition with Russia for influence and power in Central Asia.[66] BRI projects have already established close links with the Central Asian "stans", several of which are now highly dependent on China for their economic development.[67] The Russians are unlikely to look well on a takeover of their Eurasian Economic Union by Chinese business. Another potential source of friction is Russia's supply of weapons to countries China considers unfriendly, such as India and Vietnam.

China has tried to unify the various interests in the region by putting in place a regional group – the Shanghai Cooperation Organization, comprising China, Russia and all of the five "stans" but one (Turkmenistan) – and recently opening to India and Pakistan. The focus is partly on economic cooperation, but also on the "three evils" of "terrorism, separatism and religious extremism". Given the disparate nature of the membership, especially now that China and India both belong, it is difficult to see the group serving an operational purpose. But it is a signal of China's attempt to establish networks in Central Asia which do not include the United States. And it is the US involvement which is central to the balance of forces in East Asia.

Multidimensional chess: China, Japan and the Koreas

The relationships in East Asia entailing China, Japan and the Koreas, together with the USA, involve serious complexity because of the interplay of economic interests, military security, territorial disputes and the history of conflict and past hatreds. There are also the problems created by the division of the Korean peninsula and the rogue state in the north.

In relation to Japan, the intensity of mutual ill feeling at a popular level is unmatched anywhere. Earlier in the decade, a survey suggested that 3% of Japanese had a favourable view of China and 73% negative, with 5% of Chinese having a favourable view of Japan and 90% negative.[68] While the rest of the world has cooled on China since, Pew surveys suggest that the opposite has happened in Japan, albeit negative ratings are still higher than in the rest of the world.[69] One factor helping improve perceptions was a strong programme of reciprocal support over the pandemic.

History plays a big part in explaining the pervasive fear and loathing. In Chinese histories, Japan played an especially ignominious role in exploiting Chinese weakness during the "century of humiliation".[70] There then followed the occupation of Manchuria and the atrocities of the Second World War, culminating in the Rape of Nanking. Lest any Chinese forget, there is a steady diet of war films on Chinese TV mostly featuring Japan as the enemy. Japanese leaders have added fuel to the fire by paying homage to people regarded in China as war criminals – and these events, in turn, have provoked anti-Japanese riots, probably encouraged by the authorities.

Remarkably, both countries have managed to compartmentalize economic issues and have built up substantial levels of interdependence. A key step forward was Deng's decision to make a visit to Japan – the first visit by any Chinese leader to Japan in recorded history – to solicit investment and development assistance.[71] Mutual trade grew from $1 billion a year before the rapprochement to around $320 billion today, accounting for 20% of Japanese trade and making China Japan's biggest trade partner. Japan also benefits from having 8.4 million Chinese tourists (the year before the pandemic) and 115,000 Chinese students. These are, after all, the biggest and third-biggest economies in the world – and, given their proximity, it would be surprising if there were not close integration.

Enthusiasm for mutual trade has also grown in the wake of Trump's tariff war with China, which was accompanied by tariffs on Japan. Indeed, there are echoes of the era before 1990, when Japan was regarded as an up-and-coming economic superpower and a threat to the dominance of the USA.[72] China's development trajectory in many ways follows that of Japan, with similar resistance from the USA and similar accusations of IP theft. Commonality of interest and experience lies behind Japan's decision to join the RCEP trading grouping, which includes China and excludes the USA. Even then, without decoupling the economies, Japan has been getting increasingly alarmed at the way it is falling behind China in digital innovation and AI especially, and we can expect to see some attempts to reassert Japanese independence of China in advanced technology.

The relationship looks different outside the compartment of economics.[73] There is the festering dispute over some barren islands remote from the Japanese archipelago occupied by Japan and claimed by China, the Senkaku Islands. The countries have come close to war over this issue and, were China to attack, Japan would be unable to defend those territories. It has turned to the USA to extend its current security guarantee from the mainland to the islands, and one of the first acts of the Biden administration has been to agree to the extension. More generally, there is a growing fear of Chinese power and what the Japanese see as Chinese over-confidence and its dangerous dependence on one man: a contrast with Japan's more collective leadership. There was, for a while, interest in partnering with Russia against China, but the Ukraine war has killed that idea. A more fundamental change has been a greater emphasis on stronger armed forces and military alliances. Japan has been more openly supportive of Taiwan. Japan is a key member of the Quad, comprising the USA, Japan, India and Australia – which, despite denials, represents the kernel of a future defence pact. A key step, in December 2022, was the launch of Japan's new security strategy, which significantly boosts defence spending, including the purchase of US cruise missiles which can reach China, strengthens military cooperation with Australia and regional allies as well as the USA and explicitly designates China as Japan's "greatest strategic challenge".

It has required considerable skill on both the Chinese and Japanese sides to maintain good working relationships and close economic ties in an environment of security threats and mutual public hostility. So far, and particularly in the long premiership of Mr Abe, this was achieved. But there are some major destabilizing factors. One is the fact that Japan has a self-denying policy of not using its undoubted technical ability to acquire nuclear weapons. Were Japan to feel seriously threatened, that could change, especially if the USA were to withdraw its support and protection. One of the threats could come from another source of instability: Korea.

The legacy of the Korean War seventy years ago, Korea is a peninsula divided between the Communist North, one of the world's most unstable and unpredictable regimes and an ally of China, and the South, which hosts US bases, enjoys US protection and has evolved, like Taiwan, into a robust parliamentary democracy.[74] Despite the military alignments and clash of values and systems (and memories of China's role in the Korean War), relations between China and South Korea are reasonably good. South Korea relies on China to restrain the North. As with Japan, leading Korean companies do good business in China, and China accounts for 25% of Korea's exports – by far its largest market. China has also worked hard to develop good neighbourly relations, which critics see as an attempt to weaken American alliances in Asia, with South Korea as the weak link.[75]

South Korea has also learnt that there is a price to be paid for antagonizing China, as it did when it installed a US THAAD missile screen in 2016. The original aim was to protect South Korea against a strike from the North, but the Chinese saw it as a hostile move towards them, because the radar would supposedly facilitate spying on China. There was a boycott of South Korea by Chinese tourists and of Korean stores in China. The economic damage was considerable – an estimated cost to Korea of $7 billion – and a year later the Koreans (under a new president) capitulated and accepted Chinese conditions for the shield. The Koreans learnt that they have to perform a delicate balancing act. They have steered clear of any suggestions to create an "Asian NATO" – though they have attended NATO meetings in Europe to signal an understanding of alliance-building with the West. They have declined the opportunity to join the Quad.

A further complicating factor is the very poor relations between South Korea and Japan, which are easily excited by memories of wartime atrocities, and which are proving especially difficult to manage between two democracies where public opinion counts. Public-opinion surveys suggest that Japan is even less popular in South Korea than China or North Korea. The South Korean balancing act could become even more difficult if the North Korean regime were to do something provocative, or if the United States were to demand more commitment from its allies to form a common front against China.[76] But as of now, the various pressures on South Korea illustrate the complexities involved in its approach to China – something we see throughout the region. A common thread, however, is that whatever the distaste or fear of China, there is a high level of interdependence with the Chinese economy which will not be surrendered easily.

South-East Asia's rainbow coalition

One of the very few success stories in regional integration is the progress south-east of the ASEAN group, bringing together the very disparate countries of Asia. Like the European Union, but unlike regional groupings in Latin America, Africa, the Arab world and South Asia, the grouping – which now counts ten countries – has survived for over half a century. Its achievements in economic and political integration are relatively modest compared to Europe, but it has managed to accommodate states of very different size, history and governance, from the nominally Communist regimes of Vietnam and Laos to the military governments of Thailand and Myanmar to the full democracies of Malaysia and Indonesia.

They have all had to respond to the growing influence of China, balancing the economic opportunities, and in particular BRI projects, against the politics of ideology and identity and against perceived or real threats to sovereignty, as in the South China Sea. What has emerged is a disparate spread of responses, ranging from high levels of dependence on China – in Laos and Cambodia – to the robustly hostile in Vietnam and a range in between, with some leaning to China (Thailand and Myanmar) and others towards the USA (Singapore and the Philippines), with Indonesia and Malaysia maintaining a delicate balance. The gradations of this "rainbow coalition" are worth some elaboration.

Vietnam is an improbable ally of the USA but is shaping up to be the mainstay of a tacit alliance – improbable because Vietnam is a former adversary in war with the USA, and one of the few solid allies of the former USSR. More recently, Vietnam was dismissed by President Trump in his trade wars as "the single worst abuser of everybody".[77] Vietnam is unapologetic about one-party rule under the Communist Party, and its approach to "human rights" mirrors that of China. But Vietnam has a long history of standing up to its bigger and more powerful northern neighbour, most recently in armed conflict in 1978, when the Chinese PLA retreated with heavy losses and a battered military reputation.

Vietnam has been involved in several violent incidents with China on disputed islands and reefs in the South China Sea and has been as assertive as China in establishing a physical presence on those that it claims. Its long coastline also means that it has more at stake than its neighbours. And it has offered the use of its ports to foreign – that is US – naval vessels while stopping short of accepting foreign bases and formal alliances. Recently it decided, like Singapore, to reject Huawei 5G technology, and it is developing its own system through a state-owned firm – Viettel – in partnership with Ericsson. The regime's show of independence from China is supported by public opinion. Asked a hypothetical question as to which side they would choose in a showdown between the USA and China, 85% chose the USA, as against a regional median of 54%.[78]

Another improbable US ally is Singapore – improbable because until recently Singapore was seen to have a special relationship with China, on account of the close personal ties between the founder and leader of modern Singapore, Lee Kuan Yew, and Chinese leaders. Lee visited China an estimated thirty-three times, dispensing advice to Deng and Jiang. Chinese ethnicity was another common factor. But more recently there have been strong disagreements over China's proprietorial approach to the Malacca Straits. Singapore, unlike its neighbours, sees China's more advanced economy as competing rather than complementary, eroding Singapore's competitive advantage as a supplier of sophisticated electronics. In addition, its role as a regional entrepôt centre, offering marine refuelling facilities, is now in competition with Chinese ports. Singapore is a small state, but with formidable defences, including US-supplied advanced fighter jets (F-35s) and submarines. It now sees itself as a "US ally", and by the Chinese as no longer "special".[79]

Traditional US allies like the Philippines seemed to have drifted away under President Duarte, despite a bitter dispute with China over the South China Sea, which the Philippines call the "West Philippines Sea". Duarte chose to downplay the Philippines' big legal victory over their territorial rights, calling the ruling a "piece of trash paper with four corners", and instead actively cultivated President Xi and embraced the BRI. Some analysts saw more subtle readjustments, with traditional strong US defence cooperation in the background.[80] And there is some resentment in the country at the presence of as many as 500,000 Chinese, mainly in Manila, involved in the online-gambling industry. Nor has the BRI delivered much, with only a tiny fraction of the promised investment materializing. And the public has shown more confidence in Western ways, as most recently with Covid vaccines. President Duarte threatened to suspend the Visiting Forces Agreement with the USA and blocked the deployment of US troops to two airbases close to the South China Sea. His own political investment in China and his antipathy to the USA meant that the Philippines remained in the Chinese column while he stayed in power. His immediate successor, "Bongbong" Marcos, son of the late, corrupt and repressive, President Ferdinand Marcos, and his running mate, Sara Duterte, daughter of the outgoing president, initially signalled their preference for close engagement with China. But subsequently President Marcos lifted restrictions on the use of four military bases which have been in place for thirty years (there are ten bases altogether, owned or to which it has access). The opening was followed by joint military exercises. Nonetheless, the Philippines government has to tread carefully on this tilt to the USA, since there is strong nationalist sentiment in the country.

Some subtlety can be detected in the positioning of Indonesia. It also has long had close relations with the USA, though these frayed after Trump's trade wars and the American Muslim ban. The government has also accepted offers of large-scale Chinese assistance to build its infrastructure, and has welcomed Huawei to develop its government cyber-security operations. One complication is a territorial dispute over waters rich in natural-gas reserves, claimed by China and by Indonesia. There is also a long-standing anti-Chinese xenophobic sentiment, which peaked with the massacres that followed a failed Communist coup is 1967 and has recently resurfaced thanks to conspiracy theories around Covid and Chinese migrants. A particular manifestation of Muslim anti-Chinese feeling was the imprisonment of the popular Christian-Chinese Governor of Jakarta, Basuki Tjahaja, on trumped-up charges of blasphemy. President Joko Widodo has become a major player in the region and in the G20. He is maintaining neutrality between the US and China, and is careful not to criticize China publicly.

The interplay of economic, ethnic and territorial issues which complicate China's relationship with Indonesia also apply to Malaysia. The Chinese minority, many of whom were heavily involved in Communist uprisings in the 1950s and '60s, has long been regarded with suspicion by the dominant Malay parties. Arguments about the South China Sea also reinforced negative perceptions of China, as elsewhere in the region. But BRI and economic interests generally have changed the balance of opinion.[81] Malaysia has around 20% of its trade with China, and Chinese companies are the largest source of investment.

The administration of Prime Minister Najib committed itself to large BRI projects, but was then discredited by evidence of large-scale corruption, some associated with Chinese projects. Najib's successor, the veteran Mahathir Mohamad, repudiated this "new version of colonialism" and undertook to reduce Chinese influence. In practice, the biggest Chinese project – the East Coast Rail Link – has been renegotiated and reinstated, and even the combative Mr Mahathir pulled his punches in criticizing China. Significantly, he failed to express solidarity with Uyghur Muslims, preferring to attack India over Kashmir. Malaysia's prolonged political instability is however preventing the emergence of a consensus around China policy and much else.

There is less equivocation in Thailand, where the traditional alliance with the USA, built up during the war against Communism in Indochina, has seemingly died out. By contrast, the military, who dominate Thai politics, and their allies in the conservative forces around the monarchy, aligned themselves strongly with China.[82] China supplied substantial weaponry to the armed forces, especially the navy, and has access to base facilities on the coast. A railway line now connects China to Bangkok, and other communications systems are linked to China, as with the acceptance of Huawei 5G and the use of Chinese technology for Internet controls and surveillance systems.[83] The election in 2023 which brought to power a reform-minded democrat may now change the balance.

The stability of China's new friendships is not totally secure, as illustrated by the ups and downs in relations with military and civilian governments in Myanmar. For centuries, Burmese rulers were dominated by China, creating a relationship characterized by both dependence and resentment.[84] In recent decades, the long isolation of Myanmar under military rule led to a high level of Chinese economic and political influence in the country. But there was simmering anti-Chinese feeling under the surface, which broke through in riots in 2011. The military regime at the time chose to ride the tiger of Burmese nationalism, accused the Chinese of fomenting rebellion on the peripheries and cancelled big projects, including a large dam.

The Chinese dream of a China–Myanmar Economic Corridor opening up communications to the coast suffered a serious setback. There was an anguished debate on how China "lost" Myanmar.[85] The setback seemed likely to deepen with the civilian government of Aung San Suu Kyi. But, in the event, relations were brought to a more businesslike level, which recognized the geographical and geopolitical links to China, together with the importance of Chinese trade and investment, but with more sensitivity to Burmese concerns over corruption and the behaviour of predatory Chinese companies. Subsequently, the international outcry over the treatment of Rohingya Muslims has once again led to Myanmar's isolation and deepened dependence on China. The reversion to military rule could reinforce that dependence.

The two countries which are closest to China, politically and economically, are Laos and Cambodia. Laos hosts some of the biggest and most prestigious projects in the BRI, including a high-speed railway link between China and Vientiane, which it is hoped will eventually be extended through Thailand and Malaysia to Singapore. Laos also demonstrates the dangers of BRI, in particular the debt problems that can result from heavy borrowing for infrastructure projects. Debts incurred to build dams have proved financially unsustainable for what was already a poor and fragile economy, and the Chinese have been seeking to take over the electricity grid to secure their assets. In addition, large numbers of Chinese have crossed the border and have effectively taken over parts of the country. There seems little the Laotians can do to exercise meaningful sovereignty.

In Cambodia, too, Chinese interests dominate, from the commercial interests of casino owners in Sihanoukville, garment factories, infrastructure projects and forest loggers to the naval facilities on the coast of the Gulf of Thailand, which give the Chinese military advantages. The strategic and political benefits which China derives from the domination of Cambodia are partially offset by the reputational damage from the large-scale corruption involved. As in Laos, Cambodia's debt position is precarious. Unlike Laos, Cambodia is semi-democratic, and relations with China rest heavily on the long-serving President Hun Sen, who will not be there for ever.

Taken as a whole, the ASEAN countries are much more under Chinese influence than when the group was founded half a century ago, or even compared to a decade ago. The opportunities provided by the BRI and the increasingly dominant Chinese economy have offered an antidote to historical and ethnic antipathies and fears of Chinese territorial control of the South China Sea and its resources. But its position is far from secure, and as Myanmar has shown, what seemed like irreversible dominance can be undone by unpredictable local politics. And the identification which President Xi has personally made with often unpopular ethnic Chinese minorities (*xin yimin*) is very double-edged.[86]

The future superpower of South Asia and the "string of pearls"

One of the seminal events in the global reassessment of China's role was a fight in a remote Himalayan valley between soldiers armed with sticks and clubs. Twenty Indian soldiers and an unknown number of Chinese were killed, and the event resonated out of all proportion to the scale of the hostilities. This was one of the very few cases of nuclear-armed powers coming into physical conflict. And the fracas could be seen as an early signal of future confrontation between the superpowers of the late twenty-first century.

On a PPP basis, India is already the world's third-largest economy, with a GDP of $8.7 trillion as against $21.8 trillion for the USA and $24 trillion for China. We have learnt in recent years about the power of compound growth rates. Were China to enter a "middle-income trap" and the USA to continue to motor at rates of 2% to 3%, and India to sustain the spectacular growth rates it has seen for much of this century, we could be dealing with a three-horse rather than a two-horse race for global strategic influence within a couple of decades.

With its famed capacity for long-range strategic vision, the Chinese leadership should be thinking in those terms, but seems instead strangely blind to the possibility and behaves condescendingly towards India.

Chinese attitudes towards India have almost certainly been framed by their different trajectories since the immediate post-war period, when India became independent in 1947 and China experienced its revolution in 1949. Any comparison of relative economic and social development is unflattering to India, with the exception of India's avoidance of large-scale famine and its successful adoption of democratic governance, in all its messiness.[87] And while China managed to retain its territory, India was partitioned, and this gave China an opportunity to take advantage of a divided subcontinent by adopting Pakistan as an ally. Chinese policy towards India has seemingly been to indulge India's aspiration to be taken seriously as a major power not aligned to the USA, but administering the occasional put-down, as a reminder of the reality of power differentials.

The first of those put-downs occurred in the 1962 border war, when China humiliated the Indian army and occupied swathes of territory, some of which it retains. The 3,500-km border has subsequently seen minor incidents, but the dispute has been essentially frozen with the implicit threat to India that there are large areas of Northeast India, which China calls "South Tibet", that could be taken if China was provoked. Since then, India has not merely modernized and improved its armed forces but has acquired a nuclear deterrent. China appears to regard the Indian deterrent as directed primarily at Pakistan rather than itself.[88] And it has ensured that Pakistan is sufficiently well armed (including with enriched uranium, to build its nuclear deterrent), so that India is preoccupied by its western rather than its northern frontier. Indian sources – not Chinese – see India as being engaged in serious rivalry with China.[89]

China's other approach to defusing hostility from India has been, as with the rest of the world, to build strong linkages of economic interdependence. That has not been easy, since India has few raw materials of interest to China, has an essentially competing rather than complementary economic structure and, even by Chinese standards, is a notoriously impenetrable and protectionist market for foreign traders and investors. Therefore, economic interdependence is very low. Total bilateral trade was $88 billion in 2020 and $95 billion the previous year. India runs a large deficit on trade, exporting only $21 billion in 2020 – mainly iron ore, cotton and uncut diamonds – while China exported $67 billion to India of electrical machinery, chemicals and other manufactures. Bilateral trade was well under 1% of GDP for both countries. For China, its trade with India is considerably less important than, say, with Brazil, and is very small in comparison with the EU, the ASEAN countries and the USA (respectively $650, $684 and $450 billion).

These facts may well have persuaded the Chinese leadership that it had little to lose in picking a fight with India. Precisely why a fight broke out on the border is unclear, and it may have happened by accident in response to a local provocation. Whatever the cause, and however limited the immediate effects, the Indian government dramatized and magnified the incident. Its Hindu-nationalist government could see big political dividends in posing as the outraged victim of aggression. India retaliated by banning the apps of Chinese technology companies, blocking some Chinese imports and creating obstacles to Chinese investors (and removing Huawei from lists of bidders for 5G contacts). In global terms these were minor setbacks for Chinese companies, which probably had few illusions, anyway, about being allowed to make deep inroads into India's protected markets.

But the real significance of India's reaction is that it gave serious momentum to the formation of a "quad" group, the USA, Australia, Japan and India, cooperating with military exercises and intelligence-sharing. The group itself may be well short of a serious military alliance, but for the USA to have been able to co-opt the world's largest democracy, which had hitherto made much of its non-alignment and its close military links with Russia, was a significant step. Partly because of Prime Minister Modi's seeming chemistry with President Trump and the

CHAPTER 6

growing influence of the highly successful Indian community
in the USA, there was growing warmth in India's relations with
America, but the border clashes greatly reinforced it. India's
carefully cultivated public equidistance between the superpowers – which was reflected in eighteen meetings between Xi and
Modi, balancing the enthusiastic reception in America – was
discarded. It is difficult to avoid the conclusion that in the long
and complicated game of Go the Chinese made a blunder,
underestimating India's long-term importance.

It is more than possible, however, that India will fail to take
advantage of the opportunity that has been created by being
taken very seriously by the United States and Japan without
losing its ties to Russia (its main arms supplier). Indeed, the
Ukraine war has exposed the contradictions within that balancing act. India has refused to criticize the Russian invasion
and finds itself, ironically, in a position very similar to China:
supporting the Russian economy by purchasing Russian oil
(at a generous discount). The growing criticism over the Modi
administration's sectarian, anti-Muslim agenda and its authoritarianism also make India a less attractive partner in President
Biden's "alliance of democracies". India remains, moreover,
an obstacle course for overseas investors, a more difficult place
to do business than China. The Indian left-wing parties, and
others, have a traditionally visceral hostility to the United
States, born of attitudes which were fashionable decades ago.
And India has so far failed to deepen its economic links on the
subcontinent, even with friendly governments like Bangladesh,
whereas China has quietly become the leading investor and
arms supplier for Bangladesh.

More generally, China has learnt that the politics of the
subcontinent and its messy but genuine democracies is difficult
to manage. The region has, nonetheless, delivered two of the
biggest and most tangible success stories on its Belt and Road.
In the case of Pakistan, alongside the long-standing military
alliance, much progress has been made on the China–Pakistan
Economic Corridor.[90] There is now a direct land link to China
from the Indian Ocean. And the port of Gwadar has the

263

potential to become, effectively, a Chinese port and potential naval base. But Pakistan is an unstable cocktail of poisonous political differences between parties, regions and the military. The former government of Imran Khan had no political capital invested in the Economic Corridor, and worried about the cost for Pakistan's fragile economy. And China is being blamed for the high levels of debt which contribute to Pakistan's financial struggles. But, in the event, the interest of the Pakistan army in keeping a close military alliance with China – to help it match India's capability – has proved decisive.

There is a political twist to the region's politics following the US withdrawal from Afghanistan, in effect acknowledging defeat as did the British, the Soviet Union and other powers in the past. China seems to want to be actively involved in Afghan affairs, though it seems scarcely believable that China will go where the USSR and the USA (and its allies) have been seen off. But China has an interest in a stable Afghanistan. It has a common border, albeit small, and a strong interest in preventing Uyghur terrorists returning to Xinjiang through a failed or hostile state. China has made overtures to the Taliban with a promise to invest in infrastructure and Afghan development. One is tempted to add: good luck with that.

Elsewhere in the subcontinent, Sri Lanka was, like Myanmar, almost "lost" to China a few years ago. Heavy Chinese investment, in infrastructure, ports and roads especially, was one of the features of the Rajapaksa government, which dominated Sri Lankan politics in the early part of the century and prosecuted the brutal but successful war against Tamil rebels (allegedly won with the help of Chinese weapons). But the debt accruing from all those undertakings was extremely onerous, and often cited as an example of the Chinese "debt trap". That and the alleged corruption around the projects, several of which were serious failures, led to the Rajapaksa family losing its grip on power. An opposition coalition won power in 2015, committed to renegotiating some of the loans and reducing the country's over-dependence on China. The approach seemed to be working, but then the coalition collapsed and, in a fresh election, the Rajapaksas were back. As was China – the "string of pearls" refurbished. The apparent demise of the Rajapaksas, in conditions of extreme economic crisis in 2022, has once again created extreme uncertainty.

If there are broader lessons from South and South-East Asia, they are that China struggles with unpredictable democracies. So far, its willingness to throw money at problems and its deep, long-term engagement with prospective allies have proved decisive. But keeping vassal states in order is expensive, and not totally reliable.

Europe: a faraway continent

If the relations between China and its Asian neighbours are complex and multifaceted, those with Europe have, until very recently, been much more straightforward – commercial and, from the Chinese side, about technological acquisition. Europeans, for their part, have not been greatly exercised about the rise of modern China other than as a big new market. Nineteenth-century history is largely forgotten. There are no Chinese minorities of any significance, other than largely welcome students and tourists. There is nothing comparable to the US history of involvement with China during the Pacific War and in the Korean War; the politics of the "loss of China"; then the long period of mostly peaceful economic engagement with China until the Trump presidency; and the continued US involvement with the defence of Japan, Taiwan and South Korea from security threats, including from China.

By contrast, China has scarcely been seen as a military threat, in contrast to the USSR (and now Russia) and Islamic terrorism from the Middle East. There are no military obligations to the Asia-Pacific (apart from those of France because of its Pacific territories). And Europe has been concerned with its own challenges: enlargement, deepening integration, the Eurozone crisis, Brexit. Europe has, for its part, been largely fixated on trade and business opportunities.[91] The most recent figures suggest that the EU, taken as a whole, has emerged as a bigger trade partner for China than the USA, but smaller than ASEAN, if that group is also treated as a whole. Since the year 2000, exports to China have been growing at 10% p.a., and services (which are quantitatively less significant than goods) at 15% p.a. on a Europe-wide basis. The EU sets its trade policy, and trade negotiations with China take place at a European level. But individual European countries frame their attitudes to relations with China in national terms, and there are big differences in outlook caused in part by the level of success of their companies in selling to China. Germany has been the main champion of boosting trade with China, no doubt motivated by the considerable success of its car industry, chemicals and capital-goods exporters, though an internal debate has opened up in Germany as to whether there is an unhealthy dependence on the Chinese market.

Bilateral trade balances are a bad guide to the costs and benefits of trade but are politically significant. The EU has had a stable deficit ($200 billion) on trade in goods for the last decade. But that overstates the imbalance, since European exports have been high and Europe runs a surplus on services trade, mainly tourism and technology, related to services like consultancy. Among European countries, Germany records a significant surplus, though that may in part be due to the so-called "Rotterdam effect", whereby imports via the Netherlands are treated as imports from Holland rather than China.

One of the effects of determining trade policy at EU level is that it has been less politicized than in the USA, and there has been remarkably little trade friction with China. That is despite the ongoing deficit on goods trade and the grumbles of European companies about unlevel playing fields and trade and investment barriers in China. A long-standing dispute over textiles was defused. Although China accounts for roughly half the EU's use of "trade defence mechanisms" (anti-dumping and anti-subsidy action), use has declined since 2006, and the EU accounts for only a small share of such interventions worldwide.[92]

A more troubling issue for the EU has been the unhappiness of some European investors in China over forced technology transfers and joint ventures and the much smaller amount of Chinese capital flows into the EU, seemingly targeted at acquiring companies for their technology. Overall, there is an estimated stock of EU investment in China of around $180 billion (2018 estimate) against $60 billion Chinese investment in Europe. The Commission has been negotiating for seven years on a Comprehensive Agreement on Investment (CAI) to improve the position. It concluded talks in January 2021, along with reported side deals, such as a favoured position for Deutsche Telekom to operate mobile networks in China, and a role for Huawei in Germany. The agreement appears to concede access for European companies in a variety of sectors and to restrain the activity of state enterprises, but sceptics point to the difficulty of enforcement.[93]

The CAI may never reach the statute book, since it must be endorsed by the European Parliament, which has expressed discontent over the lack of linkage to human-rights issues, in particular the use of forced labour. The unhappiness will have grown in 2021, with the naming of several MEPs by the Chinese as the subject of travel bans, as well as other sanctions in retaliation for those imposed by the EU and USA on China over human rights. And that illustrates a wider problem: the long-standing lack of clarity and consistency over the over-arching objectives in dealings with China. This problem was apparent thirty years ago, when several member states sought to relax export controls on arms sales to China, which had been put in place after the Tiananmen Square killings. After strong pressure from the USA and Japan and some member states, the controls were retained. Then, in 2013, the issue resurfaced when the EU agreed on a "strategic agenda" that took into account China's concerns over "territorial integrity", to the displeasure of some member states.

Nonetheless, growing worries about China led to an agreement among the European member states in 2019 that the country was a "systemic rival", and there was talk of a new consensus centring on "imbalance, disappointment and unease".[94] On the other hand, following the CAI negotiations, China claimed that the two blocs were "comprehensive strategic partners, not systemic rivals", directly contradicting the earlier EU official position.[95] In the meantime, members like Poland showed great dissatisfaction at the EU's determination to exercise "strategic autonomy", mainly at French prompting, thus weakening its ties with the USA. This, combined with Germany's commercial self-interest, has appeared to undermine the newly elected President Biden, who appealed in vain to the EU to wait.[96] The change in government in Germany and the retirement of Angela Merkel, who was the main champion of the CAI, has however lessened the areas of disagreement with the USA.

The CAI hasn't been the only source of discord within the EU. The Chinese have established a framework for dealing with BRI initiatives which cut across the EU's negotiating authority. Its 17+1 group (the number varies) includes most Eastern European members, Greece, Italy, as well as Balkan non-members. Some of the 17 have developed close links with China, notably Serbia and Hungary, both of which achieved high vaccination rates through Chinese Covid vaccines. There are collective advantages to these countries from BRI investments in terms of improved connectivity, and country-specific benefits of being able to borrow for large infrastructure projects without the fiscal restrictions and conditions of EU institutional finance. But there is some suspicion that the 17+1 formula is an attempt to split the EU further and secure a tactical advantage thereby. There are also frustrations within the 17 that BRI has not delivered what the Chinese promised, leading to some disillusionment. Lithuania has withdrawn, and in a subsequent row over Lithuania's relations with Taiwan, China resorted to sanctions and threats which had the effect of uniting Europe behind the Baltic state. When China sought to "punish" Lithuania by blocking EU exports to China which might have Lithuanian components, the Commission and member states were unanimous in opposition. That episode was one factor in persuading Italy to leave the BRI group, and the conservative Greek government is also cooling on it.

The departure of the divisive President Trump, with his public disdain of the European Union, and the arrival of much friendlier President Biden and his determination to build a coalition of democratic states has however changed the political dynamic. There is now a US–EU trade and technology council which is working on common technological standards, seemingly to head off Chinese leadership in areas such as facial recognition and batteries. There has been agreement on steel and aluminium tariffs, apparently designed to exclude economies with "carbon intensive" industries such as China. Although there are differences within the EU, the human-rights agenda has gained ground, particularly with the new German coalition government. Overall, the EU can be described as "not neutral, but resistant to being asked to choose", and there is a clear wish to engage with China on environmental issues – to press China to do more following COP 26 – and on trade, including by strengthening rules on state subsidy within the WTO.

Beneath the diplomatic positions, there is also public opinion. One of the most striking polls in recent years was the big (15,000) survey of the public in eleven European countries, including Britain.[97] Although the general view of the European public about China has become negative, when asked about whether European countries should support China or the USA in any future conflict, there was strong support for neutrality: 66% in Germany; 58% in the UK. That opinion appears to be based on pessimism about the USA, whose system was judged to be "broken" (by 72% of Germans and 71% of the British), and which was likely to be overtaken by China within a decade. Those results just pre-date Biden and the common position taken on human rights in China by the USA and EU, but they may simply reflect the geographical fact that the Asia-Pacific is a long way away. In any event, the Ukraine war has injected new energy into the NATO alliance and strengthened transatlantic ties – as well as working relations with the UK – in common cause with Ukraine, all of which has widened the gulf in understanding with China, which has tacitly supported Russia.

The ambiguities in European attitudes to China were captured in a comment from President Macron, who, after meeting president Xi (in April 2023), cautioned that Europe "should not get caught up in a crisis over Taiwan which is not our own" [...], "driven by American rhythm and a Chinese over-reaction". Macron may have been saying publicly what European leaders – and the public, according to polls – think privately, but his comments were roundly attacked in the USA and in the EU, and he was obliged to reaffirm support for the "status quo". Macron's comments came in the wake of a big trade-oriented visit to China which was celebrated with numerous trade deals, including a big order for Airbus. A similar trade-focused visit to China was made by Chancellor Scholz of Germany with a large industrial delegation, and he spoke out strongly against decoupling. The German-French position is easily explained: exports of goods and services plus revenues from German companies in China amount to around 10% of German GDP. For France the share of GDP is 5% (and growing), and for the UK 4%. Having taken a big hit to distance itself from Russia, Germany in particular is not in a hurry to bin another valuable commercial relation-ship, though there are powerful voices in Germany urging a rethink of the China connection.

In order to maintain a common front within the EU, Ursula von der Leyen has coined the phrase "de-risking, not decou-pling", which was then adopted by the G7. A good phrase does not however end the discomfort or add clarity. The European Commission has put forward a series of concrete proposals for de-risking which involve reducing dependence on Chinese rare earths, solar panels and pharmaceuticals. The details however do not remove the underlying problem that China represents a large market and trade partner not easily replaced – but the EU is very dependent for defence on the USA and cannot realistically embark on "strategic autonomy", as Macron has advocated.

CHAPTER 6

British exceptionalism

Post-Brexit Britain may be a place where government think-ing, if not yet public opinion, is shifting towards a much more committed role in the Asia-Pacific. There are few coun-tries whose position on China and perception by China have changed as radically as the UK. There have been specific events like the turmoil and crackdown in Hong Kong, but the key factor has been Brexit: severing links with the EU and forc-ing a rapid realignment to the USA and traditional allies in the Anglosphere. For China, the UK has simply become less important: no longer an entry point for Chinese firms to the European single market for goods and finance, and no longer able to influence EU trade and investment policy.

There was a very sharp break between the first half of the decade, characterized as the "Golden Era", culminating in the visit of President Xi to the UK in 2015, and the post-referendum environment. But as a result of the acceleration of trading activi-ties, China progressed from being the UK's 24th-largest export market at the turn of the century to the third-largest after the USA and Germany in 2019. Chinese imports grew from being the 15th-largest source to the second. There has been a consistent deficit in China's favour throughout the last decade of around £20 billion, and a modest surplus of £3 billion on services.[98]

More important than trade, there was a big build-up of direct investment in both directions, with the stock of Chinese invest-ment in the UK currently around £85 billion. There have been major, high-profile investments in the UK by Huawei, Jingye (which has taken over the integrated steel plant at Scunthorpe), Geely making electric taxis, SAIC seeking to revive the former MG car company and in the nuclear-power sector at Hinkley Point. China has become a major source of revenue and profit for British overseas investors: Jaguar Land Rover, HSBC, GSK, AstraZeneca. UK universities have invested heavily in attracting Chinese students to the UK and in campuses in China. China is especially important for the UK luxury-goods sector through sales in China or to Chinese tourists in London.

How much that will change from the Chinese side now remains to be seen, but several big specific decisions signal a shift in the UK position. The first was the choice to block Huawei from 5G and gradually to remove it from legacy systems. Until very recently, Huawei's presence was managed in such a way as to safeguard security concerns. When the issue of 5G arose, the May government agreed a compromise which provided security safeguards alongside access to Huawei's advanced systems, so that the Chinese company could operate on the periphery, but not in core functions. But when the USA sought to prevent Huawei gaining access to American microprocessors, the UK was forced to change policy again, excluding Huawei entirely, after concerns were raised that Chinese-sourced components would not be secure.

Secondly, the Chinese response to the prolonged demonstrations in Hong Kong, and the effective repudiation of the "one country, two systems" formula, has led to the offer of a route to settlement in the UK for a large group of UK passport holders hitherto excluded. Granting immigration rights to British passport holders was, one would have thought, a reasonable response to a potential refugee situation. But it has become part of a bigger, acrimonious exchange about the future of Hong Kong and democracy itself.

A third issue is new legislation designed to screen foreign investment for "national security" concerns. Although it is not mentioned explicitly, the debate around the legislation makes it clear that China is the main target. The government's intentions were put to the test with the attempted acquisition of the semiconductor manufacturer Newport Wafer Fab by a Chinese company based in Holland, Wingtech, the owner of Nexperia. After strong criticism of the initial passive response, especially from the Conservatives' China Research Group (CRG), the matter was referred to the National Security Adviser, who judged that there was little security risk. But political demands continued to be made to exclude the Chinese company – and in the end the deal was blocked. With semiconductor technology at the heart of the tech "cold war" between the USA and

China, suspicions will arise over any Chinese company looking to acquire technological know-how in the sector.

There has also been criticism of Chinese (minority) investment in the nuclear-power sector and other "critical infrastructure". There have been calls from the Conservatives' China Research Group of MPs to block Chinese investment in the industry, currently in the form of a minority financial stake in EDF's Hinkley Point project. The financial investment is not particularly problematic, but Hinkley was seen as an entry point for Chinese investment in future projects at Sizewell C and Bradwell B, the latter using a new Chinese technology which the Chinese are looking to export. Putting aside James Bond fantasies of sabotage and exploding nuclear plants, the worry about Bradwell is that it could make the UK dependent on Chinese equipment and components that could be caught up in US trade embargoes or wider commercial conflict in the future. In any event, the Chinese investor (CGN) appears to be looking for an excuse to quit the potentially loss-making Hinkley project. If it does quit, the UK will be left with the daunting prospect of finding a new investor for the industry.

The former Prime Minister, Boris Johnson, spoke up in favour of economic engagement with the Chinese and its benefits (especially for services exporters), and against what he called an "anti-China spirit". But it is difficult to weigh economic factors against "security threats", especially when the political consensus across parties and in the UK's main ally is dominated by an "anti-China spirit". His successor Liz Truss was openly hostile to all forms of engagement with China, and attacked Chinese-owned companies like TikTok.

Government supporters have even questioned the undoubtedly considerable economic benefits from hosting Chinese students and researchers. There were an estimated 120,000 Chinese students in the UK (2019/20, pre-Covid), 35% of all overseas students. They earned £1.7 billion in tuition fees, which would otherwise have to be raised from British and other overseas students. The argument being advanced is that "academic freedom" is being compromised by the fact that some students, researchers and academic donors may be politically aligned with the Chinese government. Some undoubtedly are. But some universities, like Cambridge, have been attacked for accepting relatively small private Chinese donations[99] and (at Jesus College) hosting Chinese studies centres with links to Chinese academic institutions. But it is the job of independent universities, not government, to defend their standards, as it is also the case when British or American donors have ideological motives or Middle Eastern students seek to introduce extreme forms of Islam or anti-Semitism. Universities which are careful of their reputation and survival will ensure that they are not over-dependent on one source of income.

The issue of disengagement is not coming only from the UK side. A major challenge to the British-based HSBC came from the Chinese insurer Ping An, a big Chinese shareholder in HSBC. Ping An wished to split HSBC to separate the UK-based operation from the Chinese business of the group. It is not clear if there were political motives, but it is certainly plausible that Chinese business interests are planning for a more divided world.

The British government is trying to reconcile its belief in an open, competitive "Global Britain" with the narrowing horizons imposed by the US–China "cold war". The difficulty is reflected in the ambiguities contained in its 2021 Integrated Review,[100] which designated China as a "systemic challenge", as opposed to an "active threat" in the case of Russia. There is a continuing argument within government, which has been under pressure from "hawks" among its backbenchers demanding that the word "threat" be used to define relations with China. Not to do so, according to Ian Duncan Smith, would be "project kowtow". In an attempt to give clearer definition, in April 2023 the foreign secretary, James Cleverly, called for a "robust and constructive" relationship with China, and he firmly repudiated the idea of a "new cold war". The overall approach is to be "calibrated", balancing the benefits of trade against the need to stand up for "human rights and the values fundamental to the world's democracies". The calibration has decisively shifted in the direction of joining US-led initiatives to contain China, and places the UK in a different position from France and Germany.

The exposed Anglosphere

If the UK is looking for precedent in terms of what to expect in the wake of a more hostile approach to China, it can be seen in the "coercive diplomacy" deployed against other members of the Anglosphere. Canada prepared to negotiate a far-reaching trade deal with China in 2017. But Premier Trudeau raised issues of human rights, labour and environmental standards during the negotiation, and the deal was suspended. Then Canada acted on an extradition request from the USA to apprehend the chief finance officer of Huawei and the daughter of its founder. China responded by cancelling the trade agreement.

The dispute escalated. China retaliated against Canada's refusal to free Ms Meng by imprisoning two Canadians – the "two Michaels" – on what appear to be trumped-up charges. In addition to this "hostage diplomacy", China responded to the arrest of Ms Meng by deploying selective trade sanctions on Canadian food exports. The Canadian government responded pragmatically, by not banning Huawei from its networks, as expected, and by muting somewhat its criticisms on human rights. The "hostage" issue has since been resolved through the release of Ms Meng – who returned to China a national hero – and the two Michaels.

Australia's experience has been even more fraught and painful.[101] It reached a trade agreement with China in 2015. But in 2020 it was one of 62 countries to call for an investigation into the origins of Covid, in terms which the Chinese regarded as insulting. In addition, it excluded Huawei and attacked China over human rights and publicized fourteen grievances about Chinese behaviour, mainly in commercial matters. The Chinese response was in effect to tear up the trade agreement; impose sanctions on $20 billions of Australian exports, 10% of total exports, covering 13 sectors; disrupt the coal trade by keeping coal-carrying vessels waiting for long periods before unloading in China; and warning off tourists.

Australia has in turn doubled down, strengthening its military links with the Quad and proposing a reinforcement of the "Five

Eyes" group for intelligence-sharing (extending it to Japan). China is also raising the stakes by launching a vituperative propaganda war and by orchestrating moves in the UN to have Australia's own human-rights record challenged, as with the offshore detention of asylum-seekers. Australia is now in the frontline of the new "cold war" with China, and this became clear with the announcement of the formation of the AUKUS defence group and the decision of the Australian government to switch from a French submarine contract to US–UK nuclear submarines, a move described by the French prime minister as "duplicitous". The contract signalled Australia's key role in any potential maritime confrontation with China – a possibility made more real by China's moves to establish Pacific bases in the Solomons and other island states.

For all the bravado, Australia depends on China for a third of its exports of goods and services, more than the combined total of Japan, Korea, India, the USA and UK; 20% of its imports are from China. China also sends 160,000 overseas students (40% of the total), and it is the biggest tourist market in terms of expenditure. Australia's well-being depends on China, and it would be surprising if there were not a move to a modus vivendi. Under a new – Labour – prime minister, that may already be happening with more emollient language, at least.

One of the "Five Eyes" countries, New Zealand, has taken a more accommodating approach to China, leading to mutual criticism and divisions with Australia. New Zealand had been reviewing its own relations with China, particularly in the light of various episodes of espionage, and its analysis of the strategic picture is not too distant from that of the Australian government. But the Chinese market is crucial to New Zealand exports, and the government has pressed ahead with an upgraded trade agreement with China which improves access for New Zealand products (and helps New Zealand specifically in areas where it is in competition with Australia).

Coalition-building

One of the considerable and distinctive achievements of the Biden administration, unlike its predecessor, has been the building of coalitions of the like-minded. The common NATO front against Russia has been a key feature of the Ukraine War, both on military supplies and economic sanctions, and a similar approach is being adopted to China, regionally and globally. Asian regional security arrangements have been strengthened through the AUKUS group (Australia, UK and USA), the Quad of the USA, Japan, Australia and India with support from Singapore, the Philippines (latterly), South Korea and, less visibly, Vietnam. The EU and Canada have also bought into the "de-risking, not decoupling" formula.

That said, the coalitions paper over some very large cracks. There are serious disagreements within the EU and with the USA over how to deal with China, and the agreed consensus approach may not long survive the end of the Ukraine War or the Biden presidency. The US itself has a high and rare degree of bipartisanship on the issue, but with Congressmen and individual states seeking to "out-hawk" each other, that may not last. Even among Asian allies there is publicly expressed frustration that the US can only offer military might and will not engage in the trade-liberalizing agenda once promised by President Obama. More seriously, much of the Global South in Africa, Latin America and the Middle East shows little inclination to be co-opted into alliances against China. The establishment of a BRICS Bank – Brazil, Russia, China, South Africa with Saudi money – symbolizes the lack of width as well as depth in the anti-China front.

Chapter 7

Competition, Conflict, Cooperation, Coalitions and Cold War

The complex, multilayered set of relationships which China has developed is very different from the two-country, zero-sum world of President Trump and his acolytes. There is a wide range of public perceptions about China, from the extremely negative (Japan and Vietnam), to varying degrees of disapproval in the Western world (with the USA, the UK and Australia at the negative end of a wide spectrum), to admiration and approval (in several countries in Africa, Latin America, the Middle East, the Balkans and Russia). The public in many countries appear to see China's rising economy as a positive influence, presenting opportunities for trade and inward or outward investment, though a few, not just in the USA, also feel threatened by China's rise and worry about Chinese competition – or, as in Europe, see overall benefit but have concerns about trading practices and non-economic issues, notably human rights.

China's importance is primarily economic, but not exclusively so. A few neighbouring countries worry about China's military capacity, but have nonetheless, as with Japan, Korea or the ASEAN countries, close economic relationships. For democratic nations there is a clash of values, but a great variation in the extent to which this is seen as relevant or more important than other considerations. There is also, for reasons of values or geography or defence commitments, a varied range of alignments with the United States – countries who share the deep-rooted concern in the USA about China as a superpower-competitor, usurping the established international order, as against those who are indifferent or see merit in a competition for influence, or even in Chinese dominance.

Perceptions and the pandemic

What is striking about some of the alignments and attitudes to China is how volatile they are. Governments of countries such as Myanmar, Malaysia, Indonesia and the Philippines – even India – have shifted backwards and forwards in terms of closeness to the regime in Beijing. The UK has performed an abrupt U-turn. Some of this volatility can be attributed to President Trump, and some to shifts in policy and more authoritarian rule under President Xi. Some is the product of circumstances, and in particular the pandemic. According to the Pew surveys of public opinion in fourteen OECD countries, the judgement that China had handled the pandemic badly was the cause of a sharp deterioration in favourability ratings of China. Sixty-one per cent of those surveyed thought China had done badly, and 37% were positive – and that contributed to a rise of more that 10% in overall unfavourability in the UK, Germany, the USA, Sweden and South Korea (and a 24% rise in Australia).[1] One consolation for the Chinese was that the USA, at least before the change in administration, was judged to have done even worse in handling the pandemic (84% negative versus 15% positive).

Critics of China were quick to politicize the pandemic. A pamphlet widely distributed in the UK was headlined: "How the Chinese Communist Party Endangered the World".[2] President Trump blamed the "China virus" for his own administration's failings in flamboyant language: "This is worse than Pearl Harbour. This is worse than the World Trade Center. There has never been an attack like this."[3] The accusations that the virus was created in a laboratory at the Wuhan Institute of Virology and then spread deliberately abroad had little scientific support, as did Chinese claims that the virus was brought in from abroad. But the possibility of accidental leakage seems plausible, even though a WHO visiting mission in February 2021 concluded that it was very unlikely to have emerged from experiments in a laboratory in Wuhan. Lab leaks have occurred before, not only in China, and they cannot be ruled out. How Covid originated remains a mystery, though zoonotic transmission from animals is the favoured explanation among many scientists.[4]

The pandemic is receding into history. China's reputation has been damaged by the initial cover-up, the extreme zero-Covid policy and its chaotic abandonment of it. But so have the reputations of countries like the USA, India and UK by their high death rates and the West's reluctance to share vaccines.

One practical consequence of the pandemic was the impact of the virtual closure of China to foreign business visitors and tourists, and the inability of many Chinese to travel abroad in a world where quarantine rules applied. These created a sense of isolation and suspicion, fuelling nationalism. These relatively short-term factors affecting perception and performance matter, but what is more important are the long-term trends, which are subject to much debate and uncertainty. I shall look at them through a series of scenarios.

Three scenarios and archetypes of future China

We cannot predict the future, but we can identify plausible stories of how it could evolve based on features that are also recognizable today. As a former practitioner of the Shell scenario system, I am attracted to a flexible and open-minded way of thinking about the future – a method which leads to questions of "what if" rather than "what will be" and which avoids the trap of simply extrapolating from the past. For the sake of simplicity, I identify three such stories. None are "true", and all are deliberate caricatures, but they are plausible accounts of what the future might hold.

There are many uncertainties, but the scenarios focus on two of these and the interaction between them. The first is the internal priority of the Chinese leadership: the extent to which China will adapt and reform to deal with the undoubted challenges posed by the "middle-income trap", seek maximum engagement with the world economy and be supportive of the Chinese and foreign private sector. In one version of China's future, economic concerns dominate, since the Communist Party leadership sees a successful economy as the basis of China's strength and the underpinning of superpower status. It also strengthens political stability within China, since the Communist Party's legitimacy rests in large part on its ability to deliver rising living standards, especially for the urban middle class. But it is also possible to envisage a different view of China's priorities in which party control trumps economic reform and growth. Such prioritization could be the result of perceived external threats from the USA and its allies or a response to domestic dissatisfaction and threats of disorder stemming from economic failures.

The other key dichotomy relates to how the USA and its allies see, and treat, China. On one hand there are those who want to engage with China – who see the relationship as commercially and politically competitive, but are not afraid of competition. They believe that, while there are big differences in ideology and interest, there should be cooperation over trade and business and common problems like climate change. On the other hand, there are those for whom the contest with China is a "zero-sum game", a fight to the death between two hegemons. They believe that China is a fundamental threat to a global order based on Western values of democracy and the rule of law. China must therefore be "contained". There has to be a "decoupling" of economies as far as possible to reduce dependence on China and in anticipation of inevitable conflict. Security trumps economics.

These two dichotomies provide the basis for several stories.

Davos China

The first such scenario story I call "Davos China". This is a China which is dominated by economic priorities, and which manages to overcome the obstacles to its continuing economic rise. And it gives substance to its oft-repeated slogan of "win-win" by maintaining engagement with the USA and its allies and upholding international rules and order. Were China seen to be fully committed to broadly liberal economic reform within its "state capitalist" system, to opening up and to being constructive in multilateral trade and wider economic negotiations, then this would also help tilt the balance of opinion in the West. Arguments from cheerleaders in the business world – Apple, Tesla and the Wall Street banks – would attract a more receptive hearing. The German-French approach would have greater credibility. Liberalization creates its own dynamic.

The Chinese leadership understands the symbolism of Davos as embodying "globalization", and identifies with it. President Xi went to the World Economic Forum in Davos in January 2017 to give a strong defence of globalization and its benefits at a time – the beginning of the Trump presidency and post-Brexit – when fashionable opinion in the West was turning against it. He had defined China's approach a few months earlier: "Sealing off and excluding others is not the correct choice [...]. China will not shut the doors to the outside world."[5] That visit could be seen as an opportunistic piece of public relations designed to embarrass the USA, highlighting the erratic behaviour and counterproductive economic nationalism of its president.

But it could also represent something deeper: a sign of how his regime saw itself and wanted to be seen, as a champion of global economic integration and the international economic order, albeit with Chinese characteristics. Xi revisited Davos (virtually) in January 2021 to make the case again and to argue for multilateral cooperation on climate change, public health, frontier technologies and economic policy. He condemned the actions against China in internationalist terms: "To build small circles or wilfully impose decoupling, supply disruption or sanctions [...] will only push the world into division and even conflict."[6]

A scenario story built around the concept of Davos China isn't to imagine a giant version of Switzerland or even a country en route to OECD status like South Korea or Chile. It is distinctively Chinese, and retains its one-party system to provide order, stability and a body of institutionalized beliefs around "socialism", which also legitimize its economic model of "state capitalism". Davos China is the Chinese version of multilateralism:

multipolarity rather than unipolarity; "inclusive multilateralism" rather than "universalism" based on Western values and dominance.[7] It envisages peaceful competition among different nation states, and different models within which its status as an economic and technological superpower is acknowledged and formally recognized by according it a bigger weight in the more inclusive decision-making of multilateral institutions and rule-setting bodies. At the Boao Forum for Asia Annual Conference (April 2021), President Xi set out a vision for a "new world order" which is multipolar, but whose economic objectives dominate: "Stability brings a country prosperity, while instability leads a country to poverty."[8]

There is plenty of evidence that, despite disagreements with other powers – and especially the United States – on specific issues, Davos China represents important elements in China's broad direction of travel. China is now the world's largest trading economy, after a long process of induction to the WTO and its rules. There are large volumes of foreign direct investment and some, albeit slow, liberalization. Chinese and China-based firms participate in internationally integrated supply chains much more than earlier pioneers of East Asian development like Japan and Korea. China takes an active role in the Bretton Woods institutions, the G20 and the Paris Accord on climate change, and is seeking better representation in all global bodies. The regime has encouraged well over a hundred million Chinese to travel abroad every year to study or for tourism (at least until the forced closure due to the pandemic). They then freely return. Chinese scientists have been encouraged to enter international competitions and collaborative projects. Leading Chinese companies seek to acquire global recognition through listing in leading financial centres overseas and the adoption of international standards of audit and governance. China has more international peacekeepers than any other country.

President Xi is sometimes described by his overseas critics as wanting to turn the clock back on the globalizing trends he inherited: his "Common Prosperity" drive has involved arbitrary attacks on some successful innovative sectors of Chinese business.

But officials who value China's economic openness and are committed to making a success of Chinese "state capitalism" remain powerful. In this scenario they prevail over officials preoccupied with national security and hostile to capitalism. Xi has some reputation as an economic reformer, including the strengthening of intellectual-property-rights enforcement, with a big rise in prosecutions, and, more recently, opening the finance sector to foreign investors. His regime is repressive but has been open to economic reform. Xi's pre-pandemic personal travel schedule overseas, to more than seventy countries, was that of a global figure, not an inward-looking nationalist. His personal project – the Belt and Road Initiative – has added considerably to connectivity, especially in the Eurasian land mass, and has contributed seriously to African development. He has overseen agreements designed to integrate China further into the global or regional economies, as with the Asian RCEP and the proposed Investment Agreement with the EU, or applying to join the successor body to the Obama administration's Transpacific Partnership, which the USA is not part of (the CFTPP). The CFTPP makes demands of China in respect of data privacy, labour rights and state enterprise which will be difficult to reconcile with Chinese reality, but the mere fact of applying is significant. The Asian Infrastructure Investment Bank (AIIB), promoted and hosted by China, enjoys wide support and conforms to international standards of governance and professionalism. In Asia, Africa, the Middle East and Latin America the story is of a confident, outward-looking China embracing the world economy.[9]

The key slogan in this version of China is "win-win": "Its approach would be non-prescriptive, consensus-based and aimed at creating a multipolar world structure, one where the old dominance of a single power alone is consigned to history."[10] And because China has a different political system and arguably different cultural norms, its view of economic globalization has "Chinese characteristics". It is pluralist, not universalist. This view of the world may not be comfortable in the USA (or the UK), whose vision of the international order has long held sway. But it is not unlike the expressed ambition of other major emerging economies like India or Brazil to play a bigger role in a system they did not design.

Cynics would say that this story is altogether too good to be true – that Chinese "win-win" means that China wins twice. And there is a major gap in this scenario. China's globalization excludes one thing that really matters: information. If people can only find out about other countries, or indeed their own, through government-approved sources (or by travelling abroad), the process of integration is necessarily superficial and distorted. If scientists cannot get access to Google Scholar and other source material, their ability to work collaboratively is stifled. There may be a bigger contradiction, in that it is very difficult to sustain a closed and controlled political system in an open and internationally integrated economy. Pessimism on that score is reinforced by the fact that some of the pluralism and flexibility on display earlier in the decade – a vigorous and irreverent social media; contested elections in localities; permitted protest and petitioning – seem to be in retreat.

There are also important respects in which China has chosen to ignore or even trash the global rules that it supports in theory, where they clash with national self-interest. The most obvious case is the Law of the Sea, of which China is a signatory and which it invokes in its own interest. When there was a strong international ruling against China in a dispute with the Philippines, the Chinese response was to reject and ridicule the finding. In rejecting the authority of international law, however, China is in good company. The United States has never acceded to the Law of the Sea and rejects the authority of judicial bodies such as the International Criminal Court. The UK has only recently argued that national sovereignty trumps international treaties in relation to the EU – echoing the Chinese view of international law.

Elizabeth Economy points to a wider failure to exercise meaningful global responsibility where there are common problems: "Even in China's own backyard – addressing North Korea's nuclear proliferation or managing the refugee crisis in Myanmar – China has not yet put forward a workable solution.

China's leadership globally is largely confined to those issues where its interests are most easily advanced."[11] In other words, Davos China doesn't match impressive words about enlightened global leadership with necessary but difficult deeds (though that could be said just as easily of the United States under Trump and the European Union or the UK). China could respond that its peacemaking between Saudi Arabia and Iran contradicts this pessimism.

A more deep-rooted problem with the Davos China scenario is that there are fundamental disagreements with the West on what an open, multilateral system would look like. There are influential Chinese intellectuals whose world view is global and well-disposed to a harmonious international order, but who insist that a future world order will have "Chinese characteristics". The concept of "*tianxia*" – roughly meaning "all under heaven" – derives from China's imperial past and describes a world in which China is at the centre, not on the peripheries.[12] That presages a future which is far from harmonious.

Even if the Chinese leadership were sincere about operating constructively within an integrated world economy, that is not the current trend. Globalization is unfashionable. Decoupling is. Faced with the prospect of a bifurcating world and serious internal pressures, the regime is moving to the idea of a 'fortress China' with more self-reliance in advanced technology, energy and food. Davos China is still a plausible scenario, but becoming less so.

China as Sparta

There is a very different view of China, which is also global in perspective, but dominated by security concerns and geopolitical competition. "Hawks" in the West would regard Davos China as a wolf in sheep's clothing. The wolf, they believe, is a comprehensive threat, especially to trusting and gentle lambs. The good shepherd's role is to protect the lambs by alerting them to the danger. China, like the wolf, is hungry, aggressive, predatory and brutally ruthless. I call this wolf-state "Spartan

China", after the martial Greek city state. I use that analogy since it links to the idea of the Thucydides Trap, in which there can only be one hegemonic power – in that case Sparta or Athens. The Thucydides Trap involves a "zero-sum" game rather than a "win-win" situation. Someone must lose. There is an influential school of thinkers in the USA which sees a close parallel with the clash between Sparta and democratic Athens and the rise of China to challenge the hegemony of the USA and the fundamental values of Western civilization.[13] American politics, across the board, is obsessed by the need to keep the USA as No. 1. President Biden was quite clear that "on my watch [...] China will not become No. 1".

The Chinese leadership provides a mirror image of this aggressive assertion of power, believing that China's time has come, not willing to be "contained" and confident that China will replace the declining USA. As Xi has put it, "The East is rising, and the West is declining." Such sentiments can tap into strong nationalistic feeling and justify the suppression of rights as necessary to maintain security. There is, within this world view, also a sense that China is under attack and is the victim of those in the USA plotting to undermine it through regime change and interference in its internal politics, as in Xinjiang and Hong Kong.[14] This strand in Chinese thinking is prepared to take on the USA over Taiwan and assert its new strength. If cooperation with the USA is no longer possible, China is preparing for a deep split and a world which is divided into respective spheres of influence. In this scenario, those in China who see the world in "zero-sum" terms come to dominate, as they do in the USA. International relations are all about "winning".[15]

In recent years the Sparta scenario has become more recognizable. The Trump presidency institutionalized the zero-sum approach to trade with China in particular, and international relationships in general. But Biden's presidency has not changed US suspicions of China, and he has made it clear that the USA will not allow itself to be displaced by China as the dominant superpower. Moreover, Biden has been successful in creating alliances based on common values and interests to contain and confront China. Many Western analysts now see China's rise as reflecting a Spartan world view, based on the desire to dominate, rather than a more cooperative Davos China. The "Made in China" strategy, for example, is seen as explicitly aimed to build Chinese technological superiority in a variety of frontier technologies which hold the key to future economic success and military dominance. Moreover, China does have an active programme of cyber warfare directed at Western targets, such as a recent alleged hacking (denied) of Covid vaccines.[16] All major countries engage in espionage and "black propaganda", but arguably the Chinese effort seems especially aggressive (or successful).

To those concerns we can add the territorial ambitions in the South China Sea; hostility to independent-minded neighbours like Vietnam and Australia; the armed confrontation with India; the use of the Belt and Road Initiative to generate markets and raw materials in the manner of imperial powers; and the build-up of military capability – which, while spending is not disproportionate to the Chinese economy, may soon enable China to have parity with the USA in some aspects of warfare. Alliances with Russia, Pakistan and Iran heighten a sense of confrontation with China's critics and adversaries.

Much of the argument about whether China is an aggressive Sparta, or a more cooperative and emollient Davos China, is at cross-purposes, and perhaps lost in translation. In Chinese eyes it is not aggressive and expansionary to claim territory that is rightfully its own. That is why the President can say, truthfully, that "China will never seek hegemony or expansion" while demanding control over Taiwan, the Senkaku Islands and chunks of northern India.[17] It is also fair to see Chinese belligerence as in part fuelled by a sense of paranoia at being surrounded by American bases and assailed by demands from Western powers to change its behaviour in territorial China (Xinjiang, Tibet and Hong Kong), which it construes and perhaps believes as attempted "regime change". By contrast, China would claim that it poses no such military or political "threat" to North America, Europe or Australasia, though the build-up of nuclear-weapon stockpiles and delivery systems generated by the new atmosphere of confrontation make it appear so.

The story of China as the modern Sparta ignores the many respects in which China is highly integrated with the process of globalization. But it is plausible, and becoming more so. Confrontational rhetoric and behaviour is reciprocated and leads into a vicious circle of recrimination and reaction. We have seen the level of mutual suspicion and paranoia which can easily be generated in the episode of the Chinese balloon floating across America and shot down on the president's orders in response to a political clamour over spying (which may or may not have been the case, or serious enough for genuine alarm). There is fevered debate in Congress around "the Chinese Communist Party's threat to America". Some of the hostility is directed against Asian-Americans in hate crimes. All of this is reported back in the Chinese state media, magnified and used to fuel Chinese nationalism.

Sanctions for "human-rights abuse" or restrictions on trade and investment on security grounds increase those already powerful nationalistic forces in Beijing preparing China for higher levels of self-sufficiency and for conflict – what some in China call the "great split". Cutting off supplies of sophisticated semiconductors makes it more likely that China will develop its own indigenous substitute. Driving away Chinese companies and researchers makes it more likely that they will develop under the control of the Chinese state without the benefit of exposure to Western influences. President Biden has continued or strengthened all these moves to "decouple" from China and tried to persuade other Western countries to follow suit. Chinese planning is no doubt based on the assumption that the China doctrine of Trump and Biden is normal rather than exceptional. It has also seen, in the West's response to the Ukraine war, a range of new sanctions like the seizure of overseas assets and disruption of the global payments system which could potentially be deployed against China. The Beijing government is clearly preparing for the use of these sanctions, should it carry through its commitment to unify China by taking

Taiwan. So, China as Sparta becomes a self-fulfilling prophecy. And, as in ancient Greece, the result is war: certainly "cold" war and perhaps "hot" war.

War over Taiwan

The Sparta scenario has two variants. In one there is a "cold war". There is a "great split". Decoupling gathers momentum as companies reassess "China risk", and it cannot be stopped despite attempts at a more nuanced "de-risking". The introduction of "guard rails" prevents open military conflict, except via proxies, but the world is effectively divided into Chinese and American spheres of influence with fierce competition for the political support, business opportunities and resources of the Global South.

A more alarming version of the Sparta scenario is that war happens. Until recently this was seen as a low-probability event – no longer. Taiwan's status is ambiguous: it exists in reality as a country of 24 million people, but it doesn't exist in theory (unlike Ukraine, whose existence as an independent sovereign state was widely accepted internationally). The ambiguity has been skilfully and pragmatically managed by the Taiwanese, the Americans and the Chinese. But the underlying positions are rigid and incompatible. In a Sparta scenario, the rigidity is tested to destruction.

For the Chinese, Taiwan is a breakaway province that must return to the PRC, by agreement if possible or by force if necessary. For the Taiwanese – 60% of whom identify as Taiwanese – Taiwan is a successful democratic country with a strong economy (albeit tied very closely to China). For the Americans, Taiwan must be defended not just for its own sake, but as a test of the security guarantees to Japan and South Korea and the wider region.

It is not difficult to see how "red lines" might be crossed. President Xi might conclude that the enormous economic damage caused by a war and accompanying sanctions is a price worth paying to unify the country. The Taiwanese ruling Liberal Party (the DPP) might decide, after winning another general election, that it is worth the risk of declaring independence and seeking wider recognition, since its allies will defend it. The Americans might be provoked into (or provoke) a clash with Chinese forces should the Chinese attempt a full or partial blockade or occupy a Taiwanese island near the mainland, or even attempt a full-frontal landing. Even without those, but with emotions running high, an accidental collision of vessels in the Malacca Strait or an unexplained aircraft disaster could easily lead to escalation.

There are numerous sub-scenarios on how conflict could unfold from limited and contained action to a wider war. Even with a limited conflict there would be far-reaching economic consequences: comprehensive economic sanctions on China; reciprocal action including measures to disrupt or destroy the TSMC factory on Taiwan which produces 90% of the world's advanced semiconductors. The "great split" would be sudden and brutal for the combatants and the world economy.

Peak China

It is perfectly plausible that neither of these two stories of a rising China will materialize. China could fail. The formidable set of "middle-income" problems facing the country could prove insurmountable. In such scenario, China becomes less important – neither a major threat nor an El Dorado offering vast commercial opportunities. In this version of events, which I call "Peak China", China has no capacity for and, ultimately, no interest in becoming a hegemonic power. It remains a powerful player in the Asian region – but nothing more. There are several reasons for believing that this is plausible. The Chinese could well come to realize that they have no hope of matching the "hard" and especially "soft" power of the USA once American influence is effectively combined with that of its allies. The Chinese language and the sense of racial exclusiveness are serious barriers to communication and building relationships across the world. It is also difficult for foreigners to fathom what a world run according to Chinese values would look like.

Moreover, there are unresolved domestic constraints on continued economic expansion: the "red flags" of demographic ageing, accumulated debt, an inconvertible currency and the "middle-income trap".[18] It could soon become apparent that trying to compete with the USA in technology is an impossible dream given American access to a global talent pool and information flows. The next decade could see a process of slowdown or stagnation in China, in which global ambitions are scaled back and the priority becomes domestic economic and political management. Projects like the Belt and Road could come to be seen by President Xi's successors, or he himself, as expensive indulgences. There is already evidence that China's massive commitment to BRI spending overseas is causing problems for overextended Chinese banks and a backlash in some recipient countries. There was a period early in the Ming dynasty in which the remarkable voyages of exploration of Admiral Zheng He were ended suddenly as an unnecessary extravagance, leading to a period of exclusion and isolation. That could happen again.

In this scenario, China reverts to being a chastened regional power trying to dominate its neighbours in East, Central and South-East Asia in a stable but asymmetric set of relationships, as it did under the imperial dynasties.[19] Countries like Thailand, Myanmar and Vietnam were never colonies in the manner of Western empires but were expected to defer to the emperor in Beijing and not cause offence. This kind of relationship could be described as "bullying", but in a way which is not dissimilar from US behaviour in relation to Mexico and Central America, the EU's treatment of peripheral countries like Greece, India's attitude to its small Himalayan neighbours or Russia's to its "near-abroad". But the bigger regional powers like Japan and India can hold their own economically and militarily. China is less engaged with the rest of the world.

If this scenario evolves, it will become clear to the USA and its allies that China is not a direct threat – that it has (like Japan after the 1980s) reached a plateau in terms of economic performance and has no aspirations to run the world. There is then a gradual loss of interest and a series of moves to avoid being caught up in regional disputes involving China. It is acknowledged that Hong Kong and Xinjiang are purely Chinese matters. Taiwan is strongly discouraged from provoking China by displays of independence and encouraged to kowtow in order to retain an element of its relative freedom. For their part, the Chinese are relaxed about a continued American presence in Japan and Korea which discourages those countries from independently developing nuclear weapons. The Peak China story can be told in different ways, but the underlying theme is of China underperforming economically, retreating from global ambitions and restricting any dominating behaviour to its neighbourhood.

Assessment

These three interpretations are all plausible, and elements are recognizable now. None is wholly right or wrong. They coexist at present, though it will be clear with the hindsight of history that one was dominant and fundamentally right. They are not predictions, but stories of the future based on today's realities, which are useful for testing out strategies for dealing with China.

Quite apart from their utilitarian value, stories matter, and President Xi sees himself as a storyteller. His story is the China Dream of China's material advance to achieve prosperity at home and respect abroad – all within the secure, stable framework provided by the Communist Party. Attempts to communicate the China Dream abroad have however been somewhat inconsistent: the soothing words of Davos China interspersed with the angry howl of the nationalistic "wolf warriors" representing Spartan China.

There are other possible scenarios which seem very improbable at present, but which could occur and for which we need to be prepared. One is that there could be a domestic upheaval in China originating in contested leadership of the Party. There is, at present, in contrast with the three decades after Deng, no system of planned succession. There could be growing dissatisfaction with the current president – and should he lose his grip or his health, or die, there is no agreed succession. The power struggle could turn ugly, with contenders for power building up regional power bases, as happened in the inter-war period and at various periods of weak government in Chinese history. Instability could quickly manifest itself on the streets. There are enough unhappy people in China to generate significant disorder (as of course the leadership warns when it justifies restrictions on political freedoms).

The value of scenario-planning is that it challenges established strategies and assumptions. We may hope for the best, but have we planned for the worst? We may be assuming the worst, but have we thought how to achieve a better outcome? After four chaotic years dominated by American presidential impulse and narrowly focused commercial disputes, there have been signs with Biden both of a more concerted and confrontational approach to China, but also an openness to thinking about alternative scenarios for China's future and how to respond to them.

Some will argue that China's basic intention is to threaten US national interests and to weaken the alliance system – to which "the smart response is for the USA to balance against China as it did once against the Soviet Union":[20] confrontation rather than engagement. An opposite view is that "China desires only to carve out a space for its security commensurate with its rising capabilities", and so "the USA should find a way to accommodate China's rightful desire for a greater voice and role in international affairs and institutions".[21] Others are agnostic, believing that there is as yet no clear way forward beyond preparing for any eventuality.[22]

From scenarios to strategy

Scenarios are a useful tool, but decision-makers have to have a clear and consistent strategy, while hedging for other possibilities at the same time. So, how do the strategies pursued in practice match the scenarios I have described? The USA from Nixon and Kissinger to George W. Bush and Condoleezza Rice believed in engagement and were in effect operating on the assumption that they were dealing essentially with an earlier version of Davos China in which Deng's injunction to China to keep its head low and bide its time prevailed.

The Obama administration dealt with the early Xi and could be said to "have steered an unsuccessful course between engagement and containment"[23] – between some engagement with Davos China – but, on the basis of more "hawkish" advice, behaved as if it were dealing with a threatening Sparta. The confusion resulted in such embarrassments as the attempts to block the establishment of the AIIB, which were simply ignored by America's allies, who were operating on a different set of assumptions about China. Indeed, the position of EU countries, including the UK, is that they were dealing with Davos China, and so there was no need for hostility.

President Trump did not initially appear to have an overarching view. He appeared to regard President Xi warmly and as a potential deal-maker. His initial response to allegations of human-rights abuse in Xinjiang was to support the Chinese counter-terrorist arguments. He was, in any event, preoccupied with bilateral trade deficits. But some of his key advisers did have a clear view and moved the USA towards a consistently hawkish position, reflecting the perception of China as an economic and strategic threat. This led to the sanctioning or the exclusion of Chinese companies, and a more general process of decoupling. This went hand in hand with an offensive against human-rights abuse, culminating in charges of "genocide" led by Secretary of State Mike Pompeo. Brexit Britain performed an awkward U-turn to reflect this hardening of position. And other countries – notably Japan and Australia – with their own reasons to be apprehensive about China's rise – have formed a tacit alliance with the United States.

President Biden hasn't changed the overall strategy – one of the few examples of continuity with the Trump administration – but is pursuing it through a wider alliance of Western democracies and with potential democratic allies elsewhere: Japan and India in particular. Within the USA there is bipartisan support for "strategic competition" rather than cooperation, and for "pushing back" rather than engagement (the Strategic Cooperation Bill, one of a succession of anti-China measures passing through Congress, is designed to "counter the malign influence of the Communist Party globally"). The view that China is a threat and bent on world domination, displacing America as the world's pre-eminent power, is almost axiomatic on the American "right" in the Republican Party and is well represented in the Biden team among officials and advisers.[24]

The Biden administration has been initially successful in its attempts to create alliances which reflect different perspectives and interests amongst allies. There was a joint US–Japan statement of support for Taiwan. The US–EU–Canada joint statement and sanctions on human rights was another. President Biden's attempt to resolve the seventeen-year-old aviation dispute (Boeing vs. Airbus) signalled a more cooperative approach to trade. But Europeans (and the Japanese) are wary of sacrificing economic interests in China, and are unsure whether Biden's alliance-building, or Trump's unilateralism, is the new normal.

The pandemic and the Ukraine war – with China tacitly supporting Russia – appear however to have accelerated a new consensus about China as the new Sparta seeking global dominance to pursue despotic ends. If this opinion consolidates, it will be used to strengthen a strategy of containment by the USA and its allies. This potentially leads down a dangerous road to conflict, cold or hot.

The limits of containment

The strategy of containment emerged under the Trump administration and is being urged on his successor by "hawks" inside and outside government. This approach to China consists of several elements: a belief that conflict is virtually inevitable and requires mobilization to fight a new "cold war", as with the former Soviet Union; a demand for comprehensive action to face a "whole of society" threat; and the need for a forceful assertion of Western values of liberal democracy and human rights, including within China. The consequences of pursuing containment rather than engagement need to be spelt out.

First, the negative expectation about Chinese behaviour is likely to be self-fulfilling. The repeated warning given by President Xi and widely believed among the Chinese elite is that the primary objective of Western and specifically US policy is to thwart China's rise – to suffocate its continued economic and technological advance and to prevent it achieving recognition of its proper status. That in turn calls for more self-reliance and a more forceful assertion of China's rightful place. Military encirclement and "interference" with China's internal affairs add to a sense of the USA and the West being a "threat", with the need to respond in kind. A key part of that response will be to strengthen the alliance with Russia and other "rogue states" like Iran and Venezuela – and, most dangerously, indulging dangerous provocations by North Korea.

Second, many of America's potential allies don't share the confrontational approach and have no wish to choose between the USA and China. An estimated 75% of countries trade more with China than with the USA. Whether it is "America First" or "China First" in terms of GDP and overall economic and technological leadership matters greatly to the self-esteem of their nationals and leaders, but not necessarily to other countries. Europeans, for example, value their economic links with China. German and French decision-makers are likely to be unattracted to an economic strategy designed to boost jobs in the United States rather than Europe. They may also judge that the calm and considered Biden regime is merely a temporary relief from some variant of Trump-style nationalism, and in any event do not agree among themselves about China. Such close neighbours and allies as Australia and New Zealand have had a different approach. Japan, South Korea and South-East Asian countries that feel threatened in security terms greatly value doing business with China. That is true even of Taiwan. And India, which feels threatened and has little trade with China, is a questionable ally in defence of a Western-led international order, not least because of its valued relationship with Russia.

China has also acquired many "friends" in the Middle East, Africa, Latin America and South-East Asia which have no wish to be conscripted as foot soldiers in a new "cold war" and appreciate the benefits of businesslike dealings with a country which is non-judgemental about their internal affairs, or share China's authoritarian model of government. They also ask, naturally, what is in it for them. Middle Eastern oil producers see that China is now a more important market than the USA. Recipients of Chinese BRI or other funding see that the USA and Europe have nothing of comparable scale and ambition. The lack of ambition extends to trade agreements, which are an obvious way to deepen relationships. For all the talk of Indo-Pacific trade cooperation, the USA makes it clear that improved market access is not on offer, while China parades its enthusiasm for new deals.

Henry Kissinger warned that "a policy which is seen as having designated China as the enemy primarily because its economy is growing and its ideology is distasteful would end up isolating the United States".[25] So far, President Biden has been successful in organizing common action, and the US-led NATO response to the Ukraine war has been impressively strong and united. But if China's opponents fail to maintain a common front, those in China who have mobilized for a confrontation will sense that they are "winning" and be emboldened to take more risks over, say, Taiwan.

Third, the high degree of integration of supply chains and collaborative research networks means that disentanglement or decoupling is damaging to both sides, and not obviously more damaging to China. A particular danger is the demonization and discouragement of Chinese researchers in the USA (and potentially the UK and elsewhere). PRC-born scientists make up a quarter of US-based researchers in artificial intelligence.[26] No doubt China would like to have them back. Chinese companies, like Chinese students, also benefit from exposure to Western standards and values. Excluding them is counterproductive. But including them, in a form of selective engagement, is difficult to sustain against a background of noisy "cold war" hostility.

Fourth, there are genuine differences in values, and democratic countries rightly wish to promote the attractions of free speech, democratic government and respect for minorities. But the values are best demonstrated by example rather than lecturing and denunciation. The United States has a particular credibility problem in defence of democracy following the Trump presidency and continued attempts by the Republican Party to weaken voting rights and judicial independence. There is also the problem that accusations directed against China may be true but are also true of other countries in any anti-China coalition. Vietnam is potentially an important regional ally, but an improbable recruit into a "league of democracies" as a Communist dictatorship, like China. India, like China, can be accused of mistreating its Muslim minority, and it is currently drifting away from its widely admired system based on democracy and free speech. Nor can we be confident that a fundamental change of political direction within China would be for the better. The experience of the USSR, Yugoslavia and the Arab world is not encouraging.

Finally, the idea that the USA and the West would "win" a "cold war" based on the experience of the Soviet Union may well be wishful thinking.[27] The Chinese economy is much bigger, stronger and more technologically sophisticated than that of the Soviet Union; the state is more competent; and there is far more integration into the global community. Moreover, carefully constructed surveys suggest that the regime enjoys high trust and satisfaction levels, even if it isn't loved. A major Harvard study shows satisfaction in Chinese central government to be consistently very high and growing.[28] Support has held up and grown after the pandemic.[29] International studies show that the Chinese government enjoys relatively high popular support.[30] The Soviet Union, by contrast, was a hollow construct which had to prevent its citizens leaving en masse.

Containment in these circumstances could well lead to confrontation and the mobilization of popular Chinese nationalism. China has no capacity or ambition to match the USA with strategic nuclear weapons as did the USSR, though it has a credible deterrent and is moving rapidly to increase and enhance its nuclear armoury. It is perfectly conceivable that conflict could erupt on one of the several flashpoints on China's periphery, and it is not to be assumed that China would back down. Would the United States then really go to war over the uninhabited Senkaku Islands or islands surrounding Taiwan – or, indeed, a frontal attack on Taiwan? Such scenarios are being publicly explored in China by people who could be described as "nationalist provocateurs".[31] There is sufficient doubt over the motives and reactions on both sides as to encourage risky behaviour and insufficient trust to prevent escalation. This is how a "cold war" could become "hot". There has to be an alternative involving engagement.

Making engagement work

It has become fashionable to describe engagement in relation to China as "naive" – the argument of those duped by exaggerated accounts of China's economic success and seduced by occasional soothing speeches by President Xi. But such an approach is essential not just to avoid confrontation – which could be dangerous, even disastrous – but to sustain the continued benefits of economic globalization. There are also various international public goods which require cooperative solutions and the cooperation of China. They include climate change (and other shared environmental problems); nuclear proliferation;

pandemic control; rules around the trading system; many areas of scientific research; rules on data flows; protocols around AI; international economic cooperation; standard-setting for new technologies; international peacekeeping and conflict resolution. The Brookings Institute has set out a comprehensive list and analysis of some of the issues involved.[32] Some are more urgent than others, and there are varying degrees of multilateralism or institution-building required. There are differences in the extent to which China is an enthusiastic or grudging participant (as is also the case of other powers). But unless we take the fatalistic view that confrontation and conflict are unavoidable, and cooperation pointless – since China is only interested in imposing its own world order – engagement is unavoidable. And the Davos China scenario sketched above, however incomplete, suggests that China wants to cooperate. I will review several of the key areas.

Climate change

China is by far the largest emitter of greenhouse gases, with around a third of the world total, more than the USA and Europe combined. About 80% by weight of these gases consists of CO_2, and most of that originates in coal-burning, which accounts for close to 60% of Chinese energy demand. Chinese coal is abundant, cheap, a major employer and – above all – a stable source of energy in a world where geopolitical tension is giving additional importance to security of supply. Without Chinese participation, little progress can be made in realizing reductions in global emissions, not least because climate-change deniers in the USA, major producers like Russia and Saudi Arabia and other major emitters like India have every reason to avoid assuming any obligations themselves. After arguing for many years that, as a developing economy, it should be exempt from any obligations, Chinese negotiators worked with the Obama administration to make a success of the Paris Agreement in 2015. China played little active part in COP 26 in Glasgow, and President Xi's absence provided a peg for criticism of China's large-scale burning of coal. An offer to stop financing coal-burning power stations overseas indicated, however, a willingness to support the COP process, and a joint declaration with the USA provided a basis for further action.

There are indications that the Chinese regime not only now takes the problem seriously but is committed to meeting demanding targets for carbon reduction.[33] Climate change is potentially very problematic for China itself, as highlighted by the recent severe flooding in Zhengzhou. President Xi has committed China to "zero net carbon" by 2060, and as an intermediate objective to reduce carbon emissions after reaching a peak in 2030. For a certain time, between 2013 and 2017, coal use was falling. And there are accounts of polluting plants being denied bank loans, others closed, and the burning of coal being politically denounced.[34] Power shortages in 2021 produced however a big shift back to coal burning. The 2030 target may be reached earlier, nonetheless, with big improvements being made in energy (and specifically carbon) efficiency and a rapid shift to renewable-energy production, behind which lies the world's largest solar- and wind-power industry and the production of electric cars. China seems to have installed more wind-power capacity in 2021 than the whole of the rest of the world in the previous five years. China has launched an emissions trading system. China appears to want not just to be compliant, but to be a global leader, and to progress beyond passive engagement to active cooperation in developing new technologies. That does not preclude vigorous competition between Chinese and other firms to develop technology: a race for glory and "green" profits should surely be welcome?

Encouraging though some Chinese statements and actions are, they are not primarily motivated by global idealism, but are more of a side effect of other domestic policies:[35] a curb on poor air quality, which was causing serious health problems in cities; an anxiety to reduce dependence on imported oil. It is also the case that in order to combat an economic slowdown the government has reactivated investment in coal-powered electricity stations (albeit ones that replace less efficient older power stations).[36] The latest Chinese Five-Year Plan, announced in March 2021, places heavy reliance on coal for power generation and appears to scale back earlier ambitions with renewables. Sceptics could also argue that global environmental commitments by an authoritarian regime have no public endorsement and are fragile. But in a world where the alternative is non-cooperation and disastrous inaction on climate change, the qualified commitment of the Chinese regime to a leadership role should surely be welcomed and then translated from vague promises to verifiable action.

Nuclear proliferation

It is debatable whether the spread of nuclear weapons is more or less of a threat to humanity than climate change, but it is of the same order of gravity. At present there are nine nuclear-weapon states, five recognized by the Nuclear Non-Proliferation Treaty, and four outside the treaty (India, Israel, Pakistan and North Korea). A largely dormant issue has been revived by the worries about North Korea's testing and improved delivery programme (which China has been unable or unwilling to stop); the revival of weapon stockpiling and modernization following failures of negotiation between the USA and Russia; and the attempts of others to break into the nuclear club (Iran). Moreover, there are at least half a dozen countries with the capacity to develop and deploy nuclear weapons who are currently being dissuaded from doing so, but may be tempted to break out.[37]

China has a key role to play in cooperating to maintain the status quo *or* destabilizing it further. It has been expanding and modernizing its own arsenal. It appears to be the one country able to restrain North Korea, though the relationship is opaque. China also played a role in developing the Pakistan bomb, and the triangular relationship (Pakistan, India, China) is currently stable but dangerous. A revival of the lapsed nuclear agreement with Iran will also require China not to undermine it under its new security agreement with Iran. China has also supplied Saudi Arabia with uranium-ore-processing technology and, separately, with rocket-engine technology. A likelier candidate for nuclear status is Japan, if provoked by China or North Korea, and if it lost confidence in American protection. South Korea is another one. Were China to play the role of a disruptor, it could set in train a new wave of proliferation in East Asia and the Middle East. Or it could be a helpful and stabilizing influence. Trust and confidence are key, and neither will be strong in a "cold war" environment.

Trade and the WTO

Some of the deterioration in relations between the USA and China, and to a lesser degree with Europe, is due to disenchantment over trade and investment. A critical factor giving impetus to Trump's aggressive trade "war" with China was the failure of American business to rally against it as it had in previous episodes of threatened protectionism directed at China.[38] And that failure had a lot to do with accumulated grievances around intellectual-property rights, "unfair" trade practices and various bad experiences in joint ventures which had come to outweigh the attractions of the China market. There has been a similar regression in Europe which the proposed Investment Agreement (CAI) was designed to resolve. A core issue for both the USA and Europe is the challenge presented to trade and investment rules by a system of "state capitalism" in which state-owned or state-controlled ventures benefit from hidden subsidies, procurement preference, access to favourable bank loans and, more generally, the hidden hand of the Chinese government.

The problem is not unique to China; India is even more protectionist and has many nationalized companies operating outside market rules and disciplines, as do Brazil and other emerging economies. But while India can continue (albeit with diminishing plausibility) to argue that it is a poor developing country meriting special and differential treatment, China cannot any longer take refuge in such arguments. Even then, among developed OECD countries, there are still structural barriers in countries which do not have a tradition of Anglo-Saxon capitalism. The long battles over "non-tariff barriers" protecting Japan Inc. and Korea Inc. are still fresh in the memory. In the case of China, what has made the problems so acute is the scale and intensity of Chinese competition, allied to the complaint that, after China was eventually admitted to the WTO, undertakings have been broken.

The current position in relation to trade and investment is "lose-lose". Trump's tariffs have been paid by American consumers, have cost an estimated 175,000 jobs and have not made China concede structural reforms. China offset much of the cut in exports to the USA by exporting more elsewhere.[39] And the tariff policy divided the USA from Europe and Japan, who together might achieve more in negotiating terms. Trump's preoccupation with bilateral deficits and "currency manipulation" was a distraction. The Biden administration would like to move away from it, though there is a strong protectionist element in the Democratic Party which was enthusiastic about Trump's economic nationalism and recognized its appeal. The misnamed "Inflation Reduction Act" and a slew of legislation designed to boost US production capacity in semiconductors and green technologies are highly protectionist in terms of trade. China has every reason to cooperate in creating a less protectionist environment, which is currently damaging its export industries and disrupting its supply chains. It could and should make concessions on the structural issues of concern to the USA and the EU where these overlap with needed domestic economic reform to support growth.

If the approach to China was conducted outside a "cold war" mindset, there is much of mutual benefit which could be negotiated in a multilateral context. Constructive negotiations could, in the process, lead to reform and revival of the currently moribund WTO.[40] China wishes to be classified as a "market economy", which gives it more protection from discriminatory action in the field of anti-dumping and "trade defence" measures. In return China would have to accept greater discipline over state enterprises and "forced transfer" of technology and be willing to accept rules around new issues such as e-commerce and digital trade. Negotiations would not be easy, but this is one area where US and EU negotiators can work together and with other countries which are broadly aligned on strengthening a rules-based multilateral trading system. There are detailed suggestions about how negotiating with China in a multilateral context could be revived based on mutual self-interest.[41]

Development

China has become a major player in the development of poorer countries, especially in Africa, through the BRI and lending from its state-owned banks. The debt from these loans is now a major part of African external debt and a significant contributor to the economic crisis which has come to Africa in the wake of the Covid pandemic, with the crippling loss of export and tourist earnings. It is estimated that at least 20% of African debt is owed to China, and more than double that in Angola, with high levels also in Zambia and Zimbabwe.

There has been a campaign led by the main multilateral bodies – the World Bank, the IMF and the G20 – to suspend debt service for seriously affected countries. Debt is not being cancelled, but suspension of servicing is a form of relief, and gives time for negotiations under the Paris Club of official creditors. China has been separately offering suspension – but, as with Western creditors, there is little indication that it is willing to forgive debt (except in a few, largely unreported cases like Cameroon). Indeed, so far, China has been as hard-nosed in dealing with debtors as its Western counterparts, seeking control over real assets like Angolan oil fields as collateral.[42]

But it does not wish to be seen as less generous than Western creditors, and has worked cooperatively with the West in some cases (for example, Ghana). That is a good reason for trying to get China inside the club of official lenders. China's lending is currently outside international norms – it is opaque. And there is also an understandable reluctance by creditors to offer debt relief if this merely helps debtors to pay back Chinese lenders. Cooperation makes sense.

China has also set up what appears to be a genuine development agency, CIDCA, which provides concessional loans and grants. China now has an incentive to respond positively to attempts to engage it. If it were to agree to join the Paris Club and coordinate debt relief, the quid pro quo could be a bigger voice in the IMF. If it were, through CIDCA, to join the Development Assistance Committee, which oversees standards of aid governance, including transparency and competitive procurement, the offer would be a bigger role in the World Bank.[43] The United States has the additional carrot in reserve of joining the AIIB. There is a strong case for making this set of issues a test of Chinese sincerity – whether it really wants to be Davos China. Core national interests and pride are not at stake, and the positive signalling would be powerful.

Cyber security

There is a messy, confusing and rapidly changing world in which cyber crime by gangsters, and security against it, merges into cyber warfare between states. As the two leading digital economies, China and the USA have a shared interest in minimizing disruption to their economies, but also diverging interests in building up a cyber-offence capability. There is scope both for more cooperation and more conflict.

There are separate issues. One is spying, state on state, to gather material for state security as well as to help favoured firms. Nations spy on each other. What is new is the scale and speed of espionage. The Chinese hacking of the American Office of Personnel Management in 2014 involved the records of more than 20 million people. But otherwise, there is no difference from the old world of secret drops and cameras with microfilm. In the case of China there are reports of dozens of espionage cases being brought against Chinese nationals in the USA, but the extent and severity of spying will depend on the overall state of bilateral relations.

A largely distinct issue is large-scale criminal activities in the form of ransomware, as in the recent attacks on Colonial Pipeline in the USA. These actions are largely driven by criminality rather than state policy, but criminal gangs get varying degrees of protection from uncooperative states like Russia, and perhaps China. China's potential as a haven could well be enhanced using a digital currency, which criminals prefer to cash. Cooperation on cyber crime is obviously of mutual benefit but isn't going to happen in a "cold war" environment. Instead, we are likely to see more hybrid cyber warfare, in which state-backed hackers attack commercial interests. An example of this was the March 2021 hack of Microsoft's email system. China has categorically denied any wrongdoing, but the USA was sufficiently confident of Chinese involvement that it issued a warning "advisory note" naming China as the sponsor of the attacks.

The potential for both cooperation and conflict is however limited by what some experts believe is an exaggerated belief in China's capability (relative to the USA).[44]

Tripwires and conflict avoidance

Wars break out by accident. There are hair-raising anecdotes of how the Cold War almost became a hot war by accident: the misreading of incoming missiles on radar screens which turned out to be flocks of birds; intercepted messages wrongly translated or interpreted. In the event, carefully prepared and agreed protocols and confidence-building – with telephone "hotlines" – prevented the worst from happening. It is not at all clear that the several potential flashpoints on China's borders have been similarly defused, especially the precise point at which Chinese harassment of Taiwan by warships or aircraft or China's response to Taiwan's provocative assertion of "independence" triggers armed intervention by the USA. Hitherto, pragmatism has prevailed on both sides. But there is a dangerous dynamic, in that events in Hong Kong have effectively killed any prospect of Taiwan being willing to accept PRC rule under the "one country, two systems" formula, while there are signs of Chinese impatience at the failure to conclude the long-awaited reunification of China. There are similar but less pressing issues in relation to China and Japan, and in the complex interaction which would be involved in a crisis between China, the two Koreas, the USA and Japan.

A positive sign was that China had a "no first use" policy in relation to nuclear weapons, but even that has been abandoned, prompting a big expansion of nuclear weapons and the development of much more rapid and manoeuvrable delivery systems. But other "tripwires" will need to be developed. In mid-2023 the Chinese military high command were refusing to meet their American opposite numbers to discuss conflict risks because the political context was too confrontational. The United States was sufficiently alarmed at the breakdown in communications in 2023 that the director of the CIA was sent to Beijing to try to start a dialogue.

There is also a set of problems which did not apply in the Cold War with the USSR. The USSR was massively armed, and China is not. But China is a technological innovator, and capable of creating lethal autonomous weapons and expanding the use of cyber technology. The development of AI and 5G raises ethical and political as well as military issues, which require international agreement on new protocols and standards. The United States would expect to lead, overall, in establishing such standards, but since China is the main alternative source of new technologies, there has to be a mechanism within which cooperation can proceed.

Conflict avoidance and "tripwires" to warn of dangerous tensions fall a long way short of active cooperation, but they create confidence, on which bigger things can be built. Kevin Rudd's recent book on China and the West[45] describes in detail how such processes can be developed.

Limits to engagement: strategic competition and coalitions

There are areas where cooperation is particularly difficult: where national-security is deemed to be at stake. "Security" can be defined narrowly or broadly, and the broad definitions are often being used in a damaging and self-defeating way to restrict flows of talent, investment and trade. But clearly there are national-security constraints on cooperation. Jeffrey A. Bader of Brookings expresses the dilemma well: "The challenge is to protect and defend [our] interests in the emerging strategic competition without pursuing decoupling from China to the point of entrenching a new Cold War [...]. Ideological differences exacerbate the rivalry, but most of the issues are inherent in major power competition. This should be handled without the need to demonize China over systemic differences."[46]

A good general principle is that the best way to succeed in economic, technological – and ideological – competition is to demonstrate superiority, not to try to suppress the competition. The best antidote to Chinese success in innovation, science and technology is for Western countries to invest more heavily in R&D, both academic and commercial; to maintain open borders to attract scientific talent, including Chinese students; and to create an environment where innovators are rewarded. The best response to China's economic success is to demonstrate that Western economic management is better at achieving growing living standards and quality of life, greater equality and stability. The best way of communicating core values around democracy, free speech and human rights is to show that we practise them, dispelling the widespread Chinese belief that the Western model is discredited and the values hollow and hypocritical.

There are however several areas where coalitions of the like-minded can take the lead in creating rules and standards in areas where China would not currently reach the relevant threshold (but might aspire to).

Commercial data flows

It has been estimated that half of global economic output in the next five years will be created digitally.[47] The potential gains from cross-border data flows, and from not restricting them geographically, are immense.[48] We have had examples of the potential benefits from international collaboration over Covid-genome analysis and vaccine-testing. But, as of now, there is little common ground between Western countries and China on the free flow of information. Nor is there much of a common understanding among the leading non-authoritarian societies about what rules should apply. European personal privacy standards are stricter than in the USA, and the gulf was revealed by the decision of the European Court of Justice to invalidate the US–EU "Privacy Shield" governing transfers of personal data on the grounds that the US system is insufficiently secure. Japan has suggested a multilateral agreement based on a "free flow of data with trust" with countries certified according to agreed standards of openness and privacy protection.[49] But without agreement between the USA and EU and other key players like India, the idea isn't going anywhere.

Meanwhile, China has been ploughing its own furrow, and is proving remarkably successful at generating vast quantities of data from its Internet platforms for internal use. But its principle of "data sovereignty" and, through the Great Firewall, its censorship of imported data deemed to be politically unacceptable, cut across the free flow of data. And the use of sophisticated and comprehensive surveillance to capture masses of data, furthermore, shows little respect for privacy. There are ways of getting a prudent balance between security and openness.[50] But unless an alternative model is offered through a common approach by the USA and EU, global standards evolving through the governing bodies of the Internet and the International Telecommunications Union will simply reflect the Chinese view of information flows based on "sovereignty".

Values and rights

There is a strong movement in civil society in Western countries, as well as from politicians of "right" and "left", for their governments to "call out" Chinese human-rights abuses, to defend "our values" and "hold China to account". To some extent, government denunciations of China are for domestic consumption. The fact that, until recently, "values" offensives were led by Mr Mike Pompeo, carrying all the political baggage of the Trump administration, has limited their appeal.[51] But there is a serious question of how to influence China's conduct from outside, and how most effectively to give support to groups within China whose rights are being compromised.

The Chinese could respond to external criticisms in one of two ways. The first is to retaliate by attacking weaknesses in the record of those governments criticizing them and expose hypocrisy and inconsistency. There would be a rich vein of material in most cases, if it came to a slanging match over values. A focus on weak US gun laws would play on the revulsion and incomprehension elsewhere. It cannot be a coincidence that motions have surfaced in the United Nations challenging Australia's human-rights record in relation to, for example, the removal of asylum-seekers to remote offshore islands. But China does relatively little of that, since it would undermine its main defence: that these are internal matters of national sovereignty. The regime has aggressively dismissed, on these grounds, attacks on its behaviour in Hong Kong, Tibet, Xinjiang and elsewhere. More generally, it disputes the whole idea that there are universal values to which it is bound – indeed it claims that non-interference is a universal principle.

That defence is widely shared by governments outside the developed-country democracies. Indeed, many other democratic and semi-democratic nations do not respond well to external criticism. There is a so-called "Like-Minded Group" including Bangladesh, Malaysia, Indonesia and Pakistan – all democracies – which has worked with China to deflect or suppress criticism in international fora, notably the UN.[52] But hiding behind a defence of sovereignty exposes China to serious and valid criticism in respect of its non-compliance of conventions it has subscribed to and the principles of organizations like the United Nations, to which it belongs. China has signed and ratified six human-rights treaties, but has only signed, not ratified, that on civil and political rights.[53] Attacking China because it does not follow Western notions of "liberal democracy" invites scornful dismissal of "colonial" attitudes and interference. But the defence of universal, law-based norms to which China has subscribed is a much stronger position.

There are several practical implications. The first is the need for critics of China to underline their own commitment to the universal status of human rights by participating in relevant UN institutions and Treaty "Special Procedures", such as country reviews. There are undoubted procedural obstacles within the UN system, and China has become skilful at mobilizing support in key bodies like the UN Human Rights Council.[54] US withdrawal from the UNHRC was regarded as a diplomatic gift to the Chinese regime.[55] Moreover, the USA has not yet ratified a range of conventions setting international standards, like those relating to discrimination against women, the rights of the child and disability. Sometimes the operating systems of the UN produce uncomfortable outcomes and frustrations, but that is the price of establishing a common set of rules against which all countries can be judged.

A second point is that it should be easier to support civil-society activists in China who are campaigning on issues that cannot be portrayed as threatening to Chinese national security: domestic violence, LGBT rights, disability and sexual harassment, for example. But even in these areas there are signs that the issues are being portrayed as the concerns of hostile foreign influences, and there is evidence of aggressive trolling of feminists, gay people and environmentalists which may have official encouragement.

A third is that there are practical ways of helping individuals threatened with persecution without intervening in China's internal affairs. One is being generous in granting asylum. For this reason, the British response to the crackdown in Hong Kong by opening its doors to its residents who wish to leave was well judged. It is compatible with Britain's claim – often not realized – to be open and inclusive, and compatible with China's own good record of encouraging its nationals to travel abroad. As a result, Chinese complaints about "interference" looked hollow and unconvincing.

A final point relates to the issue of "punishment" for non-compliance with agreed norms. In practice the main punishment is reputational damage, and that is a powerful weapon when delivered by bodies whose impartiality is beyond doubt. China's disregard for an international panel of judges in relation to the Law of the Sea has had a far bigger impact on attitudes in South-East Asia than any amount of lecturing from aggrieved or unfriendly governments. Sanctions however give the impression of seriousness but are usually symbolic and lack credibility when applied by the usual suspects. And China will simply retaliate in kind.

The issue of enforcement of human rights is the context in which to view the decision of the USA, supported by UK and others, to accuse China of "genocide" in Xinjiang. To charge China with the most horrific of all crimes against humanity invites the obvious supplementary question: what action is to be taken to stop it and to prosecute the perpetrators in the provincial and national leadership? The move is undoubtedly shrewd, since China is a signatory to the convention on the Prevention and Punishment of the Crime of Genocide. The practical problem is that there is a wide range of legal interpretations. Virtually no one is alleging that China is engaged in the mass killing of Uyghurs or any other group. Rather, a very wide legal definition of genocide is being used to encompass serious human-rights abuse against members of an ethnic and religious minority – but it is so wide as to be applicable to a good many other countries. And it thereby devalues the significance of a particularly horrific accusation.

The decision of Western governments (conspicuously not supported by governments of leading Muslim countries) to make the Uyghur Muslims the focus of their human-rights policy raises the obvious question as to what is happening. The issues have been discussed in Chapter 5.

China's treatment of its minorities is dire, but far from being unique. As discussed earlier, the "genocide" campaign is questionable in its own terms. It is also dangerous: either it will lead to sanctions and arrests on international warrants – in which case China will retaliate by means of hostage diplomacy in an already tense environment – or, more likely, nothing will happen beyond token sanctions (as now), in which case the accusers will appear weak, and the accusations devalued. The publication of the UN's Bachelet report on Xinjiang was a far more influential mechanism.

Contrasting scenarios

China isn't going to go away. Basic realism demands engagement at some level. The greater likelihood is that China's influence on the world's economy, environment and politics will grow (though there is the possibility of what I call the Peak China scenario, where it retreats inward in the face of economic difficulties at home and overreach abroad). As countries seek to define their relations with China, there is a range of possibilities: cooperation, competition, confrontation and conflict. Currently, almost all the political energy and analysis comes from the United States – and, to a degree, from Australia. That is unsurprising, giving American centrality in the international economic system and its military dominance in the Asia-Pacific based on its defence commitments to its Asian allies – Japan, South Korea and Taiwan (as well as Australia, Singapore and New Zealand). Within the last decade, American policy has been through major mutations, starting with an emphasis on engagement, primarily for economic reasons, followed by trade conflict, followed in turn by more comprehensive hostility based on the idea of China as an economic, technological, military and political threat. The Biden administration has sought to build alliances to confront this threat, whilst allowing for a degree of engagement in commercial matters and in areas of common global concern such as climate change.

By contrast, Europe has looked at China largely through the lens of trade and investment, though the interest of civil society in human rights and China's emergence as a global power have forced a deeper and wider look.[56] The fact that the main countries of Europe are allies of the USA in NATO has also led to a sharing of American analysis of China and, to a degree, the adoption of common positions, a trend strengthened by the Ukraine war. An attempt has been made by the European Union, through the Commission, to define a common approach to China, but there are also differences of approach reflected in the all-purpose formula which includes describing China as a "partner", "competitor" and "strategic rival" at the same time.[57]

Two broad approaches have emerged in Europe. The first is the British position, which has been, after an abrupt U-turn, to align itself closely with the USA to become an ally in a new "cold war" with China – what I have described elsewhere being part of the "posse" riding against the outlaw state.[58] The other approach, associated with France and Germany, is one of accommodation and engagement with China, reluctance to join the "posse" and a focus on a beneficial economic relationship together with collaborative working on important "public goods" like climate change. Both are caricatures, with the British seeking, in practice, to maintain businesslike relations with China, and Germany re-examining its dependence on the Chinese market.

As described in the previous chapter, Germany's involvement with China encompasses a long and profitable set of business relationships, through trade and investment, based on its engineering prowess: top-of-the-range car manufacturers, capital goods and engineering conglomerates like Siemens. China accounts for more than 40% of Volkswagen's sales; Audi, Mercedes and BMW all have great exposure to the Chinese market. Germany is also one of the few countries to run a trade surplus with China. It has not all been sweetness and light.[59] German Mittelstand companies have had their share of complaints about technology extracted through joint ventures and IP theft. The ambitions of the "Made in China" report in 2015 alarmed some German industrialists.[60] The takeover of a German robotics company, KUKA, caused further apprehension about the scale of Chinese industrial ambition. Germany reacted to these events by pushing for stronger anti-dumping action by the EU, and more thorough screening of inward investors.

But various factors have put back the positives into the relationship. Much of that was due to Mrs Merkel's personal diplomacy: she visited China on numerous occasions. The British referendum and Brexit also undermined the leading role which China had accorded to the UK as a partner within the EU, which has now passed to Germany. The establishment of the Duisburg terminus to the BRI has strengthened German communications to the East across the Eurasian land mass.

A key factor in the evolution of German policy appears to have been an agreement between Deutsche Telekom and Huawei, which gives the former a major role in the development of Chinese telecoms and Huawei a foothold in Europe after being shut out by the UK, France, Sweden and other countries. The consolidation of Germany's economic links with China has, however, coincided with the deterioration in the political climate, and there is a growing influence of geopolitical "hawks" as well as the Greens and Social Democrats in the new coalition government, concerned about human rights, to pursue a more combative and confrontational approach to China. The Ukraine War has led to a lot of recrimination about Germany's overdependence on Russia, and the same argument is being made over the export sector's dependence on the China market. Chancellor Merkel stood for economic engagement. Now she has departed the scene, German policy is more likely to reflect the views of Germany's main ally, the USA, albeit tempered by a degree of "strategic autonomy", as advocated by the French.

With the UK, there has been a sharp decline since the "Golden Era" of 2015. Several factors have contributed to the process. First, the decision to ditch Huawei went against national interests, defined by an earlier compromise. It was a decisive break, and demonstrated that, faced with a choice between China and the USA, the UK had little choice. Second, the crisis in Hong Kong has put the legacies of empire into the spotlight and made it unavoidable that the UK would have to defend the "one country, two systems" model which it negotiated. Offering safe haven to UK passport holders was morally right but has brought the UK into direct confrontation with China.

Third, a powerful cross-party momentum has built up in Westminster, led by the Conservatives' China Research Group (CRG) but endorsed by opposition parties, to take a particularly vigorous line on human rights, and particularly the accusations of "genocide". There are also those in the CRG who are pressing to disengage from Chinese investment in the nuclear-power industry and other sectors. The decision of Mr Nigel Farage to devote his considerable political talents to campaigning against Chinese "influence" in the UK suggests that there is substantial untapped potential for a populist anti-Chinese movement.

One big change, underlying this change in mood, is Brexit. Brexit has led inevitably to a move to shift alignments away from Europe to the United States, in pursuit of an elusive "trade deal", but reflecting a deeper attachment captured in the British belief that there is a "special relationship" based on language and history. This realignment, in turn, has prompted the adoption of a position on China closer to that of the United States. There has also been some excitement about the prospects for a "global Britain", unshackled from the constraints of the EU, to become an "Indo-Pacific" power and to exploit the economic opportunities presented by the economic growth and the trade openings offered by Asia. Problematically, however, many of those opportunities originate with China, and one of the regional trading groups which Britain could join, the RCEP, is seemingly led by China and excludes the United States. Instead, Britain has identified the legacy body from Obama's stalled TPP, which excludes the USA and potentially includes China. There also appears to be an appetite to join a loose alliance, confronting China, of the USA, Japan, Australia and possibly India. Britain's membership of the AUKUS grouping with Australia and the USA was a firm statement of military intent.

To try to make sense of this mixture of influences, the recent government launched an Integrated Review. It sets out an approach to China which treats China, on the one hand, as a commercial opportunity, building on the rapid growth of trade and investment of the last decade, but also as a "systemic challenge".[61] The dilemma is not unique to Britain, but "cakeism" – "having one's cake and eating it" – could prove elusive. As Australia has discovered, China can switch on and off the trade tap if provoked, and Britain could suddenly find that valuable business is put at risk.[62] Sending warships to the South China Sea in a display of military strength is the kind of gesture which has consequences. There is little indication that the new British approach has been thought through.

Britain on one hand and Germany and France on the other have represented two different models of how Europe should deal with modern China. Britain has a declared intention to redefine itself as an Asian power, with preferential trade links and military involvement in an embryonic alliance with the USA, Australia and other countries in the region confronting China in a new Cold War. Germany, with France and others, is potentially offering a model based on engagement with China which is nuanced, ambiguous and transactional. There is little doubt that the latter accords more closely with the political and economic realities of a world where China is emerging as the next superpower. But the former is in tune with the more confrontational spirit within the USA. The overall approach, however, is still very far from settled, and rests, at present, on the somewhat opaque formula that the West should "de-risk" from overdependence on China, but not "decouple".

Conclusion

It is still an open question as to whether future relations between the West and China will be characterized by confrontation, attempted containment and disengagement on the one hand or attempts at cooperation, coexistence and engagement on the other. At present there is an awkward mix of the two different approaches: angry confrontation with China over Taiwan, regional security, cyber warfare, "unfair" trading practices, technology "theft" and human-rights issues, and attempts at businesslike cooperation over economic matters and shared international problems like climate change.

It is perfectly possible that such a complex and hybrid approach can be sustained for a while with diplomatic skill. It also reflects the reality that, as between the USA and the EU, and many other countries outside the Western world, there are very different interests and different appetites for the benefits of trade and the costs of confrontation. The approach is however somewhat unstable, since conflict, once ignited, can easily escalate. China does not compare militarily with the United States on a global scale, but is increasingly well matched, should disputes in China's neighbourhood, as with Taiwan, spin out of control. "Taking a stand" on human rights within China, reinforced by sanctions, leads to retaliation; then counter-retaliation and counter-counter-retaliation. Unpicking supply chains on "security" or "de-risking" grounds affects both sides and quickly leads to competitive decoupling and protectionism.

A long-term, considered approach to China must start from a base of fact. What is surprising (and alarming) is that, even among "experts", there are wildly different assessments of where China currently is – big disparities over such apparently straightforward matters as the size of the economy, its growth, the level of technological development and the relative importance of the state and private sectors. There is a wide gulf between economic "bulls", who see a continuation of China's impressive growth, and "bears", who see an economy weighed down by challenges such as debt, demographic ageing and a "middle-income trap". The "bulls" point to a successful, dynamic, entrepreneurial model of "state capitalism"; the bears see a sclerotic, unreformed Communist-state machine. Politics is full of contradictions: an increasingly authoritarian, dictatorial regime which also seems to enjoy public trust and support; a suppression of personal freedoms at the same time as (pre-pandemic) 130 million Chinese freely leave and return to their country every year; leadership with a long-term vision but no succession plan.

To predict the future, due to the extreme uncertainty, is quixotic and, for someone who is not a "China expert", would be extremely presumptuous. I have endeavoured instead to sketch out three very different scenarios, describing possible, plausible futures. Each is recognizable today, and it is only with future hindsight that we will be able to say with more confidence which was essentially right.

The West, led by the USA, appears now to believe that it is dealing with what I call "Spartan China" – that "assertive" China is a "threat", aiming for global supremacy and rejecting the fundamental truth of Western values, and must be confronted and contained through alliances prepared for a new "cold war". There are certainly elements in current Chinese behaviour and rhetoric which justify that reaction – but, overall, a strategy based upon it leads down a very dangerous path.

There is, as a counterpoint to that downbeat scenario and the "threat" of Spartan China, a more optimistic outlook. I call it "Davos China". This is a China that wants to engage globally, through trade and investment, participating in multilateral institutions and contributing to dealing with collective problems. But it is not the China which was, until recently, envisioned by Western leaders as a pliant country which would become more "like us" and sign up to the existing international order. Davos China is closer to the Chinese concept of *tianxia*: a peaceful and harmonious international order with China at its centre. It retains its distinctive political system and can be a difficult partner, rejecting the imposition of Western values and insisting on a share in decision-making appropriate to its superpower status: a new security and economic order reflecting China's rise. This is "engagement with Chinese characteristics" and it is uncomfortable for the West, used to engagement on its own terms.

Engagement with China is currently unfashionable, and likely to be dismissed as "naive" or even as "appeasement". The alternatives however are worse: a sacrifice of economic opportunities, a neglect of shared threats to the planet and war – war which will certainly be cold and probably hot. Catastrophic war is a real risk, but also avoidable.[63]

It is worth, in conclusion, drawing on the wisdom of Henry Kissinger, now a hundred years old, who has devoted as much high-quality thought to the issue of how China and the USA can coexist as anyone on the planet. He warns that "neither side has much margin for political concession, and any disturbance of the equilibrium can lead to catastrophic consequences". But he also believes that it is possible to create a world order on the basis of rules that China (with Europe and India) can join.[64]

Notes and Sources

PREFACE

1   Oliver Letwin, *China v America: A Warning* (London: Biteback 2021).
2   Vince Cable, *China and India: Economic Reform and Global Integration* (London: Royal Institute of International Affairs, 1995).
3   Vince Cable, *China: Engage! Avoid the New Cold War* (London: Bite-Sized Books, 2020).
4   Stein Ringen, *The Perfect Dictatorship: China in the 21st Century* (Hong Kong: Hong Kong University Press, 2016), p. 39.
5   www.tinyurl.com/tztdufz7.

CHAPTER 1

1   Pew Research Center. Little more than a decade ago, in 2010, Americans' view of China was strongly positive, and three years ago "favourable" and "unfavourable" views were equally split. Now, roughly four times as many rate China as "unfavourable" as "favourable". There has been a similar shift in Europe and Australia.
2   The quote has been variously attributed to Lord Amhurst (who visited Napoleon on St Helena), Lenin (citing Napoleon) and the script of a film starring David Niven. The history of the quote is covered in Peter Hicks's article '"Sleeping China" and Napoleon' (Napoleon.org).
3   Parag Khanna, *The Future Is Asian: Global Order in the Twenty-First Century* (London: Weidenfeld & Nicolson, 2019); Gideon Rachman, *Easternisation: War and Peace in the Asian Century* (London: Bodley Head, 2016).

4   Gideon Rachman, *The Age of the Strongman: How the Cult of the Leader Threatens Democracy around the World* (London: Bodley Head, 2022).

5   Martin Jacques, *When China Rules the World: The Rise of the Middle Kingdom and the End of the Western World* (London: Allen Lane, 2009).

6   Kishore Mahbubani, *Has China Won? The Chinese Challenge to American Primacy* (New York: PublicAffairs, 2020).

7   Arvind Subramanian, *Eclipse: Living in the Shadow of China's Economic Dominance* (New York: Columbia University Press, 2011).

8   C. Fred Bergsten, *The United States vs China: The Quest for Global Economic Leadership* (Cambridge, UK: Polity Press, 2022).

9   Rush Doshi, *The Long Game: China's Grand Strategy to Displace American Order* (Oxford: Oxford University Press: 2021).

10 Michael Beckley, *Unrivalled: Why America Will Remain the World's Sole Superpower* (Ithaca and London: Cornell University Press, 2018).

11 William Bernstein, *A Splendid Exchange: How Trade Shaped the World* (London: Atlantic Books, 2009), pp. 2–4.

12 Angus Maddison, *Contours of the World Economy, 1–2030 ad* (Oxford: Oxford University Press, 2007) and *Chinese Economic Performance in the Long Run* (Paris: OECD Publishing, 2007).

13 Peter Frankopan, *The Silk Roads: A New History of the World* (London: Bloomsbury, 2015), p. 185.

14 Voltaire, *An Essay on the Customs and Spirit of Nations*, cited in Jonathan Spence, *The Search for Modern China* (New York: W.W. Norton, 1990), p. 133.

15 Spence, ibid., p. 134.

16 Adam Smith, *An Inquiry into the Nature and Causes of the Wealth of Nations*, ed. Edwin Cannan (Chicago: University of Chicago Press, 1977), p. 70.

17 Ibid., pp. 70–72.

18 Spence, op. cit., p. 121.

19 Ibid., p. 117.

20 Michael Greenberg, *British Trade and the Opening of China 1800–42* (Cambridge, UK: Cambridge University Press, 1970),

pp. 6–8, and Hsin-Pao Chang, *Commissioner Lin and the Opium War* (Cambridge, MA: Harvard University Press, 1964), pp. 212–13.

21 Quoted in *An Embassy to China: Being the Journal Kept by Lord Macartney During His Embassy to the Emperor Ch'ien-lung, 1793–1794*, ed. J.L. Cranmer-Byng (London: Longmans, 1962), pp. 212–13.

22 R.K. Newman, *Opium Smoking in Late Imperial China: A Reconsideration* (Cambridge, UK: Cambridge University Press), cited in Bernstein, op. cit., p. 289.

23 Chang, op. cit., pp. 85–91.

24 Jacques, op. cit., p. 88.

25 Jonathan Fenby, *The Penguin History of Modern China* (London: Penguin, 2008), p. 10.

26 Bernstein, op. cit., p. 297.

27 Ibid., pp. 297–98.

28 Franz Michael, in collaboration with Chung-li Chang, *The Taiping Rebellion* (Seattle: University of Washington Press, 1966).

29 Cited in Fenby, op. cit., p. 22.

30 Jonathan Spence, *The China Helpers: Western Advisers in China, 1620–1960* (London: The Bodley Head, 1969), p. 74.

31 Karl Marx, 'Revolution in China and in Europe' (1853).

32 Michael H. Hunt, *The Making of a Special Relationship: The United States and China to 1914* (New York: Columbia University Press, 1983), pp. 92–93.

33 John Kuo Wei Tchen and Dylan Yeats, eds., *Yellow Peril!: An Archive of Anti-Asian Fear* (London: Verso, 2014).

34 Joseph W. Esherick, *The Origins of the Boxer Uprising* (Berkeley and Los Angeles: University of California Press, 1987).

35 Fenby, op. cit., p. 91.

36 Ibid.

37 Victor Purcell, *The Boxer Uprising: A Background Study* (New York: Cambridge University Press, 1963).

38 Jacques, op. cit., p. 381.

39 George T. Yu, *Party Politics in Republican China: The Kuomintang, 1912–24* (Berkeley and Los Angeles: University of California Press, 1966).

40   John K. Fairbank, ed., *The Cambridge History of China,* Vol. 12, *Republican China, 1912–49, Part 1* (Cambridge, UK: Cambridge University Press, 1983).

41   John K. Fairbank and Kwang-Ching Liu, eds., *The Cambridge History of China,* Vol. 11, *Late Ch'ing, 1800–1911, Part 2* (Cambridge, UK: Cambridge University Press, 1980).

42   Spence, op. cit., p. 382.

43   Jacques, op. cit., p. 67.

44   Fenby, op. cit., p. 304.

45   Spence, op. cit., p. 470.

46   Merle Miller, *Plain Speaking: An Oral Biography of Harry S. Truman* (New York: G.P. Putnams, 1973), pp. 258–59.

47   Spence, op. cit., p. 527.

48   Ibid., p. 524.

49   Joseph R. McCarthy's book *America's Retreat from Victory: The Story of George Catlett Marshall* (1963) features in Richard M. Fried, *Nightmare in Red: The McCarthy Era in Perspective* (New York: Oxford University Press, 1990) and David M. Oshinsky, *A Conspiracy So Immense: The World of Joe McCarthy* (New York: Free Press, 1983).

50   Jung Chang and Jon Halliday, *Mao: The Unknown Story* (London: Jonathan Cape, 2005), p. 3.

51   Ibid., pp. 456–57.

52   Ibid., pp. 457–58.

53   Fenby, op. cit., p. 496.

54   Spence, op. cit., p. 623.

55   Chang and Halliday, op. cit., p. 601.

56   John K. Fairbank and Albert Feuerwerker, eds., *The Cambridge History of China,* Vol. 13, *Republican China 1912–49, Part 2* (Cambridge, UK: Cambridge University Press, 1986).

57   Dwight Chaplin, *The President's Man: The Memoirs of Nixon's Trusted Aide* (New York: William Morrow, 2021). See *The Economist* of 26th February 2022, p. 80).

58   Margaret MacMillan, *Seize the Hour: When Nixon Met Mao* (London: John Murray, 2006), p. 6.

59   Ibid.

60   Quoted in Fenby, op. cit., p. 506.

61 Ezra F. Vogel, *Deng Xiaoping and the Transformation of China* (Cambridge, MA: The Belknap Press, 2001), Chapters 7 and 8.

62 Ibid., p. 294.

63 Quoted ibid., p. 304.

64 Spence, op. cit., p. 658.

65 Ki-ichirō Fukasaku and David Wall, *China's Long March to an Open Economy* (Paris: OECD Publishing, 1994), pp. 43–44.

66 Vogel, *Deng Xiaoping and the Transformation of China*, op. cit., pp. 466–68.

67 Ibid., pp. 487–511 (in particular p. 507).

68 Penelope Hartland-Thunberg, *China, Hong Kong, Taiwan and the World Trading System* (Basingstoke and London: Macmillan, 1990).

69 Helen Hughes, ed., *The Dangers of Export Pessimism: Developing Countries and Industrial Markets* (San Francisco: ICS Press, 1992).

70 Vogel, *Deng Xiaoping and the Transformation of China*, op. cit., p. 487.

71 Ibid., p. 423.

72 Ibid., p. 600.

73 Ibid., p. 649.

74 Bob Davis and Lingling Wei, *Superpower Showdown: How the Battle between Trump and Xi Threatens a New Cold War* (London: HarperCollins, 2020), p. 59.

75 Michael Pillsbury, *The Hundred-Year Marathon: China's Secret Strategy to Replace America as the Global Superpower* (New York: Henry Holt & Co., 2014).

76 Song Qiang et al., *China Can Say No*, published in Chinese by the China Federation of Literary and Art Circles in 1986.

77 The phrase was coined by James Carwell, Bill Clinton's strategist in his successful 1992 presidential campaign.

78 Davis and Wei, op. cit., p. 83.

79 Jean Bovin, President of the OECD Development Centre, in his preface to Fukasaku and Wall's book (op. cit., p. 9).

80 See note 1 above.

81 The phrase is attributed to Robert Zoellick, the Deputy Secretary of State, at the 2005 National Committee Gala.

82 Pillsbury, op. cit.

83 Kerry Brown, *China's Dream: The Culture of Chinese Communism and the Secret Sources of Its Power* (Cambridge, UK: Polity Press, 2018); Kerry Brown, *Xi: A Study in Power* (London: Icon Books, 2022).

84 Vogel, *Deng Xiaoping and the Transformation of China*, op. cit.

85 Elizabeth Economy, *The Third Revolution: Xi Jinping and the New Chinese State* (New York: Oxford University Press, 2018).

CHAPTER 2

1   *New Scientist*, 21st September 2020.

2   There is a summary in Christopher Mills's 'Sizing the Chinese Market Using PPP Exchange Rates', World Markets Executive Overview, October 1994.

3   George Magnus, *Red Flags: Why Xi's China Is in Jeopardy* (New Haven, CT: Yale University Press, 2018), pp. 208–9.

4   Subramanian, op. cit.

5   'China: Statistical System in Transition', World Bank Group, 1992.

6   Daniel H. Rosen, 'A Better Abacus for China', Rhodium Group, 12th December 2014.

7   Quoted in K. Sarwar Lateef, 'China and India: Economic Performance and Prospects', IDS Discussion Paper 118, Sussex University, June 1976.

8   Angus Maddison, *Monitoring the World Economy 1820–1992* (Paris: OECD Publishing, 1995).

9   Dwight H. Perkins, *Agricultural Development in China: 1368–1968* (Chicago, Aldine Publishing Company, 1969).

10 Harry X. Wu, '*The "Real" Chinese Gross Domestic Product (GDP) for the Pre-Reform Period 1952–77*', Review of Income and Wealth, March 1993. Congressional Joint Economic Committee, 'The Chinese Economy, Post Mao', Washington, 1978.

11 Maddison, op. cit., p. 145.

12 The mechanism is explained in Matthew C. Klein and Michael Pettis, *Trade Wars Are Class Wars* (New Haven, CT: Yale University Press, 2020), pp. 114–15.

13 Harry X. Wu, 'Re-estimating Chinese Growth', The Conference Board, China Center Special Briefing Paper, New York, 2014.

14 Cable, *China and India*, op. cit.

15 Quoted by Jacques, op. cit., p. 80.

16 Mark Elvin, *The Pattern of the Chinese Past: A Social and Economic Interpretation* (Stanford, CA: Stanford University Press, 1973).

17 Peter Harrold, 'China's Reform Experience to Date', World Bank Discussion Paper 180, 1992. 'China – Updating Economic Memorandum: Managing Rapid Growth and Transition', World Bank Group, 1993. Fukasaku and Wall, op. cit.

18 Jacques, op. cit., p. 154.

19 Klein and Pettis, op. cit., p. 104.

20 Nicholas R. Lardy, *China in the World Economy* (Washington: Peterson Institute for International Economics, 1994).

21 Dwight H. Perkins and Shahid Yusuf, 'Rural Development in China', World Bank Group, 1984.

22 Justin Yifu Lin, Jikun Huang and Scott Rozelle, 'China's Food Economy: Past Performance and Future Trends', in *China in the 21st Century: Long-Term Global Implications* (Paris: OECD Publishing, 1996).

23 Christopher Findlay, Will Martin and Andrew Watson, *Policy Reform, Economic Growth and China's Agriculture* (Paris: OECD Publishing, 1993).

24 Vincent Cable, 'The Outlook for Labour-Intensive Manufacturing in China', in *China in the 21st Century*, op. cit.

25 Leslie T. Chang, *Factory Girls: From Village to City in a Changing China* (New York: Penguin Random House, 2009).

26 The trend is discussed in Alexander J. Yeats, 'China's Foreign Trade and Comparative Advantage: Prospects, Problems, and Policy Implications', World Bank Discussion Paper 141, 1991.

27 Masaru Yoshitomi, 'The Comparative Advantage of China's Manufacturing in the Twenty-First Century', in *China in the 21st Century*, op. cit.

28 Klein and Pettis, op. cit., p. 108.

29 Alexander Gerschenkron, *Economic Backwardness in Historical Perspective* (Cambridge, MA: The Belknap Press, 1962).

30 *McKinsey Quarterly*, September 2010.

31 Peter Nolan, *Transforming China: Globalization, Transition and Development* (London: Anthem Press, 2004), pp. 185–90.

32 Thomas Rumbaugh and Nicolas Blancher, 'China: International Trade and WTO Accession', IMF Working Paper WP/04/36, 2004.

33 The former by Larry Summers in a speech in Washington in 2004; the latter by Niall Ferguson and Moritz Schularick in an article in *International Finance*, Vol. 10, 2007.

34 IMF Survey, 'China's Difficult Balancing Act', September 2007, cited in Adam Tooze, *Crashed: How a Decade of Financial Crises Changed the World* (London: Penguin, 2018), p. 246.

35 Shahrokh Fardoust, Justin Yifu Lin and Xubei Luo, 'Demystifying China's Fiscal Stimulus', World Bank Policy Research Working Paper 6221, 2012.

36 Tooze, op. cit., pp. 248–49.

37 Kerry Brown, *The World According to Xi: Everything You Need to Know about the New China* (London: I.B. Tauris, 2018).

38 Magnus, op. cit., p. 57.

39 Carl Walter and Fraser Howie, *Red Capitalism: The Fragile Financial Foundation of China's Extraordinary Rise* (Singapore: John Wiley & Sons Pte. Ltd, 2011).

40 Jamil Anderlini, 'The Chinese Chronicle of a Crash Foretold', *Financial Times*, 25th February 2016.

41 *The Economist*, 27th February 2016, p. 60.

42 Kenneth S. Rogoff and Yuanchen Yang, *Peak China Housing* NBER Working Paper, August 2020.

43 Iain Cunningham, *China Has Pivoted and No One has Noticed*, Investment Monitor, 21st February 2022.

44 Magnus, op. cit.

45 Brown, *China's Dream, op. cit.*

46 Indermit S. Gill and Homi Kharas, 'The Middle-Income Trap Turns Ten', World Bank Policy Research Working Paper 7403, Washington 2015.

47 Raj Nallari, Shahid Yusuf, Breda Griffith and Rwitwika Bhattacharya, 'Frontiers in Development Policy: A Primer on Emerging Issues', World Bank, 2011. Barry Eichengreen, Donghyun Park and Kwanho Shin, 'Growth Slowdowns Redux: New Evidence

on the Middle-Income Trap', NBER Working Paper, January 2013.

48 Wing Woo, 'China Meets the Middle-Income Trap: The Large Potholes in the Road to Catching-up', *Journal of Chinese Economic and Business Studies*, Vol. 10, No. 4, 2012, pp. 313–36.

49 W. Arthur Lewis, 'Economic Development with Unlimited Supplies of Labour', Manchester School, May 1954.

50 Ross Garnaut and Yiping Huang, 'Continued Rapid Growth and the Turning Point in China's Development', in Ross Garnaut and Ligang Song, eds., *The Turning Point in China's Economic Development* (Canberra: ANU Press, 2006), pp. 12–34.

51 China National Bureau of Statistics, reported in the *Financial Times* of 5th May 2015.

52 Yue Parkinson, *China and the West: Unravelling 100 Years of Misunderstanding* (London: Bite-Sized Books, 2021).

53 Loren Brandt et al., 'China's Productivity Slowdown and Future Growth Potential', World Bank Policy Research Working Paper, June 2020.

54 People's Republic of China: 2021 Article IV Consultation-Press Release; Staff Report; and Statement by the Executive Director for the People's Republic of China, IMF Staff Country Reports, 28th January 2022.

55 *The Economist*, 5th February 2022, p. 69.

56 Barro and Lee Long-term Educational Attainment by Country (1870-2040), Knoema, 2018.

57 Scott Rozelle and Natalie Hell, *Invisible China: How the Urban-Rural Divide Threatens China's Rise* (Chicago: Chicago University Press, 2020).

58 George Magnus, 'China's Reckoning Cannot Be Deferred Indefinitely', *Financial Times*, 1st May 2016.

59 Moritz Schularick and Alan M. Taylor, 'Credit Booms Gone Bust: Monetary Policy, Leverage Cycles and Financial Crises, 1870–2008', NBER Working Paper 15512, November 2009.

60 Sally Chen and Joong Shik Kang, 'Credit Booms: Is China Different?', IMF Working Paper 18/2, January 2018. See also Terry E. Chan and Kim Eng Tan, 'China Debt after Covid-19: Flattening the Other Curve', *S&P Global*, July 2020.

61 Richard C. Koo, *The Holy Grail of Macroeconomics: Lessons from Japan's Great Recession* (Singapore: John Wiley & Sons Pte. Ltd., 2009).

62 Rogoff and Yang, op. cit.

63 Mahinthan Mariasingham and John Arvin Bernabe of the Asian Development Bank, cited in Gregory C. Smalley, 'Measure the Most Important Sector of the Universe', Amiya Sahu 27th November 2021.

64 Andrew Tilton, 'Takeaways from China's Economic Data', Goldman Sachs, 20th April 2020.

65 Martin Wolf, 'Time to Rein in the Debt Boom', *Financial Times*, 26th July 2018.

66 'Targeting Practice', *The Economist*, 13th February 2021, p. 66.

67 Thomas Orlik, *The Bubble That Never Pops* (New York: Oxford University Press, 2020).

68 Daron Acemoglu and James A. Robinson, *Why Nations Fail: The Origins of Power, Prosperity and Poverty* (London: Profile Books, 2012).

69 Yuen Yuen Ang, *China's Gilded Age: The Paradox of Economic Boom and Vast Corruption* (Cambridge, UK: Cambridge University Press, 2020), p. 1.

70 Paulo Mauro, 'The Effects of Corruption on Growth, Investment and Government Expenditure', IMF Working Paper 96/98, 1996.

71 Transparency International Corruption Perception Index, 2019–20.

72 Ang, op. cit.

73 doingbusiness.org, World Bank.

74 Ang, *China's Gilded Age*, op. cit.

75 OECD/ILO Labour Share in G20 Economies, Report for G20 Meeting 2013.

76 Peter Nolan, *China at the Crossroads* (Cambridge, UK: Polity Press, 2004), p. 15.

77 Sonali Jain-Chandra, Niny Khor, Rui Mano, Johanna Schauer, Philippe Wingender and Juzhong Zhuang, 'Inequality in China: Trends, Drivers and Policy Remedies', IMF Working Paper 18/127, June 2018.

78 Ibid., p. 6.

79 Simon Kusnetz, 'Economic Growth and Income Inequality', *American Economic Review*, Vol. 45, March 1955.

80 *Shenggen Fan, Ravi Kanbur and Xiaobo Zhang, eds., Regional Inequality in China: Trends, Explanations and Policy Responses (Abingdon: Routledge, 2009).*

81 Chao Li and John Gibson, 'Rising Regional Inequality in China: Fact or Artefact?', *World Development*, Vol. 47, July 2013, pp. 16–29.

82 Rozelle and Hell, op. cit.

83 Winnie Yip et al., '10 Years of Health-Care Reform in China: Progress and Gaps in Universal Health Coverage', *The Lancet*, 28th September 2019.

84 Neil Stern, 'China to Become the World's Largest Retail Market, Even with a Slowdown', *Forbes Magazine*, 5th February 2019.

85 Tricia McKinnon, *Indigo9 Digital*, 12th November 2020.

86 Rainer Zitelmann, 'State Capitalism? No, the Private Sector Was and Is the Main Driver of China's Economic Growth', *Forbes Magazine*, September 2019. The numbers are from the All China Federation of Industry and Commerce.

87 Magnus, *Red Flags*, op. cit., p. 215.

88 Ringen, op. cit., p. 15.

89 Richard McGregor, *Xi Jinping: The Backlash* (Sydney: Lowy Institute and Penguin, 2019).

90 Nicholas R. Lardy, *The State Strikes Back: The End of Economic Reform in China?* (Washington: Peterson Institute for International Economics, 2019).

91 Orange Wang and Zhou Xin, *South China Morning Post*, 8th January 2020.

92 Cited in Gabriel Wildau, 'China's State-Owned Zombie Economy', *Financial Times*, 29th February 2016.

93 Amir Guluzade, 'How Reform Has Made China's State-Owned Enterprises Stronger', World Economic Forum, 21st May 2020.

94 Magnus, *Red Flags*, op. cit., p. 45.

95 Davis and Wei, op. cit., pp. 154–56.

96 Duncan Clark, *Alibaba: The House That Jack Ma Built* (New York: Ecco, 2016).

97 Speech on 'Seeking Truth' referred to in Davis and Wei, op. cit., p. 158.

98 David Dollar, Yiping Huang and Yang Yao, *China 2049: Economic Challenge of a Rising Power* (Brookings Institution, January 2020). See also 'China and India Will Overtake US Economically by 2075, Goldman Sachs Economists Say' (*Forbes*, 6th December 2022).

98 Roland Rajah and Alyssa Leng, *Revising Down the Rise of China* (Lowy Institute, 14th March 2022).

CHAPTER 3

1 IMF growth accounting estimates based on changes in GDP on a PPP basis.

2 Ruchir Sharma, 'China is Faltering, But the World Is Not Feeling the Effects', *Financial Times*, 6th December 2021.

3 The issues are set out in Vincent Cable, 'What Is International Economic Security?', *International Affairs*, Vol. 71, No. 2, April 1995, pp. 305–24.

4 David Held and Anthony McGrew, *Globalization/Anti-Globalization* (Cambridge, UK: Polity Press, 2002). Ian Bremmer, *Us vs. Them: The Failure of Globalism* (London: Portfolio Penguin, 2018).

5 Pillsbury, *op. cit.*

6 Graham Allison, *Destined for War: Can America and China Escape Thucydides's Trap?* (Boston: Houghton Mifflin Harcourt, 2017).

7 Speech by Wang Yong, Director of the Center for American Studies, Beijing University, reported in 'How China Sees America', *The Economist*, 7th November 2020, p. 58.

8 Kathrin Hille, 'Why US Pressure Will Multiply Supply Chains', *Financial Times*, 7th October 2020. Alternative view in Yukon Huang and Jeremy Smith, 'Why US–China Supply-Chain Decoupling Will Be More of a Whimper Than a Bang', *South China Morning Post*, June 2020.

9 'China's "Dual-Circulation" Strategy Means Relying Less on Foreigners', *The Economist*, 7th November 2020. Michael Pettis, 'The Problems with China's "Dual-Circulation" Economic Model', *Financial Times*, 25th August 2020.

NOTES AND SOURCES

10 Klein and Pettis, op. cit., p. 29. Chunlai Chen, 'Foreign Direct Investment in China: What the Figures Don't Tell Us', The University of Warwick, 2008. Gordon H. Hanson and Robert C. Feenstra, 'Intermediaries in Entrepôt Trade: Hong Kong Re-Exports of Chinese Goods', NBER Working Paper 8088, 2002.

11 Shaun K. Roache, 'China's Impact on World Commodity Markets', IMF Working Paper 12/115, 2012.

12 'Does China Pose a Threat to Global Rare Earth Supply Chains?', China Power, 24th September 2020. Sophia Kalantzakos, *China and the Geopolitics of Rare Earths* (New York: Oxford University Press, 2018).

13 Davis and Wei, op. cit., p. 30.

14 Stephen D. King, *Losing Control: The Emerging Threats to Western Prosperity* (New Haven, CT: Yale University Press, 2010).

15 Ricardo J. Caballero, Emmanuel Farhi and Pierre-Olivier Gourinchas, 'Global Imbalances and Policy Wars at the Zero Lower Bound', NBER Working Paper 21670, 2015.

16 Davis and Wei, op. cit., p. 181.

17 'The Yuan Has Been One of the World's Most Stable Major Currencies', *The Economist*, 11th June 2020.

18 Swarnali Ahmed, Maximiliano Appendino and Michele Ruta, 'Global Value Chains and the Exchange Rate Elasticity of Exports', IMF Working Paper 15/252, 2015.

19 Niall Ferguson, 'Don't Let China Mint the Money of the Future', Bloomberg, 4th April 2021.

20 David and Wei, op. cit., p. 133.

21 Benjamin Powell, *Out of Poverty: Sweatshops in the Global Economy* (Cambridge, MA: Cambridge University Press, 2014). Deepak Lal, *Resurrection of the Pauper-Labour Argument* (London: Trade Policy Research Centre, 1981).

22 David Greenaway, Robert C. Hine and Peter Wright, 'An Empirical Assessment of the Impact of Trade on Employment in the UK', *European Journal of Political Economy*, Vol. 15, No. 3, September 1999, pp. 485–500. Vincent Cable, *Protectionism and Industrial Decline* (London: Hodder and Stoughton in association with the Overseas Development Institute, 1983). Eddy Lee and Marion

Jansen, *Trade and Employment: Challenges for Policy Research* (Geneva: ILO/WTO, 2007).

23 David H. Autor, David Dorn and Gordon H. Hanson, 'The China Syndrome: Local Labor Market Effects of Import Competition in the United States', NBER Working Paper 18054, May 2012.

24 Davis and Wei, op. cit., p. 127.

25 Fabian Jintae Froese, Dylan Sutherland and Jeoung Yul Lee, 'Challenges for Foreign Companies in China: Implications for Research and Practice', *Asian Business & Management*, Vol. 18, 2019, pp. 249–62.

26 Hui Feng, *The Politics of China's Accession to the World Trade Organization: The Dragon Goes Global* (New York: Routledge, 2012).

27 Ann Harrison, Marshall Meyer, Peichun Wang, Linda Zhao and Minyuan Zhao, 'Can a Tiger Change Its Stripes? Reform of Chinese State-Owned Enterprises in the Penumbra of the State', NBER Working Paper 25475, January 2019.

28 Dani Rodrick, 'The WTO Has Become Dysfunctional', *Financial Times*, 5th August 2018.

29 Petros C. Mavroidis and André Sapir, *China and the WTO: Why Multilateralism Still Matters* (Princeton, NJ: Princeton University Press, 2021).

30 Peter Navarro and Greg Autry, *Death by China: Confronting the Dragon – a Global Call to Action* (Upper Saddle River, NJ: Prentice Hall, 2011).

31 Interview on Fox News, Reuters, 17th May 2019.

32 Donald Trump's tweet, 2nd March 2018.

33 Davis and Wei, op. cit., p. 132.

34 Ibid. Quote of comment made on 2nd May 2016.

35 'Findings of the Investigation into China's Acts, Policies, and Practices Related to Technology Transfer, Intellectual Property, and Innovation under Section 301 of the Trade Act of 1974', Office of the US Trade Representative, 22nd March 2018.

36 Mark Zandi of Moody's Analytics, reported in Davis and Wei, op. cit., p. 340.

37 Dubravko Lakos-Bujas, J.P. Morgan's Head of U.S. Equity Strategy, 7th June 2019. For global estimates of the cost, see Davide Furceri,

Swarnali A. Hannan, Jonathan David Ostry and Andrew K. Rose, *Macroeconomic Consequences of Tariffs*, IMF Working Paper 19/9, January 2019.

38 Davis and Wei, op. cit., p. 401.

39 Gideon Rachman, 'Europe Has Handed China a Strategic Win', *Financial Times*, 4th January 2021.

40 Gerard DiPippo, 'Could the West Punish China the Way it has Punished Russia?', *The Economist*, 23rd April 2022. *Economist* estimates based on research by the Center for Strategic and International Studies.

41 Data from American Enterprise Institute, China Global-Investment Tracker.

CHAPTER 4

1 *Final Report, National Security Commission on Artificial Intelligence*, March 2021.

2 *Financial Times*, 'How to Manage the New World of Cyber Risk', 11th March 2021.

3 Joseph A. Schumpeter, *The Theory of Economic Development: An Inquiry into Profits, Capital, Credit, Interest, and the Business Cycle*, Translated by Redvers Opie (Cambridge, MA: Harvard University Press, 1934). Paul M. Sweezy, 'Professor Schumpeter's Theory of Innovation', *The Review of Economics and Statistics*, Vol. 25, No. 1, February 1943, pp. 93–96.

4 David Romer, 'Endogenous Growth', in *Advanced Macroeconomics*, Fourth edn. (New York: McGraw-Hill, 2011), pp. 101–49. Robert M. Solow, 'Technical Change and the Aggregate Production Function', *The Review of Economics and Statistics*, Vol. 39, No. 3, August 1957. Gene M. Grossman and Elhanan Helpman, *Innovation and Growth in the Global Economy* (Cambridge, MA: MIT Press, 1991).

5 Douglass C. North, *Institutions, Institutional Change and Economic Performance* (Cambridge, UK: Cambridge University Press, 1990).

6 Michele Boldrin and David K. Levine, *Against Intellectual Monopoly* (Cambridge, UK: Cambridge University Press, 2008).

Joel Mokyr, 'Intellectual Property Rights, the Industrial Revolution, and the Beginnings of Modern Economic Growth', *The American Economic Review*, Vol. 99, No. 2, May 2009, pp. 349–55.

7   Nagesh Kumar, 'Intellectual Property Rights, Technology and Economic Development: Experiences of Asian Countries', *Economic and Political Weekly*, Vol. 38, No. 3, January 2003, pp. 209–26.

8   David I. Jeremy, 'Damming the Flood: British Government Efforts to Check the Outflow of Technicians and Machinery, 1780–1843', *The Business History Review*, Vol. 51, No. 1, Spring 1977.

9   Peter Andreas, *Smuggler Nation: How Illicit Trade Made America* (New York: Oxford University Press, 2014).

10 W.G. Beasley, *The Meiji Restoration* (Stanford, CA: Stanford University Press, 1972). Andrew Gordon, *A Modern History of Japan, from Tokugawa Times to the Present*, Fourth edn. (New York: Oxford University Press, 2019).

11 Keith Maskus, *Intellectual Property Rights in the Global Economy* (Washington, DC: Peterson Institute for International Economics, 2000).

12 Michael Hobday, *Innovation in East Asia: The Challenge to Japan* (Aldershot: Edward Elgar Publishing Co., 1995).

13 Alice H. Amsden, *Asia's Next Giant: South Korea and Late Industrialization* (New York: Oxford University Press, 1989). Linsu Kim, *Imitation to Innovation: The Dynamics of Korea's Technological Learning* (Boston: Harvard Business School Press, 1997).

14 Linsu Kim and Richard R. Nelson, *Technology, Learning, and Innovation: Experiences of Newly Industrializing Economies* (Cambridge, UK: Cambridge University Press, 2000). Robert Wade, *Governing the Market: Economic Theory and the Role of Government in East Asian Industrialization* (Princeton, NJ: Princeton University Press, 1990).

15 Arie Y. Lewin, Martin Kenney and Johann Peter Murmann, eds., *China's Innovation Challenge: Overcoming the Middle-Income Trap* (Cambridge, UK: Cambridge University Press, 2016). Xiaolan Fu, *China's Path to Innovation* (Cambridge, UK: Cambridge University Press, 2015). Dan Breznitz and Michael Murphree, *Run of the Red*

    Queen: Government, Innovation, Globalization, and Economic Growth in China (New Haven, CT: Yale University Press, 2011).

16 Joseph Needham et al., *Science and Civilisation in China*, seven volumes (Cambridge, UK: Cambridge University Press, 1954–2004).

17 Menita Liu Cheng and Can Huang, 'Transforming China's IP System to Stimulate Innovation' in *China's Innovation Challenge*, op. cit., pp. 152–88.

18 David Ahlstrom, Garry Bruton and Kuang Yeh, 'Venture Capital in China: Past, Present, and Future', *Asia Pacific Journal of Management*, Vol. 24, No. 3, September 2007, pp. 247–68.

19 European Union Chamber of Commerce, *China Manufacturing 2017*, quoted in Davis and Wei, op. cit., p. 124.

20 *Made in China 2025: Global Ambitions Built on Local Protections* (Washington, DC: US Chamber of Commerce, 2017).

21 'China's Hybrid Capitalism', *The Economist*, 15th August 2020, p. 17. Davis and Wei, op. cit., p. 293.

22 Yu Yongding in 'China's Hybrid Capitalism', op. cit., p. 17.

23 Carsten A. Holz, 'Industrial Policies and the Changing Patterns of Investment in the Chinese Economy', *The China Journal*, Vol. 81, October 2018, pp. 23–57.

24 'China Leads the Way on Global Standards for 5G and Beyond', *Financial Times*, 4th August 2020.

25 Naomi Wilson, 'China Standards 2035 and the Plan for World Domination – Don't Believe China's Hype', cfr.org, blog article, 3rd June 2020.

26 Kai-Fu Lee, *AI Superpowers: China, Silicon Valley, and the New World Order* (Boston: Houghton Mifflin Harcourt, 2018).

27 Matt Sheehan, 'The Chinese Way of Innovation: What Washington Can Learn from Beijing about Investing in Tech', *Foreign Affairs*, 21st April 2022

28 Mahbubani, op. cit., p. 131.

29 National Science Board, *Science and Engineering Indicators 2020*.

30 Ibid.

31 Carsten A. Holz, 'University Rankings: Comparing Apples and Pears', Hong Kong University of Science and Technology, 19th November 2020.

32 Paper for the US Senate by Rob Portman and Tom Carper, reported in Dennis Wang, *Reigning the Future: AI, 5G, Huawei, and the Next 30 Years of US–China Rivalry* (Potomac: New Degree Press, 2020).

33 Nina Xiang, *US–China Tech War: What Chinese Tech History Reveals about Future Tech Rivalry* (Independently published, 2021).

34 Yingzhi Yang, 'China Surpasses North America in Attracting Venture Capital Funding for First Time as Investors Chase 1.4 Billion Consumers', *South China Morning Post*, 5th July 2018.

35 Douglas B. Fuller, 'China's Political Economy: Prospects for Technological Innovation and Growth', in *China's Innovation Challenge*, op. cit., pp. 121–51.

36 Ross Brown and Augusto Rocha, 'Chinese Start-Ups Are Being Starved of Venture Capital – with Worrying Omens for the West', *The Conversation*, 24th April 2020.

37 Douglas B. Fuller, *Paper Tigers, Hidden Dragons: Firms and the Political Economy of China's Technological Development* (Oxford: Oxford University Press, 2016).

38 Dan Wang, 'China's Hidden Tech Revolution: How Beijing Threatens US Dominance', *Foreign Affairs*, March–April 2023.

39 Robert Hannigan, 'Wake Up to the Security Risks in Chinese Tech Dominance', *Financial Times*, 27th July 2018.

40 James Kynge, 'China's Tech Juggernaut Steams Ahead', *Financial Times*, 24th July 2020.

41 Isabel Hilton, 'The Huawei Dilemma', *Prospect Magazine*, August–September 2019.

42 Dennis Wang, op. cit.

43 Fuller, *Paper Tigers, Hidden Dragons*, op. cit., pp. 96–97.

44 Industry statistics from the Dell'Oro Group.

45 IPlytics, *5G Patent Study 2020*.

46 Dennis Wang, op. cit., p. 122.

47 '"Weapons of Economic Warfare": Huawei Has 56,492 Patents – and It's Not Afraid to Use Them', *South China Morning Post*, 15th June 2019.

48 Davis and Lei, op. cit., p. 381.

49 *The Times*, 19th June 2020, reporting a radio interview with Eric Schmidt on 'The New Tech Cold War'.

50 Christopher Balding and Donald C. Clarke, 'Who Owns Huawei?', SSRN, 17th April 2019.

51 George Parker, Helen Warrell and Kiran Stacey, 'Huawei Decision Jolts UK–US "Special Relationship" at Sensitive Time', *Financial Times*, 28th January 2020.

52 Constanze Stelzenmüller, 'Europe Faces a Fateful Choice on Huawei', *Financial Times*, 17th July 2020. 'Huawei and 5G', *The Economist*, 18th July 2020.

53 Wang, op. cit., p. 125.

54 Kai-Fu Lee, op. cit.

55 Fuller, *Paper Tigers, Hidden Dragons*, op. cit., Chapters 5 and 6.

56 Kathrin Hille, *Financial Times*, 3rd November 2020 and 1st January 2021.

57 Margaret E. Roberts, *Censored: Distraction and Diversion Inside China's Great Firewall* (Princeton, NJ: Princeton University Press, 2018).

58 James Griffiths, *The Great Firewall of China: How to Build and Control an Alternative Version of the Internet* (London: Zed Books, 2019).

59 Remarks by President Xi Jinping of the PRC at the opening ceremony of the Second World Internet Conference, Ministry of Foreign Affairs, Beijing, 16th December 2015.

60 Economy, *The Third Revolution, op. cit.*, pp. 85–87.

61 Chris Stokel-Walker, *TikTok Boom: The Inside Story of the World's Favourite App* (London: Canbury Press, 2021)

62 Nina Xiang, *Parallel Metaverses: How the US, China and the Rest of the World Are Shaping Different Virtual Worlds* (Independently published, 2022).

63 Byron Reese, *The Fourth Age: Smart Robots, Conscious Computers, and the Future of Humanity* (New York: Atria Books, 2018). Max Tegmark *Life 3.0: Being Human in the Age of Artificial Intelligence* (London: Allen Lane, 2017).

64 'The Digital Divide', *The Economist*, 18th January 2020.

65 Graham Allison and Eric Schmidt, 'Is China Beating the US to AI Supremacy?', *The National Interest*, 22nd December 2019.

66 Nicholas Chaillan, 'The Pentagon Needs a New AI Strategy to Catch Up with China', *Financial Times*, 22nd November 2021.

67 Allen Institute for Artificial Intelligence, 2020.

68 Edward Tse, *China's Disruptors: How Alibaba, Xiaomi, Tencent and Other Companies Are Changing the Rules of Business* (London: Portfolio Penguin, 2015).

69 Wang, op. cit., pp. 292–93.

70 Sara Hsu and Gabrielle Green, 'Blockchain in China', Stimson Center, 16th August 2021.

71 Wang, op. cit., p. 296, citing Elsa B. Kania and John Costello, 'Quantum Hegemony? China's Ambitions and the Challenge to American Leadership'.

72 Jenny J. Lee and John P. Haupt, 'The "China Threat" and the Future of Global Science', *Scientific American*, 7th January 2020. Andrew Silver, Jeff Tollefson and Elizabeth Gibney, 'How US–China Political Tensions Are Affecting Science', *Nature*, 18th April 2019. Liming Li, Kean Wang, Zhuo Chen and Jeffrey P. Koplan, 'US–China Health Exchange and Collaboration Following Covid-19', *The Lancet*, 8th April 2021.

73 Yanzhong Huang, 'US Dependence on Pharmaceutical Products from China', Council for Foreign Relations, 14th August 2019.

74 Jacqueline Varas, 'US Dependence on Chinese Pharmaceuticals is Overstated', American Action Forum, 20th May 2020.

75 Christian Shepherd and James Kynge, 'China's Ambitions in Space: National Pride or Taking on the Americans?', *Financial Times*, 9th May 2021.

76 Press comment reported from the White House summit on climate, 21st April 2021.

77 James Kynge, 'As Digital Trade Grows, So Does Western Distrust of Beijing', *Financial Times*, 22nd March 2021.

CHAPTER 5

1 Jacques, op. cit., pp. 409–13.

2 Quoted by McGregor, op. cit., p. 20.

3 R.W. Davies, 'Lenin, Stalin and the New Economic Policy, 1921–5', in *Soviet History in the Yeltsin Era* (London: Palgrave Macmillan, 1997), pp. 135–45. Vince Cable, 'Lenin: From War Communism

to State Capitalism' (Chapter 4), in *Money and Power* (London: Atlantic Books, 2021).

4 Ringen, op. cit., Chapter 3.

5 'Ruler for Life: China's Leader Xi Jinping Will Be Allowed to Reign Forever', *The Economist*, 26th February 2018. David Shambaugh, 'Under Xi Jinping, a Return in China to the Dangers of an All-Powerful Leader', *South China Morning Post*, 1st March 2018.

6 *Freedom on the World Report* (Washington, DC: Freedom House, 2020).

7 Edward N. Luttwak, *The Rise of China vs. the Logic of Strategy* (Cambridge, MA: The Belknap Press, 2012), p. 235.

8 Henry Kissinger, *On China* (London: Allen Lane: 2011), p. 337.

9 Mahbubani, op. cit., p. 136.

10 Brown, *The World According to Xi*, op. cit., p. 95.

11 Vogel, *Deng Xiaoping and the Transformation of China*, op. cit.

12 'Why Bother Counting', *The Economist*, 16th January 2021, p. 51.

13 Brown, *The World According to Xi*, op. cit., p. 99.

14 Kevin J. O'Brien, ed., *Popular Protest in China* (Cambridge, MA: Harvard University Press, 2008). Teresa Wright, *Popular Protest in China* (Cambridge, UK: Polity Press, 2018).

15 Bruce Dixon, *The Party and the People* (Princeton, NJ: Princeton University Press, 2021).

16 Brown, *The World According to Xi*, op. cit.; McGregor, op. cit.; Economy, op. cit.

17 Economy, op. cit.

18 Brown, *The World According to Xi*, op. cit., p. 48.

19 Economy, op. cit., p. 31.

20 Desmond Shum, *Red Roulette: An Insider's Story of Wealth, Power, Corruption and Vengeance in Today's China* (London: Simon and Schuster, 2021).

21 Ang, *China's Gilded Age*, op. cit.

22 Yongnian Zheng and Wei Shan, 'Xi Jinping's "Rule of Law" with Chinese Characteristics', blog post on University of Nottingham website, 28th May 2015.

23 Xi Jinping, *The Governance of China* (Beijing: Foreign Languages Press, 2014), p. 162.

24 Tom Mitchell, 'Xi's China: Smothering Dissent', *Financial Times*, 27th July 2016.

25 Economy, op. cit., p. 46.

26 Joseph Fewsmith, *Rethinking Chinese Politics* (Cambridge, UK: Cambridge University Press, 2021).

27 Jude Blanchette, 'Xi's Gamble: The Race to Consolidate Power and Stave Off Disaster', *Foreign Affairs*, July–August 2021.

28 Daniel H. Rosen, 'China's Economic Reckoning: The Price of Failed Reforms', *Foreign Affairs*, July–August 2021.

29 Edelman Trust Barometer 2020.

30 Ringen, op. cit., p. ix.

31 Brown, *The World According to Xi*, op. cit., pp. 100–1.

32 Roger Garside, *China's Coup: The Great Leap to Freedom* (Oakland, CA: University of California Press, 2021).

33 Tony Saich, *From Rebel to Ruler: One Hundred Years of the Chinese Communist Party* (Cambridge, MA: The Belknap Press, 2021), p. 466.

34 Mahbubani, op. cit., pp. 140–43.

35 Jacques, op. cit., p. 260.

36 Cheng Li, 'Avoiding Three Traps in Confronting China's Party-State', in Ryan Hass, Ryan McElveen and Robert D. Williams, eds., *The Future of US Policy Toward China: Recommendations for the Biden Administration*, John L. Thornton China Center, Brookings Institution, November 2020, p. 3.

37 Vogel, *Deng Xiaoping and the Transformation of China*, op. cit., p. 507.

38 William A. Callahan, *Contingent States: Greater China and Transnational Relations* (Minneapolis: University of Minnesota Press, 2004).

39 Mahbubani, op. cit., p. 50.

40 Nury Vittachi, *The Other Side of the Story: A Secret War in Hong Kong* (Hong Konk: YLF, 2020).

41 Brown, *The World According to Xi*, op. cit., pp. 57–59.

42 Jonathan Sumption, 'Britain Should Avoid Undermining the Hong Kong Judiciary', *The Times*, 18th March 2021.

43 Isabel Hilton, 'Beijing's Hong Kong Takeover Is a Masterclass in Creating Fear', *Financial Times*, 3rd July 2020.

44 Jacques, op. cit., pp. 250–51.

45 Bill Hayton, *The Invention of China* (New Haven, CT, and London: Yale University Press, 2020).

46 John Gittings, *The Changing Face of China: From Mao to Market* (Oxford: Oxford University Press, 2005), p. 313.

47 Nick Holdstock, *China's Forgotten People: Xinjiang, Terror and the Chinese State* (London: I.B. Tauris, 2015).

48 Tom Miller, *China's Asian Dream: Empire Building along the New Silk Road* (London: Zed Books, 2019), pp. 62–63.

49 'Xinjiang's Shadow', *The Economist*, 23rd January 2021, pp. 47–48.

50 BBC reports, 22nd March 2021.

51 Colum Lynch, 'State Department Lawyers Concluded Insufficient Evidence to Prove Genocide in China', *Foreign Policy*, 19th February 2021.

52 Charles Parton, 'The Truth about China's Genocide against the Uyghurs', *The Spectator*, 3rd February 2021.

53 'Xinjiang: The Evidence' (www.tinyurl.com/tztdufz7).

54 Adrian Zenz, '"Thoroughly Reforming Them towards a Healthy Heart Attitude": China's Political Re-Education Campaign in Xinjiang', *Central Asian Survey*, Volume 38, No. 1, 2nd January 2019, pp. 102–28.

55 'China Is Doubling Down in Xinjiang', *The Economist*, 10th December 2020.

56 Vicky Xiuzhong Xu, Danielle Cave, James Leibold, Kelsey Munro and Nathan Ruser, 'Uyghurs for Sale: "Re-education", Forced Labour and Surveillance beyond Xinjiang', Australian Strategic Policy Institute, Policy Brief No. 26, 1st March 2020. Adrian Zenz, 'Coercive Labor and Forced Displacement in Xinjiang's Cross-Regional Labor Transfer Programme', Special Report, The Jamestown Foundation, March 2021.

57 Pun Ngai, *Migrant Labour in China: Post-Socialist Transformations* (Cambridge, UK: Polity Press, 2016).

58 Adrian Zenz, 'Sterilizations, IUDs, and Coercive Birth Prevention: The CCP's Campaign to Suppress Uyghur Birth Rates in Xinjiang', *China Brief*, Vol. 20, No. 12, The Jamestown Foundation, 2020.

59 Quoted in Parton, op. cit.

60 Sheena Chestnut Greitens, Myunghee Lee and Emir Yazici, 'Counterterrorism and Preventive Repression: China's Changing Strategy in Xinjiang', *International Security*, Vol. 44, No. 3, Winter 2019/20.

61 Ibid., p. 46.

62 Atlantic Council, *China Discourse Power* (Washington, DC: Scowcroft Center for Strategy and Security, 2020).

63 Joseph S. Nye, Jr., *Soft Power: The Means to Success in World Politics* (New York: PublicAffairs, 2004).

64 *Global Soft Power Index 2021*, 16th March 2021.

65 Portland Communications and University of Southern California Center for Public Diplomacy.

66 Atlantic Council, op. cit.

67 Ying Zhou, 'Establishing Confucius Institutes: A Tool for Promoting China's Soft Power?', *Journal of Contemporary China*, Vol. 25, No. 100, 2016, pp. 628–42. Falk Hartig, *Chinese Public Diplomacy: The Rise of the Confucius Institute* (London: Routledge, 2017).

68 Rachelle Peterson, 'China Is Rebranding Its Confucius Institutes', RealClearEducation, 22nd July 2020.

69 Xi's quote from the 19th Communist Party Conference in 2017.

70 Kristine Lee, POLITICO, 15th April 2021.

CHAPTER 6

1 Quoted in its original and in Chinese in Economy, op. cit., p. 188.

2 Brown, *The World According to Xi*, op. cit., pp. 80–81.

3 Wang Xiaodong, 'China's Nationalism under the Shadow of Globalization', lecture at the LSE, 7th February 2005. Christopher R. Hughes, *Chinese Nationalism in the Global Era* (London: Routledge, 2006).

4 Yingje Fan, Jennifer Pan, Zijie Shao and Yiqing Xu, 'How Discrimination Increases Chinese Overseas Students' Support for Authoritarian Rule', 21st Century China Center Research Paper No. 2020-05, 30th June 2020. 'China Youth', *The Economist*, 23rd January 2021.

5   Janan Ganesh, 'The USA Is Not Responsible for China's Rise', *Financial Times*, 14th December 2021.

6   Doshi, op. cit.

7   Wang Jisi, 'The Plot Against China? How Beijing Sees the New Washington Consensus', *Foreign Affairs*, July–August 2021.

8   Interview with Henry Kissinger, *Financial Times*, 14th–15th May 2022.

9   Michael Beckley, 'Enemies of my Enemy: How Fear of China Is Forging a New World Order', *Foreign Affairs*, March–April 2022.

10   Allison, op. cit.

11   Speech during the 19th National Congress in 2017, US–China Economic and Security Review Commission, US Congress, 20th June 2019.

12   'The Military Balance', Stockholm International Peace Research Institute, 2020.

13   RAND Corporation, 'The US–China Military Scorecard: Forces, Geography, and the Evolving Balance of Power, 1996–2017'.

14   Gordon Lindsay Maitland, 'Briefing on China's Modernizing Military Council for Foreign Relations', 2020.

15   Ibid. and US Department of Defense, 'Military and Security Events: China', 2020.

16   Report of the National Security Commission on Artificial Intelligence, March 2021, reported in *Financial Times*, 3rd March 2021.

17   Elbridge A. Colby, *The Strategy of Denial: American Defense in an Age of Great Power Conflict* (New Haven and London: Yale University Press, 2021). Reviewed in the *Financial Times* of 4th November 2021 by James Crabtree.

18   *The Wall Street Journal*, 5th December 2021.

19   David Vine, Lists of US Military Bases Abroad 1776–2021, American University Digital Research Archive 2021.

20   ChinaPower Project, 'Is China a Military Superpower?', 26th August 2020.

21   RAND Corporation, op. cit.

22   Lindsay Maitland, op. cit.

23   Kurt M. Campbell and Jake Sullivan, 'Competition without Catastrophe: How America Can Both Challenge and Coexist with China', *Foreign Affairs*, 13th September–October 2019.

24 John Bolton, 'Revisit the "One-China" Policy', *Wall Street Journal*, 16th January 2017.

25 Report of the National Security Commission, op. cit.

26 Chi-kin Lo, *China's Policy Towards Territorial Disputes: The Case of the South China Sea Islands* (London: Routledge, 1989).

27 Merwyn Samuels, *Contest for the South China Sea* (London: Routledge, 2013).

28 Discussed in Miller, *China's Asian Dream*, op. cit., pp. 211–12.

29 Peter Frankopan, op. cit.

30 Xi Jinping on BRI. See Miller, *China's Asian Dream*, op. cit., p. 30.

31 OECD, *Infrastructure to 2030*, 2 Vols., International Futures Programme, 2006.

32 David Dollar, 'Seven Years into Belt and Road', Brookings, 1st October 2020.

33 Benn Steil and Benjamin Della Rocca, 'Belt and Road Tracker', Council on Foreign Relations, 2019.

34 There is a good discussion of Chinese motivation in Miller, *China's Asian Dream*, op. cit., pp. 30–34. See also Andrew Chatzky and James McBride, 'China's Massive Belt and Road Initiative', Council on Foreign Relations, 28th January 2020.

35 Vladimir Lenin, *Imperialism: The Highest Stage of Capitalism* (1917). J.A. Hobson, *Imperialism: A Study* (1902).

36 Yuen Yuen Ang, 'Demystifying Belt and Road: The Struggle to Define China's "Project of the Century"', *Foreign Affairs*, 22nd May 2019.

37 Chan Kung and Yu (Tony) Pan, 'How China's Belt and Road Initiative Went Astray', *The Diplomat*, 7th May 2020. Yiping Huang, 'Understanding China's Belt & Road Initiative: Motivation, Framework and Assessment', *China Economic Review*, Vol. 40, 2016, pp. 314–21.

38 Centre of Global Development, Washington and London, 2018.

39 *Financial Times*, using World Bank and Grisons Peak data, 14th October 2016, p. 11

40 Dollar, op. cit.

41 Chatham House, 'Debunking the Myth of "Debt-Trap Diplomacy"', 23rd October 2020.

42 Kathrin Hille and David Pilling, 'China Applies Brakes to Africa Lending', *Financial Times*, 11th January 2022.

43 AidData Project (2000–17), William & Mary's Global Research Institute, Virginia.

44 Owen Churchill, 'Mike Pompeo Warns Panama and Other Nations about Accepting China's "Belt and Road" Loans', *South China Morning Post*, 20th October 2018.

45 Deborah Brautigam, *The Dragon's Gifts: The Real Story of China in Africa* (Oxford: Oxford University Press, 2009).

46 Chris Alden, *China in Africa* (London: Zed Books, 2017).

47 Data from Johns Hopkins China–Africa Research Initiative.

48 Li Anshan, *China and Africa in the Global Context: Encounter, Policy, Cooperation and Migration* (Cape Town: Ace Press, 2020). Deborah Brautigam, Jendayi E. Frazer and C.D. Glin, 'China's Growing Footprint in Africa', Council on Foreign Relations Seminar, June 2020.

49 Deloitte data cited in *The Economist* of 19th February 2020.

50 Center for Global Development, Washington, D.C., 2020.

51 Axel Dreher, Andreas Fuchs, Bradley Parks, Austin Strange and Michael J. Tierney, *Banking on Beijing: The Aims and Impacts of China's Overseas Development Program* (Cambridge, UK: Cambridge University Press, 2022).

52 Haley J. Swedlund, 'Is China Eroding the Bargaining Power of Traditional Donors in Africa?', *International Affairs*, No. 93, 2017.

53 Data from Johns Hopkins China–Africa Research Initiative.

54 Lina Benabdallah, *Shaping the Future of Power: Knowledge Production and Network-Building in China–Africa Relations* (Ann Arbor, MI: University of Michigan Press 2020).

55 Zhiqun Zhu, *China's New Diplomacy: Rationale, Strategies and Significance* (Abingdon: Routledge, 2017).

56 Pew Research Center, December 2019.

57 Howard W. French, *China's Second Continent: How a Million Migrants Are Building a New Empire in Africa* (New York: Alfred A. Knopf, 2014).

58 Daniel Large, *China and Africa: The New Era* (Cambridge, UK: Polity Press, 2021).

59 Elizabeth Economy and Michael Levi, *By All Means Necessary: How China's Resource Quest Is Changing the World* (New York: Oxford University Press, 2014).

60 *BP Statistical Review*, 2019.

61 Ibid.

62 'Nuclear Proliferation', *The Economist*, 30th January 2021.

63 David R. Mares and Harold A. Trinkunas, *Aspirational Power: Brazil on the Long Road to Global Influence* (Washington, DC: Brookings Institution Press, 2016).

64 Harold A. Trinkunas, 'Testing the Limits of China and Brazil's Partnership', article on Brookings website, 20th July 2020.

65 Jonathan E. Hillman, 'China and Russia: Economic Unequals', Center for Strategic & International Studies, 15th July 2020.

66 Colin Mackerras and Michael Clarke, eds., *China, Xinjiang and Central Asia: History, Transition and Crossborder Interaction into the 21st Century* (London: Routledge, 2011). Marlène Laruelle and Sébastien Peyrouse, *The Chinese Question in Central Asia: Domestic Order, Social Change and the Chinese Factor* (London: Hurst & Company, 2012). Michael Clarke, 'Understanding China's Eurasian Pivot', *The Diplomat*, 10th September 2015.

67 Miller, *China's Asian Dream*, op. cit., pp. 73–85.

68 Surveys conducted by BBC World Service in conjunction with the polling from Globe Scan and the Programme of International Policy Attitudes at the University of Maryland.

69 Figures from Pew Research Center, end of 2019.

70 Ezra F. Vogel, *China and Japan: Facing History* (Cambridge, MA: The Belknap Press, 2019).

71 Ezra F. Vogel, *Deng Xiaoping and the Transformation of China*, op. cit.

72 Dennis B. Smith, *Japan since 1945: The Rise of an Economic Superpower* (New York: St Martin's Press, 1995). Richard McGregor, *Asia's Reckoning: China, Japan, and the Future of US Power in the Pacific Century* (New York: Viking, 2017).

73 Ryosei Kokubun, Yoshihide Soeya, Akio Takahara and Shin Kawashima, *Japan–China Relations in the Modern Era* (Abingdon: Routledge, 2017). Chien-peng Chung, *Contentious*

Integration: Post-Cold War Japan–China Relations in the Asia-Pacific (Farnham: Ashgate, 2014).

74 Jonathan D. Pollack, 'Order at Risk: Japan, Korea, and the Northeast Asian Paradox', Brookings, September 2016. Ji-Young Lee, 'The Geopolitics of South Korea–China Relations: Implications for US Policy in the Indo-Pacific', RAND Corporation Perspectives, 1st November 2020.

75 Jung H. Pak, 'Trying to Loosen the Linchpin: China's Approach to South Korea', Brookings, July 2020.

76 Chung Min Lee, 'South Korea Is Caught Between China and the United States', Carnegie Endowment for International Peace, 21st October 2020.

77 Cited in 'Trump Warns China Is "Ripe" for New Tariffs and Suggests Vietnam Could Be Next', *The Guardian*, 27th June 2019.

78 Huong Le Thu, 'Rough Waters Ahead for Vietnam–China Relations', Carnegie Endowment for International Peace, 30th September 2020.

79 Felix K. Chang, 'The Odd Couple: Singapore's Relations with China', Foreign Policy Research Institute, 3rd December 2019.

80 Brenda Tan, 'Friend or Foe? Explaining the Philippines' China Policy in the South China Sea', E-International Relations, 10th August 2020.

81 Felix K. Chang, 'A Faint Breeze of Change: Malaysia's Relations with China', Foreign Policy Research Institute, 8th January 2020.

82 Zachary Abuza, 'America Should Be Realistic about Its Alliance with Thailand', Texas National Security Review, 2nd January 2020.

83 Ibid.

84 Peter Church, ed., *A Short History of South-East Asia* (Singapore: John Wiley & Sons Pte. Ltd, 2009).

85 Miller, *China's Asian Dream*, op. cit., Chapter 4.

86 *The Economist*, 27th February 2021.

87 Vince Cable, *China and India*, op. cit.

88 Tanvi Madan, 'Emerging Global Issues: The China–India Boundary Crisis and Its Implications', Brookings, 9th September

2020. Lora Saalman, *The China–India Nuclear Crossroads* (Washington, DC: Brookings Institution Press, 2012).

89 *Samudra Manthan, Sino-Indian Rivalry in the Indo-Pacific* (Washington, DC: Carnegie Endowment for International Peace, 2012).

90 Andrew Small, *The China–Pakistan Axis: Asia's New Geopolitics* (London: Hurst & Company, 2015).

91 There is a comprehensive review of trends in a report of the Breughel Institute for the European Parliament and Commission, 'EU–China Trade and Investment Relations in Challenging Times', May 2020.

92 Ibid.

93 'What Is in the EU–China Investment Treaty?', *Financial Times*, 30th December 2020.

94 Janka Oertel, 'The New China Consensus: How Europe Is Growing Wary of Beijing', European Council on Foreign Relations, 7th September 2020.

95 Helen Thomson, 'The New EU–China Trade Deal Is Driven by a Commercial Realpolitik – and the World Knows It', *New Statesman*, 27th January 2021.

96 Gideon Rachman, 'Europe Has Handed China a Strategic Victory', op. cit.

97 Survey by the European Council on Foreign Relations, 19th January 2021.

98 Andrew Cainey and Veerle Nouwens, 'Assessing the UK–China Commercial Relationship', RUSI, 12th June 2020.

99 Ian Williams, 'How China Bought Cambridge', *The Spectator*, 10th July 2021.

100 'Global Britain in a Competitive Age: The Integrated Review of Security, Defence, Development and Foreign Policy', gov.uk, March 2021.

101 McGregor, *Xi Jinping: The Backlash*, op. cit., pp. 88–94; 'Australia Can Teach the UK a Lesson in Chinese Wrath', *Financial Times*, 20th March 2021.

CHAPTER 7

1   Laura Silver et al., Pew Research Center, 6th October 2020.

2   *The Epoch Times*, May 2020.

3   Reported by the BBC on 7th May 2020.

4   Reported in *The Lancet* in February 2021.

5   Quoted in Economy, op. cit., p. 231.

6   Speech in Geneva, 25th January 2021.

7   Yan Xuetong, 'Becoming Strong: The New Chinese Foreign Policy', *Foreign Affairs*, July–August 2021.

8   Sam Olsen, blog article on China's new Global Security Initiative, 5th May 2022.

9   World Bank, *Doing Business 2020*.

10 Brown, *The World According to Xi*, op. cit., p. 7.

11 Economy, op. cit., p. 231.

12 William A. Callahan, 'Chinese Visions of World Order: Post-hegemonic or a New Hegemony?', *International Studies Review*, Vol. 10, No. 4, December 2008, pp. 749–61.

13 Allison, op. cit., John Mearsheimer, *The Tragedy of Great Power Politics* (New York: W.W. Norton & Co., 2001).

14 Jisi, op. cit.

15 Jacques, op. cit., Mahbubani, op. cit.

16 *New York Times*, 13th May 2020. Reuters, 30th July 2020. *The Guardian*, 22nd November 2020.

17 Speech on 3rd October 2015 referenced in Miller, *China's Asian Dream*, op. cit., p. 245.

18 As in Magnus, *Red Flags*, op. cit., Chapter 7.

19 David C. Kang, 'Getting Asia Wrong: The Need for New Analytical Frameworks', *International Security*, Vol. 27, No. 4, Spring 2003, pp. 57–85. Jacques, op. cit., pp. 374–75.

20 Robert D. Blackwill and Ashley J. Tellis, 'Revising US Grand Strategy toward China', Council on Foreign Relations, March 2015.

21 Lyle J. Goldstein, 'Is It Time to Meet China Halfway?', *The National Interest*, 12th May 2015, quoted in Economy, op. cit., p. 234.

22 Thomas J. Christensen, *The China Challenge: Shaping the Choices of a Rising Power* (New York: W.W. Norton & Co., 2016).

23 Miller, *China's Asian Dream*, op. cit., p. 247.

24 Doshi, op. cit.

25 Henry Kissinger, *Does America Need a Foreign Policy?: Toward a Diplomacy for the 21st Century* (New York: Simon & Schuster, 2001), p. 135.

26 MacroPolo, *The Global AI Talent Tracker*, The Paulsen Institute, 2020.

27 Cheng Li, op. cit.

28 Edward Cunningham, Tony Saich and Jessie Turiel, 'Understanding CCP Resilience: Surveying Chinese Public Opinion through Time', Ash Center for Democratic Governance and Innovation, Harvard Kennedy School, July 2020.

29 Lei Guang, Margaret Roberts, Yiqing Xu and Jiannan Zhao, with Young Yang and Jiannan Zhao, 'Pandemic Sees Increase in Chinese Support for Regime, Decrease in Views towards the US', China Data Lab, University of California, San Diego, 30th June 2020.

30 Andrew Nathan, referred to in Cheng Li, op. cit.

31 'How to Kill a Democracy', *The Economist*, 20th February 2021, p. 49.

32 Ryan Hass and Michael H. Armacost, 'Designing a New Diplomatic Framework for Dealing with China', in *The Future of US Policy toward China*, op. cit.

33 Anita Engels, 'Understanding How China Is Championing Climate Change Mitigation', *Nature*, 14th August 2018.

34 Fergus Green and Nicholas Stern, 'China's Changing Economy: Implications for Its Carbon Dioxide Emissions', *Climate Policy*, March 2016.

35 'Working Together, But in Parallel', *The Economist*, 13th February 2021.

36 Ma Jun, *Time Magazine*, 12th September 2019.

37 'Who Will Go Nuclear Next', *The Economist*, 30th January 2021.

38 Davis and Wei, op. cit., p. 247.

39 David Dollar, 'Forging an Alternative Economic Strategy for Dealing with China', in *The Future of US Policy Toward China*, op. cit.

40 Mark Wu, 'Managing the China Trade Challenge: Confronting the Limits of the WTO', Working Paper for the Penn Project on the Future of US–China Relations, Harvard Law School, 2020.

41 Mavroidis and Sapir, *op. cit.*

42 Alex Vines, 'China's Southern Africa Debt Deals Reveal a Wider Plan', Chatham House, 10th December 2020.

43 Dollar, op. cit.

44 'Cyber Capabilities and National Power: A Net Assessment', International Institute of Strategic Studies, Research Paper No. 28, June 2021.

45 Kevin Rudd, *The Avoidable War: The Dangers of a Catastrophic Conflict between the US and Xi Jinping's China* (New York: PublicAffairs, 2022)

46 Jeffrey Bader, 'Meeting the China Challenge: A Strategic Competitor, Not an Enemy', in *The Future of US Policy Toward China*, op. cit.

47 Cited in Samm Sachs, 'Addressing the Data Security Risks of US–China Technology Entanglement', in *The Future of US Policy Toward China*, op. cit.

48 Joshua P. Meltzer and Peter Lovelock, 'Regulating for a Digital Economy: Understanding the Importance of Cross-border Data Flows in Asia', Brookings, 20th March 2018. Robert K. Knake, 'Weaponizing Digital Trade: Creating a Digital Trade Zone to Promote Online Freedom and Cybersecurity', Council on Foreign Relations, September 2020.

49 Samm Sachs, op. cit.

50 Anne-Marie Slaughter, 'How to Succeed in the Networked World: A Grand Strategy for the Digital Age', *Foreign Affairs*, Vol. 95, No. 6, November–December 2016.

51 Mike Pompeo, 'Communist China and the Free World's Future', 23rd July 2020.

52 Yu-Jie Chen, 'China's Challenge to the International Human Rights Regime', NYU *Journal of International Law and Politics*, Vol. 51, 2019, pp. 1179–222.

53 UN Treaty Bodies and China (hrichina.org/en/un-treaty-bodies-and-china).

54 Yu-Jie Chen, op. cit.

55 Frances Eve, 'The US Withdrawal from the UNHRC Is Perfect for Xi Jinping and China', *The Guardian*, 22nd June 2018.

56 Oertel, op. cit.

57 'EU–China Strategy Outlook', European Commission, March 2019.

58 Cable, *China: Engage!*, op. cit.

59 McGregor, *Xi Jinping: The Backlash*, op. cit.

60 Jost Wübbeke, Mirjam Meissner, Max J. Zenglein, Jaqueline Ives and Björn Conrad, 'Made in China 2025: The Making of a High-Tech Superpower and Consequences for Industrial Countries', Merics, Mercator Institute for China Studies, December 2016.

61 'Global Britain in a Competitive Age', op. cit.

62 McGregor, 'Australia Can Teach the UK a Lesson in Chinese Wrath', op. cit.

63 Rudd, cit.

64 'Henry Kissinger Explains How to Avoid World War Three', *The Economist*, 17th May 2023

CURLEW COAST

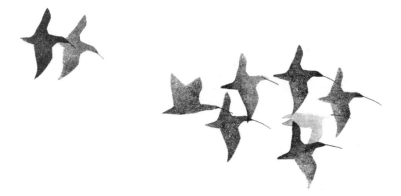

Judith Ellis

CURLEW COAST

Diversions on Maritime Suffolk

with illustrations by the author

( and a few red herrings)

Two Points East: A View of Maritime Norfolk by Judith Ellis
was shortlisted for the East Anglian Book Awards in 2017

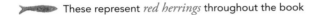 These represent *red herrings* throughout the book

Published by Red Herring Publishing
© Judith Ellis 2018

Designed by **studio medlikova**
Edited by Jenny Wilson

ISBN 978-1-9997839-3-8

A CIP record for this book is available
from the British Library

Printed and bound in the UK by the Pureprint Group

WORLD
LAND
TRUST™
www.carbonbalancedpaper.com
CBP0001908250418028

The moon has risen,
The river breeze is blowing,
The Curlew River
Is flowing to the sea.

William Plomer, from the libretto to Benjamin Britten's *Curlew River*

CONTENTS

INTRODUCTION

There are two Suffolks. One is the gentle, arcadian landscape painted by Constable and others, a landscape of woods and fields, with the occasional flash of water glimpsed between undulating hills betraying the presence of a distant river. It is scattered with pink-washed thatched cottages, small market towns, and some unusually large and very beautiful medieval churches; it is edged with beaches, shingle and salt marshes alive with plant and bird life.

The other Suffolk is a wild and desolate place, where a grey sea, whipped up by northeasterly winds, constantly challenges the land in a never-ending battle for territory which it is always going to win. Just up the coast from Southwold at Covehithe, the road simply disappears over the cliff and a huge half-ruined church stands nearby, waiting its turn. To stand on the shingle beach there, under a forbidding sky with a penetratingly cold wind, one can only marvel at how our predecessors managed to find a living in such an unforgiving environment. This is the Suffolk which Benjamin Britten conjures up so well in his music, and which suffuses the scores of his operas, capturing the bleakness of the sea and the hardship of the lives played out by its inhabitants.

The coast of East Anglia is a shifting thing. It is an indistinct, blurred edge-land that does not remain in the same place for very long. The present coastline is only the most recent edge between water and land. It is a liminal thing; a threshold between one form and another, made of the sand, shingle and boulder clays that were left behind on the retreat of the last glacier that once covered Britain down as far as the Thames Valley. These elements of gravel, mud and silt are themselves in transition, on their own journey in geological time to becoming, perhaps, sandstone and shale in the long millennia which lie ahead. This rim is neither one thing nor another; a place of transition between sea and land, with the memory of past tidal surges and floods a forever present reminder that nothing is fixed about this coast. For centuries storms and surges have ravaged this ever vulnerable edge of Britain, and will continue to do so, changing its contours year by year.

This is the continuing story of a journey around the coast of East Anglia which began in King's Lynn and has grown into a fascination with how the coast has shaped the lives of its inhabitants over the centuries, and how it has altered since people first came here to live by its shores. It is a story of ships and fishing, storms and lifeboats, maritime trade and transport, and some of the remarkable people who have made their mark in some way along this coast over the last few hundred years.

It is also the story of lighthouses and piracy, of navigators and saints, of Egyptian funerary barges and the crossing of the River Styx, as we touch upon some of the maritime-related legends that have enthralled the world for hundreds of years.

But let us begin close to home, with the history of the East Coast edge-land.

IN THE BEGINNING

The eastern edge of Britain has not been hardened in the fires of the earth's core like the igneous rocks of the west; it does not present an impenetrable barrier to the ocean forever pounding at its door. Rather, it is soft and yielding, made of sand and shingle, an infant coast, a neonate, the edge of the lost country of Doggerland which now lies forgotten under the North Sea.

Doggerland was the last remaining landbridge between Britain and Northern Europe, and its inundation with glacial meltwater happened only ten thousand or so years ago, severing our last physical connection to continental Europe and making us an island, the effects of which have been reflected in our history ever since.

It is hard to believe that until ten thousand years ago humans lived and hunted in Doggerland, raised families, made tools and told stories. Seven thousand years ago, in around 5000 BC, the Suffolk coast lay a good six miles further out to the east, under the sea now, and it was a land wooded with oak, elm and lime trees. Another two thousand years on people arrived from Europe, bringing with them their farming skills. They also mined flints at Grime's Graves near Thetford, and by 2500 BC they were making bronze by smelting copper with tin. Settlers from the Netherlands arrived in 500 BC and they brought with them the new alchemy of making iron, and it was into this Iron Age that the Romans first came.

The fifth and sixth centuries saw the arrival of as many as a hundred thousand Angles, Jutes and Saxons, driven partly by rising sea levels from their coastal homelands of what is now Denmark and Germany; they were to be followed in the ninth century by more Scandinavians. Long seafarers and fishermen, they ate fish and dug peat for fuel.

The coastline gradually began to retreat as sea levels continued to rise. Water crept up into tidal channels, creeks and river valleys, and shingle spits advanced slowly southwards as longshore drift began the ceaseless defining and redefining of this soft, yielding land's edge.

With safe moorings, sheltered estuaries and not too many offshore shoals (reef-like ridges or banks), it was a good coast for shipping, and attracted both trade and invaders from up the coast and across the North Sea. Essex, by contrast, with its extensive mudflats and treacherous shoals, had a much less strong connection with the North Sea than Suffolk did, looking more to the Thames Estuary, London and northern France.

The river valleys of the Lark and Gipping, known to geologists as *the Lark-Gipping corridor*, stretch across the south of the county from Bury St Edmunds to Ipswich, once forming both a physical and a cultural barrier across East Anglia. When the Romans first came, the Iceni were living to the north of the corridor in Norfolk and Suffolk, and the Trinovantes to the south, occupying Essex and the southwest of Suffolk.

The strip of marsh, heath and arable land along the Suffolk coast is called the *Sandlands*, or *Sandlings*. The soil here is mainly the sand and gravel laid down in the last glaciation and it overlies the much older *crag* to a depth of about ten metres. South of Aldeburgh the soil is sandy, acid and infertile with a few silt deposits, and there are long shingle spits and some large rivers. North of Aldeburgh there are areas of more fertile soil, some unclaimed fen and a few small rivers which are blocked from flowing out to sea now by the accumulation of shingle. In places the shingle has formed into banks creating small lagoons which have gradually filled with the peat produced by the slow, undisturbed decomposition of trees over the centuries.

It was Bronze Age people who lived mainly in the Sandlands as their simple plough, the *ard*, was unable to work the heavier but much more fertile soils found further inland, and this is why most of the Bronze Age settlements in Suffolk are to be found in the Sandlands. They kept sheep, folding them on the heath in small areas for a few nights at a time, and the dung improved the fertility of the soil enabling crops of barley, wheat and oats to be grown for one or two seasons. Without the sheep to keep the heather and gorse down, the land would quickly revert to heath again.

When the Iron Age people came to settle, they brought with them their stronger ploughs which allowed them to work the better land, and agriculture continued to thrive under the subsequent Roman occupation, only to fall into decline after the Romans left in AD 410 so that, by the time the Anglo-Saxons arrived, the population was largely living near the sea again.

During the Anglo-Saxon period, East Anglia underwent enormous changes which took it from a tribal culture to a collection of separate kingdoms, with all the increase in social complexity that entailed, followed by the embracing of Christianity.

This is the beginning of the story of the Suffolk coast.

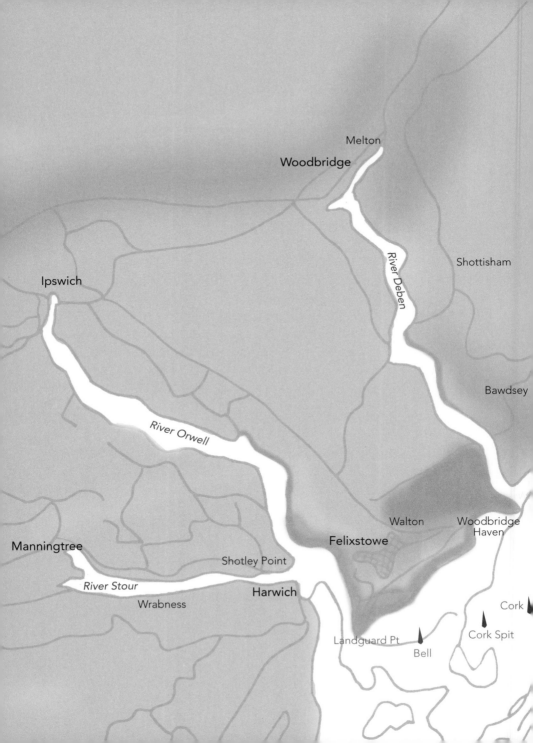

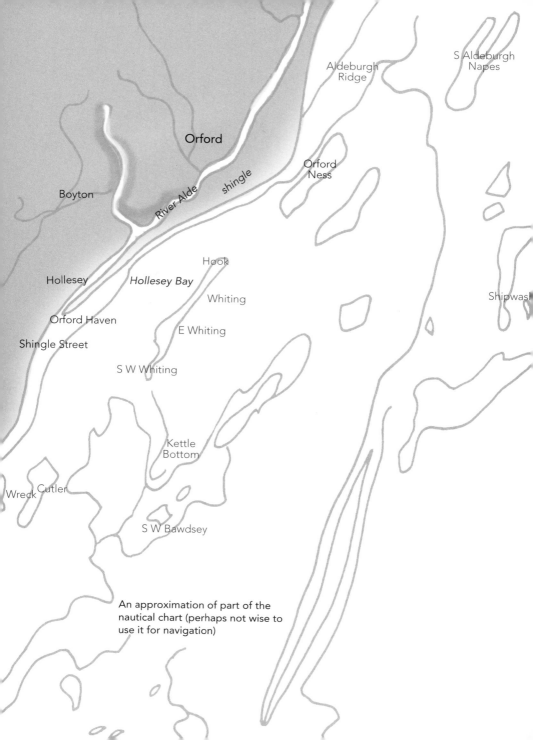

S Aldeburgh
Napes

Aldeburgh
Ridge

Orford

Orford
Ness

Boyton

River Alde   *shingle*

Hook

Shipwash

Hollesey   *Hollesey Bay*

Whiting

Orford Haven

E Whiting

Shingle Street

S W Whiting

Kettle
Bottom

Wreck Cutler

S W Bawdsey

An approximation of part of the
nautical chart (perhaps not wise to
use it for navigation)

Chapter 1
LOWESTOFT

Walking down the High Street in Lowestoft today gives one little clue to the past of this largely forgotten town. The observant will notice signs of a maritime trail, a few carved fish let into some of the paving stones in strategic places pointing up something of interest, and some badly corroded metal plaques on the passages leading down towards the sea, almost unreadable now. If you walk down one of these steep passages – they were known as *scores* – you no longer find yourself on the shore where the old fishermen's huts once stood. Instead, you come to a road with factories blocking all sight of the sea which lies behind them; this part of the old fishing town seems to have severed any connection with the sea.

If we should go back to the thirteenth century, however, the original settlement on the north side of the River Waveney had by then developed into a fishing village. The men worked from the beach where they built their fishing huts, but they had their dwellings on the cliffs above – today's High Street – with access to the shore by way of the series of paths which they called scores. These were tracks in the cliffs that had been made by surface water as it drained down to the beach, each scoring a path as it went.

Many of the scores are still there, leading off the High Street as steep, narrow, tarmacked paths, often with wide shallow steps for the final descent

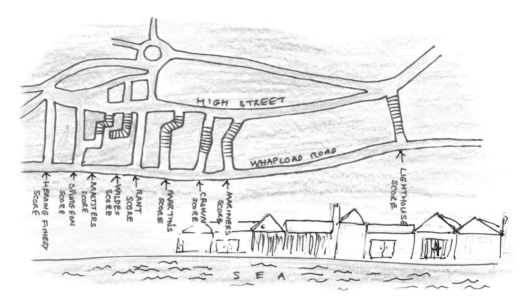

The Scores

down to Whapload Road. This road was built as part of the industrial development when the fishing sheds were finally demolished, thereby removing
the last physical remains of Lowestoft's connection to its fishing past. The
names of Cart Score, Martin's Score, Wildes Score, Crown Score, Maltsters
Score, Spurgeon Score, Lighthouse Score, Rant Score and Herring Fishery
Score are still there, and you can walk down towards the sea as countless fishermen have done before you. The walls either side of the paths are made of
flints interspersed with bricks.

Back in medieval times the population grew in number as the town
thrived on its fishing and associated trades, and in 1306 it was granted a
market to be held on Wednesdays, and two annual fairs on 12th May and
10th October. The fairs are thought to have been held on the site where the
Town Hall is now.

The drying racks

Just north of Lighthouse Score is the area known as The Denes, and it is here where rope was once made and nets were dried on large wooden racks, some of which are still there — the last, dying statement of a former past. The fishing nets were steeped overnight in catechu bark as a preservative and hung out to dry before being fitted with cork floats.

>━━━ *Catechu is a variety of the acacia tree and its bark was also used to tan sails, giving an almost black colour to the sailcloth*

ROPE-MAKING

Huge quantities of rope were needed for sailing ships, and wherever there was a shipyard a whole industry of related trades would spring up, from rope- and sail-making to metal-working. Blacksmiths were needed to make chains, anchors and the copious quantities of nails that were used in the building of a ship.

Hemp, from the plant *Cannabis sativa* (yes, the same plant as the drug), was the preferred material for rope, its fibres also used for caulking (when it was known as oakum), and hemp was grown extensively in East Anglia in the sixteenth century just for this purpose. Its importance can be inferred from a law passed at the time of Elizabeth I which required anyone farming more than sixty acres to grow a crop of hemp.

Flax was also grown for spinning into linen, the word 'linen' being derived from the plant's Latin name Linum, and fields of flax can still sometimes be seen in East Anglia, painting a haze of blue among the patchwork of barley and rape

Hemp fibre was also woven into cloth for sails; the word 'canvas' has its root in the word 'cannabis'

There are several different strains of *Cannabis sativa* and the one that produces the best fibres for rope contains much less of the psychoactive component. Hemp always made the strongest ropes but needed to be waterproofed with tar to prevent it from rotting, leading to sailors becoming known as *tars*. A sailor was required to spend a lot of time applying tar to the rigging, and anyone who has spent any time on an old sailing vessel will be familiar with the all-pervading smell which clings to their clothes and hair, but, despite all this, the average lifespan of a rope was only five years.

Manila, a sort of banana growing mainly in the Philippines, produced fibres which did not need waterproofing but it made a much weaker rope, while the rope produced from the fibrous leaves of the **sisal** plant was stretchy, a quality which made it best for mooring lines. **Coir**, from the coconut shell, did not rot at all in saltwater but its rope was very weak and so it was largely reserved for net-making.

Rope was made on a ropewalk, the length of the walk determining the length of rope that could be made. The ropewalk at Chatham Naval Dockyard is a quarter of a mile long and housed inside a long shed – the longest one in the country.

The tough fibres were first stripped from the stems of the hemp plants and the resulting tangled mess combed using a piece of wood covered with metal spikes which was called a *hatchel*. The fibres were then spun into a *yarn*, and six of these yarns were twisted together to make a *strand*. Three or four strands were then twisted together in the opposite direction to make a rope; one direction of twist was called an S twist and the opposite way was called a Z twist. The strands were attached to hooks placed on a revolving disc at one end of the walk. Facing the disc, the rope-maker would hold the ends of the strands and walk slowly backwards while the disc was turned. A well-made rope should be of even tension throughout and will lie straight when dropped on the ground; any rope not of this standard will develop tensions under use and it will gradually break down.

➤ *A hawser is made up of three strands, while three hawsers twisted together make a* cable

The quality of rope was of huge importance, as the safety of the ship relied on rope that would not part in the stressed conditions of sailing in heavy seas. To this end, the Royal Dockyards set up under Henry VIII required each rope-maker to mark his rope by adding a coloured strand from which its origin could be identified. With the invention of the engine, the process became more mechanised as machinery could then drive the discs, and a carriage running on rails meant that no-one had to walk backwards anymore.

Up until the nineteenth century Lowestoft's river, the Waveney, was blocked from flowing into the sea by a bank of shingle which allowed water to pool into lake-like bodies of water. Crossing over the roadbridge on the A146 at Mutford Lock I was always puzzled by the topography until I realised that my confusion was caused entirely by the fact that the expanse of water on either side of the road is given two different names. The wide stretch of water on the landward side is known as Oulton Broad, and that on the other side as Lake Lothing, but both are just a widening of the River Waveney as it nears the sea. Another lock, built at the seaward end of Lake Lothing in the

Oulton Broad

nineteenth century, finally allowed access from the river through the shingle bank to the sea, but more of that later.

HERRING

Vast shoals of the Atlantic herring, *Clupea harengus*, swim the ocean feeding on plankton in the surface layers. They migrate around the coast to spawn, only staying for a week or two in each location. In the early summer they are to be found off the west coast of Scotland; swimming north, by mid-summer they are off the Shetlands, and then, moving east along the north coast, they come down the east coast to arrive at their breeding ground off Great Yarmouth in August. The Smith's Knoll ridge on the seabed twenty-five miles east of Yarmouth was once the world's biggest spawning ground for herring.

For our coast-dwelling ancestors herring were plentiful, cheap and nutritious, being high in protein and fats, and they could be salted to preserve them for a little while. But things were to change in the fourteenth century when a fisherman from northern Flanders named Willem Beukels is reputed to have invented a new way to preserve the herring. According to the story, which first appears in fifteenth-century texts, he removed the guts and gills from the fish, leaving the liver and pancreas in for flavour,

19

and then soaked the fish in brine. This superior method of preservation was to transform the fishery, allowing large numbers of fish to be caught and sold, and herring became a staple food forming an important part of the medieval economy.

The Hanseatic League of merchants were quick to pick up and control herring fishing in the Baltic, which worked well with their control of the salt trade in northern Germany. But Holland was not slow to realise the importance of the fishing industry in the North Sea and soon started to develop more efficient ways to catch herring. The most significant improvement they made was their invention of the *drift net*. This is a very long net suspended from floats, which forms a vertical curtain into which the unlucky shoal of herring swim, quickly becoming entangled by their gills. Casting their nets at dusk the boats would drift slowly with the tide while the fish coming to the surface to feed as usual at night would swim instead into this wall of netting – the very first industrial fishing.

There was no stopping the Dutch now in their bid to dominate the North Sea fishery and they built massive fishing boats which they called *busses*. These large, cumbersome vessels could store huge numbers of fish, which were gutted and salted on board by the crew. Smaller faster boats, *jaags* (from which we derive our word 'yacht'), would take the catch ashore, which allowed the busses to stay at sea for long periods of time. Some say the Dutch Empire was built on the back of the herring.

> *The Dutch word* jaag *meaning 'yacht' can also mean 'hunt'*

When is a herring really a sprat?
All the world's herring belong to the family Clupeidae, and there are a number of familiar fish under this general umbrella. The herring found in European waters is the Atlantic herring, *Clupea harengus*, but there are many other species all over the world.

Herring

Sprat

The Clupeidae family also includes the sprat, of which there are in turn a lot of different species; the one found in European waters is known as *Sprattus sprattus*.

This brings us to the sardine and the pilchard. These are colloquial names used for various different types of small fish within the herring family, and which name is used largely depends on the region in which they are fished. What is called a pilchard in one neck of the woods can be called a sardine somewhere else. At the time of writing, the fish previously referred to in the West Country as the pilchard is now being marketed as the Cornish Sardine, no doubt to put people in mind of those delicious grilled sardines to be had on Mediterranean holidays, which of course may well be yet another species within the herring family... They still taste delicious, though, whatever you choose to call them.

The domination of the herring fishery by Holland was a constant source of irritation to the East Coast fishermen, who soon started to copy their methods of fishing and to build similar bigger vessels, and the fishery which developed at Great Yarmouth became more than a match for the ambitious Dutch. Although rivalling Yarmouth in medieval times, Lowestoft just a little further down the coast could not continue to compete as it lacked a hinterland of waterways and roads for transporting fish to the markets, and by the mid-eighteenth century Lowestoft had less than half the number of fishing boats that Yarmouth had working out of its harbour.

But the town's future was about to change, with an ambitious plan to open up the navigation.

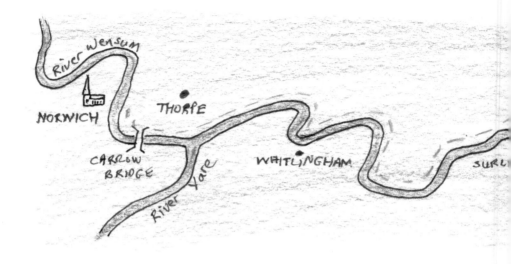

A HARBOUR TO RIVAL GREAT YARMOUTH

The proposition

In the early nineteenth century Norwich was thriving on the wealth generated by the textile industry. The Norwich merchants sent their goods by river to the port of Great Yarmouth, but the River Yare and Breydon Water had become rather neglected, and the difficulties of navigation were compounded by the narrowness of the channel at Yarmouth's Haven Bridge. To make matters worse the Port Commissioners were levying an exorbitant tax on every ship using the harbour, and this is what finally moved the merchants to look for a cheaper way of getting their goods to the coast. It was proposed to develop Lowestoft as their alternative port by building a harbour there and improving its river access. These major alterations required an Act of Parliament to be passed, and in 1827 the Norwich and Lowestoft Navigation Act received its royal assent and the Company of that name was formed.

The plan

Norwich's river, the Yare, was to be dredged, widened and straightened, and a canal cut to link it directly with Lowestoft's river, the Waveney, thus bypassing Breydon Water altogether. Oulton Dyke would be enlarged, with a lock to be installed at Mutford Bridge, and finally a sea-lock would be built in the shingle bank at Lowestoft, joining Lake Lothing to the sea and thus creating a small harbour. All this would cut ten miles off the journey to the sea for ships leaving Norwich.

The River Yare

The new harbour

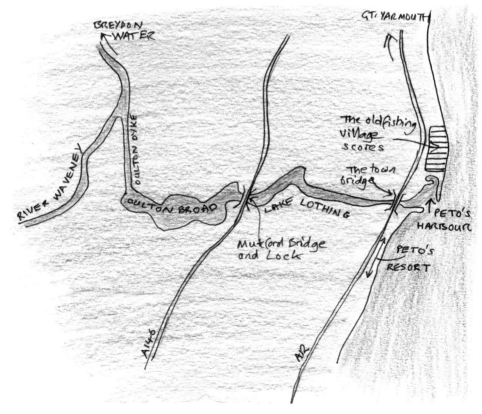

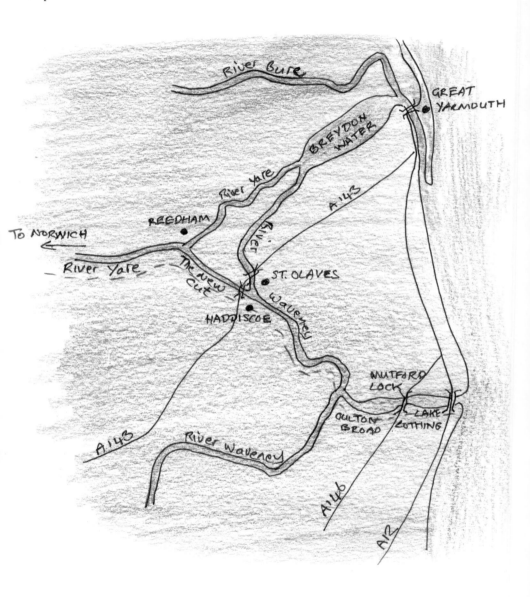

The New Cut

The consequences

The harbour was opened in 1831 and the New Cut was completed two years later, but the maintenance costs of the opening-bridges and locks, and the wages of the keepers needed for them, proved to be prohibitively high. Then the harbour began to silt up with sand swept down from the north on every high tide and, to compound the problems further, the port of Great Yarmouth then decided to reduce its tolls. By 1835 the losses were so great that the mortgage lenders foreclosed on the Company and it went up for sale. But Lowestoft's future was about to change once more.

ENTER SAMUEL MORTON PETO (1809–1889)

The civil engineer, entrepreneur and Member of Parliament Samuel Morton Peto moved to Somerleyton Hall in 1844, bought the Company, acquired the Lordship of the Manor, and proposed an ambitious plan to build both a railway and a new harbour for the town. His Lowestoft Railway and Harbour Company received Parliamentary approval in 1845 for building a track between Lowestoft and Reedham, and for improving the existing harbour. Peto was one of the foremost rail contractors of his time, a hardworking man committed to his Non-Conformist faith, with a reputation for combining his strict moral code with fair and humane treatment of his employees.

He worked at astonishing speed and within the space of three years he had built his railway, enlarged the harbour to the size of twenty acres, and made extensive new quays in the inner harbour of Lake Lothing. New warehouses and a covered fish market completed this stage of his plans. At a stroke the new railway opened up the town as a pleasure resort and rejuvenated the fishing industry with its new access by rail to the London markets.

Steam packets then began to use the facilities for running passenger and freight services to Rotterdam, Hamburg, Norway, Sweden, Denmark and St Petersburg, and timber, stone and coal were landed in the inner harbour. Industry then began to grow up around the port.

Peto now turned his energies to developing a new town on the south side of the river with elegant new houses, a pier and an esplanade where visitors could enjoy the sea, well away from the working side of the harbour across the river. With the construction of further railway links Lowestoft began to attract ships away from Great Yarmouth and by 1864 it had over two hundred fishing boats based in its harbour. Smacks and drifters were being built in shipyards on the north shore of Lake Lothing and were supplied by the nearby thriving iron foundries and timber yards.

The First World War saw the decline of fishing but Lowestoft was able to maintain a bigger fleet than that at Yarmouth and did not suffer the terrible bomb damage that Yarmouth sustained.

The lack of good road links from Lowestoft has stunted its further growth, but it can look back with pride to its brief flowering in the years when Peto transformed a small fishing town of five thousand people into a flourishing harbour and seaside resort.

>—— *During the Second World War, dummy tanks and naval ships were placed in the harbour to fool the Germans into thinking that the D-Day landings were being planned from there*

>—— *Christopher Cockerell invented the hovercraft in 1955 at Ripplecraft Boatyard in nearby Somerleyton*

THE EXTRAORDINARY LIFE OF JOSEPH CONRAD (1857–1924)

In 1877 Joseph Conrad came to Lowestoft looking for work, taking his first job as a paid ordinary seaman on a coaster working out of Lowestoft. But his story begins a little further back in Poland.

Poland had been annexed by Russia when Conrad was born in 1857 (today his birthplace is located in present-day Ukraine). His parents were wealthy but his father, who went by the terrific name of Apollo, was a romantic who spent his life, and his money, chasing dreams and schemes which never quite worked out. A natural revolutionary, he became involved with a movement to free Poland from its oppressors, getting himself exiled with his family to Russia as a dissident in the process. By the time the young Joseph was eleven, both his parents had died and the boy was taken in by his mother's brother, Thaddeus, who had always been a staunch and loyal friend to his father. Thaddeus showed Joseph immense generosity and forbearance throughout the young man's teenage years as he began to show his father's weaknesses for drink, gambling and general aversion to work.

At the age of seventeen Joseph was keen to go to sea so his uncle paid for him to go as a passenger on a sailing ship bound for Martinique, hoping that a long tedious voyage would cure him of the idea, but instead it had the opposite effect. Joseph helped to work the ship voluntarily and began to get a taste for sailing. After another of these passages, and with an allowance from his generous uncle, he went to live in Marseille where he became fluent in French, spending his time in the bars and cafes, among the intellectuals, revolutionaries and sailors who made up life in the lively port at that time.

He was later to tell the story of how, falling in with a Corsican sea captain, he was persuaded to join a syndicate being formed to run guns into Catalonia as part of a plot to restore King Carlos II to the Spanish throne. There were two other members of the syndicate – the captain's nephew Cesar and a mysterious woman called Doña Rita, who was probably Joseph's first lover. Captain Dominic Cervoni had a large moustache and a beautiful little lateen-rigged sailing ship bearing the equally beautiful name of the *Tremolino*. Conrad later described her as having two forward-raking masts, bearing two long curved yards that carried sails which resembled *'the pointed wings on a seabird's slender body'*.

Begging more money from his uncle, he converted three thousand francs into gold coins and stashed them in his locker on the little ship, unaware that Cesar had betrayed them. Having been tipped off, the coastguards were ready for them, giving chase off the Spanish coast, and when Joseph went to his locker to retrieve his coins he found that the blackguard Cesar had got there first. Realising they could not outrun the coastguard's fast cutter, Captain Cervoni decided to abandon his lovely little ship, and ran her deliberately onto the rocky shore, in order to make an escape overland. This they managed to do but in the general melee Cesar was knocked out of the dinghy and drowned – his demise no doubt hastened by the weight of all the gold coins in his pockets.

Escaping with his life, the young Joseph made his way back to Marseille and borrowed more money. Gambling it away in an attempt to repay all his debts, and ridden with despair, shame and guilt at losing everything that his patient uncle had given him, he tried to commit suicide by shooting himself in the chest. This desperate measure failed but brought his long-suffering uncle to Marseille to find him. When Joseph had recovered from his injuries, Thaddeus insisted that he find paid work in the British merchant navy and paid for him to join a steamship going to London via Constantinople. When Joseph wired his uncle from London asking for more money, Thaddeus's patience finally snapped and he responded by cutting off Joseph's allowance altogether. From now on the young man would have to make his own way.

Heading up the coast, he found work in Lowestoft, on a coaster called the *Skimmer of the Sea*, which sailed in and out of the East Coast ports. For three months he laboured on board as an ordinary seaman, loading and unloading the cargo as well as working the ship, before moving on to London to find a more interesting vessel to join. Always drawn to beautiful ships, he was lucky to find a berth as an apprentice officer on an old tea clipper, the *Duke of Sutherland*. The days of the fast clippers were numbered by now, with the invention of the steam engine, and like most of the old tea clippers she was working the Australian wool-run instead. On his return from Australia, Conrad took the Board of Trade examination for his Second Mate's certificate. Working through various other ships, his First Mate's ticket was to follow, and he finally qualified as Master Mariner at the age of only twenty-four.

Looking for new adventures, he took command of a river steamer in the African Congo, where he came across the most terrible atrocities and suffered

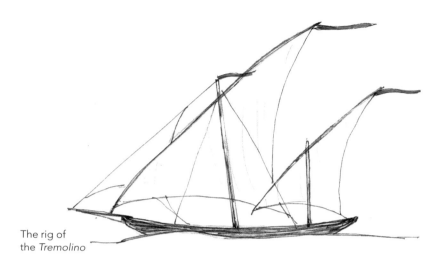

The rig of
the *Tremolino*

badly with his health. It was while recovering from this back in London that
Captain Cope offered him the job of First Mate on his then-famous passenger clipper ship, the *Torrens*.

The great period of the clippers was to be a brief one. Most were built in
the second half of the nineteenth century and, of all the fast and sleek ships
built, the *Torrens* was perhaps the most successful. Fast and beautiful she
could slip through the water with ease in the lightest of airs, working between
London and Adelaide using the Cape of Good Hope route rather than the
shorter but far more treacherous one around Cape Horn. Conrad worked
two round voyages on her, meeting John Galsworthy who was travelling as
a passenger on one of the trips and who was to remain a lifelong friend. He
finally left the sea at the age of thirty-six with enough adventures to furnish
a lifetime of writing.

No-one has ever written more movingly of the sea than Conrad. In his
memoir *The Mirror of the Sea*, he writes: *'No man … ever saw the sea looking
young as the earth looks young in Spring'*, and the wind he describes as *'the wild
and exulting voice of the world's soul'*.

Chapter 2
SOUTHWOLD

Southwold
town sign

Southwold makes its first appearance in the Domesday Record of 1086, where it is described as a small hamlet on a peninsula with thin sandy soil, no natural resources, and a population of just thirteen men and their families. The villagers were required to provide the monks of the abbey at Bury St Edmunds, who owned the land, with twenty-five thousand herring a year. As there is no evidence that they were actually fishermen, it seems rather a lot for only thirteen men to find, and they would have had to catch the fish the old way in wooden *weirs* placed in the sea, which trapped the herring as the tide went out.

Life in the village ticked over for many years punctuated by the granting of a charter in 1220 which allowed it to hold a weekly market and also an annual fair, but, as the century drew to a close, things were going to change for the population of this small coastal village.

At that time Southwold did not have a harbour. The River Blyth ran south, parallel to the shore inside the long shingle spit, and flowed into the sea at Dunwich. Dunwich was a major port on the east coast in those days, blessed by a large natural harbour at the mouth of the river, sheltered from the north and east winds by the lee of the shingle headland. One night in 1286 a savage storm blew up, which raged along the coast for three days.

It washed thousands of tons of shingle into the mouth of the river, permanently destroying the beautiful harbour and blocking the river's exit to the sea forever. This catastrophic event reversed the course of the River Blyth, which now flowed back up towards Southwold, where it burst through the shingle bank and gave Southwold the makings of a harbour for the very first time. Quick to recognise this opportunity, it was not long before the inhabitants enlarged the breach and built a harbour which allowed fishing and trade to flourish as it had never been able to before. By the end of the fourteenth century Southwold was serving boats fishing for cod in Iceland and herring off the east coast, and had become one of the few ports licensed to carry pilgrims to Santiago de Compostela, a lucrative business in medieval Europe.

Ships took corn, malt, and the butter and cheese from Suffolk's dairies up the coast and across the North Sea to the Low Countries. Shipyards were busy with orders for new boats, and all the associated trades built up and thrived – the sail- and rope-makers, the blacksmiths and riggers.

As the town continued to grow in prosperity it was granted another charter, this time by Henry VII in 1489, which gave Southwold its freedom at last, with the right to appoint a mayor and bailiffs to administer the town's affairs. It also, significantly, removed the rights from Dunwich to levy duties on ships coming into the river, transferring them to Southwold instead, along with jurisdiction over the foreshore and the right to salvage shipwrecks.

Under this charter a second annual fair was granted – there was one now held on St Bartholomew's Day and the other on Trinity Monday – and a second weekly market was licensed.

MARKETS, FAIRS AND CHARTERS

The *market* was an important part of life in medieval times, both for the buying and selling of food and other goods and for the exchange of news and gossip. They were always held once a week on the same day, usually in a churchyard, on the main street or at an intersection of two roads. They were often marked with a stone cross. The right to hold a market had to be granted by the Crown, which collected dues for the stalls, and this meant that the entry and exit points had to be controlled. Sometimes the rights to a market were held by the Lord of the Manor, who could be the local landowner or the Church and, as times prospered and towns grew in size, market places came to be built into the infrastructure, the market cross sometimes being replaced with a covered shelter.

Unlike the weekly market, a *fair* took place annually and would last for several days, often attracting visitors and merchants from great distances. The coastal towns of Suffolk were part of a wider North Sea community, and traders from the Low Countries and northern Germany would have been regular visitors. The annual Herring Fair at Great Yarmouth was one of the great fairs of Europe and lasted for forty days, attracting merchants from all over the continent, the herring being an important staple of the medieval diet.

The red herring, which was soaked in brine and smoked for far longer than the normal cure, could be kept for months; it sustained pilgrims and armies all across Europe. The strong smell of a red herring was used by criminals to put dogs off their scent when being pursued by the law – hence its colloquial use now.
There were approximately one thousand fairs licensed in the thirteenth century

The thirteenth century saw the beginning of the devolution of a limited amount of power from the Crown in exchange for a tax; the bargain was usually struck to finance whatever war the king was pursuing at the time. This early devolution involved the granting of a *charter*, which was the document a town needed to license its own markets, fairs and guilds, and to appoint a mayor with bailiffs to oversee the administration of the town's affairs. In return for paying a regular tax to the Crown, the town could then regulate and levy taxes on its citizens for the benefit of the community. Many of these charters were granted during the twelfth and thirteenth centuries by King John and King Richard to finance their foreign wars.

The granting of a charter was a significant development in social history and was accompanied by the striking of a *seal*. These seals usually portrayed some aspect of the life of the town, and the seal of a coastal town often showed fishing boats. They have become an important source of information about the design of ships of the period.

BREWING

Famous for its Adnams brewery now, Southwold pioneered the brewing of English bitter back in the fifteenth century. Before the days of freely available clean water, beer was routinely drunk as a safe alternative and every small town had its maltings for the making of malt from barley. But the East Coast sailors were developing a taste for the bitter beer brewed in the Low Countries where the brewers added hops to the malt as a preservative, giving the beer a characteristic bitter taste. The local breweries began to import hops for brewing and by the sixteenth century Suffolk was growing its own and it had become known for English bitter.

above right George Child designed and built some of England's early gasometers in Southwold and made the church gates, the trough outside the Swan Hotel, and the town pump with the three herrings as finials

WILLIAM GODELL (d. 1509)

William Godell owned a large estate as well as a fleet of ships, and in 1485 Henry VII appointed him as victualler to the official ships which protected the North Sea coast from piracy. Already a wealthy man, in that same year Godell became a member of the Company of Merchant Staplers of Calais, who at the time held the monopoly of the English wool trade. Four years later, when Henry gave the town its charter, Godell and Robert Bishop were appointed as bailiffs to run the affairs of the town.

When he eventually died in 1509, Godell bequeathed all his land and property to the town and inhabitants of Southwold, which five hundred years on is still benefiting from his foresight and generosity. Much of the land has been sold over the years to raise money for the borough council but the extensive common to the east of the town, now administered by a charitable trust, is protected for the benefit of the townsfolk and visitors.

THE GREAT FIRE

By the early seventeenth century, the relentless onslaught of longshore drift was causing shingle to persistently clog up the harbour and, with piracy on the increase, fishing and trade began to decline, but worse was yet to come. One day in 1659 a stray spark, fanned by strong winds, started a fire which burnt nearly all of the buildings in the town down to the ground. They had been built of timber and thatch, and the entire property-owning population of some three hundred families were ruined at a stroke.

Collections were held as far afield as Yorkshire for the relief of the inhabitants, a reminder that these coastal towns have always been a community linked by the sea. Since first being colonised by those early Angle and Saxon settlers arriving on these shores by boat, seafaring had been in the blood of the inhabitants of this coast. The North Sea to them was a natural means of transport and it would have been both safer and faster to travel by sea

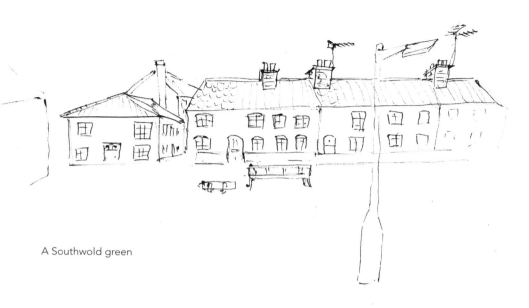

A Southwold green

than to use the inadequate roads of the time with the added risk of attack from robbers. For many years there had been a thriving trade in coal from Yorkshire, brought down the coast by the *collier brigs*, and news of the devastating fire would have spread quickly.

As the town was slowly built again, a large number of greens were incorporated as fire-breaks between the houses – an example of early town planning.

THE SOUTHWOLD SALTWORKS

A year later, in 1660, a charter established the Southwold Saltworks. Water at the high spring tides was allowed to flood into a lagoon, in this case a creek off the River Blyth, where it was left to evaporate, and this concentrated brine was stored in a well. From the well it was pumped to the saltworks by a canvas-sailed wind pump, where it was blended with mined salt brought in from Cheshire – the technique known as *salt on salt*. This super-concentrated brine was then evaporated in a succession of coal-fired pans to produce crystalline salt of differing grain size, the coarsest of which was used for salting fish. In 1702 the Salt Tax, administered by the newly created Salt Office, led to a decline in the industry and only the coarse salt for salting fish, which was free from the tax, remained in demand.

SALT

We take salt for granted now, as it is so freely available, but it is not that many years since the production of salt was vital for ensuring that food would last long enough for survival through the winter months, and it still remains an important source of the iodine needed for the thyroid gland to function.

>━━ *The table salt we use now has magnesium or calcium carbonate added to it to absorb moisture, thus keeping the salt from solidifying, but in earlier times it was contaminated naturally with many other chemicals*

The Ancient Egyptians were the first to discover that meat and fish could be preserved for long periods of time with salt. It works in several ways. Osmosis draws out water from the flesh of the fish, making it difficult for the bacteria to digest, and in addition fatally drying out the actual bacteria. Salt also produces chemical changes in the muscle proteins very similar to those brought about by cooking, a process still familiar to us in the preparation of gravadlax, hams and salamis. When salting is combined with smoking (smoke contains antioxidants as well as more antimicrobial chemicals), food can be preserved for many months on end, and the curing of hams and fish such as the herring became important skills for living through times of food shortage. Fat on the surface of a fish will prevent saltwater from penetrating the flesh, which makes leaner fish such as the cod better for salting.

With little surface fat to go rancid on exposure to oxygen in the air they were ideal for air-drying before salting, which made them last for a very long time. If you visit Norway you can still see rows of wooden racks with cod gently drying in the wind.

Our ancestors found many ways of obtaining salt, and its production was a common industry in fishing ports. The simplest method was to evaporate seawater in shallow lagoons, and variations on this were to scrape naturally evaporated salt water from the shore or to boil seawater in shallow pans. The Romans filled clay pots with seawater, boiling the water away and topping up with more until the pot contained a solid block of salt; the clay was then smashed to release it. Salt-marsh plants could also be burnt and the salt extracted from the ashes; and rock salt could be mined, as it was in Cheshire.

The importance of salt is reflected in the politics of our past. In the thirteenth century the Venetians made more money from trading in salt than from actually making it. By paying merchants a subsidy to land their supplies of salt in Venice, they soon built up a monopoly over its supply and could thus control the price; they even destroyed the saltworks on Crete and banned its further production in order to reduce the competition.

In northern Germany, the town of Lüneburg produced salt of particularly fine quality, it being relatively free of impurities. It was taken along the 'Salt Road' to the coastal port of Lübeck, from where it could be shipped, but such a valuable commodity in transit was at constant risk from attack. This inspired the twelfth-century merchant traders to organise themselves into a group for its protection, and so the Hanseatic League was born. It was to become one of the most powerful organisations in Northern Europe, dominating trade and controlling shipping for the best part of three hundred years. The Hanseatic merchants were also known as Easterlings, which is the origin of the word *sterling* which we still apply to something of assured quality.

→ Henry VIII added Wednesday to the already long list of fast days in order to boost the fishing trade which was losing out to the Dutch, thereby increasing again the need for salt

Taxing the salt
Monarchs were not slow to realise the value of salt and were inclined to slap a tax on it whenever they needed some more revenue. In more recent times, the imposition of a salt tax in India by the British was a key component in the struggle led by Gandhi for independence. France also had a salt tax, the *gabelle*, which started in the fourteenth century: the most hated tax of all, it was a contributing factor in the run-up to the French Revolution and was only finally repealed after the Second World War.

Five facts you may not know about salt
• The Ancient Egyptians discovered how to use olives by first soaking them in water to remove the bitter taste, and then soaking them in brine which softened the flesh sufficiently to make them edible.

• The Romans salted their greens, hence our word 'salad' which comes from the Latin word *sal* meaning salt.

• The Romans sometimes paid their soldiers in salt and so gave us the word 'salary'.

• Salt was used for curing leather and for glazing pottery.

• The salting of the Mediterranean mollusc, the Murex, produced the purple dye so loved by the Romans, who only allowed purple clothes to be worn by Caesar.

→ The Venetian islands were once a lot further from the mainland than they are now, and the area between was known as the Seven Seas. They were treacherous to navigate because of the extensive sandbanks. In AD 600 the Venetians began to fill in the Seven Seas with mud to make the landmass that now has Chioggia as its port.

Fishermen's sheds

THE FREE BRITISH FISHERY

By the seventeenth century the continual problem of trying to prevent the harbour from clogging up had led to a decline in the fortunes of Southwold. This must have been an on-going headache for the mayor and bailiffs, at a time when piracy was on the increase from the privateers working out of Dunkirk and the wars with the Dutch. As if this wasn't enough, the Dutch were now dominating the North Sea herring fishery. By 1654 the town was destitute, with many of the menfolk either killed or away in the wars. In the Battle of Sole Bay (Southwold Bay) in 1672, two thousand sailors were lost on both sides and the town had to care for eight hundred wounded men.

In 1750 George II tried to revive the nation's fishing industry in an attempt to compete with the Dutch for the dominance of the European herring markets. He established the Free British Fishery by Act of Parliament and gave the considerable sum of £500,000 to Southwold for the building of wharves, warehouses, net-houses, coopers' workshops and a row of cottages which were built in Church Street. Two piers were constructed at the entrance to the harbour, and fifty *herring busses* were built at the Buss Creek shipyards.

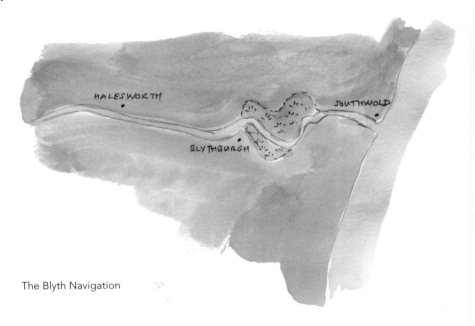

The Blyth Navigation

There followed a boom during which the saltworks increased their production of coarse salt, and several more public houses were licensed for the entertainment of the populace. But it was not to last and the combination of several bad fishing seasons, the often treacherous harbour and the general incompetence of the managers of the fishery led to all its assets being put up for auction in 1772 at the Old Swan Inn, and the unemployed fishermen turned to the old standby of smuggling.

THE BLYTH NAVIGATION

An Act of Parliament in 1757 had established the opening up of the River Blyth by its widening and dredging and by the building of locks as far upstream as Halesworth. The tidal marshes were drained for grazing, and the canal provided a valuable commercial route until the arrival of the railway in 1872. However, by 1884 the enterprise was insolvent.

The old Cromer lifeboat shed

THE LIFEBOAT *ALFRED CORRY*

The *Alfred Corry* was commissioned as Southwold's new lifeboat by the RNLI (Royal National Lifeboat Institution) in 1893. It was named after its sponsor, a civil engineer from Wandsworth and a member of the Royal Institute of Naval Architects. Alfred Corry died at the young age of thirty-four, leaving a legacy of £15,000 for the building of a new lifeboat, not specifying where it should be.

The boat was designed to be powered by both sail and oar, carrying fourteen oars and two masts, but after twenty-five years' service she was considered to be no longer worth repairing, and a boat with the recently invented diesel engine fitted was commissioned. The old boat was sold, later to be converted to a ketch-rigged yacht. She passed through the hands of several owners and was used as a houseboat before finally being rescued by John Craigie, who was the grandson of her very first coxswain.

After four years of restoration she became a family cruising yacht again until, approaching her hundredth year, the cost of maintaining her became too much, and a charitable trust was set up to restore her back to her original form as a sailing and pulling lifeboat. The National Maritime Museum still had her original plans and they were able to supply copies of the original drawings along with details of her construction.

By 1995 she was ready but there was nowhere to house her permanently until the Trust learned that the old Cromer lifeboat shed was to be replaced. So in 1998 the beautiful old blue and white Cromer shed was dismantled and brought round by sea to Southwold, where it now stands as a fitting home for the Alfred Corry Lifeboat Museum.

BEACH COMPANIES

A beach company was an informal group of boatmen who worked together to help launch and land their fishing boats from the beach but their role gradually expanded into salvage, rescue and the provision of services to the port, which included pilotage, loading and unloading cargo and ferrying passengers. The beach companies on the east coast used shallow drafted *yawls*; the ones at Southwold were two-masted, with a dipping lugsail on each mast. There are models and photographs of them in the Sailors' Reading Room in the town.

A Southwold Beach yawl

THE SAILORS' READING ROOM

This 'Room of Rest and Recreation' was built in 1864 by the widow of Captain Rayley RN. It was a quiet place for fishermen to meet, smoke and read as an alternative to the pub, providing tea, books and periodicals. The walls are covered with paintings of ships and fishing boats, and portrait photographs of weatherworn fishermen look down from the walls on their visitors below. Glass cases display a chaotic collection of model ships, and newspapers and journals are laid out on a central table. Comfortable worn armchairs arrayed against the walls allow the visitor to sit and read to the gentle sound of the clicking of billiard balls as a game of snooker is played in the inner members' room.

FANNY FOSTER (1891–1975)

Fanny Foster was a remarkable and much-respected resident of the town but is little known now outside Suffolk. She was educated at Saint Felix School where she showed a talent for languages and music, but her academic studies were cut short when she had to leave to care for her ailing mother. Not being one to resign her life away stranded in Southwold, she worked part-time as a secretary, taught the violin, and took up the study of photography (this would have been around the time that Olive Edis, working from her studio further up the coast in Sheringham, Norfolk, was making her portrait studies of local fishermen and experimenting with colour, in the process known as 'autochrome').

During the Balkan crises of the early twentieth century, Fanny provided a home for a young Yugoslavian boy. She taught him English while he taught her Serbo-Croat and this fired her with a life-long passion for the culture, literature and language of Yugoslavia. Her mother died in 1922 and now, with money and her freedom, she was at last able to spread her wings. In the spirit of the intrepid women of that time, she took her photographic equipment and booked a passage on a cargo ship sailing for New Zealand.

On her return to Britain, pursuing her interest in the language and culture of the Balkan countries, it was not long before she was working with the Yugoslavian government, becoming involved with various cultural projects which led her to the award of the Order of St Sava in recognition of her services. This unusual experience made her very useful to the British government during the Second World War and they soon had her working in the War Office translating correspondence from Eastern Europe.

Fanny was passionate about the conservation of Southwold and after the war served on the borough council for thirty-two years, twice becoming mayor, before her death in 1975. Some of her papers can be found at the Pitt Rivers Museum in Oxford, as well as in the Lowestoft Record Office.

Chapter 3
DUNWICH

SAXON DUNWICH

The early kings of East Anglia came from the Swedish Wuffinga dynasty and their seat was at Rendlesham, near Woodbridge. The most well-known of the dynasty there is Raedwald, who is thought to be the king buried in the ship at Sutton Hoo, but more of that later.

It was King Sigeberht who was on the throne in AD 630 when Felix, an abbot from Burgundy, arrived in East Anglia. He had been sent by the Archbishop of Canterbury to evangelise the population coming by sea and river to land at Babingley in Norfolk, if legend is to be believed. The Wuffingas, who were Christians at this time, had long had associations with the Church in France and, when Felix arrived, the Anglo-Saxon king gave him a bishopric at Dunwich and later helped him to establish a school for the education of local boys. Felix was in due course joined by East Anglia's other famous saint-to-be, Fursey, a monk from Ireland, who went on

above The Dunwich seal

to found a monastery in the region which was probably at the old Roman site of Burgh Castle, a little further up the coast near Great Yarmouth.

But Felix's priory fell victim to the Viking raiders who plundered the east coast throughout the ninth and tenth centuries, attacking towns and monasteries, taking slaves and generally terrorising the population. The bishopric collapsed in the face of this terror and Dunwich was never to regain its episcopal status again.

Felix's remains were reputedly stolen in the twelfth century by monks from Ramsey Abbey. Enthusiastic collectors of relics, they made their escape through the Fens by boat under cover of a dense fog with their sacred trophy on board.

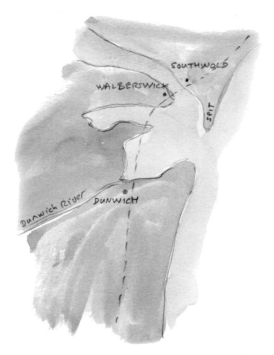

Saxon Dunwich

MEDIEVAL DUNWICH

For many years a shingle spit had been advancing slowly down the coast from Southwold until by the eleventh century it had become long enough to reach Dunwich, making a large and exceptionally well-sheltered harbour at the mouth of the River Blyth. Once the threat of marauding Scandinavians had passed, Dunwich grew to become one of the largest and most important ports

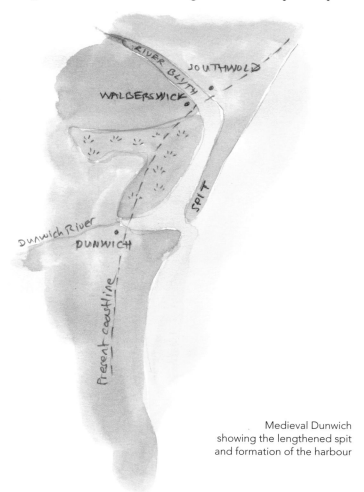

Medieval Dunwich
showing the lengthened spit
and formation of the harbour

on the east coast, and in 1199 received a charter from King John making it a free borough with the right to have a Guild of Merchants. This was followed by a second charter in 1215, giving it the additional right to have a mayor and four bailiffs.

Nearly a hundred years on, in 1290, a group of Franciscan monks – known as the Greyfriars, from the colour of their habit – arrived and built their priory at the western edge of the town. The priory extended over seven acres of land and was surrounded by a continuous stone wall, much of which is still there today, along with the remaining two of the four very fine gates.

Dunwich was on a roll by now, with a thriving ship-building industry, several churches and the town large enough to be able to supply no fewer than eighty ships to the King's Service in 1241. The busy port traded in fish, furs and timber from Iceland and the Baltic, fine cloth from the Low Countries and wine from France, and exported grain and wool.

However, as the thirteenth century drew to a close, the relentless encroachment of the sea was about to bring this prosperity to an end.

THE DEMISE OF DUNWICH

The thirteenth and fourteenth centuries saw a time of rising sea levels and the severe storms known as *rages* which could wreak devastating damage to the coast, sometimes wiping out a substantial part of a village in just one storm. In 1286 the three-day rage that swept tons of shingle down the coast resulted in the harbour at Dunwich becoming so completely filled that the exit to the sea was blocked and the course of the River Blyth changed forever (see p. 31). With its harbour so badly compromised, Dunwich would never regain its status as one of the east coast's finest ports.

By 1346 the once important town had reduced in size so much that it lost its right even to have a mayor. The Black Death in 1348 accelerated this decline, while continued coastal erosion led to more and more buildings being lost to the sea.

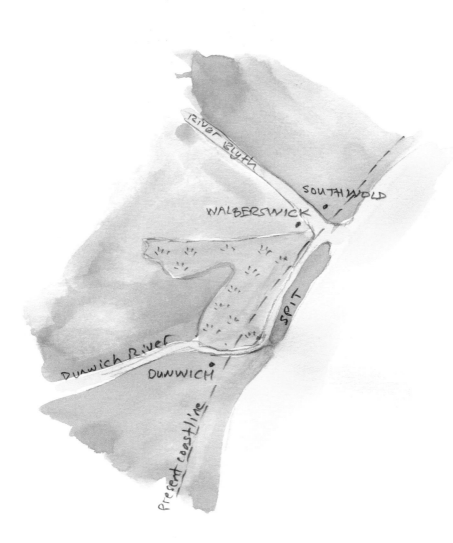

Sixteenth-century Dunwich
showing the River Blyth
now entering the sea at Southwold

Over the ensuing years the men of Dunwich cut various channels through the shingle in an attempt to get shipping to enter their bit of river before going further up the coast to Southwold, so that Dunwich could collect the tolls, but these channels kept silting up and the rights to levy duties on ships going up the Blyth were eventually transferred to Southwold.

THE BLACK DEATH

The plague known as the Black Death swept through Europe in 1348, wiping out nearly half of its population. The first known case in England was supposed to be a sailor landing in Weymouth from where it spread to the whole country, going on to kill somewhere between forty and sixty percent of the entire population of England.

It is generally accepted that the cause of the plague was the bacterium *Yersinia pestis*, carried by the flea of the rat, but there are epidemiologists who dispute this interpretation, suggesting that it may have been a virus similar to Ebola, although it is difficult to confirm these theories within the limitations of available archaeological evidence. We do know, however, that there are three types of plague and they probably all occurred concurrently.

• **bubonic plague**, where the infected flea bites a human and the bacteria enter the lymph system causing the swelling of the lymph nodes which were called *buboes*.

• **pneumonic plague**, an airborne infection where the bacteria enter the lungs directly from an infected person.

• **septicaemic plague**, where the flea bite introduces the bacteria directly into the bloodstream. This version would kill the victim within a few hours.

The knock-on effects from such a dramatic reduction in the population were enormous. There were not enough men to tend the fields and livestock, which led in turn to a shortage of grain, with the subsequent price inflation of bread and real hardship among the poor. The feudal system of serfdom began to break down as peasants could demand higher wages for their work and could go elsewhere if they were refused; this was likely to be the very first seeds of the Peasants' Revolt.

As a consequence of the loss of labourers, landlords began to enclose their land and pasture sheep on it instead, which gave a boost to the wool trade and led the way to the first inklings of the *enclosures* which were to cause so much hardship among the people evicted from their grazing land in later years.

Apart from these changes, the king's military capacity was reduced, with fewer men to recruit as soldiers, and this was to lead to the winding down of the Hundred Years' War fought for the throne of France.

The men of God had not been spared from the dying either, and the Church suffered the blow of losing large numbers of its clergy, who had to be replaced with less educated men. The subsequent loss of its authority may well have contributed to priming the ground ready for the arrival of the Reformation.

A ROLL CALL OF DUNWICH CHURCHES

The gradual loss of nearly all its churches makes a poignant time marker for the long decline of this once prosperous town.

• St Michael's and St Bartholomew's churches were lost to the sea in the thirteenth century, and St Leonard's and St Martin's went in the fourteenth.

• The church of St John stood near the market place once in the centre of the town, but by 1540 the sea had encroached so much that the towns-people dismantled it to prevent it falling over the cliffs.

• The chancel of St Peter's went over the edge in 1688, to be followed by half of its steeple in 1697. Its lead, timber and bells were removed before the rest finally followed in 1702.

• The church of St Nicholas was lost later in the eighteenth century, and the last remaining tower of All Saints church went into the sea in the early twentieth century.

To stand on the dunes at Dunwich and look out to sea, imagining the huge town which once stretched for quarter of a mile out to the east and is now under the water, is a moving reminder of just how fragile this coast is.

The maps in this section show the changing topography of Dunwich under the influence of storm surges and longshore drift.

WHERE IS THE EDGE?

The changing coastline

The soft coastline of East Anglia is forever on the move, its pace measured sometimes in centuries, sometimes in decades and sometimes in just the few hours it takes for a storm surge to do its worst, but whatever the timescale you can never pin it down. At Dunwich the coast has retreated by a quarter of a mile since 1587, and at Southwold, although you can still find the name of Sole Bay on the maps, there is a bay there no longer, just a straight piece of coast with no trace of its former long curve.

Erosion has not been uniform along this part of the coast and the major changes have been largely confined to the stretches just north of Southwold, and from Dunwich south to Aldeburgh. Neither has it always occurred gradually but sometimes in periods of dramatic deterioration during storms. Looking at the 1587 map of Aldeburgh, the Moot Hall and market place are shown firmly in the centre of the town, with three whole streets running parallel to the sea between the market place and the beach. Another map made two hundred years later shows no trace of the three streets and the sea only a little way from the Moot Hall. This is much where it remains now, which would at least seem to indicate a fairly long period of stability.

Longshore drift

The strong northeasterly winds that blow here whip up waves which constantly gnaw away at the shore, eroding the cliffs and washing sand and shingle down the coast. This slowly builds up long shingle spits, which gradually extend southwards in the process known as *longshore drift*. Between

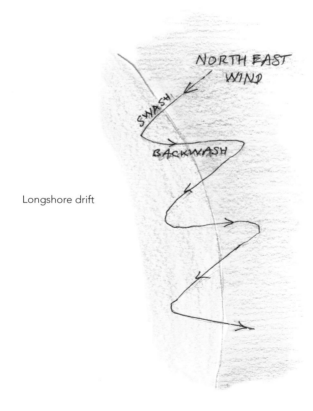

Longshore drift

the twelfth and nineteenth centuries the long spit of Orford Ness grew at the astonishing speed of thirteen metres a year. Land gradually builds up on the inside of a spit, in a slow trade-off between loss of land in one place and gain in another. Orford, once a busy port, now finds itself marooned inland and bears no trace of the waterside quays that once bustled with activity there.

Longshore drift has sometimes caused whole rivers to disappear. There are thirteenth-century documents which describe rivers at Benacre, Kessingland, Dunwich and Minsmere that once flowed into the sea, each with a haven for boats to shelter in. The advancing shingle spit has completely cut them off from the sea now, leaving the water to seep out through the shingle and sometimes to back up, making a small lake such as Benacre and Covehithe Broads, and Thorpe Meare, all of which are the remains of estuaries long since vanished.

Chapter 4
ALDEBURGH,
SNAPE AND ORFORD

The town sign

ALDEBURGH

As you approach Aldeburgh by car down the steep hill past the church, there comes a point when the sea, seen ahead through a gap in the houses, for a moment appears to be above your head. This trick of perception never fails to quicken my pulse, arousing the feeling that this place is not quite of this world. An early walk along the shore in the thin light of morning, the fishermen preparing their catch, eyed up by ranks of hungry gulls, the vast steep bank of shingle and the sun rising over the sea, which always seems to be a little higher than it should be, is a scene like no other I know. This is an unusual stretch of coast with a strange, ethereal atmosphere, at once inhospitable and beautiful, fascinating and dangerous.

The rise and fall in the fortunes of Aldeburgh over the centuries has always been linked to the changing topography of the shore, with winds and

Aldeburgh High Street

tides constantly shifting shingle from one place to another. Walking down
the High Street today past pretty terraced cottages and cafes, gift shops and
galleries, it is hard to imagine the Aldeburgh of a former time when the sea
lay much further out than it does today. The Moot Hall, once in the centre
of the town, now stands rather self-consciously not a stone's throw from the
beach, and the once-thriving fishery is now just a small collection of sheds
serving the handful of local men who still catch sole, bass and shellfish from
their small boats launched now by tractors from the beach.

left Boats on the beach;
opposite The town seal

Aldeburgh does not feature very much in the historical records until the Dissolution of the Monasteries in 1536, when the monks at Snape lost their jurisdiction over the town. The main port had always been at Orford, a little further down the coast, which had a good harbour sheltered by the shingle spit which we now know as Orford Ness, except in those days the spit was a fraction of its current length and the town of Orford was by the sea.

But back to Aldeburgh. With no safe anchorage off the shore, ships had also been using the sheltered expanse of water a little way up the coast called the Haven on the old maps, and now known as Thorpe Meare. It had once been the mouth of the Hundred River which flowed out to sea here, but had become blocked by a shingle bar. Ships could enter on the flood when the bar was covered with water and leave when the next tide would allow them to float off again, providing them with a safe place to load and unload their goods and some protection from the weather.

The years immediately following the loss of the monastery at Snape brought prosperity to Aldeburgh. The monks had not paid much attention to its potential as a port, but the long steep shingle beach had never provided a safe anchorage and the Haven kept silting up, making it less and less useful. Orford further down the coast was experiencing similar problems with its harbour. Aldeburgh now saw the opportunity to both solve its own immediate problem and to take shipping away from its rival, by improving the quay at Slaughden, which was at the time just a small collection of buildings at the south of the town.

Another change around this time was the granting of Aldeburgh's first charter, in 1547, making the town a borough and giving it some autonomy over its affairs. Henry VIII was worried about the threat of Dutch invasion and was keeping a close eye on his east coast, improving defences and encouraging ship-building.

Three years on and the population had reached a peak of two thousand inhabitants, the increase in wealth was being generated by the town's now thriving port, which was exporting wool and fish, while sailcloth woven in Suffolk and timber from the famous Suffolk oak forests were being sent to the Thames dockyards where Henry was starting to build his Royal Navy.

By the end of the century Aldeburgh had eclipsed Orford, building almost as many ships for the new Navy as Ipswich. But this was not to last.

Under Elizabeth's reign, the shipyards at Aldeburgh built both of the ships that made Francis Drake famous – the Pelican, *later named the* Golden Hinde, *and the* Greyhound

The seventeenth century saw the rise of piracy, which made the passage of the collier brigs, bringing coal from Newcastle, increasingly dangerous and led in turn to the levying of a Ship Tax to finance the building of more ships for defence. By the end of the century Trinity House (see p. 152) was putting into place a system of channel markers in the Thames Estuary which made navigation of the restricted channels up to London a great deal easier. This, combined with the newer ship designs which were producing much handier vessels, meant that orders for building of naval vessels in the Slaughden ship-yards began to dwindle and, along with that, the wealth of the town.

Fishing boats continued to be built here, though, one of the most well-known of the boat-builders being William Hunt, who built smacks for cod fishing, and sprat boats, up until 1880. He always carved the head of a grey-hound on his tillers as his signature.

During the eighteenth century many of the larger of the East Coast ports were employing Dutch engineers to improve their harbours, but Aldeburgh was in no position to afford this and it was to remain with just its memories of a prosperous past until awakened once more by the arrival of the railway, which brought the first flowering of tourism and, later still, the arrival of Benjamin Britten.

Little is left now of the complex of houses and shipyards at Slaughden, with all the industries that accompanied ship-building at the time – the

ropewalks, the coopers and sail-makers. Only one boatyard remains, servicing the yachts and pleasure boats of the current generation of sailors who still navigate the quiet waters of this remote river.

Just a scattering of fishermen's huts now stand on the shingle at Aldeburgh, the only sheds allowed here since the 1953 floods swept all away.

SNAPE

W.G. Arnott in his book on the Alde records that there is a large map of the world painted on one of the walls in the Vatican, decorated with the first gold leaf that Columbus brought back from South America. There are only two places in England that are marked on it: one is Walsingham and the other is Snape Bridge. I have not been back there to check this out.

After the Norman invasion, one of William the Conqueror's barons, William Martel, was given the Manor of Snape and Aldeburgh, which included the rights to everything washed up on the shore from Thorpe down to Orford. It must have provided rich pickings from the large numbers of ships which regularly went down off this coast. He rebuilt the churches at Iken and Aldeburgh, and not only built a priory and a watermill at Snape but also improved life considerably for the inhabitants by the addition of a bridge over the river. Bridges were expensive to build and it was often

 Sprats

a local benefactor who provided one, sometimes with a chapel, so prayers could accompany the crossing of the river. The maintenance of a bridge was often a cause for dissension and the Lord of the Manor could levy a tax on his tenants for carrying out repairs, although disputes over their repair frequently became the stuff of court proceedings.

The church at Iken had a Saxon stone cross mounted outside to ward off demons and to make a landmark for sailors. It is now in the floor of the church.

Martel gave the monks of the priory the manorships of both Snape and Aldeburgh, but the monks took little interest in the fishing, although they owned the fishing weirs and demanded a *tol* of herrings each year from the fishermen, which was known as *Christ's Dole*. When the Prior managed to gain independence from the Crown in 1446 (meaning that his taxes went to the Pope instead of the King), he immediately slapped on a tax of ten shillings to be paid by every fisherman during the spratting season, which caused poverty and a great deal of resentment. But this state of affairs only lasted two years, much to the relief of the locals, and was reduced to just two pence before finally being abolished when Cardinal Wolsey took over the Manor. The fishery at Aldeburgh still sends a gift of sprats each year to the Mayor of London.

BENJAMIN BRITTEN (1913–1976)

The Aldeburgh poet, George Crabbe, who recorded that eleven houses were washed away by a storm in 1779, tells in his poem 'The Borough' of a fisherman who brutally mistreated his apprentices. Benjamin Britten used this story for his opera *Peter Grimes*, which was first performed at Sadler's Wells in 1945.

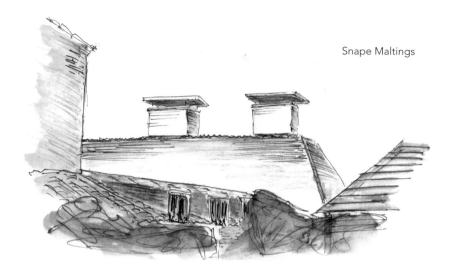

Snape Maltings

Crabbe, who worked on the docks at Slaughden before escaping his drunken father to go to London, got himself ordained as a clergyman and eventually returned to Aldeburgh, where he wrote his popular but gloom-laden poems.

Aldeburgh came to more recent fame with the music festival started by Benjamin Britten in 1948 with tenor Peter Pears, his life-long companion, and librettist Eric Crozier. This was to lead eventually to the building of the concert hall at Snape Maltings.

The 'Scallop' sculpture standing on the beach was made by artist Maggi Hambling in 2003 and consists of two interlocking, broken scallop shells pierced by the words from Peter Grimes, 'I hear those voices that will not be drowned'

The hall, converted from the old nineteenth-century maltings, was ravaged by fire only two years after its completion in 1967, but was rebuilt, and the complex of buildings now offers facilities for the training of young musicians from all over the world.

Snape Maltings lies on the banks of the River Alde by the bridge and looks across a wide expanse of marsh towards Iken church in the distance. The reedbeds are home to kestrels and marsh harriers, bearded tits and reed warblers, and, among the reeds, sculptures stand sentinel over this wild, beautiful and strangely moving place.

Britten, who in the last year of his life became Baron Britten of Aldeburgh, is regarded as one of the central figures of twentieth-century classical music. Born in Lowestoft in 1913, he died in Aldeburgh in 1976.

ORFORD

It is hard to imagine that the village of Orford, now separated from the sea by the long arm of Orford Ness, was once a busy port. Back in the twelfth century, however, the spit extending south from Aldeburgh only reached as far as here and was just long enough to give Orford a good sheltered harbour.

The fine castle still standing in the village was built by Norman engineers under Henry II in 1165, the stones being brought round by sea and transported along a specially dug canal to the building site. If you stand and look up Quay Road now, you can see a long depression in the ground which marks the edge of the long-since vanished quay.

For two hundred years Orford's ships served the east coast, taking provisions to the King's Guard at Newcastle and ferrying cattle across to the Ness for grazing, while its fishing boats drew their nets in Hollesley Bay. Many ships were built, much wool was exported and local merchants made their fortunes, rebuilding Orford church with some of their wealth.

But as Aldeburgh began to blossom, after the improvements to its quays at Slaughden in the mid-sixteenth century, and with its superior access to timber in the oak forests at Framlingham and Saxmundham, Orford gradually became less important. Its decline continued as the harbour increasingly silted up and the slow but relentless advance of the Ness distanced it further and further from the sea.

ORFORD NESS

The sixteen-kilometre-long spit, which is continuing to grow down the coast from Aldeburgh, ends in a mass of land called the Ness. The surface of the Ness is marked by a series of long shallow ridges which provide shelter for rare plants and make it a classic example of a *vegetated spit* – the largest of its kind in Europe. This unusual habitat is formed when shingle is thrown over the crest of a beach by the large waves whipped up by many storms over a number of years. Once over the highest point of the beach, the newly deposited shingle forms a low ridge which is now protected by its high position from any further disturbance. Over the years a series of parallel ridges is gradually built up. This salty, dry habitat can only be colonised by plants which have adapted to life in such inhospitable conditions and, in return for the favour of shelter, their roots help to stabilise the shingle, slowing down its further erosion.

Another rare habitat to be found here is known as *acid shingle heath* and Orford Ness is the second largest example of it in Britain, home to Sea campion, Sea pea and no fewer than a hundred and sixteen different species of lichen.

Despite its remote location, there were once several houses here occupied by the marshmen who looked after the grazing cattle, but the last of these houses were lost to the sea in the 1920s. The lighthouse standing on the edge of the shingle beach was built in 1792; the two earlier ones have long since been washed away, but some of the remains of the foundations can still sometimes be seen at a low spring tide.

The Ministry of Defence used the Ness for a research station developing radar during the First World War, and during the Second World War

above Sea Campion

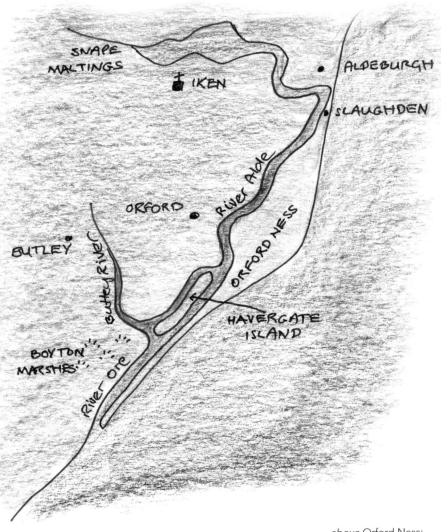

SNAPE MALTINGS

IKEN

ALDEBURGH

SLAUGHDEN

River Alde

ORFORD

ORFORD NESS

BUTLEY

Butley River

HAVERGATE ISLAND

BOYTON MARSHES

River Ore

above Orford Ness;
opposite Orford Ness 'Pagodas'

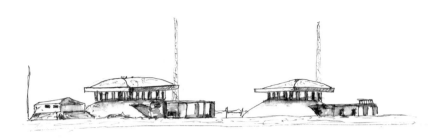

the Atomic Weapons Research Establishment used it for testing ballistics. This continued under their jurisdiction until the more recent end of the Cold War. Although there was never any nuclear material here, the strange pagoda-like buildings visible from a long way off were erected for the testing of the highly explosive initiator charges which were needed for nuclear weapons. These buildings were designed to absorb the effects of any catastrophic explosion: the roof was supposed to collapse on top of the building below, thereby sealing it with a lid of concrete and shingle. Now the strange outlines of the pagodas against the sky, like a collection of eastern temples, add to the air of mystery which still haunts this site.

While the Ministry of Defence were working here, all sorts of rumours circulated about the research they were undertaking, ranging from biological warfare to the bizarre idea of the placing of a system of pipes under the sea carrying petrol that could create an inferno in the case of German invasion. A rumour is claimed by some that the badly charred bodies of a number of soldiers were once found on the beach, but this was never substantiated. The MoD files, which were meant to be kept secret for seventy-five years but were actually made public in 1992, revealed no such information but no doubt any sensitive materials would have been redacted first.

The austere, functional Ministry of Defence brick buildings remain, as does the network of tarmac roads. The Ness has now been turned over to the National Trust who allow only limited access in order to protect the fragile habitat and the colony of Little Terns which breed here.

I joined the ferry from Orford with seven others at ten o'clock in the morning on a cold windy day in July. After the short trip across the water we were met by two volunteer wardens who took our (named) tickets and gave us each a map; if anyone failed to return by five o'clock, a search party would be sent out to find them.

Under a sunless sky with a cold northeast wind blowing, I set off on the recommended route. Within the space of half an hour my fellow passengers had all dispersed and there was no-one to be seen. It would be easy to imagine that one had been abandoned among the derelict buildings dotted, seemingly randomly, all around. All were locked.

I walked the couple of miles towards the lighthouse, stopping at the only building which was open on the way to read the brief display. When I reached the lighthouse, a grey sea was crashing on the shingle and I was suddenly unnerved by the strangeness of this post-apocalyptic landscape.

Feeling very chilled by now I made my return, becoming more and more affected by the eeriness and desolation of this extraordinary place, relieved only by the sound of whinchats and whitethroats singing cheerfully from almost every bramble bush.

I read the following passage from Longfellow in the guide book:

Not far away we saw the port,
The strange, old-fashioned, silent town,
The lighthouse, the dismantled fort,
The wooden houses, quaint and brown.

CROSSING THE RIVER

Rivers were the arterial roads of the medieval world, the main transport for people and goods deep into the country. A river was busy. It was used by millers and fishermen, washerwomen and reed cutters, dyers and tanners. The river drew people to it, as rivers still do, and news and gossip travelled fast up and downstream.

The reedbeds were the territory of marshmen who cut reed and sedge for thatching, keeping their stretch of water clear for navigation, and the marshes provided good hunting for those who trapped birds or sought their eggs for the table.

As dusk fell and activity ceased, the river could become itself once more – a ribbon of stillness disturbed only by the occasional flop of an otter after a fish and the quiet voices of eel-fishers laying their setts. As night descends the river starts its own secret life: deer come to drink at the water's edge, foxes prowl the banks on the lookout for unwary birds, a pair of owls hunt for mice, their cries piercing the muffled sounds of night. Dawn brings nesting birds to wakefulness with their first stirrings of song, swallows dip over the surface, and swifts return from their night on the wing high above; the light gradually brightens to reveal a solitary bittern standing motionless in the reeds; someone appears on the riverbank, maybe for a bit of early fishing or perhaps simply to enjoy a last undisturbed hour, and another day begins.

The beaver is thought to have become extinct in England around 1300

There are many ways to cross a river. A bridge was expensive to build and maintain but a ford was very simple if the water was shallow enough to walk across, with wet ankles the only price to pay. The prevalence of fords is given away on every map by the names of so many places which end in 'ford', while 'wade' would indicate a rather wetter experience, but still perfectly possible for cattle, horses and people to get to the other side. A *hard*, sometimes called a *stone* as it is made up of gravel and flints, is a give-away for a river crossing, as in Woolverstone on the Orwell and the well-known hard at Pin Mill.

But another way was by ferry and, like so much else in medieval life, it became an opportunity for the extraction of a tax. The Lord of the Manor usually owned the rights to a ferry, under

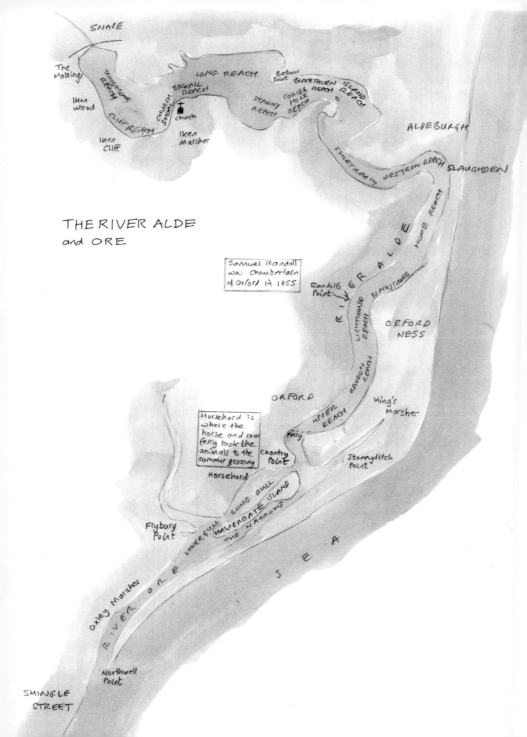

THE RIVER ALDE
and ORE

Samuel Randall
was Chamberlain
of Orford in 1855

Horsehard is
where the
horse and cow
ferry took the
animals to the
summer grazing

licence from the Crown, and he in turn licensed a ferryman, charging him an annual rent but often providing him with a house as well. A good look at the place names on a map will indicate old crossings, such as Felixstowe Ferry at the mouth of the River Deben, and Ferry Cliff across the river from Woodbridge (a ferry remained in use there right up until 1974). But the taxation system soon caught up even with the less formal ways of getting across, with the building of official landing stages and the construction of new fords where a fee could be charged for the privilege of use.

There are still two rowing-boat ferries left in East Anglia, one across the Butley River at Orford manned during the summer by volunteers, and the other between Walberswick and Southwold, rowed by Dani Church who took over the role from her father in 2001. The Walberswick Ferry, in service since 1236, has been run by the same family for the last one hundred and thirty years. Dani Church is the fifth generation to run it, taught by her father and now assisted by five others at busy times. In 1885 the first of her family to run the ferry replaced it with a hand-cranked floating bridge, but it became impractical when the harbour changed and the crossing soon resumed its guise as a rowing ferry.

WHO PAYS THE FERRYMAN?
Crossing the river in myth and legend

There are many myths surrounding rivers and river crossings, and, like all myths, they know no cultural divides. A river symbolises many things, from the water of life to the boundary between life and death. The crossing of a river can represent the struggle to overcome a particular difficulty in life. Meanwhile, the constant movement of a river's water, through a world that appears to remain still, is a reminder of the flowing of time. A river is a liminal space where one world meets another, with just the possibility of slipping silently through.

The legend of **Christopher**, the patron saint of travellers, bearing the Christ child across a river is widely known in different versions all over the Christian world. The story is basically as follows: Christopher was a giant who longed to be able to put his great size and strength to good use and went on a journey in search of Christ. Coming across a hermit by a river, he asked the old man how he could best serve his Lord and the answer came that he could use his physical might to help pilgrims cross the dangerous waters of the river. One day a child appeared on the riverbank and asked to be taken to the other side. Raising the child up on his shoulder, Christopher started to walk across but found that as he waded through the water the child became heavier and heavier until he could bear his weight almost no longer. Setting the boy down, exhausted, on the other side, he said, *'I do not think the whole world could have been as heavy on my shoulder as you'*, whereupon the child replied, *'You had on your shoulder not only the whole world but also him who made it – I am Christ your King.'*

The fifteenth-century Japanese *noh* play about grief at the loss of a child being healed by the crossing of a river was the inspiration for Benjamin Britten's opera *Curlew River*. In his version there are just three principal characters: The Madwoman, The Traveller and The Ferryman. The Madwoman asks the Ferryman to take her across the Curlew River, but, put off by her strange behaviour, he at first refuses. Taking pity on the poor woman, the Traveller persuades the Ferryman to consent and at last he agrees to take them both across. During the passage he tells them the story of a child who a year ago was abandoned on the bank of the river by his cruel master who had kidnapped the boy from the Black Mountains. The child had become sick and was no longer of any use to him. Taking pity on the young boy, the local people took care of him but he knew he was dying and asked to be buried by the path to the chapel, *'then, if travellers from my dear country pass by this way, their shadows will fall on my grave'*. The Madwoman, whose child it was, recognises him from the Ferryman's story and, as she prays at the little grave, the spirit of her child speaks to her and her madness is cured.

The River Styx of Greek myth was one of the seven rivers of the Underworld where the ferryman **Charon** would take the souls of the dead across to the other side. He expected a fee for his trouble and it was usual to place a coin in the mouth of the dead to ensure their safe passage. Charon was invariably described as an uncouth, dirty and dishevelled figure, and this image was taken up by Dante and by the Renaissance painters. Odysseus and Orpheus were two among many who risked the journey to the Underworld, putting their trust in Charon to return them safely.

The crossing of a river remains a powerful myth.

MAKING A LIVING ON THE COAST

When the Normans first came to East Anglia, fishing was thriving, large flocks of sheep were being grazed, and by the twelfth century the region was on a roll producing large amounts of wool which were to make many a fortune for the landowners and merchants. The number of large, beautiful churches that they built in the counties of Norfolk and Suffolk stand witness to this wealth built on the wool trade.

Many monasteries were endowed by the local Lords along the coast at this time (they could save their souls from a little time in Purgatory and find a use for poor-quality land in one stroke – what's not to like about that?). There were Augustinians at Butley, Blythburgh and Woodbridge, Benedictines at

Snape, and both Franciscan and Dominican friars at Dunwich. Although saltings have always been a paradise for birds, as well as producing an important part of the diet of a medieval coast-dweller, salt-marsh plants do not provide much nourishment for a sheep, and the monks often carried out land improvement such as embanking their marshes to improve the quality of the grazing.

Ports began to develop all along the coast and charters were granted for markets, as the economy began to grow. Oyster pits were dug on the Ore and Butley rivers, and fish were caught in traps. The salt that was such an important part of life then was being produced everywhere.

KEEPING THE WATER OUT: WARPING, INNING, AND HOW TO DATE A DRAIN

The early Anglo-Saxons reclaimed marsh by a process they called *warping*. They would build a low wall of earth and timber on the shore which would allow the silt-laden water to flood over it at high tide, but prevented the silt from returning with the water on the ebb. The steady deposition of mud, tide on tide, gradually raised the level of the land, making the marshes higher than the river.

This rather subtle way of going about things fell out of favour, however, and a much more popular way of draining a marsh, known as *inning*, became the way to do it. This method involved building a substantial embankment to completely stop water entering the marsh. Understandably, this bold message delivered to the river was favoured by the Romans. Over a period of years, rain gradually washes the salt out of the soil, allowing more nutritious grasses to grow, but the resulting fenland is lower than the river. This can be seen on a spectacular scale in the Fens.

The reclamation of land reached a peak in the eighteenth century as Dutch engineers, the most well-known of these being Cornelius Vermuyden, came over to drain the Fens. A local Commission of Sewers composed of the local landowners and tenants was set up to oversee the work. They drained the land and then charged rent for the maintenance of the banks and sluices. The Commissions came and went as the need arose and they carried out some major drainage works around the River Alde.

Numerous enclosure acts in the 1750s allowed drainage of the wet-fen common land north of Aldeburgh, but the wind-powered pumps of the day were not really up to the job being demanded of them and the system did not work very well until mechanised drainage pumps were built much later, in the nineteenth century.

In 1812 the geologist and civil engineer William Smith was consulted on the problems of keeping Benacre Levels drained, but his ambitious plans to build a higher bank and bigger sluice proved to be too expensive. At Minsmere Level, Smith designed a more sophisticated iron sluice connecting to an eleven-metre-long iron pipe, with a complete system of drains, which are sometimes called *dykes* or *sokes*.

You can roughly date a drainage system by looking at a map and examining the course the drains take. Prior to 1700 a drain tended to follow the natural course of the channels in the marsh, making for an irregular, rather serpentine appearance, whereas after 1700 they tended to be dug in straight lines, thus creating a more rectilinear pattern.

In the first half of the twentieth century some of the marshes were neglected and they soon reverted to the now environmentally important reedbeds at Blythburgh and Walberswick. After the floods of 1953 a new, higher sea-wall was built, pumps were installed and drainage was carried out on a massive scale reclaiming land for arable farming, and there are now only three hundred hectares of wetland left out of an original ten thousand.

William Smith drew the first geological map of Britain, publishing it in 1799. His work as a civil engineer, surveying the building of canals, led him to notice that the same types of fossils were found consistently in the same geological strata wherever he was in the country. Not of the right class to be accepted into the scientific community, he was finally honoured for his pioneering work by the Royal Geological Society in 1831.

Decoys were introduced from Holland in the 17th century to catch wildfowl

RABBITING

Rabbits lived on the Sandlands, reintroduced by the Normans, but the medieval rabbit was not the hardy species we know today and had to be fed during the winter. The *warrener* in charge of the warren bred them in *pillow mounds* – raised banks about fifty feet long and five feet wide – and some of these mounds can still be found. There is one near Sutton Hoo, and they are also common on Dartmoor. The adult rabbit was called a *coney*, the term 'rabbit' being reserved for the young ones which were culled for food by catching them in nets or by using ferrets or lurcher dogs.

Chapter 5
WOODBRIDGE

Woodbridge sits at the head of the River Deben, which must be one of the most beautiful estuary rivers in the country. There are very few places where it can be accessed from the shore, and many a boat has been discouraged from venturing in from the sea by the ominous shifting sand bar across the entrance. This has allowed the river to retain its air of peaceful quietude, with little to disturb the wooded banks, mudflats and wading birds. Sailing up the final reach to the head of the river, the most striking sight to a visiting yacht is the white weather-boarded, red-roofed tide mill. Closed in 1957, it has now been restored and is milling flour once more. There can be few more pleasing scenes on a summer's evening than the late sun over the wide tidal basin with redshanks picking over the mud and the piping of oystercatchers flying overhead.

The Angles and Saxons coming up the river by boat a few centuries earlier would have appreciated its qualities of deep, sheltered water and abundance of wildfowl, but the story begins further back than that. When the Romans left Britain in AD 410, they left behind them a sophisticated infrastructure of roads and plumbing but no system in place for supporting its maintenance.

above The Sandlings Way sign at Woodbridge Quay

The wide tidal basin

With no-one in charge it was not long before everything began to unravel and much of the urban population, by now a mixed race of Roman, Briton and Celtic people, gradually abandoned the cities to return once more to rural life (there must be a fascinating story to be uncovered about the gradual disintegration of London, which was one of the largest cities in Europe at that time). The political vacuum left by the collapse of Roman Britain triggered many years of struggles for power between neighbouring warlords. The Roman legions occupying Britain were a cosmopolitan lot (multiculturalism is nothing new) and there were soldiers from North Africa as well as from all over Europe, including the Germanic races we refer to as Angles and Saxons.

It was into this fragmented country that Anglo-Saxon settlers from across the North Sea began to arrive. Some of the earliest ones came up the river to the small peninsula of Kingston, where Martlesham Creek forms

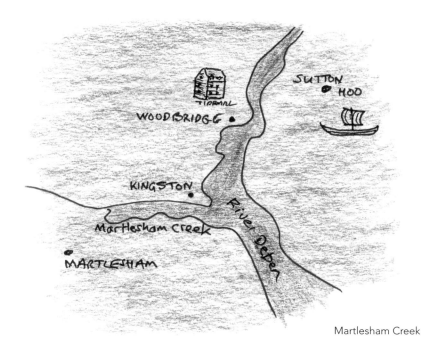

Martlesham Creek

an arm to the River Deben. The name Deben means 'deep' and the river remained navigable as far upstream as Rendlesham, where the Anglo-Saxon kings were to establish their capital. It is only recently that excavations at Rendlesham have revealed a large building thought to be a royal hall.

The first settlement at Kingston in time moved a little further upstream to a place which became known as Uderbrygge, or Woodbridge as we call it now (*uder* was the old word for 'wooden' and *brygge* meant 'jetty'). There followed the Viking invasions, and numerous tales are to be told from that disturbing time until King Alfred had the wisdom to bring the conflicts to an end by sharing his kingdom with the Danes, establishing the *Danelaw* in the east (see p. 95).

After the Norman invasion, the Domesday Record was commissioned, which noted that nearly half of the peasants in Norfolk and Suffolk were

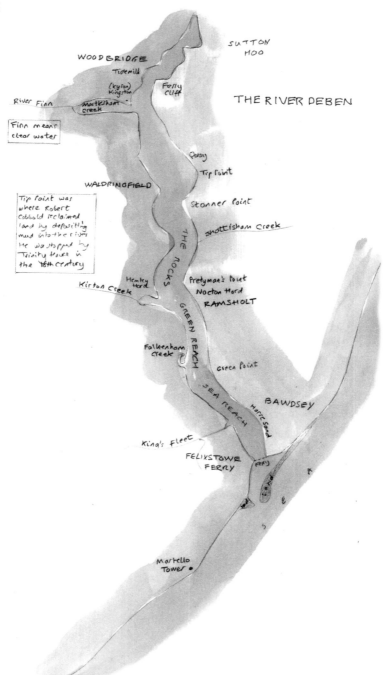

THE RIVER DEBEN

SUTTON HOO

WOODBRIDGE

Tidemill

(Kyton)
Kingston

Ferry
Cliff

River Finn

Martlesham
Creek

Finn means
clear water

Quay

Tip Point

WALDRINGFIELD

Stonner Point

Tip Point was
where Robert
Cobbold reclaimed
land by depositing
mud into the river.
He was stopped by
Trinity House in
the 18th century.

Shottisham Creek

THE ROCKS

Hemley
Hard

Kirton Creek

Pretyman's Point
Nocton Hard
RAMSHOLT

GREEN REACH

Falkenham
Creek

Green Point

SEA REACH

BAWDSEY

Horse Sand

King's Fleet

FELIXSTOWE
FERRY

Ferry

Martello
Tower

freemen compared with only fourteen percent nationally: this was probably linked to the earlier Danelaw where freemen were allowed to hold land without having to provide services in return to the Lord of the Manor. At this time the wool trade in East Anglia was booming and as a consequence Norfolk and Suffolk were the most populous shires in Britain. An Augustinian priory was established in Woodbridge in the last years of the twelfth century, on a site near the present Abbey House, and in 1227 it was endowed with the rights to the market held round the corner on Market Hill. Nothing remains of it now. Settling into its growing prosperity, the town began to operate as a port, building ships and attracting trade. Hemp for rope was grown nearby, and the local linen-weaving industry supplied *poldavis*, a coarse linen cloth, for the sailmakers.

By the second half of the fifteenth century, Woodbridge was a busy town and its merchants wealthy enough to rebuild the church of St Mary in the new *perpendicular* style. The considerable sums raised in taxes on the wool trade also led to the establishing of the town's first Custom House in 1589, which took over an existing building on the quayside. Another hundred years on and Suffolk had become an important area for keeping dairy cattle. Large amounts of cheese and butter were exported from Woodbridge, as well as the wool, silk and cloth from local weavers. Ship-building was becoming a major industry, which would reach its height in the mid-seventeenth century with the building of warships.

THOMAS SECKFORD (1515–1587)

The Seckfords had been Lords of the Manor since the thirteenth century and Thomas's father had built Seckford Hall, which is now a hotel just outside the town. Thomas Seckford was the Member of Parliament for Ipswich for eighteen years, building a mansion there so he could keep in touch with his constituents, and in 1560 he bought the Manor of Woodbridge Priory, which came with the tide mill attached. He built a very fine house in the

town on the site of the old priory, which you can still get a glimpse of if you look up the drive leading to Abbey School.

Seckford's list of public offices expanded to include Steward of the Liberty of St Ethelreda, Master of the Court of Requests, and Surveyor to the Court of Wards and Liveries. These were some of the highest legal offices in the kingdom and require a little explanation.

The *Liberty of St Ethelreda* was an old Anglo-Saxon legal entity, independent of the Crown, dating back to the monastery founded by St Ethelreda at Ely in 673. It was responsible for the courts in a large area of southeast Suffolk. St Ethelreda, also known, confusingly, as St Audrey, was the daughter of an Anglo-Saxon king bearing the unlikely name of Anna. She reigned under the third name of Queen Aethelthryth before finally taking Holy Orders and retreating to a simpler life. Her monastery at Ely ran the courts in the *liberty*, receiving the fines paid and any goods that it forfeited. When Thomas Seckford became Steward of the Liberty he moved its Session Courts to Woodbridge, building the Sessions Hall on the Market Hill which is now the Shire Hall. In those days, the ground floor was open and used as part of the market, but the arches have long since been bricked up.

>—⋙ *A fair took place annually in Ely on St Audrey's Day,*
the twenty-third of June, where silks, lace and necklaces were sold.
It gained a reputation for selling items of such poor quality that
the word 'tawdry' was coined to describe shoddy goods.

The *Court of Requests* was set up, thanks to Cardinal Wolsey, during the reign of Henry VIII, to settle the complaints of the poor man, under the instruction that compassion should always be exercised wherever possible.

above and opposite The Shire Hall

Complaints were presented to the monarch by petition as the royal court moved around the country, and the king was always accompanied by one of the two Masters of the Court. Seckford held this post for twenty-seven years, during the reign of Elizabeth I, accompanying her on her progressions around the country.

Finally, the *Court of Wards and Liveries* was the court responsible for the legal affairs and welfare of orphans and wards of court. In this capacity Thomas Seckford would have had responsibility for managing various estates until the orphaned beneficiary became of age. It may not be too much of a flight of fancy to imagine him as a kind and compassionate man acting as mentor to his young wards. I wonder if he was the inspiration for Matthew Shardlake, the hunchbacked lawyer and Master of the Court of Requests created by C.J. Sansom in his novels set in the time of Thomas Cromwell.

After a life of public service, Thomas Seckford then devoted most of his wealth to helping others less fortunate, building the Seckford Almshouse which gave a home to thirteen single men.

THE SECKFORD CHARITIES

On his death, in 1587, Thomas Seckford left Woodbridge the income from four Woodbridge streets and his Clerkenwell Estates in London, and by 1840 the value of these endowments to the town had increased so much that it was possible to double the number of almsmen and to build another 'hospital' to accommodate them. This building is just a little further up Seckford Street; nothing remains now of the original building as it was burnt down in the eighteenth century. In 1861 the funds allowed for the endowment of a grammar school, and Woodbridge School is still funded by the Seckford Charitable Trust.

➤ *Thomas Seckford's brother was a well-known pirate at a time when piracy was licensed by the Crown*

➤ *Thomas Seckford commissioned the first atlas of all the counties of England and Wales, produced by Christopher Saxton*

THE TIDE MILL

The earliest evidence of a tide mill at Woodbridge dates from 1171, when it was owned by the Canons of Butley Priory who sold it to the Augustinians shortly after they built their priory in 1195. After the Dissolution of the Monasteries in 1537, the mill entered into royal ownership where it was to remain until Elizabeth I sold it to Thomas Seckford in 1564. Seckford's family owned it for about a hundred years before it was sold on again, passing through various other hands until 1793 when it was replaced by the present mill, built on the site of the earlier ones.

In 1899 it was clad in corrugated iron to protect the wooden weatherboard exterior, and by 1933 it was one of only nine tide mills left still working

The Tide Mill

in the country. Closing in 1957, by now the last working tide mill in the country, it retained a quietly dignified presence on the quay, the rusting corrugated iron exterior, tall angular shape and mansard roof a feature of the waterfront for so long. The mill pond was turned into a yacht harbour in 1962 but the mill itself was saved six years later by a generous benefactor. Eventually restored with a new, smaller, mill pond, it opened to the public in 1973 and is now working as a tide mill once more.

The first commercial steam engine was invented by Thomas Newcomen in 1712 and paved the way for the Industrial Revolution. The first steam-powered mill – the Albion – was built in Southwark in 1786.

MILLSTONES

The millstones at the Woodbridge Mill are made from French burr stone which comes from a quarry in northern France. Each millstone is made up of twenty separate pieces of stone bonded together with plaster of Paris and the whole thing encircled by a metal band. Each stone weighs about a ton and has to be carefully balanced with lead weights to give an even grinding surface. There has to be a gap between the stationary bed-stone and the moving runner-stone, for if the two should ever make contact a spark could cause a fire – a disastrous event for an entirely wooden structure. The stones are *dressed*, that is incised with a pattern of grooves. The pattern has to be the same on each one, causing a scissor-like action when the stones are grinding.

MILLING

As the tide comes in, the pressure of the incoming water opens the mitred sluice gate, filling the mill pond. As the mill pond fills, the subsequent build-up of pressure of water on the exit gate causes this gate in turn to open and the water then flows through a channel delivering it to the water-wheel which now begins to turn. Milling traditionally took place at half ebb tide for approximately four to five hours and went on day and night, dictated entirely by the tides.

SHIP-BUILDING

The defence of the east coast from French invasion was long a preoccupation of the State and it led Henry VIII to institute the Royal Navy, setting up his royal dockyards on the Thames at Deptford, Chatham and Woolwich for the building of naval ships. Up until then, the king had commandeered local fishing boats and merchant ships, along with their crews, to fight his battles

above A dressed millstone

at sea, a custom that often caused great hardship among the small coastal communities which relied so heavily on the sea for their livelihood.

By the seventeenth century Woodbridge was rivalling Ipswich for ship-building, the ships being built at Lime Kiln Quay, a little way up the river from the Tide Mill. The oak forests in High Suffolk supplied large amounts of good oak, making it easier to build the ships there than to cart the wood to the London dockyards.

PHINEAS PETT (1570–1647)

Phineas Pett and his family were ship-builders on the Thames, Phineas becoming Master Shipwright at Deptford in 1599 building ships for the Navy. He came to Woodbridge regularly to buy timber, where he lodged at the Crown Inn which belonged to local landowner Thomas Cole. The two men struck up a friendship and when Pett's son Peter married Thomas Cole's daughter, the family acquired property in Woodbridge, which included the Lime Kiln Dock. When Peter Pett rose, like his father before him, to the position of Master Shipwright at Deptford, and later on Navy Commissioner as well, he would favour the ship-builders in Woodbridge with contracts. Between 1630 and 1700 fifteen *men o' war* were built for the Navy at Lime Kiln Dock. After launching, the ships were generally sailed round to London under a *jury*, or temporary rig, to be fitted out on the Thames.

THE DECLINE OF SHIP-BUILDING

The expansion of the London dockyards, combined with the depletion of the local oak forests, was compounded by Peter Pett losing his post at Deptford, and with Pett no longer able to pass contracts out to Woodbridge, the industry began to decline. By the second half of the eighteenth century, the east coast of Canada had become such a cheap source of timber that businessmen started to have their ships built in Nova Scotia and New Brunswick instead of at home. Unrestricted by the boundaries of land-based life, the maritime world has always had an international flavour.

By the time the nineteenth century arrived, the commonest types of boat on the Suffolk coast were the *brig*, a rather tubby two-masted, square-rigged vessel often used for carrying coal down the coast from Yorkshire, and the *schooner*. The schooner had one or two masts, with a fore-and-aft sail and a square-rigged topsail above; it also had rounded bows, a square stern and marked *tumblehome*, that is to say the width of the boat was narrower at deck level than it was lower down, giving the vessel greater stability.

➤ *The last schooner to be built at Woodbridge, by William Garrard, was the* Ellen *in 1853; she was to sink off Yarmouth 22 years later*

➤ *It was common practice for a ship to belong to a group of shareholders; by custom there were 64 shares divided between her owners, usually local tradesmen, and often including the ship's master*

The Woodbridge shipyards were now mostly building schooners, which were faster than brigs and became much more popular, but they drew about ten feet of water and often had to wait for spring tides for there to be enough water under the keel for the passage up to Lime Kiln Quay. Spring tides only occur once a fortnight, and the schooners sometimes had to have up to thirty tons of cargo removed by lighter at Kyson Point before being able to continue upriver.

Four schooners made the passage regularly to London from Woodbridge each week, taking flour and cement south, and returning with wine, porter, sugar, tea and various manufactured goods. This continued until the railway arrived in 1859, which provided a cheaper and much more reliable method of transport. The time was primed for the arrival of the *Thames sailing barge*.

THE THAMES SAILING BARGE

Efficient and designed to sail on rivers and estuaries, as well as able to make coastal passages, these capacious and well-designed barges could be sailed

opposite above A Thames sailing barge; *opposite below* with the sails brailed by just two men. This was partly due to the ingenious sail plan. The enormous, heavy mainsail remained hoisted to the top of the mast all the time but could quite quickly be 'brailed' up out of the way if the wind was too strong or just to slow the vessel down. She set a number of much smaller sails which could be used in various permutations according to the sailing conditions and these were relatively easy to handle due to their much lighter weight. A large heavy *leeboard*, pivoted on each of the outer sides, removed the necessity for having a keel; by raising and lowering one at a time, the pilot could use the heavy leeboards to resist the tendency of the barge to slip sideways through the water. Being flat-bottomed, the craft could also beach in creeks at low tide to load and offload grain, sugar beet, coal and hay, without the need for a quay. This gave them the versatility to serve farms near the coast throughout East Anglia, and they would take hay back to London for the carriage horses, returning with manure for the fields.

Woodbridge, however, did not at first embrace the new way to trade and had only one local barge, whereas Maldon further down the coast on the River Blackwater had over one hundred sailing barges, mostly owned by tradesmen and skippers in the town.

Frank Mason, who owned the cement factory at Waldringfield, downriver from Woodbridge, did however invest in sailing barges, buying seven altogether – *Petrel, Elsie, Bertha, Jumbo, Excelsior, Augusta* and *Orinoco* – all sporting his emblem of a white moon on their topsails. Mason's factory made cement by mixing chalk with river mud which was first fired and then milled to a powder, before being shipped upriver to Ipswich. Having delivered its cement the barge would then take on oil-cake from the Ipswich mills to deliver it round the coast to London. They would take up to twenty-five tons of mud at a time on one tide, which must have helped to keep the channel dredged, but in 1907 Mason closed down his operation at Waldringfield and opened another cement works at Claydon, selling off all of his barges to Cranfields, who, incidentally, retained the moon emblem on the topsails.

At the time of writing, Orinoco *is still sailing, based at Faversham and competing in local barge matches. She was built at East Greenwich in 1895. The other Mason barges have all long disappeared.*

Two pilots were needed for ships entering the River Deben, one for crossing the Bar and one for navigating from Waldringfield to Woodbridge

Fishing smacks came to the Deben from Essex each summer, trawling for eels on the reach between Melton and the Tide Mill, and dredging for oysters at Ramsholt

THE MARTELLO TOWER

The Suffolk coast has always been vulnerable to invasion from Europe since the days of the Romans who built the Saxon Shore defences, and we have seen that Henry VIII started the Royal Navy and built his ships here, as well as putting fortresses all along the south coast.

A curious feature of this part of the East Anglian coast is the presence of the fortified circular buildings on the cliffs known as Martello towers. There were one hundred and forty of them built as a defence against invasion on the south and east coasts and they stretch from Seaford in Sussex to Aldeburgh in Suffolk. The origins of these towers lie in Corsica, where in 1565 one of them managed to hold off a prolonged attack from two British warships. The ship's

The Martello Tower at Bawdsey

officers were deeply impressed with this resistance to their attack and brought the idea of building something similar here back to Britain.

Engineers were employed who successfully copied the design but managed to misspell the name *mortella*, which their Corsican designer had given, calling them *martello* towers instead. Martello is actually the Italian word for a hammer. It is an ingenious design. Each tower is about forty feet high, with two floors and accommodation for up to twenty-five men, topped with a flat roof for a gun emplacement: from this high circular platform the gun could fire around three hundred and sixty degrees. Each mini-fortress is made of roughly seven hundred thousand bricks, the majority of which were brought up to the east coast by sea from London.

The garrisons in the towers communicated with each other through a system of red flags and beacons, and six of them were built between the River Deben and the Orwell, the one at Shingle Street being completed in 1812, but with the development of more powerful, rifled artillery, they eventually became redundant.

The most recent army garrison was established in Woodbridge in 1750. Large numbers of troops were stationed here and in 1803 barracks were built, along with a number of Georgian houses for the officers. The barracks were eventually pulled down in 1815 after the defeat of Napoleon, but many of the houses remain today.

1859 saw the arrival of the railway and with it the decline of shipping and subsequent shrinking of the size of the population. There were, however, some interesting characters living in the town.

THE WOODBRIDGE WITS

Edward FitzGerald (1809–1883), scholar, wit and eccentric, was born to wealthy parents in the village of Bredfield, near Woodbridge. He studied at Cambridge and, while there, became close friends with William Makepeace Thackeray and Alfred Tennyson. Never marrying, he moved to a cottage in Boulge just outside the town, which became the focus for a lively group of writers and intellectuals who became known as the Woodbridge Wits.

FitzGerald produced a small body of literary work and an extensive correspondence with writers, but his highest achievement was to translate 'The Rubaiyat of Omar Khayyam', which, through his brilliant translation, was to become so widely known and well-loved. FitzGerald had been introduced to the Persian language by Edward Cowell from Ipswich, who had first given him a copy written in Persian.

FitzGerald was also well known locally for sailing his forty-foot ketch, the *Scandal*, built in Wivenhoe in 1856. Calling his boats *Scandal*, as nothing travels faster than that, and her tender *Whisper*, FitzGerald employed a crew to sail as he preferred to just enjoy the river unencumbered by the responsibility of sailing himself. He became a familiar if eccentric figure for many years, sailing for pleasure on the Deben long before 'yachting' became popular.

The year after FitzGerald's death, a journalist, William Simpson, collected seeds from roses growing on Omar Khayyam's grave in Naishapur:

these were germinated at Kew and later planted on FitzGerald's grave at Boulge, and in 1972 a member of the Persian Embassy planted six more roses there to honour the man who made the Persian poet so popular.

The Woodbridge Wits also included the local Quaker poet Bernard Barton and the painter **Thomas Churchyard** (1798–1865). Churchyard had trained as a lawyer but he was far more interested in painting than he ever was in pursuing a career in law. He bought and copied Constable's work, developing his great talent as an artist of the English Landscape school.

Working at the Suffolk courts, he loved to defend the underdog, often getting local poachers off the hook, until eventually the Marquis of Hertford paid him a retainer to act as the prosecuting solicitor in all game cases.

There is a story told about him that he was once in the shop of a certain Mr Barrit, when his retriever managed to eat several of Barrit's sausage rolls. A few days later, passing the shop again, Barrit accosted Churchyard, telling him that someone's dog had eaten a number of his sausage rolls. Churchyard said he could recover Barrit's loss against the dog owner, whereupon Barrit asked him to hand over one shilling and a penny, as it was his dog that had eaten them. Quick as a flash, Churchyard replied that he would charge him six and eightpence for his advice, so Barrit now owed him five and sevenpence.

DINOSAUR DROPPINGS AND LEVINGTON COMPOST

The fossil-rich sands and clays which outcrop in East Anglia are known to geologists as *crags*. *Coralline crag* is the oldest of these and mainly confined to Suffolk, while the youngest one, *red crag*, was formed only three million years ago and contains an abundance of fossilised shells with occasional mammal bones and teeth as well. The red crag also contains a lot of phosphate-rich, mud-stone pebbles which were called *coprolites* as it was thought, quite wrongly, that they were fossilised dinosaur droppings. These were exploited commercially in Suffolk for fertiliser and pits were dug as early as 1717 to extract them. Some deposits were just a few feet below the surface, while others went down to as far as one hundred feet, but it had to remain open-cast mining as the crag was too soft to support tunnelling. In the 1870s ten thousand tons were being sent to Ipswich every year for milling. Coprolite was also milled at Snape, but by the turn of the nineteenth century, phosphates were being surface-mined in North America and it became cheaper to import them from there. Levington, on the north side of the Deben, was a good area for coprolite mining and the fertiliser firm Fisons still have a presence there with their research laboratories, giving the name 'Levington' to their compost.

> *Barley for malting was one of the few crops that would grow well on the local, very light land in the pre-irrigation days, and by 1860 large malthouses were being built; Woodbridge alone had thirty*

Chapter 6
THE ANGLO-SAXONS,
SHIP BURIALS
AND SUTTON HOO

The Dark Ages, suspended between the departure of the Romans in AD 410 and the arrival of the Normans in 1066, are gradually becoming a little less dark as archaeology reveals more about Anglo-Saxon society. Historical research on any period generally relies on four basic sources for its material, and the study of Anglo-Saxon times is no exception. These sources are:

1. Narrative – the writings of The Venerable Bede, The Anglo-Saxon Chronicles, The Irish Annals, and the writings of the monks Alcuin and Nennius.
2. Documentary records – the laws, wills, charters and writs.
3. Material objects – the coins, artefacts, manuscripts, embroideries and archaeological findings.
4. Literature – the letters, poems and sagas.

The Anglo-Saxon Chronicles, begun in the 890s under the great King Alfred, chart the history of Britain from Roman times. Several copies were made but individual monasteries continued to update their own copies so each one gives a slightly different perspective.

The scholar Alcuin spent much of his time at the court of Charlemagne, teaching at the Palace School in Aachen, as well as the Archbishop's School in York. Never actually getting round to taking his monastic vows, he wrote about the Viking raids in England, although he was in fact in Aachen at the time they were happening.

The **sagas** are an important literary source for these times and they come in several different versions. *The king's sagas* are stories of the dynasties of the twelfth-century rulers. *The thirteenth-century sagas* are the most well-known and relate the stories of individuals from less noble families, usually through several generations. *The sagas of the knights* were adaptations of European romances for an Icelandic audience, while the *legendary sagas* are a record of mythical stories.

Drawing on all of these resources, a picture of the Anglo-Saxon Age is continuing to emerge. The political vacuum left by the departure of the Romans was soon filled by various factions competing for power over various pieces of territory. The Romans had employed Anglo-Saxon mercenaries to boost their army, and these men were just part of the mix of competing tribes and warlords who sought to hold power. Out of these struggles there were to emerge three great Anglo-Saxon kings: Offa, Alfred and Athelstan.

OFFA (*c.* AD 757–796)

The King of Mercia, and of Offa's Dyke fame, unified the whole of England below the Humber and in his later years became a statesman well-known at the Papal Court as well as developing a friendship with Charlemagne, exchanging gifts and protection with the first of the great Carolingian kings. Offa's death was closely followed by the death of his son who had been the next in line, and under this double blow the overlordship of Mercia gradually began to crumble as England descended once more into rival factions all fighting for power. It was time for the Saxons in the west to rise with their leader Alfred.

ALFRED THE GREAT (*c.* AD 849–899)

The much-loved legend of Alfred, living rough in the Somerset Levels and burning cakes when left in charge of the fire by a peasant woman, is often all that is remembered about this English king. But his is a great story to be told.

The 'Danelaw' was a term first coined by Wulfstan, the eleventh-century Archbishop of York, to describe the area which maintained Danish legal procedures. The treaty between Alfred and Guthrum described the area, which was south of the Humber, as *'up the Thames, and then up the Lea and along the Lea to its source and then to Bedford, then up the Ouse to Watling Street'*.

MAP OF THE DANELAW

YORK

NOTTINGHAM

BEDFORD

LONDON

Born into a world where England was divided into the separate kingdoms of East Anglia, Mercia, Northumbria and Wessex (with the additional minor kingdoms of Essex, Kent and Sussex), there was a constant struggle for power with the invading Danes, and the concept of ever having a united England must have felt very remote. As a boy, Alfred learnt Latin and, never very strong, always relied more on his intellect than his physical prowess; there is some suggestion that he may have suffered from Crohn's disease.

As a young man, Alfred became king of Wessex in 871 following the death of his brother, just at the time when the Danes had conquered Mercia as well as East Anglia, and were well settled at York. In the ensuing wars Alfred managed to drive them out of Wessex back into Mercia but they soon returned, taking him unawares at Christmas, defeating his army and forcing him into hiding in the marshes of Somerset. This must have been the lowest ebb in the era of the Saxons, but somehow rallying his remaining forces Alfred engaged the Danish leader Guthrum in a battle at Edington in 878 and, in a complete reversal of fortunes, managed to defeat his bitter enemy. This is where Alfred showed his abilities and courage as a leader by negotiating a peace with the Dane. Instead of yet more slaughter, he made Guthrum convert to Christianity, becoming his godfather, and divided the kingdom, giving the East to the control of what became known as the Danelaw which included part of east Mercia as well as Northumbria. It was defined by the courses of the rivers Thames, Lea and Ouse.

It was a commonly used tactic by the Danes to surprise the enemy by attacking them at their times of feasting. They must have studied the religious calendar to spot the dates when the Christians would be the worse for drink.

Town planning and education: how to build a nation

Alfred then began developing an infrastructure in his kingdom for the first time since the Roman occupation, and a great urban expansion took place throughout southern England. He was the first town planner, creating towns as a centre for refuge and defence as well as for commercial life. The towns were called *burhs* and plots of land were given to anyone who would commit to maintain and man the defences in times of war. The streets were laid out in a linear pattern within a fortified wall, and remains of this layout can still be seen in many places today. No part of the kingdom was to be more than twenty miles from a guarded burh, and there were strong-points made on all of the river routes: no longer were the Vikings going to take them by surprise with their longships.

Alfred also recognised the importance of education and language as an essential part of political life. You cannot govern a country where the people cannot read and understand its rules and laws. But a hundred years of the destruction of monasteries and manuscripts by Viking raiders had taken its toll on education, and the standard of Latin and book production was at an all-time low.

With this in view, Alfred embarked on the translation of Latin texts into Anglo-Saxon. The Anglo-Saxon Chronicles and the writings of Bede, Boethius and St Augustine were all systematically made available to men who could not read Latin.

It is this attention to the civic lives of his people, as well as their defence, that makes Alfred one of our greatest kings.

The linear pattern of streets designed by Alfred can be seen in many towns today; particularly good examples are in Cricklade and Wallingford, and, in London, the streets between Cheapside and the Thames

ATHELSTAN (*c.* AD 894–939)

It was to fall to Alfred's grandson Athelstan to finally unite the country into one kingdom. Burning to achieve this goal, he systematically dismantled the hold of the Danes by a relentless onslaught of battle and diplomacy. To consolidate the kingdom, he introduced a fairer system of justice, reworked Alfred's design of fortified towns and then turned his attention to the commercial life of the country. He allowed trade to take place only in the burhs, thereby controlling taxation, and he centralised the coinage by controlling the number of *moneyers* (those licensed to mint coins) in each city, standardising the weight and quality of silver in their coins. To this end, they were required to stamp each coin with the name of the mint.

By the time Athelstan died, aged only 44, he was recognised as an elder statesman both at home and in Europe, and together with his grandfather Alfred left a legacy of government that we still benefit from today.

>━━ *Under Athelstan, the whole of England was divided into* shires *and this was not to alter until 1974*

WHO'S WHO IN THE ANGLO-SAXON WORLD

aethel   a member of the king's family (for example, Athelstan is also written 'Aethelstan')

thegn   someone engaged in the service of a king or a nobleman. There were three levels: *earl's thegn*, *king's thegn* and *median thegn*. The term *thegn* largely disappeared after the Norman Conquest to be replaced with the class of *knight*.

ceorl   a freeman. He could rise to *thegn* if he owned sufficient land, and pleased the king enough.

bretwalda   an overlord king who ruled over the kings of smaller kingdoms.

BEOWULF

Beowulf is an epic poem in the tradition of *The Iliad*, written in this country somewhere between the middle of the seventh century and the end of the tenth. It is set in Scandinavia and was written in Anglo-Saxon (also known as Old English), and some say it was commissioned by King Alfred.

The poem tells the story of the Swedish warrior Beowulf who goes to the land of the Danes to slay a man-eating monster named Grendel. He kills the monster, and then the monster's mother, and returns home to rule over the land of the Geats, as southern Sweden was known then. After fifty years of rule, a dragon begins to roam in the land and Beowulf, now an old man, has one final and fatal battle in which he slays the dragon and dies to pass into legend as a great hero.

The poem, which had long been studied by academia for its historical and linguistic material, was brought into the world of literature by J.R.R. Tolkein who wrote a paper that drew attention to its value as a piece of writing. Seamus Heaney published a beautiful translation of it in 1999.

SHIP BURIALS

The only ship burials discovered so far in the world are in Egypt, Scandinavia and Great Britain.

THE SOLAR BARGES OF EGYPT

In 1954 an Egyptian archaeologist, Kamal el-Mallakh, discovered one of the oldest ships ever to be found. It was lying in over a thousand pieces in a long pit beside the Khufu Pyramid at Giza just outside Cairo. But the ship had not fallen to pieces; it had been buried like this in 'kit' form, all the pieces laid out in the right order ready for assembly. Although there is evidence that it had been used in water, there was not really enough room on board for oarsmen, neither was there any rigging for a sail, so it was very probably built as a funerary barge, just to carry the body of the Pharaoh to his tomb.

It has now been assembled and can be seen in all its magnificence in a building alongside the pyramid. Built of overlapping Cedar-of-Lebanon planks which have been sewn together with hemp rope, it is forty-four metres long and six metres wide. It was buried here when the pyramid was built in around 2500 BC.

A number of these so-called solar barges have been discovered in Egypt, for conveying the resurrected body of a dead king across the heavens with the sun-god Ra. Fourteen more were discovered in the year 2000 at the ancient city of Abydos. Here they were built of tamarisk wood and, although they were fully assembled, none of the joints had been pegged, suggesting that the boats were designed to be easily taken to pieces for transport through the desert. The idea of the flat-pack seems to have begun in Ancient Egypt.

The Abydos barges were all buried with their prows pointing towards the Nile

ANGLO-SAXON SHIP BURIALS

These are the earliest ship burials outside Egypt, dating at around the sixth and seventh centuries, and only three have been found to date. One was unearthed at Snape, where just a few remaining rivets were discovered in a grave that had been robbed, and the other two are both at Sutton Hoo, near Woodbridge (see p. 105).

VIKING SHIP BURIALS

Viking ship burials are all a little later than the Anglo-Saxon ones, dating from the eighth century, and several of these have been found in Britain, notably on the Isle of Man, Orkney and more recently at Ardnamurchan in Scotland. They are all boat burials, being small compared with the ship burial at Sutton Hoo, and each was probably the grave of a Viking chieftain.

A number have been found in Norway, Denmark and Sweden, of which the most well-known are the ships found at Oseberg and Gokstad near Oslo. Unlike the Sutton Hoo ship, where the wood had disappeared completely, leaving just the compacted impressions in the earth, these Norwegian ships have been largely preserved in the clay soil and have been relocated and put on display in the Viking Ship Museum at Oslo.

The Oseberg ship contained the bodies of two women, one aged about fifty, and the other, in her eighties, is thought to be of Persian ancestry. There are many beautiful grave goods, including four highly decorated sledges and an intricately carved wagon, along with textiles, jewellery and food. The construction of the ship, and the performance of the replica which was subsequently constructed, suggests that it was probably built as a ceremonial ship, it being of very shallow draft and the mast step not really built strongly enough to take the weight of a heavy sail.

The Gokstad ship is less highly decorated than the Oseberg one and, despite being robbed at some point, still has a wonderful collection of equipment such as tents, three boats, a gaming board, hunting weapons and silks. Twelve horses, six dogs and two peacocks were buried with the occupant of the tomb who had been killed in battle.

Ship and boat burials in Norway are usually orientated pointing south and often towards water

VIKING FUNERALS

Although occasionally written about in Norse mythology, there is no archaeological evidence that ships were ever set on fire at a Viking funeral. There is, however, an eyewitness account written by the Arab traveller **Ahmad ibn Fadlan** dating from the tenth century. He attended the ritual funeral of a *Rus* chieftain where a *thrall* girl, apparently a volunteer, was given intoxicating drinks in a long and elaborate ceremony which involved the killing of two horses and much singing. She was then raped by several men before being slain and burnt along with the king and his ship.

It is thought that the funeral in question was that of a Swedish chieftain who had been travelling with his men along the Volga River. This was a route well-known to the Viking traders who took their ships from the Baltic deep into the heartland of Eastern Europe and Asia. They were known there as *Rus* due to their fair hair, and subsequent settlers there came to be called *Russians*.

UP HELLY AA

Despite the lack of any evidence that the Vikings ever set fire to their ships, the exuberant celebrations each year of *Up Helly Aa* at Lerwick in Shetland continue to keep the idea alive. Starting in the 1880s the festival has taken place on the last Tuesday in January every year with only three exceptions – the death of Queen Victoria, and for the duration of both the First and Second World Wars. The street lights are switched off and a thousand *guizers* dressed in Viking costume process by torchlight through the town, burning the model of a galley at the Market Cross and singing the traditional Up Helly Aa songs. They also preserve the fictitious conceit of wearing winged or horned helmets to add to the atmosphere. An excellent way to escape briefly from the cold and darkness of a Shetland winter…

VIKING SHIPS

There can be few ships ever built of more elegant lines than those of the Viking Age. Lean, long and graceful, they epitomise the simple, spare forms that we still associate with Scandinavian design.

They were built in the *clinker* style, overlapping planks each nailed to the next with wooden or iron nails, although the very early ones would have been fixed with twine lashings. Internal wooden frames, fitted after the planks have been fixed together, hold the shape. This method of building gives a boat great longitudinal rigidity while still allowing the hull to flex a little with the waves, and some wooden boats are still built like this today. Viking ships were steered with an oar fixed over the right side of the hull. The now familiar rudder fixed to the stern did not become standard until well into the twelfth century and the fascinating story of how this developed can be read in *Two Points East*, the version of this book on maritime Norfolk.

Where did the idea for clinker building come from?

First imagine that you want to make the most basic of boats, a dugout canoe. Hollowing out a tree trunk gives you a perfectly serviceable boat, but then you find that adding some shaping to the outside of the log makes it go faster. Happy with this improvement to begin with, you then start to think that it would be better if it was a little wider which would make it less tippy and able to carry more stuff. So someone came up with the bright idea of heating the wood, which meant the sides could then be bent outwards, thus making the boat a bit wider. All was well to start with, but this bending had the effect of weakening the wood, making it rather liable to spring leaks, until the light-bulb moment came when someone realised that by adding internal frames to the boat at intervals down its length, the sides would be held much more rigidly. It was only a small step now to stitching a plank along each side to make it less susceptible to swamping in a heavy sea and, suddenly, you have very nearly made a clinker-built boat.

Before the saw was invented, planks were made by hammering in wedges along the grain of a log until the wood split along its length. A plank *riven* in this way is much stronger than a sawn one, as it uses the natural strength of the longitudinally running grain. The Viking ships were all built from riven oak which gave them both the strength and flexibility needed for a safe sea passage. A row of oars, and sometimes a single square woollen sail to speed passages when the wind was favourable, completed the ship and the Viking influence can still be easily seen in the traditional boats to be found all round the coasts of Scandinavia and Scotland to this day.

The Viking Ship Museum in Oslo houses the oldest Norwegian ship found to date – the *Oseberg*, named after the place where it was found. Built in AD 820 it is twenty-one metres long, with an extraordinarily low free-board, and this beautiful ship with wonderfully intricate carvings on her stern and stem would not have been very stable at sea.

The Gokstad ship, built a little later in AD 890, by contrast with its deeper draught, higher sides and a strongly built keel and mast step, would have been a fast, versatile and very seaworthy vessel indeed. It is a breathtaking moment to enter the simple white-painted hall where she is displayed and to first catch sight of her achingly beautiful lines curving gracefully up towards the narrow prow.

Just a little way north of Copenhagen lies the little town of Skudelev, where in 1957 some amateur divers came across the biggest haul of Viking ships ever found at that time. There were no fewer than five ships, all of which had been deliberately sunk as a blockade to prevent enemy ships entering the harbour. The subsequent excavation was to pioneer the archaeology and experimental reconstruction of Viking ships, and all five ships have now had replicas built which are rowed and sailed from the harbour. When a site was found at nearby Roskilde for a museum, nine more ships were discovered there, including the largest Viking warship ever to be found. Known as Roskilde 6, this ship is thirty-two metres long and was built in the early eleventh century during the reign of Cnut.

The replica of Skudelev 2, thirty metres long and named the *Sea Stallion*, completed a journey from Roskilde, around Scotland to Dublin, in 2007. Video footage of her at sea, manned by volunteers living, eating and sleeping in the open with little protection from the sea and the weather, can be seen at the museum. Life for a Viking may have been adventurous but it was certainly not comfortable.

The Gokstad ship

SUTTON HOO

In 1926 Edith Dempster, the daughter of a wealthy manufacturer from Yorkshire, married the love of her life, Frank Pretty. Edith had travelled widely with her father before the outbreak of the First World War, developing an interest in archaeology after seeing the treasures being found in Egypt. She worked with the Red Cross during the War both in Britain and France, and she was forty-two years old when she married Frank. With her inherited family fortune, Edith and Frank were able to buy a house at Sutton Hoo near Woodbridge which stood in a fine position on high ground overlooking the River Deben. They soon settled into a happy marriage but it was to be short-lived as Frank died only eight years later, leaving Edith alone with her grief and a four-year-old son.

An energetic and educated woman, since moving to the estate her curiosity had been roused by the group of grass-covered mounds in the grounds of the house. There had been various attempts at excavating these mounds since they were first recorded in 1601 but they had never really attracted any serious investigation. By now it was 1934 and the events leading up to the Second World War were beginning to cause unease in Europe. It was against this background of foreboding that Edith, in an effort to cope with her grief, threw herself into instigating a properly conducted archaeological dig.

The dig

On the recommendation of the Curator of Ipswich Museum, Edith Pretty employed Basil Brown, who was a self-taught but experienced archaeologist working at the museum at the time. There were thirteen mounds on the site and his work began in 1938. Starting with Mound Three, Basil unearthed the remains of a horse, a man and various grave goods including pottery from the Eastern Mediterranean, all dating from around the sixth and seventh centuries.

Mound Two revealed another body with more grave goods from the same period and, to great surprise, evidence that a boat had once been buried there, which possibly linked it to a boat burial that had been found at Snape in 1862. There was just time to open Mound Four before the onset of winter, when it would be hard to protect the delicate work of the dig against the elements, and the site was covered until the following year.

Work began again in May when Basil returned to the site to investigate the largest of the mounds, Mound One. By now he had been joined by Edith's gardener and the gamekeeper who he trained to assist in the excavation, with the expectation that this time they might find another ship. So, paying close attention to any signs of change in colour of the soil, which could indicate the presence of wood or metal, the three men resumed their painstaking work and before long they were rewarded with the discovery of a ship's rivet.

Realising the significance of this find, Brown contacted Guy Maynard, the Curator of the Ipswich Museum who had first suggested he should undertake the project. On visiting the site, Maynard confirmed its importance and brought Charles Phillips over from Cambridge University to see it. Basil and his small team continued to carefully scrape away more earth, revealing what would turn out to be the impression in the earth of a vessel twenty-seven metres long – the largest ship burial ever to be found in Britain.

Now the news was out about the significance of the site, the Ancient Monuments Inspectorate put Charles Phillips in charge of the excavation and, within two months of Basil's discovery, the site was taken over by the Crown. Basil Brown must have had mixed feelings about being superseded by the academic establishment, but his careful and professional work was acknowledged by the new team and he continued to work with them as they uncovered the treasures that had for so long lain hidden beneath the earth. They continued the excavations until late into August when the site was backfilled as the Second World War was about to begin.

The finds

There was nothing remaining of any of the wooden planks of the ship, just the impressions they had left in the surrounding soil – acid sandy soil destroys organic matter quite quickly – but the rows of metal rivets remained. The ship had measured twenty-seven metres long and four and a half metres wide, with a roofed chamber amidships which contained astonishing treasure. The discovery of a large silver dish was closely followed by weapons, a shield, a highly decorated gold buckle, a chainmail shirt and a pair of beautiful shoulder clasps, coins, drinking vessels, silver dishes from Byzantium and many different textiles. But the most memorable finds were the helmet and the ceremonial whetstone.

After the end of the War, conservators at the British Museum examined the finds more closely and began to rebuild the helmet which was in over five hundred fragments. The final reconstruction showed an iron skull cap onto which had been rivetted a grid of fluted bronze. The spaces in the grid had been filled with embossed decorative bronze panels, one of which shows two warriors with linked arms, apparently dancing, and another showing a mounted warrior brandishing a spear, riding over a fallen horse; all the other bronze panels had been lost. A blackened iron crest inlaid with silver runs from the front to the back of the helmet, with a gilt bronze dragon's head at either end; the gilt bronze nosepiece and eyebrows make the form of a flying bird when viewed from the front.

Similar helmets have been found in some of the Scandinavian ship burials, but one of the most interesting things about these treasures is the demonstration of such outstanding craftsmanship by the goldsmiths and metalworkers of the time, as well as the presence of objects from overseas, showing that the continent of Europe was very much part of their world.

top right The helmet; *above right* The whetstone

Although she was granted *treasure trove*, Edith Pretty donated the finds to the British Museum, and declined the suggestion that she should have her name put forward for an honour.

➤━━ *If a treasure is found which has been deliberately hidden it belongs to the Crown, but if that cannot be proved it becomes treasure trove and belongs to the person on whose land it is found*

No trace of a body was found and there are various explanations for this: it could be due to the acidity of the soil which causes bones to decompose rapidly, or this could have been a cremation burial site or possibly even a cenotaph, but despite further excavation in 1965 no definitive explanation has been found. However, the forensic evidence of high phosphate levels within the chamber indicates that there probably was once bone there, and the very presence of personal grave goods would indicate that this was a royal burial. The date of between AD 595 and 640 would put Raedwald, or possibly his son Raeganhere, as the hottest contenders.

THE FORGING OF A SWORD

In the museum at Sutton Hoo there is a fascinating account and a video of the making of an Anglo-Saxon sword. The craft of forging a sword that would not break in use, which would hold a good sharp edge and would balance well in the hand was a highly skilled one and, along with the beautiful highly decorated buckles and jewellery-settings found in the grave, reveals that these were people with a highly advanced technology.

To make a sword, the smith would first forge a number of iron and steel billets into strips and then weld them together in alternate layers. The resulting strip of metal would then be repeatedly folded and welded, up to as much as a hundred times.

The prepared metal strip was beaten into a square-section rod and twisted; three of these twisted rods were then welded together. The process is still not finished, as two of these resulting rods are welded one to each side of an iron core, which is then beaten flat.

The cutting edges of the sword are made separately by sandwiching wrought-iron and carbon-steel strips together. These are wrapped around the core and welded into place.

Finally the sword is ground and polished, revealing in the finished blade the beautiful folded patterns of its making – a work of art and a devastating weapon.

Chapter 7
IPSWICH

The importance of Ipswich as a port, sitting at the head of the Orwell Estuary, is rather eclipsed now by the vast container port downriver at Felixstowe. One of the largest in the country, the latter's row of angular gantries makes a strangely beautiful statement against the sky at the mouth of the estuary. The huge cranes dwarf the containers, which look the size of matchboxes; it is only when you pass a lorry carrying one on its back that you remember the sheer scale of the operation. At Ipswich, the commercial dock operates a little further downstream from its original position and was developed at the Millennium. The modern waterfront now thrums with offices and cafes and the campus of the University of Suffolk, all overlooking the yacht harbour.

But a walk around the town behind soon begins to reveal some of its past, if only by the sheer numbers of Tudor and Elizabethan buildings to be found here, some stating their pedigree clearly in half-timbering and carved bressumer beams, others where their age is given away only by a jettied upper storey jutting out over the street. If you were then to start stripping away the façades added in the eighteenth century, many more of these buildings would begin to reveal their earlier origins.

Sitting at a pavement cafe on the Waterfront in the warm June sunshine with students of all nationalities mingling with the visitors and office workers it is not too difficult to imagine there was a time, not too long ago, when the docks would have also rung with the sounds of many different languages, as young sailors from Germany, the Low Countries, Scandinavia and beyond would be walking along the same dockside as these students are now.

Timber-framed houses are very draughty as the wind gets in between the wood and the lathe, so the timber was often plastered over

The new waterfront

River Gipping

IPSWICH

Belstead Brook

NEW CHANNEL

ORWELL BRIDGE

CATHOUSE POINT

FRESTON REACH

DOWNHAM REACH

Cat House

Cat House
A black cat was placed in the window to warn smugglers of the excise men. A white cat meant the coast was clear

Clamp House
Beet was stored here in clamps

Holbrook Creek

New Mill Creek

HOLBROOK BAY

SEAFIELD BAY

R I V E R   S T O U R

COPPERAS BAY

MANNINGTREE

MISTLEY

JAMES'S BAY

THE RIVER ORWELL
and THE STOUR

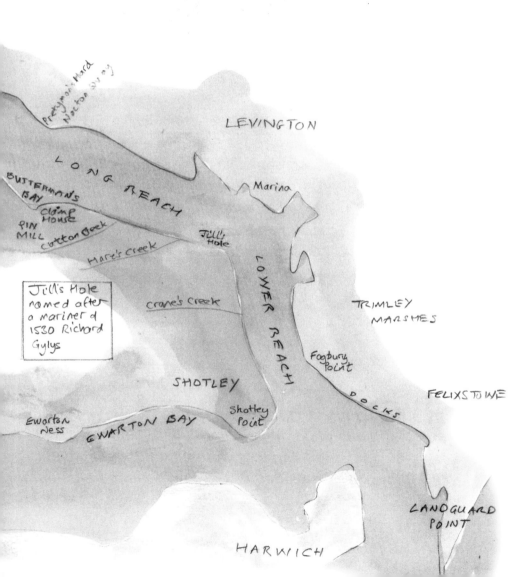

LEVINGTON

Pretyman's Hard
(Norton Quay)

LONG REACH

BUTTERMAN'S BAY

Clamp House

PIN MILL

Cotton Dock

Hare's Creek

Marina

Jill's Hole

LOWER REACH

Jill's Hole named after a mariner of 1530 Richard Gylys

Crane's Creek

TRIMLEY MARSHES

Fagbury Point

SHOTLEY

Shotley Point

DOCKS

FELIXSTOWE

Ewarton Ness

EWARTON BAY

LANDGUARD POINT

HARWICH

THE EARLY YEARS

Ipswich suffered two devastating attacks by the early Viking raiders, the first in AD 991 and the second just nine years later, when many of the town's buildings were burnt down. But, despite these setbacks, during the ensuing centuries Ipswich grew fat on the export of wool produced in the Gipping and Stour valleys. King John granted the growing town a charter in 1200, and quays were built along the river to serve the increasing trade up and down the coast and across the North Sea.

By 1500 the ship-building industry in Ipswich had grown so big that the port became known as 'the shipyard of London', building many ships of up to a hundred tons to serve the fleets of the Iceland cod fishery and the coastal trade in coal from Newcastle. With the arrival of weavers from Flanders escaping religious persecution in the fifteenth century, the port soon began to export their new cloths which were far superior to those produced by the local weavers.

THE SIXTEENTH CENTURY

Towards the end of the sixteenth century, the increase in piracy on the North Sea, combined with the much more interesting cloths being produced by the weavers of the Low Countries, started a slow decline in the wool trade. Traders instead started to turn their attention to importing other goods such as wine from Bordeaux, stone from Caen, and iron from Germany and Spain. The prosperity of these merchants can be judged by the number of fine houses that they built for themselves, some of which remain in the town today. But times never stand still, and as the sixteenth century marched on, the City of London began to drain much of the trade away from the East Anglian ports. Navigation of the Thames Estuary had become vastly improved with a system of channel markers in place, overseen by the newly established Trinity House. The silting up of harbours on the coast was a perennial problem, and it was difficult and costly to maintain enough deep water for the ever-increasing size of ships wanting to come up the river beyond Woolverstone.

CARDINAL WOLSEY (1479–1530)

A massive, carved, lime-washed corner-post supports the jettied first floor of a building jutting out over the pavement on the corner of Silent Street and St Peter's Street. Sitting with his back to it, on the other side of the road, is the bronze figure of Cardinal Wolsey, looking towards the site where his school for the poor people of the town once stood. Born in Ipswich, the son of a landowning grazier, Wolsey was loved by the poor and, making as many enemies as friends, rose to become a key figure in our history.

As Lord Chancellor to Henry VIII he initiated the *Court of Requests* whereby a poor man could petition the monarch for justice without the payment of a fee. He prosecuted well over two hundred landlords who tried to enclose their land illegally, thus depriving many rural people of their livelihoods. He attempted to regulate the price of meat, and started the practice of buying grain after a poor harvest when its price was high in order to sell it cheaply to the needy.

His last act was to try to bring education to the poor of his home town by the building of a school, The College of St Mary, for fifty children, in 1528. A year after its inauguration, however, Henry in his impatience to marry Anne Boleyn, needed an annulment from his current marriage to Catherine of Aragon. Not able to achieve this fast enough to please the difficult king, Wolsey found himself stripped of his office and his property including the beautiful Hampton Court. In a bitter twist to the story, Henry closed Wolsey's college in Ipswich and had its bricks transported to London

above right The carved post on the corner of Silent Street and St Peter's Street

to build an extension onto York Place, another of the properties he confiscated from him, renaming it Whitehall Palace. Nothing is left of Whitehall Palace now, just a plaque on the Thames Embankment as a reminder of a time long gone.

The base around the plinth on which Wolsey's statue sits reads: *'Thomas Wolsey born Ipswich 1479 died Leicester 1530. Cardinal Archbishop Lord Chancellor and teacher who believed that pleasure should be mingled with study so that the child may think learning an amusement rather than a toil.'*

Statue of
Cardinal Wolsey

Of his college in Ipswich, all that remains is an elaborate doorway off College Street, leading to nowhere.

A plaque on a wall somewhere drew my attention to Thomas Cavendish, one of the early circumnavigators of the globe who lived near Ipswich. My curiosity aroused, I found the following extraordinary story of his voyage.

THOMAS CAVENDISH (1560–1591)

Born in 1560 into a wealthy family from the nearby village of Trimley St Mary, the future navigator, explorer and privateer Thomas Cavendish was inspired by the voyage of Francis Drake. Orphaned and inheriting his father's wealth as a boy, Cavendish spent two years at Corpus Christi College, Cambridge, leaving at the age of seventeen with no degree, too much money and not enough to do. Wasting all of these potentially valuable assets for a few years, he was twice returned as a Member of Parliament before finally having his passion awakened when he took ship with Sir Richard Grenville on the voyage to Roanoke to establish a military colony on the island off the coast of North Carolina.

Fired with enthusiasm for adventure at sea he obtained permission from the Crown to follow Drake's example in raiding the coast of the Spanish colonies and capturing their ships in the Pacific. He commissioned the building of a sailing ship, which he named the *Desire*. Sailing from Plymouth in July 1586, accompanied by two smaller, heavily armed ships, the *Hugh Gallant* and the *Content*, and with one hundred and twenty-three men between them, they crossed the Atlantic to the coast of South America, sailing through the Strait of Magellan in the following January. It would have been bitterly cold that far south and food was running short so they took advantage of the large number of penguins, slaughtering the birds and salting them in barrels before turning up the west coast and into the Pacific. Pursuing his newfound career as a privateer, Cavendish sank and captured a number of Spanish ships, looted a few towns and deliberately scuppered the *Hugh Gallant* in order to use her crew as replacements for the men he had lost so far.

Tipped off by a pilot from one of his captured ships, he then laid plans to capture one of the two Manila galleons that were expected to arrive off the Californian coast that autumn, laden with silver, gold and silks from the Far East. It was a prize too tempting to miss, and Cavendish took his two ships to the Baja Peninsula to lie in wait for them.

But misfortune had met both of the ships and they had been wrecked off the coast of Japan. Only the *Santa Ana* was able, after repairs, to resume her passage and this was the ship spotted by the lookout at the masthead early on the morning of 4th November. She was a huge vessel of six hundred tons, dwarfing the sixty-ton *Content* and the 120-ton *Desire*, but she had made the fatal error of removing her cannons to make more space for the treasure she was carrying. A chase ensued, lasting several hours, which ended with the firing of cannon and grape shot into the *Santa Ana* until she struck her colours from the mast in an act of surrender.

The two small English ships were not large enough to take all of her goods on board, but they took as much as they could manage before landing her two hundred crew ashore with food and weapons and setting their ship on fire. The *Santa Ana* was not to be defeated, however, and she drifted slowly onto the shore where the men put out the fire and sailed her on to Acapulco.

The *Content* disappears from the story now and she never returned, but the *Desire* continued on to the Philippines and the Spice Islands. Laden with her treasure she could do no more raiding and just traded some of her goods in return for supplies of water, provisions and fuel. The crew, reduced in number now to just forty-eight men, made themselves new clothes out of their newly acquired silk damask and headed for home via Africa and the Cape of Good Hope, sailing into Plymouth on 9th September 1588.

The news of Cavendish's voyage and capture of the Spanish treasure, along with the defeat of the Spanish Armada earlier that year, must have been sweet to the ears of the monarch and Cavendish was knighted by Queen Elizabeth I as Drake, his hero, had been before him. He was only twenty-eight years old.

It is recorded that the Desire *sailed up the* Thames *into London with sails made of some of the blue silk taken from the* Santa Ana

THE NINETEENTH CENTURY

By the end of the eighteenth century, much of the trade in coal on the coast was avoiding Ipswich in favour of Great Yarmouth, which was maintaining its harbour rather more effectively. It was not until 1805 that an Act of Parliament was finally passed allowing the major improvements needed to be carried out under the direction of the New River Commissioners. Money was raised by all those with a vested interest – the landowners, merchants and ship-builders – and work began to cut a deep channel in the river using a steam-powered dredger, and to straighten out two of the bends.

The ensuing programme of works over the next thirty years made Ipswich a busy port once more and her shipyards went on to build many

The Custom House

ships of well over a thousand tons, such as the East Indiamen – large, armed sailing ships which traded across the oceans of the world.

>━━━ *During the Napoleonic Wars, twenty-six warships were built at Ipswich*

By 1840 they were building the new iron steamships as well as sailing vessels but the railway was beginning to eclipse shipping, and traders such as the wealthy Cobbold family, merchants in Ipswich for so many decades, turned their attention away from ship-building and looked to brewing, banking and the railway instead.

>━━━ *The streets did not have names until the eighteenth century, when they were mostly named after pubs*

>━━━ *There is a large coat of arms displayed on a wall above one of the shops in Ipswich which has the faces of two men on it. It is not known who they are but they could possibly be the two Ipswich men who accompanied the newly restored Charles II back to England.*

Despite these changes it was decided to build an entirely new dock, and in 1837 the Ipswich Dock Act was passed. Vastly exceeding its budget (times do not change), at three acres it became the largest wet dock in Britain at the time. The river was channelled through a New Cut protected with an embankment, the watery equivalent of a modern bypass, and a huge new basin dredged beside it. Water could enter the basin at high tide and was trapped inside by a lock built at the entrance, thereby ensuring that the water could be maintained at a high enough level at all states of the tide.

This facility gave the town an enormous boost, and industries sprung up all around the new dock with feedmills, iron foundries and sawmills importing their timber from the Baltic. When the rail link to Colchester was established in 1843, yet more industry developed with fertiliser plants, coke ovens, corn merchants and malting.

Soon large steamships were superseding the old sailing vessels, and the lock was no longer big enough to serve them, so yet another Dock Act was passed and in 1877 a new lock was built, twice the size of the old one.

Near to the dock, the church of St Mary-le-Tower was largely rebuilt and has some beautiful carving on the ends of all the pews, including some cogs. The pulpit was carved by a pupil of Grinling Gibbons, who always carved a peapod into his work. If it was closed, it meant he had not been paid.

THE STORY OF MARGARET CATCHPOLE (1762–1819)

In a churchyard in Richmond, New South Wales, lies the grave of Margaret Catchpole, and sooner or later anyone expressing an interest in the region of the River Orwell will be told the story of this remarkable woman.

Born just outside Ipswich in the village of Nacton, Margaret was the daughter of the head ploughman on the estate belonging to the Denton family, where she was encouraged from an early age to ride the great Suffolk Punches that were used to draw the ploughs and pull the carts in those days. She was said to be as fearless as a Newmarket jockey.

When Margaret was just thirteen years old, Mrs Denton, the wife of her father's employer, fell into an epileptic fit which caused panic among the servants. But the quick-thinking girl, realising that medical help was needed, leapt onto one of the carthorses and rode bareback to Ipswich to fetch the doctor, George Stebbings. The doctor recognised the potential of the young girl and was to befriend her later when she fell into trouble with the law.

As she grew into her teens Margaret met and fell in love with Will Laud, the son of a local boatbuilder. Will was expected to join his father in the family business but he longed to go to sea and his father finally relented, allowing the lad to join a ship belonging to a certain Captain Bargood. The captain was to be a thoroughly bad influence on the boy and it was not very long before the two of them were engaged in the much more profitable business of smuggling. Will tried desperately hard to persuade Margaret to marry him, but she steadfastly refused unless he was prepared to give up his smuggling career.

In the meantime, the young customs officer John Barry had fallen in love with Margaret, but she swore to marry no-one but Will, still hoping she could persuade him to give up smuggling. Will, however, was relishing his way of life far too much to give it up, even for Margaret, and made a plan with an accomplice, John Luff, to get Margaret down to the shore on some ploy where he hoped he could persuade her to elope with him. The plan came unstuck, though, when the two men were spotted by the customs officers and a fight broke out during which Will shot and wounded John Barry. Dr Stebbings saved the life of the young customs officer, who continued to plead hopelessly with Margaret for her hand in marriage.

Margaret was by now in service, working for several different families in turn but always hoping for news of Will, which would occasionally be brought to her by sailors calling at the house in which she worked. Then one day, John Barry brought her the news that Will's boat had been wrecked off Bawdsey Ferry and the bodies of four men, including Will's, had been washed up on the shore. Stricken with anguish she rushed down to the shore to find that Will was not among the bodies and reaffirmed her vow never to marry another. At this point in the story the heartbroken John Barry emigrated to Van Diemen's Land.

By that time, Margaret was working for the well-known Suffolk family, the Cobbolds, and was much loved and valued by both her employers and their seven children, but when she heard news that her lover was now in London waiting for her, she was persuaded to steal a horse, riding nine hours to London to meet him. Unfortunately she was caught and, despite character references from the doctor, she was sentenced to be hanged. Elizabeth Cobbold stepped in at this point and managed to persuade the judge to commute the sentence to seven years' transportation, the first year to be spent in Ipswich Gaol, before taking ship to Australia.

Entering the gaol, Margaret soon became an asset as a prisoner, respected and trusted by gaolers and prisoners alike, and it was not long before her qualities were noticed by the prison governor's wife, Mrs Ripshaw, who took her into her own personal service. One day Margaret was hanging out the laundry in the yard when, looking over the wall, who should she see but Will Laud, who was in the debtor's gaol next door. Margaret had never used the money that Will had been sending her over the years, as she knew it was gained dishonestly, so she was able to secure his release by paying off his debt. Will then persuaded her to escape by climbing onto one of the laundry racks, using the clothes as a line to let herself down on the other side. Dressed as a sailor she made her escape with Will but their plans were again thwarted by the customs men, and this time Will was shot and fatally wounded. They were both taken to the Ship Inn at Orford, where Margaret was arrested and this time around she really was deported to Australia.

On her arrival in Sydney she was assigned to the service of John Palmer, who had been purser on one of the first transport ships. Ever resourceful and seemingly loved and respected wherever she went, she worked as a midwife and when she was pardoned in 1814 settled happily into Australian life running a small farm and nursing wherever she was needed. She died just five years later and, despite her lack of education, is regarded as one of the best convict-chroniclers of the time.

The above story has been gleaned from the book by the Revd Richard Cobbold, *The History of Margaret Catchpole*, which was published in 1847. There are no doubt a few embellishments, but it certainly was a truly remarkable life.

Chapter 8
THE NAVIGATORS

Why was it the European navigators who first explored the world and not the Chinese or Arabs?

The Chinese built huge sailing ships. Their junks were highly seaworthy and even then were constructed with watertight compartments long before anyone else thought of the idea. They also had good accommodation for the crew, another first. They already had invented the magnetic compass and were skilled at celestial navigation, so why did they not set out to explore the world?

The answer lies partly in the sheer size of their own country, and partly in their own self-belief. China was a vast country, rich in natural resources, which meant they saw little need for trade with the rest of the world. The Chinese also regarded themselves as the most civilised of all the nations and did not really see what anyone else could offer them; indeed they feared contamination of their culture by other civilisations, which led to the building of the Great Wall. When Admiral Zheng He returned from his three-year-long voyage covering quite a lot of the world (see p. 128), they even shut down all further sea exploration considering it to be rather pointless.

The Arabs were skilled seafarers as well and had adopted the use of the compass from the Chinese, but their geographical position on the land-bridge between East and West meant that all trade had to pass through their hands anyway, without them having to go anywhere. Why would they want to risk losing their lives and money by making expeditions into the unknown world? The extent of their commerce stretched all the way from Africa to the Spice Islands of the Far East, and the world's trade came to them.

The Europeans, however, came from a number of small individual nations all competing for commodities from the East. The Crusaders in the eleventh century had brought back spices and silks from the Arabs and once people had tasted nutmeg, cinnamon and pepper, their everyday winter diet of bread, salted fish and pickled vegetables must have seemed very dull indeed. These goods were expensive to buy as they came via the Levant and the Arabian middle-men all took their cut. Each of the trading posts along the Silk Road had its merchants making a profit and by the time goods had reached Europe the prices were very high.

The prospect of trading directly with the East, cutting out the Arabs, was the incentive for the opening up of sea-routes, and it inspired monarchs and adventurers to explore beyond their known world. Europe needed alum for dyeing cloth, and gums and resins for making varnish, inks and glues; ivory and silk were highly valued luxury goods, as well as the coveted spices.

The Portuguese Prince Henry the Navigator was an early sponsor of exploration and, although he spent very little time at sea himself, his School of Navigation at Sagres near Cape St Vincent trained many men for the sea. The compass rose laid out in flints on the ground is still there to be seen, and a rather splendid bronze statue of him looks out to sea from Lagos harbour, a reminder of the days when the world was still a vast unexplored place.

Who were these European navigators?

The drive to establish sea trading routes with Asia became particularly acute after the fall of Constantinople to the Turks in 1453. Up until this point the Silk Road between the East and West was protected by the hegemony of the Mongolian Empire – the *pax mongolica* – but, with the Turks in control of the gateway into Europe, trade with Asia for silks and the so-valued spices of pepper and cinnamon became difficult.

The Portuguese navigator Bartolomeu Dias (see p. 129) was the first to sail east in search of Asia in 1487, but he was forced to turn back after reaching the east coast of Africa.

The Genoese sailor Christopher Columbus was sponsored by the Spanish King Ferdinand in 1492 to find a route to the Indies, as South and Southeast Asia were then called, by going west, but as we all know he found South America instead and that is a whole story of its own.

Vasco da Gama (see p. 129), another Portuguese, came next in 1497 following the eastern route taken by Dias but going on further this time, as far as the west coast of India, and this voyage was to give Portugal the monopoly over the spice routes for the best part of a hundred years.

Ferdinand Magellan (see p. 131), yet another Portuguese, was next in the line-up, sponsored by Spain in 1519 to find the route to the west that Columbus had first set out to discover. Magellan found a way into the Pacific Ocean round the tip of South America and on to the Indies, and his expedition finally completed the world's first circumnavigation.

Drake's circumnavigation is also claimed to be the first, as Magellan died on his voyage and it was Magellan's expedition, not the man himself, who actually completed the journey.

But the very first recorded navigator was far earlier than any of these. He was a Greek living in Marseille around the time of Alexander the Great.

PYTHEAS THE GREEK (4TH CENTURY BC)

Pytheas was a Greek merchant who lived in the Greek colonial trading post of Massalia, as Marseille was known then, in around 330 BC. Little is known about Pytheas, and his writings have long been lost, but he lives on in the accounts of his voyage around Britain and into the North Sea, through the manuscripts of later Greeks such as Pliny.

Pytheas was a man of the sea. He was skilled in astronomy and navigation, and became famous for his exploration of the sea and lands to the west of the Mediterranean. His quest for adventure was to take him beyond the limits of the known world to 'discover' Britain, the northeast coast of Europe and the mysterious land of Thule. The account he wrote of his exploration was called 'On the Ocean' and was considered to be so extraordinary at the time that many of his contemporaries simply did not believe it was possible.

Marco Polo was also disbelieved when he gave his account of his travels, although these were written many years after he completed his journeys and may well have been highly embellished

What makes a man an explorer? What spirits bewitch him until he can no longer stay on the shore but has to risk his life journeying over uncharted oceans? Is it the call of the unknown that bids him to test the limits of his courage and endurance? Is the invitation to dance with danger too much to resist? Or is it just a burning curiosity that, in his youth, he refuses to recognise any potential for disaster?

One can imagine the young Pytheas bored with his comfortable shore-life as a merchant, looking out to sea and longing for the feel once more of a boat under his feet, the wind in his face and the magical pull of the sail driving his little ship forward into unknown waters. The sea has always enchanted sailors and the very language that is used to describe this longing is that of seduction: a ship is referred to as female, and the spirits of the sea are the sirens, the water-witches, the mermaids.

Pytheas probably set out on one of the typical trading ships of the time, the *holkos*, a capacious, round-hulled, flat-bottomed cargo ship with a square sail. His voyage took him through the Straits of Gibraltar (the Pillars of Hercules as they were called then) and out into the Atlantic, where he sailed north along the coast of Spain and France, landing in Brittany before sailing on down the English Channel to Cornwall, where he noted the extent of the tin-mining and its export to France where it was smelted with copper to make bronze, the strongest known metal before the knowledge of how to use iron.

Making many observations on the geography, natural history and anthropology of the places he visited, Pytheas continued from Cornwall up the west coast to the Isle of Man, sailing on through the Hebrides until turning right to sail along the north coast of Scotland and into the North Sea from where he reached the land of Thule where the sun never set (it was probably Iceland) and saw a sea full of ice. From there he headed south down to the coast of Kent and, still hungry for more, he ventured up the coast of Northern Europe and may even have reached the Baltic Sea, travelling as far as Poland before finally turning for home.

The loss of his work 'On the Ocean' is the loss of a significant piece of writing from a man of intense intellectual curiosity, an acute observer of the peoples of the coasts he explored, and a true man of science as we would call him today.

THE CHINESE ADMIRAL ZHENG HE (1371–1433)

Did the Chinese really sail round the world in 1421?

In 2002 a book was published claiming that in the year 1421 the Chinese admiral Zheng He commanded a large fleet of sailing junks which sailed round the world. It is full of fascinating detail such as the use of captive otters to drive fish into fishing nets to feed the crew, and the use of sprouting beans to prevent scurvy. Evidence is produced of wrecked Chinese ships off the coasts of both Australia and California, and it is a rollicking good read.

However, a meeting with Frances Wood, once Curator of Chinese History at the British Library, was to bring disappointment, and apparently most scholars dispute the author's spinning of pieces of archaeological evidence into a story which has little basis in fact. All the same, it is a very good story, and now there is another book claiming that the Chinese sailed into Italy in 1434, thereby triggering the Italian Renaissance…

BARTOLOMEU DIAS (*c.* 1450–1500)

A knight at the royal court of the Portuguese King John II, Bartolomeu Dias was commissioned by the king to find a trade route to India by sea. He was also charged to find the land of the legendary Prester John. His two caravels, the *São Cristóvão* and the *São Pantaleão*, accompanied by a support ship captained by his brother Pêro, set out in 1487. Their voyage took them around the southern tip of Africa and up the east coast, where they landed at Mossel Bay. Experiencing some hostility from the native people and running low on food, his crew threatened to mutiny if they continued on towards India, so Dias reluctantly agreed to turn for home. Naming the Cape of Good Hope on the way back, they returned after a total of sixteen months away at sea. The opening up of the passage to India was to be left for another explorer – Vasco da Gama – some ten years later.

> *Prester John was the priest-king of a Christian nation somewhere in Africa, possibly of the Nestorian sect. The origin of the legend remains cloaked in mystery but has fired the imagination of many since the twelfth century.*

VASCO DA GAMA (*c.* 1460–1524)

Born in the Portuguese city port of Sines in around 1460 to a noble family, the young Vasco da Gama followed in his father's footsteps by becoming a knight in the Order of Santiago. He was chosen by the Portuguese king to lead another expedition to carry on from where Bartolomeu Dias had turned back. The quest, as ever, was to bring back spices from the East.

Da Gama left Portugal in 1497 with a small fleet of four ships consisting of two carracks of 180 tons each, the *São Gabriel* captained by Vasco da Gama himself and the *São Rafael* captained by his brother Paulo, another smaller caravel, the *Berrio*, and lastly a small provision ship which carried their supplies. Of the four vessels which set out, only two were to return.

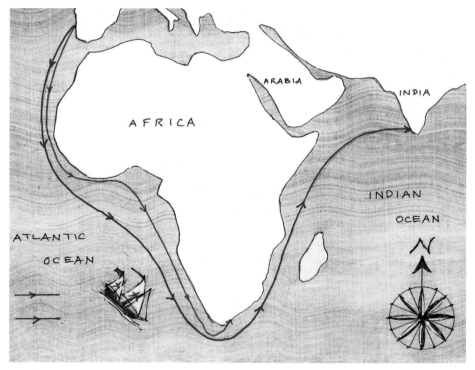

Map showing the voyages of Bartolomeu Dias and Vasco da Gama

The little fleet followed the route Dias had taken to the Cape and then turned up the east coast of Africa, naming the part of the coast they passed on Christmas Day 'Natal'. They arrived on the Malabar coast of west India (modern-day Kerala) in 1498.

Their return journey was fraught with troubles. Setting off in the stormy season against local advice they had to wrestle with monsoons, and the journey across the Indian Ocean which had earlier only taken twenty-three days, this time took a gruelling one hundred and thirty-two.

Paulo fell gravely ill during the passage and, consumed with worry for his ailing brother, Vasco stopped at Santiago Island, sending his remaining two ships on ahead. The two men eventually took passage on a caravel home but Paulo died while still at sea. The grief-stricken Vasco buried him in the

Azores before returning home to a hero's welcome. His exploration gave Portugal a monopoly over the spice routes which went unchallenged for the next hundred years.

The first spices to be brought to Europe were pepper and cinnamon, and they commanded fantastic prices

There is a crater on the moon named after Vasco da Gama

FERDINAND MAGELLAN (*c.* 1480–1521)

The first circumnavigator

Ferdinand Magellan, yet another Portuguese, was orphaned by the age of ten, but being of noble birth he was brought up at the royal court as a page, where he studied cartography, astronomy and celestial navigation. After many voyages as a young man sponsored by the Portuguese king, he fell out of favour at court so went to Spain where Charles I, shortly to become Charles V Holy Roman Emperor, asked him to try to find an alternative route to the Spice Islands. Portugal had held the monopoly over the trade route to the east ever since Vasco da Gama had led his expedition there in 1497, and it rankled with the Spanish who longed to get in on the act.

The thirty-nine-year-old Ferdinand must have been thrilled by the idea of using the skills he had developed as a navigator since he was a child, and proposed travelling west this time to see if he could find a way round the tip of South America, thus reaching southeast Asia from the opposite direction to his Portuguese rivals. Leaving Spain in the August of 1519 with a fleet of five ships, commanding the 110-ton *Trinidad* as his flagship, Magellan set off on what was to become a voyage of epic proportions. The journey was fraught with troubles which would ultimately end in his death, but not before he had achieved his aim of finding a passage through to the Pacific Ocean – the Strait of Magellan. He named the Pacific ('the peaceful sea'), as it must have seemed so calm after leaving the fearsome gales of the South Atlantic behind.

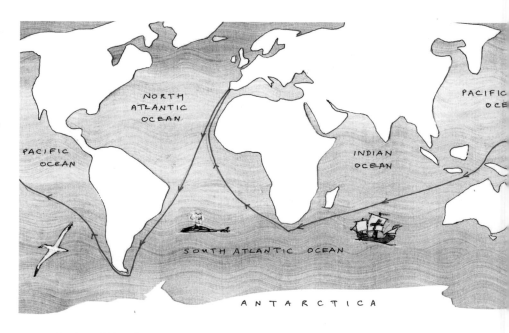

Ferdinand Magellan's voyage

➤ *The Strait of Magellan is approximately three hundred and seventy-three miles long*

On reaching the Philippines, the crew initially struck up good relations with the native people but it soon all began to fall apart and Magellan was killed in a skirmish ashore. By this time the fleet had been reduced to just two ships – the *Trinidad* and the *Victoria*. Continuing on to the Spice Islands without their leader, the ships returned to Spain via the Indian Ocean, managing to lose the *Trinidad* on the way. Juan Sebastián Elcano was the officer in command when they completed their voyage on 6th September 1522, three years after setting out, finally sailing back into harbour with only eighteen men left.

Magellan has two craters on the moon, and one on Mars, named after him

FRANCIS DRAKE (1540–1596)

Piracy and treasure on the Spanish Main

Born in Tavistock, Devon, in 1540, Francis Drake first went to sea at the age of twelve and rose to become the most celebrated sea commander and explorer in the realm, hated by the Spanish and loved by the English. A battle against the Spanish enemy early in his career, in which many of his shipmates were killed, led him to dedicate the rest of his life to taking revenge on the Spaniards.

Armed with *Letters of Marque* from the Queen which licensed him as a privateer, he headed straight for the Spanish colonies in South America and famously attacked the Silver Train, a mule-train carrying many tons of silver and gold. His raiding party took twenty tons of it, but unable to carry it all they buried part of the plunder and took what they could with them on the eighteen-mile trek back through the jungle to where they had left their raiding boats. But when the exhausted men reached the shore they found that their boats had gone. Rallying his by now dispirited crew, Drake got them to build a raft, and burying the rest of the loot on the beach, took one man with him to sail up the coast to where his flagship lay, returning later to pick up the rest of his men and the buried treasure.

The Isthmus of Panama was known in those days as the Spanish Main

Well known at the court by now, he led an expedition to circumnavigate the globe in 1577, commanding his ship, the *Pelican*, along with several supporting ships, all of which he lost for various reasons by the time he reached Tierra del Fuego. There is no evidence to support the claim that he either found Drake's Passage or rounded Cape Horn, but, travelling through the Strait of Magellan instead, he continued up the Chilean coast attacking

Spanish ships whenever the opportunity arose. By now he had renamed his ship the *Golden Hinde* and, sailing across the Pacific Ocean, reached the Molucca Islands where he befriended the Sultan-King and joined him for a while in his intrigues against the Portuguese. Returning home via the Cape of Good Hope he sailed into Plymouth on 26th September 1580, hailed as a hero and the first Englishman to have completed a circumnavigation.

Knighted by the Queen, he was Vice-Admiral in command of the English fleet which defeated the Spanish Armada in 1588.

> *As he was dying of dysentery off the coast of Panama in 1596, Sir Francis Drake asked to be dressed in his armour. He was buried at sea in a lead-lined coffin and divers are still searching there, hoping some day to find it.*

WALTER RALEIGH (1552–1618)

Tobacco and the fabled land of El Dorado

Contemporary with Francis Drake and cousin to Richard Grenville, Walter Raleigh was a soldier, spy and poet in favour at the court of Elizabeth I and a key figure in the colonisation of North America. The story of him laying his cloak over a puddle of water to prevent the queen from getting her feet wet is sadly a fabrication, probably made up by Thomas Fuller, the seventeenth-century historian well-known now for his colourful embellishment of any facts, but Raleigh is today remembered mostly for introducing us all to tobacco.

He was put in the Tower in 1603 by Elizabeth's successor James I for his alleged part in a plot to depose him, but James released him in 1616 on the condition that he would lead an expedition in search of El Dorado, the fabled City of Gold, believed to be somewhere near the mouth of the Orinoco River. Some years earlier Raleigh had published a fictitious account of the legendary city, thereby fuelling rumours of its existence. It was to do him no good in the end, though, as unable to resist attacking a Spanish settlement on the way out, he was executed on his return in order to appease the Spanish king.

JAMES COOK (1728–1779)

Son of a farm labourer who rose to become a farm manager, the young James Cook after leaving school was taken under the wing of a ship-owning Quaker family living in the coastal port of Whitby on the East Yorkshire coast. Serving a three-year apprenticeship in the Merchant Navy, he learnt his trade working the collier brigs up and down the coast. Passionate about the sea, he joined the Royal Navy to speed up his career and was to become renowned for his skills in navigation and chart-making.

In 1768, Cook was sponsored by the Royal Society as part of the quest to find a means of determining longitude by observing and recording the transit of the sun across Venus. He chose the collier barque *Endeavour* as his flagship. Such ships he knew well and trusted from his early days in the Merchant Navy, and this one underwent a refit in the Royal Naval Dockyard at Deptford to prepare her for the long expedition ahead.

Cook was to be accompanied on the voyage by two scientists – Joseph Banks, a young naturalist who would go on to found the Royal Botanic Gardens at Kew, and the Swedish botanist Daniel Solander who had studied under Carl Linnaeus at Uppsala University and had come to Britain to promote Linnaeus's system of classification. The pair were there to collect, record and draw the specimens of plants, birds and animals found on the expedition.

Cook's second mission was to look for an Australasian continent which had long been surmised to lie somewhere in the Pacific Ocean. Instead, he found and circumnavigated New Zealand and then charted what was later found to be the southeast coast of Australia before returning home.

His next voyage, in the ship *HMS Resolution*, accompanied by a second collier *HMS Adventure*, was another attempt to locate the Australian continent but this time the problem of longitude had been largely solved by the clockmaker John Harrison, and Cook took with him an improved pocket version of Harrison's timepiece, the Kendall K1 chronometer. Still not circumnavigating the Australian continent, however, Cook explored Antarctica and the South Atlantic, landing in South Georgia and sailing around the notorious Cape Horn before once more returning home.

Now a Post-captain and Fellow of the Royal Society, his last voyage was to be a fatal one for him. Departing once more in the *Resolution* and this time accompanied by the *Discovery*, he was now charged with finding a northwest passage into the Atlantic through the Arctic. He surveyed the west coast of North America as far as the Bering Strait, which he reached in 1778, and then returned to the Pacific, sailing into the Hawaiian Islands early in 1779, where he was to meet his untimely death in a skirmish on the shore.

Many a book has been written about the life of this man of extraordinary abilities and of the enigma of his later years at sea before his sudden death.

> *The story of the race to discover a means of determining longitude at sea is a fascinating story in its own right*

Chapter 9
HARWICH AND MISTLEY

EARLY HARWICH

Lying at the mouth of the Orwell Estuary, the old town of Harwich appears forgotten when I arrive one Monday morning in June: there are no carparks, parking meters or even parking restrictions, as no-one seems to come here any more. The narrow streets and Tudor buildings stand unnoticed, and the streets are deserted. Like so many of these coastal towns, Harwich seems to be lying dormant. The Halfpenny Pier attracts a few visitors at the weekend, but there is plenty to see for those who trouble to discover its once important maritime past.

There was a time when the town was thronging with mariners from all parts of Europe and the dockyards were building ships, though now the shipwrights and carpenters, blacksmiths and sail-makers, merchants and tradesmen are all barely a memory. Harwich has always had a good deep harbour, but its position, effectively on the end of a promontory with no network of rivers and roads behind, made it inevitable that in time it would be superseded as the major port on the estuary by Ipswich, which had the advantage of good inland connections – an essential element of a successful trading port.

Harwich first comes to attention under the rule of the Norman baron, Roger Bigod, the fourth Earl of Norfolk, who owned the nearby Manors of Trimley, Walton and Dovercourt as well as land at Harwich. Assuming control over the harbour, he forced ships to put into the port where he could extract tolls from them on their way up to Ipswich. His successors were to license the building of fish traps in the harbour, which caused so much danger to shipping that pilots were needed to guide incoming ships up the river.

The Andrews Shoal is named after the owners of the fishing weir which was once there

The size of a port can be guessed at by looking at the records which were kept of the number of local boats it could supply to the king in times of war, and in 1294 Harwich and the neighbouring town of Bawdsey supplied Edward III with eleven ships between them. Before the days of the Royal Navy, the king would commandeer local boats for a sort of pop-up navy. The fishing boats would be converted to temporary warships by the addition of a castle at each end to house the marines, and this is the origin of the term *fo'csle*, a contraction of the word 'forecastle', given to the accommodation at the front end of a ship. It was not until Henry VIII founded a dedicated Royal Navy in response to the threat of invasion from across the North Sea that this practice was no longer necessary.

Harwich was granted its first charter in 1318, which gave it the right to hold its own courts and manage its own affairs. This was a time of great rivalry between the fishermen of Harwich and those from Great Yarmouth over the rich pickings which were to be made by fishing herring off the east coast. The breeding ground for the herring was just offshore from Yarmouth, which always regarded it as rightfully theirs.

When Edward III fought the French at the Battle of Sluys in 1340, he assembled his fleet of some two hundred ships off Harwich, with the king himself aboard the cog *Thomas*.

As the town gradually grew in size, by the end of the fifteenth century there were no fewer than eight quays on the waterfront along with numerous warehouses. When Henry VIII visited Harwich in 1543, he recognised its value in the defence against attackers, and gave the town £400 to make improvements to the harbour.

Harwich continued to flourish, as did neighbouring ports, on the export of wool and cloth to Calais and Antwerp, and the import of wines and other goods from Gascony. The town grew steadily on its income from the taxes extracted on herring, wheat, rye and salt, and from the *groundage* charged for a ship to lie in the harbour as well as for the dredging of shingle for ballast.

The yards built, repaired and victualled ships, and Harwich took its share of income from the lucrative trade of carrying pilgrims to the important shrines of Walsingham in Norfolk and Santiago de Compostela in northern Spain. Tin, pewter and lead, saffron, coal and firewood were all being exported from the town, and a great many curing houses were busy salting and smoking herring. Harwich was on a roll.

But the massive push for ship-building under Henry VIII had depleted the Suffolk oak forests to the extent that timber became in short supply and, now that the Royal Naval Dockyards were dedicated to building warships, Harwich turned its sights more to the business of trade. The port records of the seventeenth century show that brandy, soap, linen, silk, thread, tobacco and sugar were all coming in through Harwich, giving a true reflection of the opening up of trade routes by the early navigators.

It took three thousand oak trees to build one man o' war

PASSENGER SERVICES

Two *hoys* of forty and sixty tons respectively carried passengers and mail between Harwich and Brielle, and a regular *packet boat* service to mainland Europe began in 1661 just after the restoration of Charles to the throne. The first requirement of a packet boat was speed, both for convenience and for safety to escape capture by the many pirates who ranged the seas between England and Holland.

Passengers would come from London to lodge in the town while awaiting suitable weather for their departure; the passage could take up to two days if there was not much wind.

As the buoyage of the Thames Estuary improved under the direction of Trinity House, ships began to use the Thames rather than expose themselves to the dangers of the sandbanks off the east coast and the port became less busy. Harwich, however, continued to supply London with *copperas*, which was obtained from stones dredged up by fishing smacks offshore.

COPPERAS EXTRACTION

Copperas is the name given to the chemical ferrous sulphate which was extracted from the copperas stones found off the Thames Estuary. Along with the sulphuric acid which was a by-product of its extraction, copperas once played a vital role in the dyeing of cloth and leather and in the manufacture of gunpowder.

If you pick up a copperas stone in the morning, wet it and put it in your pocket, by lunchtime it will have burned a hole right through the fabric. This is because it is made of *iron pyrites* (ferrous disulphide), a chemical which becomes unstable when wet, turning spontaneously into a mixture of hydrated ferrous sulphate and sulphuric acid – hence the hole in your pocket.

Factories for processing copperas stones were built all along the Kent and Essex coasts as early as the sixteenth century, and demonstrate an unexpectedly early knowledge of chemistry. Tanks were placed on the shore, filled with copperas stones and left to be washed over by the tides for up to four years. The resulting liquor that built up in these tanks was the mixture of sulphuric acid and hydrated ferrous sulphate which we last met in your pocket. This chemical soup was channelled into a large cistern, where it was boiled with some scrap iron for three weeks, which had the effect of turning it into ferrous sulphate, or copperas. It was then left to crystallise before being packed into barrels for sale to the textile industry. Such a lengthy and hazardous process made it a costly material to produce and it commanded a very high price.

The Fisons agricultural chemical plant at Ipswich is built on the old copperas works

Samuel Pepys became MP for Harwich in 1679, and again in 1685

GEORGIAN HARWICH

The early eighteenth century was a time of great prosperity and many fine new houses were built in Church Street and West Street, while some of the older buildings were given brick façades. This prosperity was due to a combination of the revival of cod fishing after the end of the Dutch wars, the thriving packet boat service to Holland, and the increased demand for the building of the smaller warships required for the war with France as well as victualling and repairing the Naval Fleet.

Daniel Defoe, on his visit to Harwich, recorded four to five hundred ships lying in the harbour, including one hundred men o' war

COD FISHING

By the mid-eighteenth century a co-operative system had developed whereby tradesmen, ship-builders and fitters all took a sixteenth share in a boat, with the fishermen taking the remainder. Each boat had to carry eight hundredweight of whelks and mussels for bait and, as there were by now several hundred boats operating from the port, a large number of them made a living by dredging for shellfish.

The cod boats fished mainly in the North Sea off the Dogger Bank but also travelled north as far as Orkney, and Iceland, where they caught the fish by *long-lining*. A line four to five hundred yards long, bearing a shorter vertical hooked line every six feet, was set out from the smack, the vertical lines having to be long enough to reach the sea-bed as cod are bottom-feeders. The fish were kept alive in a deep central well built into the ship until returning to port, whereupon they were killed with a club called a *codbanger*.

RECREATIONAL SAILING

The nineteenth century saw many changes, one of which was the rise of the gentleman sailor. The Royal Harwich Yacht Club, its flag the 'defaced' blue ensign, was one of the earliest yacht clubs. Formed in 1843, its first patron was Queen Adelaide, followed by Queen Victoria and then Prince Albert.

>*The annual Harwich Regatta saw the great J-Class yachts Endeavour, Britannia and Velsheda racing off the coast. The club has moved now to the quieter waters of Woolverstone just up the river from Pin Mill.*

The invention of the steam engine at this time was to transform shipping but the Harwich Packet Captains, taking pride in their fast sailing boats, were reluctant to install engines and in 1832 the Packet Service transferred to Tilbury, which also had the benefit of a railway by now. The long uncertain hours of waiting for suitable weather for a journey to Holland were over.

The cod fishing was declining, too, and the fortunes of the town now turned to the unlikely industry of harvesting *septaria nodules* for the manufacture of cement.

SEPTARIA STONES AND ROMAN CEMENT

Septaria nodules are found in the old London Clay which dates from the Eocene period, and their formation still remains a mystery to this day. Trapped in the ancient clay, some of the nodules dried out, forming internal cracks which then filled with calcite crystals. When these nodules are broken open, they reveal a beautiful pattern of crystal-lined cracks and these were popular in gemstone and fossil shops. But nodules in other layers of clay are free from such cracks, and these were the ones that were used as building materials for Colchester Castle and many of the churches along the east coast. They could also be used for manufacturing cement.

Septaria stones were taken from Beacon Cliff and West Rock and also dredged from the shore at Cobbold Point at Felixstowe. The stones were first fired in a kiln and then milled to a powder before being exported, mainly to London. Approximately fifty boats were engaged in this activity, which was based at Pin Mill, a little further up the estuary from Harwich. When water was added to this powder, it made a cement which set very quickly and could be used, as the Romans employed it, under water for sealing pipes and conduits. A four hundredweight barrel sold in London for seven and sixpence, and in 1835 there were five factories producing it in Harwich, but by 1890 it was having to make way for the new, cheaper Portland cement.

The removal of large quantities of septaria stone from the cliffs, and also from the natural stone barrier ridge on the seabed, caused considerable land erosion, which widened the estuary and consequently reduced the scouring effect of the tides. This in turn led to the build-up of silt and shingle in the harbour, until in 1843 the removal of all stone was forbidden, the harbour was dredged and the building of an eight-hundred-yard-long breakwater commenced.

Cement is made from a mixture of calcium carbonate (chalk or limestone being the commonest source) and any rock containing silica and oxygen (with clay being the commonest source). These two materials are ground up and mixed together. Adding water to this mixture would produce nothing other than a sludgy paste, but if it is heated up to a temperature of 1450 degrees Celsius, the bonds between the atoms break up and they form *calcium silicate*. When this cement powder is mixed with water, the calcium and silicate molecules dissolve and produce thread-like crystals called *calcium silicate fibrils*. These 'threads' form a skeleton-like mesh which traps the individual water molecules, locking them up until the sludgy gel finally becomes a solid rock. The fibrils bond to each other and to other rocks, making it a sort of glue for bonding bricks or stones together. The addition of small stones to the mixture makes it into *concrete*.

The Romans first discovered cement and used it extensively, but because they did not know how to reinforce it with internal steel rods, as we do now, they were not able to use it for supporting structures such as beams. They had struck lucky in their discovery, as they used a naturally occurring form of powdered silicate rock which had already been forced up to well above the necessary temperature by volcanic activity. This was a stone called *pozzuoli*, which had the added bonus of already being reduced to ash so there was no need even to grind it first. All they had to do was work out the addition of lime and, hey presto, they had their building material.

➤ *The dome of the Pantheon in Rome, one of the largest domes ever to have been built, is made of cement, but as it is under compression it does not have to bear any weight*

Reinforced concrete was invented in 1867 by a Parisian gardener, Joseph Monier, who needed to make large pots for his plants. Finding that once over a certain size concrete pots were simply not strong enough, he tried inserting some steel rods he had ly-ing around for added strength. Luckily steel and concrete both expand at the same rate so there were no problems with the concrete breaking up with changes of temperature, and he had stumbled across the most versatile building method ever to have been invented.

One of the problems with reinforced concrete is that cracks even-tually open up in it which let in air and water with the consequent rusting of the steel. An ingenious solution to this has recently been discovered, which involves the addition of a particular bac-terium that secretes calcium silicate. Colonies of these bacteria are mixed with starch powder and incorporated into the con-crete. As soon as any water seeps in, the dormant bacteria, using the starch for food, begin to replicate, producing their calcium silicate in the process, which in turn fills up the crack. This 'self-healing system' is now being developed for use in engineering.

THE MAYFLOWER PROJECT

Following a sign to the Mayflower Project brought me to the old railway yard on George Street. At first the site appeared to be empty apart from two Portacabins and a huge pile of unsawn oak at the far end, piled up as if a giant game of spillikins was about to begin. Arching up against the sky was the stark outline of a ship's frame, the midsection shape of the yet-to-be born new *Mayflower*. This ambitious project was first conceived in 2009 – to build a replica of the famous ship which sailed to America cap-tained by her owner and master, Harwich man Christopher Jones. The ship is due to be

The sign for the *Mayflower*

Timber ready for use

completed in time to reenact the voyage for the four hundredth anniversary of her sailing to the New World, in 2020.

Knocking on the door I received a warm welcome from Sean, the project manager, who soon supplied me with a hi-vis jacket and a chair so I could sit outside and sketch. There is a lofting floor above the office where the timbers are drawn out accurately according to the naval architect's plans. All the curves and angles needed for the different shapes will be found amongst

Christopher Jones's House

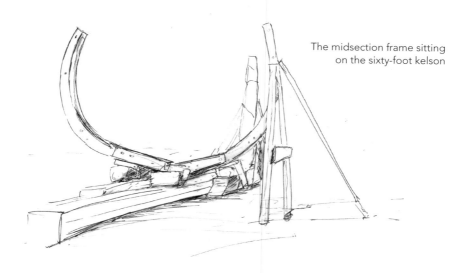

The midsection frame sitting
on the sixty-foot kelson

the carefully labelled unsawn oak lying in the yard. In the old days of ship-building it was customary to use 'grown oak' rather than cutting a piece to shape, and the ship's carpenter would carefully select which trees to fell, sometimes using ropes to adjust the angle at which a bough was growing for future use.

The Project is giving young people basic skills, no-one is turned away, and they have trained hundreds of local youngsters to different levels of skills. The old railway station building is now a college giving apprenticeships in marine engineering and carpentry, construction and business manage-ment. The practical skills learnt through the Project will be used to help begin the regeneration of the old part of Harwich, restoring buildings and promoting tourism.

Looking at the sixty-foot-long kelson, the one midsection frame and the mighty stem post, it all at first seemed hopelessly unrealistic, but Harwich goes on surprising the curious and I signed up as a friend of the scheme and left with an unexpected feeling of optimism.

THE VOYAGE OF THE *MAYFLOWER*

The background

After the death of Elizabeth I in 1603, religion continued to be contentious for those who did not conform to the approved faith. Elizabeth's successor, James I, had been brought up as a Calvinist, but he acknowledged the authority of the bishops and tried to bring them together with the Puritans at a meeting held at Hampton Court in 1604; his show of tolerance, however, did not extend as far as the Catholics, who were not invited to the party. The conference confirmed the entrenchment of the Established Church in civil life and the ordering of a new translation of the Bible, but did not bring about the reconciliation of the Puritans with the Church of England, and after the Catholic Guy Fawkes attempted to blow up the Houses of Parliament a year later, James proceeded to persecute both radical Puritans and Catholics with equal enthusiasm.

This all led to a large-scale emigration of Puritans to the New World and, by 1620, when the *Mayflower* set out on her voyage across the Atlantic, it is estimated that some eighty thousand Britons had already made the journey to America.

Many ships had made this crossing, but the *Mayflower* is remembered particularly for the signing on board of the *Mayflower Compact* – a document which established a basic form of democracy, requiring a pledge from each member of the community to contribute to the welfare of all.

The ship

The *Mayflower* was a merchant ship sailed by her master and owner, Christopher Jones. Built in his home town of Harwich, she is thought to have been about a hundred feet long and twenty-five feet wide. Built as a merchant ship for carrying cargo, she would have sported three masts and a castle at each end for defence against pirates. By the time she set sail with the emigrants destined for the New World, she was already forty years old in a world where most ships had a working life of only around fifteen. The hundred or so passengers slept, all crowded together, on the gun deck, with their belongings and provisions for the voyage stashed in the cargo hold below. Captain Jones's ship had been chartered for the pilgrim voyage by Thomas Weston, a member of the Company of Merchant Adventurers, although he did not accompany them on this particular passage.

The ship's master

Christopher Jones (1570–1622) spent most of his life in Harwich, where he first acquired the ship that was to become so famous. He was a *burgess* of the town, having some responsibility for the running of the town's affairs, but spent the last eleven years of his life in Rotherhithe on the Thames, where there was more work to be found. He was fifty years of age when his ship was chartered by the Merchant Adventurers to take passage to America. The voyage was long and it was too late in the year to expect favourable weather so when they finally arrived at Cape Cod it was bitterly cold, with snow lying on the ground and the passengers ill-equipped to cope after their long arduous voyage. It is a measure of the man that, although he had no obligation to help any further, he stayed on to help them find somewhere to settle. They had intended to join the colony at Virginia, but conditions on that coast in November were too treacherous to allow them to continue the voyage south, and they lived on board ship until March 21st 1621, during which time many, including some of the ship's crew, died from disease.

Christopher Jones finally set sail for the return passage on 5th April 1621, arriving at Rotherhithe a month later. He died the following year aged fifty-two and his ship disappears from all records two years after that.

The voyage

Around sixty-five passengers embarked at Rotherhithe on the Thames in July 1620. She sailed first to Plymouth to await the arrival of a Dutch ship, the *Speedwell*, which was carrying members of the Leiden church from Holland and had been chartered to sail in company with the *Mayflower*.

But the *Speedwell* proved to be an unseaworthy vessel and had to put into Dartmouth for repairs to her leaking hull, thus delaying their departure until early September. This month is notorious for the strong westerly gales which make the crossing of the Atlantic from east to west particularly hazardous for sailing ships, and when the *Speedwell* developed another leak two hundred miles off Land's End, she had to abandon the voyage altogether and return home, amongst rumours that her master had deliberately spiked the ship to avoid making the dangerous crossing. As the *Speedwell* went on to make many profitable voyages after this, maybe Captain Reynolds really had sabotaged the mission…

There is a plaque on a wall by the harbour at Newlyn in Cornwall which states that the *Mayflower* put in there for fresh water. It is thought that the water she took on board earlier, at Plymouth, may have been contaminated with cholera.

> *Newlyn has the Ordnance Survey benchmark, which marks the datum point for measuring height above sea level throughout the country. Benchmarks, marked on OS maps, are usually a horizontal line with an arrow beneath and can be found carved into walls everywhere. At Newlyn the benchmark is a brass bolt set into a wall.*

The *Mayflower* had a compass for navigation and a *log* with an hour glass for measuring speed. The log was a piece of wood shaped as a quarter of a circle, with a line attached to it which had knots tied at regular intervals. A sailor would drop the log over the stern and pay out the line over a measured period of time. The log, weighted with lead, would stay more or less in the same place as the line ran out, and by counting the number of knots over a set time, the speed of the vessel could be estimated. The knots were generally eight fathoms apart, a fathom being six feet, and with a standard of just over six thousand feet for a nautical mile, sand glasses were carried aboard which could measure fourteen-second and twenty-eight-second intervals, for ease of calculation of the ship's speed. The modern knot is standardised as one nautical mile per hour, a nautical mile being one degree of latitude, but the name 'knot' has been kept.

The *Mayflower* is unlikely to have travelled faster than six knots. She arrived at Cape Cod on 9th November, having had to undergo repairs to her gundeck main beam on the way. Two children were born while at sea, two passengers died during the long uncomfortable journey, and just two days after her arrival, on the 11th of November, the Mayflower Compact was signed on board.

There were twenty-six ships registered at that time with the name of 'the Mayflower'

THE MERCHANT ADVENTURERS OF LONDON

A guild of merchants trading in the export of broadcloth mostly to Northern Europe, the Merchant Adventurers of London were granted their first charter by Henry IV in 1407. By the time of their second charter under Henry VII in 1505 they had affiliated members in Ipswich, Norwich, Hull, York, Newcastle and Exeter. These affiliated members were required to pay tariffs to the Guild when trading overseas and, after much complaining, Henry VII reduced the fee for such transactions from twenty to just ten marks. The rat-race of mercantile competition is nothing new, and when the Merchants of the Staple tried to get in on the act of exporting cloth as well as their main trade of raw wool, they were heavily taxed by the Guild and squeezed out.

The Hanseatic League, having dominated trade in Northern Europe for the best part of four hundred years, were beginning to lose their ascendancy by the mid-sixteenth century, but there were many trade wars still to be fought over the Merchant Adventurers' use of the Hanseatic ports of Emden and Hamburg. The Crown then revoked the rights of the Hansa in England and, with the continuing Spanish Wars and the rise of the Dutch Golden Age, these trading cartels gradually became less powerful. The Merchant Adventurers, however, continued to exist right up to the early part of the nineteenth century and financed much of the exploration of the New World.

TRINITY HOUSE

In 1513 a guild of mariners from Deptford petitioned Henry VIII for a licence to control the pilots on the River Thames. There had been many incidents of poor pilotage resulting in the loss of ships in the Thames Estuary and the mariners' guild wanted to be able to control it.

The king granted the charter in 1514, giving the new body the snappy name of the Guild of the Most Glorious and Undivided Trinity and of St Clement in the Parish of Deptford Strond, St Clement being one of the patron saints of mariners. The first Master of the Guild was Thomas Spert, who was also the sailing master of Henry's two great ships, the *Mary Rose* and the *Henry Grace à Dieu*. Future Masters of the Guild were to include Samuel Pepys, William Pitt the Younger and the first Duke of Wellington.

In 1566 Elizabeth I passed the Seamarks Act to improve navigation by the building of beacons and other seamarks. Her Act enabled the Guild *'at their wills and pleasures, and at their costs, [to] make, erect and set up such and so many beacons, marks and signs for the sea ... whereby the dangers may be avoided and escaped, and ships the better come into their ports without peril'.*

Under this act it became an offence to remove any land-based structure that could be used as a navigation mark for the sea, such as a church tower or mill. The effect of the powers granted to the Guild was to greatly improve the safety of ships navigating the Thames Estuary up to London, and in time the North Sea coast and the English Channel were to come under their remit as well.

Some two hundred years after the granting of its charter, the Guild's brief was to be described as: *'to improve the art and science of mariners; to examine into the qualifications, and regulate the conduct of those who take upon them the charge of conducting ships; to preserve good order, and, when desired, to compose differences in marine affairs, and in general to consult the conservation, good estate, wholesome government, maintenance and increase of navigation and seafaring men; and to relieve decayed seamen and their relatives.'*

Still licensed under its royal charter, the Guild is now known by the less elaborate title of Trinity House, and it still controls navigation around the British Isles. It has three main functions. The first of these is to be responsible for the provision and maintenance of navigational aids such as lighthouses, buoys, lightships, and all maritime communication systems. Funding for the lighthouses comes from the *light dues* which are levied on all commercial ships calling at ports around Britain. The rate is set by the Department of Transport and is based on the tonnage of the vessel. The second function is to provide pilots for the ships trading in Northern European waters. Thirdly it is a maritime charity, and funds are granted for the welfare of retired seamen, the training of cadets and the promotion of safety at sea.

In 1609, petitioned by ship owners and seamen who were losing their ships on the sandbanks off the east coast, Trinity House built a lighthouse at Lowestoft. It was not a lighthouse as we know it now, rather a high and a low light – *leading light* – each placed on a separate wooden tower on the shore, one behind the other. When a ship out at sea sailed into the position where the two lights lined up, they knew they were at the entrance to the Stamford Channel, a navigable channel between Lowestoft and Winterton which is no longer there. The towers were lit with tallow candles. Up until the eighteenth century lighthouse lamps were fuelled with candles, wood, coal or whale oil; lenses did not come into use until 1823.

THE LIGHTHOUSE

The earliest form of lighthouse was a fire raised on a hilltop or platform used to help guide ships into harbour. The very first recorded lighthouse was in Piraeus harbour at Athens in the fifth century BC and it was basically a stone pillar with a fire on top.

The famous **Lighthouse of Alexandria**, one of the Seven Wonders of the Ancient World, was built by Ptolemy I, who had pronounced himself king in 323 BC when the death of Alexander the Great left the post vacant. The lighthouse which was to become so famous took twelve years to build and was constructed of interlocking blocks of limestone with all the joints sealed with molten lead.

The engineer and architect for the massive tower was Sostratus of Cnidus, although there are some that dispute this. There is a story that Sostratus had his own name incised into the stone underneath the bit of plaster which bore Ptolemy's name, so that if the plaster should ever fall off it would be the name of its architect which would last forever.

It is described fairly consistently in all the early writings as being a tapering tower of around three hundred and fifty feet in height, standing on a base roughly a hundred feet square. The lower third of the tower was square in section, the middle third octagonal, and the last third circular. For good measure the whole structure was topped off with a statue of Poseidon. A mirror was placed at the top to reflect sunlight during the day, and a fire was lit at night. The Pharos of Alexandria, as it was also known, stood proudly in the harbour for nearly twelve hundred years before partially collapsing in a huge earthquake in AD 956. Subsequent earthquakes went on to inflict more damage until the last remnant of the mighty structure finally disappeared into the sea in 1480.

The remains of the tower were discovered in 1968 but not investigated until a group of Greek archaeologists discovered them all over again, bringing some of the stones up from the floor of the eastern harbour in 1994.

The other Six Wonders of the Ancient World were: the Hanging Gardens of Babylon, the Great Pyramid at Giza, the Temple of Artemis at Ephesus, the Statue of Zeus at Olympia, the Mausoleum at Halicarnassus, and the Colossus of Rhodes

The oldest working lighthouse in Europe lies on the Hook Peninsula at the entrance to Waterford Harbour in Ireland. The Hook Peninsula is known in Irish Gaelic as *Rinn Dubhain*, after Saint Dubhain who brought Christianity to this part of Ireland in the fifth century, but the word *dubhain* got confused with *duan*, a fish hook, and so the peninsula came to be called Hook instead.

Standing over a hundred feet high, and a good forty feet wide, the lighthouse here was built of limestone blocks, early in the thirteenth century, and manned by monks from the nearby monastery. There are three vaulted rooms in the lower section connected by a stairway which has been built within the thick walls to the upper section in which the beacon fire was lit. Both the fire and the monks were replaced as time went on with a lantern and lighthouse keepers respectively. In 1911 a clockwork mechanism was installed, which fulfilled the double function of allowing the light to flash and keeping the duty lighthouse keeper entertained during his long shift as he was required to wind it up every twenty-five minutes. No sleeping during his watch... It is now all electric and run remotely by the Commissioners of Irish Lights.

The oldest lighthouse in Britain is the ruined Roman tower beside Dover Castle

MISTLEY

The road from Manningtree towards Harwich passes through a dozen or so small villages, giving the odd tantalising glimpse of water through the trees on the left. This is the River Stour, made famous through the paintings of John Constable. This part of the river, which flows into the Orwell Estuary, is delightfully secret from the road and is only really accessible to the land traveller at Manningtree, Mistley and the tiny hamlets of Ramsholt and Wrabness which lie about halfway down its southern shore.

When I stopped at Mistley on my way to Harwich, a freighter lay at the quay unloading barley for the malt extraction works over the road and there was a faint scent of malt on the air. I left the main road and dropped down to the waterside to find a range of tall empty warehouses standing with an air of dignified dereliction along a largely deserted quay, while pallets of breeze-blocks stacked alongside spoke of their fate as future luxury apartments. A pair of shelduck were waddling over the shore as the tide receded, and the bones of a wreck of a ship were sticking out from the mudflats on the other side of the water, black ribs against the soft grey mud – all that remains now of the Thames sailing barge, the *Bijou*, left to quietly return to the waters she once sailed over.

There is little clue for the casual visitor as to exactly what happened to reduce this extensive and clearly once important dockside to its present silent and deserted state. The tall brick chimney of the factory on the road above declaring 'Edme Malt Extraction Works' in white paint down its length, bears witness to the large economy that built up in East Anglia around the growing of barley for malting, after the decline of the wool industry.

Once a haven for weavers from the Low Countries escaping religious persecution in the sixteenth century, some of the cottages in Mistley date from this period. The Huguenots were to follow them a hundred years later, but the port did not come into its own until the

above right Mistley town sign;
left The chimney at the maltworks

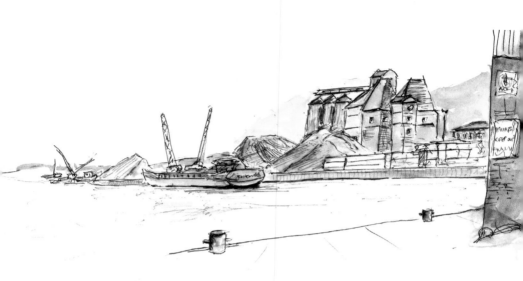

Mistley dockside

eighteenth century, with the building of the quay in 1720 and the development of a ship-building industry, largely constructing small warships for the Royal Navy.

The port then received a makeover in the 1770s from the wealthy and ambitious landowner Richard Rigby. Coming from a moneyed background, he had become Paymaster General for the Armed Forces and had a vision to use his wealth to turn Mistley into a fashionable spa. Employing Robert Adam as his architect, his idea was to build a seawater bathing pool and a new church and to expand the port into a centre for the malting business. Many of Mistley's buildings went up under Rigby's scheme, and the port thrived for a while trading in barley and malt and importing coal from Yorkshire. But Rigby fell from grace, losing his job in the Civil Service and a great deal of money with it. All was abandoned and the quayside, which had once been alive with ships loading and unloading their goods, fell into disuse, leaving the warehouses to the jackdaws, and the shore to the shelduck and redshanks.

The church, begun by Adam in 1776, was to an unusual design, with a tower at both the east and the west ends, and a semi-circular portico on each side. It was demolished before it was completed but the two towers were kept and the visitor is greeted by the incongruous sight of two Robert Adam towers standing in magnificent isolation on the green at the entrance to the town.

Another unusual aspect to Mistley is its resident flock of some two hundred and fifty mute swans which have been there since the seventeenth century. The flock is reputed to have built up its numbers by feeding on the barley blowing off the decks of the barges as they sailed up the river.

Looking equally out of place is a large stone pool with a fountain, by the High Street, complete with a stone swan for a water-spout. Painted white and pale blue, the Swan Fountain was also designed by Robert Adam, but now sits empty by the roadside, its flaking paint and gathering debris adding to Mistley's air of a ghost town.

A derelict shed

Chapter 10
THE SAILING SHIP

There are an extraordinary number of different names for sailing ships, some of which refer to their hull shape, such as the barge, and some referring to their sail plan. A lifetime of trying to fit together some kind of linear order in the development of the ship from medieval times finally came to an end for me one afternoon in the library at the National Maritime Museum when I realised that there is no direct line.

All round the coasts of Europe, since coastal dwellers first took to the water, men were building boats that were slowly evolving to suit the waters in which they had to sail. A boat working out of the deep harbours of the west coast of Britain would have a deep keel for stability but would not be able to get anywhere near the ports on East Anglia's coast with its shoals and shallow waters. This meant considerable variation in design from one part of the coast to another – except the boats then were not really designed at all. There were never any drawn plans and each shipwright would use his knowledge and skill to build, by eye, a boat appropriate for its purpose. The large number of different traditional sailing craft around Britain alone reflects the diversity of our coastal waters.

Consider the Mediterranean ships. In early medieval times it was difficult for ships to navigate west beyond the Gibraltar Straits. The strong currents and prevailing winds made sailing dangerous for the fairly primitive boats that they had then, and this meant that, with so little contact between them, boat-building methods developed quite separately in Northern and Southern Europe. But as ships became more seaworthy and able to travel longer distances, the two building traditions began to cross-fertilise.

MEDIEVAL SHIPS

How to tell your cog from your carrack

There are no fewer than sixty different names for the types of medieval ship found in the English records alone, but very few of them can now be identified. Some are recognisable only from descriptions in manuscripts with their accompanying illuminations, but with no archaeological evidence of their existence having ever been found. Port records noted the vessels entering and leaving a harbour, but local harbourmasters would often use a different name for the same type of ship, making it even more difficult to try to understand what anyone was talking about. But here is a small foray into the world of medieval ships.

Viking ships changed very little between the ninth and twelfth centuries. The familiar, elegant, double-ended ships with high stem and stern were used for transport and trading, as well as raiding foreign coasts, and were powered by a row of oars each side, assisted by a single square sail for use if the wind was favourable. Viking ships could be carried overland for short distances, which made them very useful for going up rivers, and they were able to penetrate deep into Russia. The larger warships had a higher freeboard for protection against the weather, and some even carried castles to give

opposite A faering; *above* A Viking ship

the advantage of some height for the warriors when attacking the enemy. The merchant ships, known as *knaars* or *keels*, also had a high freeboard for making a deep hull, which gave them a greater carrying capacity for cargo. The *faering* was a very small Viking craft, which bears no relation to the biscuit of the same name.

The small Shetland sixareen *is a very similar boat to the* faering

The **cog** was a Northern European vessel of the eleventh to the fourteenth centuries and is usually associated with the merchants of the Hanseatic League, but it could be armed for warfare as well. This ship was also clinker-built (see p. 103) and pointed at each end, but much deeper in the hull than the Viking ships. It had a flat bottom with a sharp angle of almost fifty degrees between the bottom and the sides, and two raked, straight end-posts. The early cogs were steered with an oar before the stern-mounted rudder was adopted.

above left An early cog; *above right* A later cog, with a stern rudder; *below* A hulc

🐟 *A number of cogs have been found and replicas made, but a British cog has yet to be discovered*

The **hulc** is a ship often referred to and illustrated in manuscripts, but one has never actually been found and there is some doubt over whether they were a separate form of ship at all. Illuminations show the hulc to be clinker-built, with a steering oar, and distinguished from the cog by its lack of a stem or sternpost. It could be rowed as well as sailed, which would have made it more manoeuvrable than the cog, which relied entirely on its sail, but the lack of both stem and sternposts would have made the hulc structurally rather unsound and could explain why none so far have survived.

left A carrack;
below A caravel

The Southern European **carrack** then began to influence shipwrights in the north, who adapted the cog over a number of years until it became a hybrid of both northern and southern ship-building traditions. The carrack was built with the planks flush to each other, a move away from its clinker-built predecessors, in a technique called *carvel* building, with the planks nailed to closely spaced internal frames. It had a straight sternpost which was raked backwards, a curved stem and a heavy keel. The vessel was now strong enough to carry more than one mast with the one at the back, *the mizzen*, carrying either a square or a lateen sail, and this rig enabled the ship to sail more into the wind than its single square-sailed predecessors which could only really sail when the wind was behind them. Strong, seaworthy and manoeuvrable, the carrack probably represents one of the most significant shifts in ship-building ever seen. One of the most well-known examples of a carrack must be the *Mary Rose*, which sank off Portsmouth in 1545.

Some historians use the terms 'carrack' and 'caravel' interchangeably, but many regard the Portuguese **caravel** as a bit of a racehorse by comparison. The caravel had the same sort of hull as the carrack, but the two or three masts all carried *lateen* sails. The caravels were fast, manoeuvrable vessels and much favoured in the Mediterranean. The lateen sail is familiar to us as the large triangular sail carried rather rakishly on a long yard by the Arab dhow. The precursor of the modern fore-and-aft sail, it allowed the ship to sail when the wind was coming over the bow, and it was later adapted to make the gaff-rig in Northern Europe.

> *The name* lateen *is derived from the word 'Latin', as the rig came from Southern Europe*

The development of the stern-mounted rudder, and the ship-building methods that allowed for the carrying of more than one mast, transformed ship design. Ships were now safer. A ship that could travel fast and put on a turn of speed was much less likely to be driven helplessly onto a dangerous shore. The deep draft of the carrack meant it could not land on a beach like its flat-bottomed ancestor and this was to change the nature of warfare. Battles were now fought out at sea. The carrack could carry inboard cannons with their muzzles sticking out of gunports, and a few small boats stowed on the deck could land parties of marines ashore. The carrack was the early ancestor of the great Ships-of-the-Line which would become the backbone of the British Navy by the time of the Napoleonic Wars.

But ships were used for carrying cargo as well as for battle, and merchant ships benefited from these vast improvements in construction as well. A plethora of different rigs now became possible.

BRIGS, PACKETS AND HOYS
The baffling world of sailing ships
These very names conjure up a picture of creaking spars, flapping canvas and a degree of waterside activity which will probably never be seen again. The

above left A brigantine; *above right* A barquentine

names given to the many different types of boats are confusing for several reasons. Some are local names, so a *fishing smack* in Maldon can become a *bawley* when in another part of Essex and you may not notice its slightly different shape favoured by the local ship-builders. Some are named for the type of fishing they do, such as a *drifter* or a *trawler*, and sometimes the same name is used for completely different types of boat; the term 'smack', for instance, is often used as a generic word for any sort of fishing boat.

A **brig**, however, was just about always a two-masted vessel carrying square sails on each mast, whereas its bigger relative – the **barque** – had three or more masts, each carrying square sails. The **brigantine** and the **barquentine** were hybrids of these, carrying a combination of square and fore-and-aft sails. The two-masted brig and the brigantine were the white vans of their day, and hundreds of these little ships would ply up and down the coast carrying everything from coal to candles, butter and cheese, landing on beaches to unload the cargo on to carts before floating off on the next tide.

The name Cart Gap given to many places on the shore is a reference to the places where carts would come down to unload coal from the collier brigs

Schooner

By the eighteenth century the two-masted **schooner**, which carried mainly fore-and-aft sails but often had a square sail set on the mainmast as well, became the vessel of choice, being both faster and handier, and many of them were built in the shipyards on the east coast. The name reflects its Dutch origin and it became the standard transport vessel, eventually superseding the ubiquitous brig.

Another boat of Dutch origin commonly found along the North Sea coast was the **hoy**, a small single-masted sloop (there goes another Dutch word), which carried passengers or goods, while the **packet** was the name given to the passenger boats which regularly ferried both people and mail across the sea to Holland.

The American schooners carried two or more masts, but were always characterised by the mast at the front being shorter than the mast or masts behind. This has been said to have been designed during the American War of Independence in order to confuse the enemy, as, when viewed on the horizon, the ship appeared to be going in the opposite direction. I don't know if this is true, but it does make a very good story.

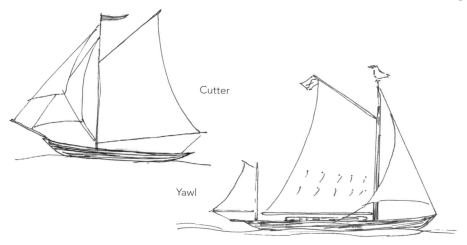

Cutter

Yawl

A **sloop** is a vessel with one mast carrying a single mainsail and just one headsail – that's the sail in front of the mast. A *cutter-rigged* sloop has more than one headsail, carried on a long bowsprit, and was the favoured rig for the fast Revenue boats designed to chase smugglers as well as for the pilots competing for work in the estuaries.

A **ketch-rigged** boat has two masts, with the mizzenmast set in front of the rudder post (unlike the **yawl**, which has its mizzenmast aft of the rudder post, and usually carries on it a much smaller sail than the ketch).

Ketch

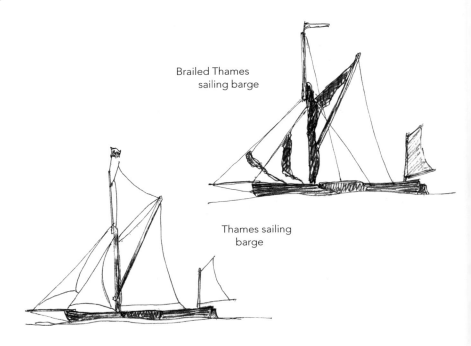

Brailed Thames
sailing barge

Thames sailing
barge

A **sailing barge** was a much more cumbersome vessel, flat-bottomed and blunt-bowed, built for carrying bulky cargo such as grain. The East Coast sailing barge was the *Billy Boy*, its tall masts carrying both square and fore-and-aft sails: it serviced the coast from Yorkshire to Essex and is frequently seen in paintings of the Norwich School. The *Thames sailing barge* was a greyhound compared to the Billy Boy: spacious, powerful and versatile, it could land on beaches, travel up rivers to remote farmsteads, make coastal passages and be sailed by just two men.

The **Norfolk wherry**, with its one huge black gaff-sail, carried sugar beet, grain and hay throughout the Norfolk Broads and rivers. With its low freeboard and shallow draft, it evolved for sailing inland waters and was not suitable for anything other than short coastal passages in favourable conditions. It is

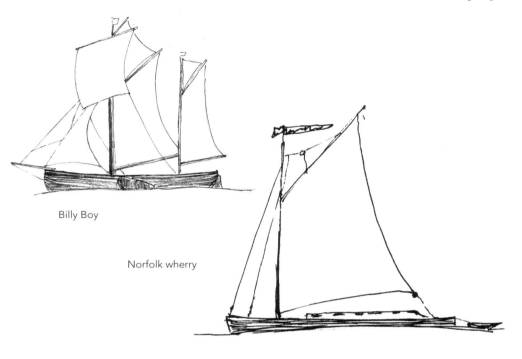

Billy Boy

Norfolk wherry

not to be confused with another sort of wherry which refers to a rowing skiff, often used as a ferry or for carrying people short distances along rivers.

The **full-rigged ship** had multiple masts carrying square as well as some fore-and-aft sails and these great windjammers were capable of long passages carrying vast amounts of cargo.

The **clipper ship** was a full-rigged ship, but it was built for speed rather than carrying capacity. Designed to carry small amounts of valuable cargo, such as tea from China, the ships that made the fastest passages could command the highest price for their wares. With beautifully fine lines and a narrow hull, their tall masts bore many extra sails with colourful names such as skysails, moonrakers and the studding sails carried on extra spars which extended

Clipper ship

the length of the yards. It was not just the design of the ship that made her so fast, as they required a skilled and daring master able to make the judgements necessary to keep her sailing at maximum speed in all conditions. The working life of one of these ships was only about twenty years. The era of these great ships was very brief, stretching from the early nineteenth century to the opening of the Suez Canal in 1869 which cut the length of the voyage to the East and made such a fast ship less necessary.

Chapter 11
DRAWING IT ALL
TOGETHER

Revisiting the coast by land has revealed its hidden history of Anglo-Saxon kings and ship burials, Vikings and invasions, fishing and philanthropy, and always against the background of a constant changing of the very contours of the land on which for centuries man has sought to make a living.

Fishing grew from the setting of a simple wooden trap in the mouth of a river to catch fish on the falling tide, to the great Dutch *busses* with their drift nets able to catch herring on an industrial scale. We have looked at the evolution of ship design, from the simple lines of the fast clinker-built Viking ships to the trading schooners of the nineteenth century; and so on to the diesel and petrol engines which took the unpredictability out of sailing ships and made life at sea easier and safer as the Industrial Age permeated every walk of life. The railway brought the next big change to the relevance of shipping, and now the world is crossed by container ships of such gigantic proportions that the old practical skills of navigation and handling sails have been largely replaced by satellite and computer technology.

The design of a boat is always relevant to the waters in which it is sailed and each part of the coast has evolved its own particular boats. Very few of the ships and boats of a former age now grace our shores, but some are still enthusiastically restored, maintained and sailed around our coasts.

You can still occasionally see the magnificent sight of a Thames barge sailing down the Suffolk and Essex rivers, its unmistakable rig and tan sails making a handsome and distinctive outline against the sky. There are still gaff-rigged fishing smacks to be seen, too, sailing out of ports along the east coast at the weekends, and tallships are, even now, still occasionally being built for the purpose of sail training. All these boats are able to provide the thrill of working a sailing ship with the teamwork, the self-reliance and the sheer wonder of feeling the power of the wind as it drives a ship forward through the waves.

So many of our coastal towns are struggling economically today: the sea is no longer an asset to a business setting up in a coastal town, it now needs a good road system instead, and as half its catchment area is presently in the sea it can only serve the community on its landward side. But, as this story has shown, there is a fascinating past to rediscover and maybe the future for these towns lies partly in remembering and taking a pride in this; there must be many visitors who come to the east coast with very little idea of what an influential part it has played in our history. There is another book to be written, too, about all the philanthropists and benefactors who have lived on this coast and made a difference by the giving of their wealth to the community and to the poor, building hospitals and schools, leaving houses and donating land. We still remember Southwold's William Godell and Thomas Seckford from Woodbridge, but there are countless more whose stories are waiting to be told.

Our coastline continues to change under the same influence of the double-act of longshore drift and tidal surge as it always has done, and there will come a time when the sea will have encroached far inland and a people, far into the future, will look over the vast waters of the North Sea and wonder about their ancestors who once lived here. But, for all its impermanence, the sun will continue to rise over the sea, the wild geese will still graze the salt-marsh and, as the tide begins another slow ebb, curlews will still call over the mudflats at the start of another day.

READING LIST

Most of my research has been in the local libraries and museums in Suffolk and at the Caird Library in the National Maritime Museum at Greenwich. There are a great many books written by local historians and I am indebted to the information they have painstakingly researched.

Here is a list of the books that I found particularly pleasurable to read.

The History of Ipswich by Carol Twinch
In Search of the Dark Ages by Michael Wood
The Conquest of the Ocean by Brian Lavery
Ships and Shipping in Medieval Manuscripts by Joe Flatman
Sea Fever by Sam Jefferson
Longitude by Dava Sobel
Alde Estuary: The Story of a Suffolk River by W.G. Arnott
Suffolk Estuary: The Story of the River Deben by W.G. Arnott
Orwell Estuary: The Story of Ipswich River by W.G. Arnott
Sailing Craft of the British Isles by Roger Finch
The Illustrated Guide to Thames Sailing Barges by Rita and Peter Phillips
Down Tops'l by Harvey Benham
Suffolk Shipping by Michael Stammers
Stuff Matters by Mark Miodownik
Herring: A History of the Silver Darlings by Mike Smylie
The Edge of the World by Michael Pye
The Ship in the Medieval Economy, 600–1600 by Richard Unger
The Dig by John Preston
The Sutton Hoo Helmet by Sonja Marzinzik
Salt by Mark Kurlansky

ACKNOWLEDGEMENTS

My thanks go to Jenny Wilson who has been such an encouraging editor as well as a pleasure to work with, and to Niki Medlik, book designer, whose skill, imagination and good company have made producing this book such fun.

Note from the author

My main source for the information presented here has been the written word found in books, museums and libraries, and the internet has also been a useful resource. It is not uncommon to find differing accounts of the same subject depending on where you look and, rather than interrupt the flow of the story through frequent provisos and footnotes, I have made a decision on what to include based solely on my judgement of the reliability of an author, whether on the internet or on the printed page, and have provided suggestions for further reading. Although I have made every effort for authenticity, any errors remain entirely mine.